LEG OF L ER DUCATION

GROUPS

GROUPS

by

Mike Robinson
Social Synthesis Unit

JOHN WILEY & SONS
Chichester · New York · Brisbane · Toronto · Singapore

Copyright © 1984 by Mike Robinson

Library of Congress Cataloguing in Publication Data:

Robinson, Mike.
  Groups.

  Includes bibliographical references and index.
  1. Social groups. 2. Social psychology. 3. Paradigms (Social sciences) 4. Small groups. 5. Cybernetics.
I. Title.
HM131.R62   1984   302.3   83-10352

 ISBN 0 471 90009 5 (Cloth)
 ISBN 0 471 90406 6 (Paper)

British Library Cataloguing in Publication Data:

Robinson, Mike
  Groups.
  1. Social structure
  I. Title
  305'.01   GN478

ISBN 0 471 90009 5 (Cloth)
ISBN 0 471 90406 6 (Paper)

Typeset by Photo-Graphics, Honiton, Devon.
Printed by Pitman Press Ltd., Bath.

Acknowledgements

Parts of the following publications have been used with permission of the copyright holders: Robert F. Bales, Fred L. Strodtbeck, Theodore M. Mills and Mary E. Rosenborough, 'Channels of communication in small groups', *ASR*, **16**, 1951. Reproduced by permission of the American Sociological Association.

Material excerpted from *Ecological Psychology* by Roger G. Barker with permission of the publishers, Stanford University Press © 1968 by the Board of Trustees of the Leland Stanford Junior University.

Gregory Bateson, 'Towards a theory of schizophrenia', *Behavioral Science*, **4**, 4, 1956. Reproduced by permission of Behavioral Science.

Stafford Beer, *Decision and Control*, John Wiley and Sons Ltd, 1966. Reproduced by permission of John Wiley and Sons Ltd.

Stafford Beer, *Platform for Change*, John Wiley and Sons Ltd, 1975. Reproduced by permission of John Wiley and Sons Ltd.

Erving Goffman, *The Presentation of Self in Everyday Life* (Pelican Books, 1971). Reprinted by permission of Penguin Books Ltd.

M. Lindaver, *Communication among Social Bees*, Harvard University Press, 1961. Reprinted by permission.

R. A. Rappaport, *Pigs for the Ancestors*, Yale University Press, 1968. Reproduced by permission of Yale University Press.

Richard Sharpe, 'Explosion of the cult of analysis', *Computing*, **9**, 8, 1981. Reproduced by permission of R. Sharpe.

Material reprinted from *Street Corner Society* by W.F. Whyte by permission of the University of Chicago Press © 1943 The University of Chicago Press.

V.C. Wynne-Edwards, *Animal Dispersion in Relation to Social Behaviour*, Oliver & Boyd. Reproduced by permission of Professor V.C. Wynne-Edwards.

Evening Argus and *Brighton & Hove Gazette*. Reproduced by permission of The Southern Publishing Company (Westminster Press Limited).

The Guardian. Reproduced by permission of Guardian Newspaper Limited.

Sunday Telegraph. Reproduced by permission of Sunday Telegraph Limited.

Contents

Contents

Introduction

But the social life of the working class is rich in institutions, and is articulated by a multiplicity of activities.

(Antonio Gramsci, 21 June 1919)

(i)

The assumption underlying this book is that *the social power of the individual is mediated by the groups to which he or she belongs.*

This is important, but not usually seen as contentious. It simply means that, except in trivial cases, individuals achieve very little on their own. This is clearest with political action. If I want to change something—a law, a policy, an injustice—my first move is to form a group of like-minded people. The individual lobbyist is a nuisance or an eccentric—which are both ways of defining them as ineffective. Groups multiply social power far faster than the mere increase in numbers. Half a dozen people can be a thousand times more effective than one or two.

If one accepts that there is a distinction between political, personal, social, and economic life, then the importance of groups holds in all these areas. My self-image is not self-contained; it is a living, changing, system of refractions, reflections, and agreements; it depends on others; lovers, friends, and enemies populate my personality—giving it the space to become organized. That my social life depends on others—on groups—is obvious. In economic life, the same thing holds. How many machines with any economic significance can be operated and maintained within a project that begins and ends with the inidividual? Just about none!

As I said, it is not very contentious to assert that the social power of the individual is mediated by groups. The question is *how*, and *to what end?*

Gramsci had it in mind that the informal, convivial institutions of the working class could replace all the useful, but oppressive capitalist functions of management and administration. This was a mixture of intuition, insight, and political assertion. He was wrenching open the door on a whole new world of the possible. In the political climate of Italy in 1919 these assertions were a call

1

to action. There was no time to stand back for a cool appraisal of sociological minutiae. How many different types of institution were there? Which could be developed and which could not? And so on.

In my view, the situation today is no less urgent. Like Gramsci, we cannot permit ourselves the luxury of mistakes. Existing social forms do not harness the creativity of the mass of the population. They suppress it. Powerlessness and alienation are only symptoms of outmoded social structures, but they can provide the motor force in the construction of a humane society. This process is revolution. It may succeed or fail, depending on uncountable events and unpredictable turns. One thing is certain. New social forms do not spring out of thin air. They must be found in everyday practice.

Groups influence us, we influence groups. What form of group is best suited to the creativity of the individual in the broadest sense? Or, simply, how can we get most out of life? In this context, it is important that we understand how groups work.

To do this, we must be careful to distinguish levels of analysis. The group and the social individual are inextricably inter-related. It is no more possible to provide a complete characterization of a group than it is of a person. Prediction—the usual method of science—is inappropriate for people and groups of people. Both generate plans and make decisions from the inside. We may *foresee* what someone is going to do: this means we *understand* that person, or can put ourselves in their place. It does not mean that their actions are 'caused', or that they had no choice in the matter.

On the other hand, it is possible to say quite a lot about forms and limits. We can account for walking and lovemaking since the details of our biology are thus and not otherwise. I believe that we can account for groups in the same way. Forms of communication, numbers of people involved, physical context—all these place limits on the possible, provide structures through which aims may be realized. For people, the account says nothing about *where* we walk, of *who* we make love to—only how we do it, *if* we do it. For groups, the account does not tell us *which* aims, or *what* we say in a conversation. It gives us the structures necessary for realizing the aims or having the conversation—structures without which these things could not be achieved, *if* we decide they are what we want to achieve.

The first step in understanding how groups work is to tease out which structures are *viable* and which are not. In other words, what sort of group is likely to help us achieve our aims; what we expect from it, and what *it* expects from us. Should we look at the group as a whole as well as its members—and if so, how? Are things that please us—like lots of new members joining— necessarily good for the group? Are things that annoy us—like people not bothering to turn up—necessarily bad for the group? When is the group 'in danger' or about to 'collapse'?

David Dickson (1974) is right when he says: 'the machines to which an individual has access coincide with the forms of possible social action that lie open to them'. He also recognizes that making technologies work is beyond the power of any single individual. It is a co-operative enterprise. Our social forms are dependent on our technologies—we can say that they are determined by them if we mean that they set the limits of the possible. Without contradicting this, we can say that some social forms will not make the technology work. *Can* informal, convivial institutions be developed to replace the oppressive functions of management and administration? How can they be developed? How can they too avoid becoming repressive? These are questions that Gramsci never had to face. Today it is necessary to provide answers that go beyond an act of faith. To this end, I have examined the structures of informal groups. In retrospect, some of the conclusions are obvious—and some are very surprising. In practice, I have found them helpful, and hope you will too.

(ii)

The only freedom open to an object is to object

In the twentieth century, groups have been studied from many different points of view. There have been groups 'in need of treatment' to improve morale or performance—often battle-units in the army, or work-teams in industry. There have been groups designed for the 'treatment' of individuals—psycho-therapy groups; T-groups for managerial skills or just for self-knowledge; brainstorming groups for enhancing creativity. Groups of university undergraduates have been solemnly scrutinized by sociologists. 'Groups' of strangers have been studied in the laboratories of experimentalists. Interaction patterns and choices about 'who you would most like to sit next to' have been analysed by computer. Conformity, leadership, and 'risky-shifts' have been discovered and argued about. The self-activity of gangs of delinquents has become an academic subject in its own right.

Along with the facts and statistics have come volumes of theory and numerous taxonomies and typologies. Many of these studies will be discussed and reviewed in Chapter 1. This is not intended to be a comprehensive review, but an examination of the way in which *paradigms* influence research. What you expect influences what you find. In addition to *paradigms*, we will look at the way *models* and *analogies* have been used in studying groups. For instance, Exchange Theory is a model derived from an analogy with Economics; attitude maintenance and resistance to change has been explained in terms of the biological analogy of innoculation; and so on.

Chapter 2 suggests an alternative, *cybernetic paradigm*. We show how this paradigm has been successfully used in many social fields from psychiatry and anthropology to ethology. Equally importantly, we look at how cybernetics and General System Theory have been misused. We see that accounts, however they name themselves, that cannot encompass instability, growth, and change, that do not deal with conflict as well as stability, are of limited value. We want to know about the circular way in which phenomena connect (or misconnect) to themselves, not about fictitious, quasi-physical 'causes'.

4

I have said *prediction* is inappropriate when we are dealing with people or groups of people. So we are looking for a way of relating to people that does not turn them into 'objects'—but at the same time allows us to make precise statements. This is almost a contradictory requirement, so in Chapter 3 we explore the implications and the methodological options.

Here we are trying to find the 'proper' method of social science. This can't be like the method of natural science, because people are actors, not 'facts'—they always have a choice in what they do. Nor can the method be *pure* politics, where everything is choice. So we need something in between. Not an ugly graft, or a 'ghost in the machine', but a special sociological dimension. This must be different from, but of equal status to 'fact' and 'choice'. The suggestion is made that this dimension can be largely caught in the idea of 'ritual'. Ritual behaves like 'fact' in that it is repeated. On the other hand, use of the idea of ritual does not deny any element of choice. If we think of ritual as the label for any describable and repeatable social phenomenon, then most forms or organization can be described in terms of sets of rituals. Chapter 3 explores this notion in detail, but the ideas can be summarized here.

Methodology	Natural Science	Systems or Social Science	Political Science
Subject matter	'Fact'	'Ritual'	'Choice'
Truth type	Correspondence	Coherence	Consensus
Method	Experiment	Modelling	Conflict
Technology	Measurement	Simulation	Ourselves

Briefly, this means that the methodologies of Natural, Social, and Political Science are entirely distinct. Each has its own subject matter, its own way of investigating and establishing truths, and its own distinctive technology.

First there is natural science, which deals with 'facts' and tries to establish 'correspondence' truths—there are things in the world that correspond with the theories. Natural science proceeds by experiment, and has a well-developed technology of measurement.

Then there is systems science (which in our view largely covers 'social' science). Here the subject matter is 'ritual' and the concern is to establish 'coherence' truth. 'Coherence' truth means that the *consistency* of the model or theory is more important than its 'correspondence' with things in the world. This is mainly because, unlike natural science, the subject matter of systems (and social) science does not stand still. There is no guarantee that yesterday, tomorrow, or somewhere else, the 'same causes' will produce the 'same effects'. Systems science proceeds by modelling, and its technology is simulation. Although (compared to measurement in natural science) this technology is not yet well developed, it is suggested that the best modelling medium we have is the computer.

Lastly, there is political science. This is the area where decision (planning, agreement, conflict) entirely replaces causality. Truth is established by 'consensus'—often as a result of conflict. In some way or other, oppositional ideas are eliminated. The subject matter is 'choice': the methods and technology are ourselves, our aims and inter-relations. We deal with facts and systems, but we live politics.

Two last points need to be made. This way of classifying sciences is controversial and non-standard. It has not been undertaken from a 'philosophical' point of view—as an attempt to arrive at some 'ultimate' classification. It is simply an attempt to 'do' social science without being lumbered with 'causality' or losing all ability to make definite statements in a welter of political indeterminacy. Second, if the schema is accepted, it should be noted that each form of science contains elements (often implicit) of the other two forms—the details of this fusion are examined in Chapter 3.

Again, if the schema is accepted, the concepts involved allow us to give a precise account of group functioning, allow us to make *projections* (concerning the future) and *diagnoses* (concerning the present) without violating the integrity (or offending the intelligence) of the people in the group.

At this point we have a research plan and an objective. The plan allows for the formal study of groups from within. The objective is to discover informal structures that are viable in themselves; that are liked by the people involved in them; and that may, on development, offer effective alternatives to hierarchic management—forms of social control that grow from within rather than being imposed from without. In this light we examine the workings of three groups, all of which are very different in form. All they have in common is that they are voluntary. No-one is forced to join, and no-one is forced to stay. If the groups continue to exist, it is because their members 'get something out of them'—if they did not, they would not come, and simply there would be no group.

The first group was a crowd of adolescents in South London, the second a community action group in Brighton, the third a local branch of a left-wing political organization. In order to illustrate the relation between the life of the group as seen by its members and the formal account, Chapter 5 gives a rich and lively history of the Brighton group. Chapter 6 mirrors this with formal analysis of the same events. In Chapter 8, the dynamics of the groups, with their similarities and differences, are computer simulated. The behaviour of the assumptions, put together as a working model, is compared with the behaviours of the groups.

It is often thought that simulation of social systems is a mechanistic—and therefore a simple—business. At one level this is true. But there is another problem. We may not be able to check computer proofs. The problem is similar to the ancient Greek conundrum about Achilles and the tortoise. In the original version, the tortoise gets a head start and Achilles has to catch her. In the first minute the tortoise covers a hundred feet. Achilles gets to the same point in a mere ten seconds. But by this time the tortoise has moved another sixteen feet. Achilles gets to this point in less than another two seconds, by which time the tortoise has travelled another three feet, and so on, infinitely. Zeno concluded that Achilles could never catch the tortoise—and that the whole idea of motion was a nonsense.

In the modern version, the computer is Achilles and we are the tortoise. This time Achilles gets the head start, and the tortoise has to catch him. Achilles does a million calculations for every ten the tortoise can manage. The problem is that the tortoise has promised to be at the finishing line first so that she can check Achilles' speed. If the tortoise does not get to the finishing line first, there can be no 'proof' that Achilles is a good runner. So far, this has not been a great practical problem in mathematics. The first proof that relied entirely on high-speed computers did not appear until recently. This was the Four-Colour Theorem, and showed that no more than four colours are needed to mark any map so that no countries with a common border are marked in the same colour (Appel and Haken, 1977). The proof is so long that it cannot be checked without the aid of another computer. The problem is similar when we computer-simulate complex social systems. If anything, it is compounded because we want to talk about possibilities and probabilities as well as consequences.

This is one aspect of the problem of *complexity*. Groups are too complex to be understood with the unaided brain. So we build models. The best model—the only fully accurate one—will be the group itself. But it is too complex to be understood. As Stafford Beer (1966) put it, 'The kinds of system under discussion exhibit literally billions of variables. There is no *rigorous* means of knowing which matter'. So, with simulation, we not only have the problem of checking the calculations. We cannot even know if our assumptions are 'correct'.

As with Zeno's paradoxes of motion, the problem here lies with our notions of correctness and proof. We tend to base our idea of science on *repeatable* phenomena that are *the same for all observers*. We leave out the frame of reference of the observer.

The many faces of science are often illustrated by the story of the four blind men and the elephant. None of them has ever come across an elephant before. As they grope around in the dark, the first blind man bumps into a leg. He announces that the elephant is a tall column. The second blind man encounters the trunk. He concludes that the first man is a fool, that the 'column' is nothing more than a hanging rope of great thickness. The third blind man, hanging onto the tail as his 'discovery' enters the spirit of the controversy. Neither a 'column' nor a 'hanging rope', but a vertical, non-poisonous snake. After some months of dispute, they conclude that the elephant is vertical and of indeterminate thickness. They employ the fourth blind man to discover whether the rope-column called elephant hangs from above, or grows from below. Guided by the learned research of his predecessors, the fourth man does not blunder about aimlessly. He reaches up to try and see if there is a top to the rope-column called elephant. He discovers the stomach. He goes away and starts his own 'the-elephant-is-a-great-Hanging-Canopy' school of science.

This story makes a great introduction to physics. The blind men have the same frame of reference—they want to know what an elephant *is*. And there *is* an elephant. But what if the blind men have different intentions? Only the first is a scientist. The second is thinking about new forms of transport. The third is simply hungry. The fourth is thinking of ways to obliterate the other three. And on top of this there is no elephant. They are feeling each other.

In social science, we must take into account the intentions and frame of reference of the 'observer'. We are not 'objects'—impartial recording instruments—any more than the people about whom (or even *to* whom) we are trying to say something. We are 'feeling each other', and must accept the situation for what it is.

Philosophers have wrestled with the problems of subjectivity and objectivity for many centuries. Some of them have dived very deep—and come up very muddy. Simulation is another tool for exploring this distinction. But we must be clear that we are exploring a representation, a reflection not a reality. This is more hopeful than it might appear. Reality is not fixed, and our representations play an important part in forming it. In social science, we are creating realities all the time. The realities of conversation or of economics—or for that matter of physics—do not exist independently of our activity. The conclusions of science are frozen activities from the past—we can call them *reifications*. Theories, and the technologies, the artefacts, that follow from them structure our present activities and amplify our range of possible activity.

A 'correct' conclusion about groups is not a disembodied truth, but a way in which future groups will be. Simulation enables us to externalize our frames of reference; to build ourselves into the model along with the 'data'. It enables us to deal with complexity without getting lost in the calculations. Truth is not just a matter of corresponding with the 'facts' (although this is a necessary condition). The truth about social structures must also gain our *agreement*. If it does, we have established a community of observers, and the possibility of repeatable phenomena.

(iii)

The groups to which we belong form, in large part, the framework of our lives. As such, they are almost invisible. We think about what goes on—the content—not about the co-ordinates. If we do reflect on groups or relationships *per se*, it is usually because something has gone wrong. In this book, I want to look at the form of groups when things are going well as a basis for understanding changes and crises. What is the difference between a viable group—one that is stable or evolves successfully—and a group that disappears? How is it that a group can be 'the same', despite the fact that most of its members have changed? Which variables are important to the functioning of the group—and how are they seen by its members? Which processes are limiting and which can be freely changed? How do these processes relate to each other?

In the last chapter we present a model that defines some limits of group stability; of processes that occur within those limits; and some consequences of going beyond the limits. The general form of the model is descriptive—but it also has a strict form as a computer program that maps our assumptions onto historical data. It should again be emphasised that the *model is not predictive* (for one thing we do not believe there is such an animal), but the model is intended to be a *diagnostic* one. It should inform the understanding without pre-empting change or political choice.

To anticipate the conclusions, the model assumes that group 'identity' is maintained if the group stays about the same size and continues to do the same sorts of things—even despite changes of membership. Such stable groups have two major components: a Normative System and a Size Regulating Subsystem.

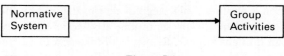

Figure I.1

The Normative System is where the politics (can) appear. It is the method (ritual) by which the group members agree on values and actions. In a general way, the Normative System determines the group activities (Figure I.1). But the sorts of activity decided on also determine the size of the group—the approximate number of people needed to carry out the activity (Figure I.2)

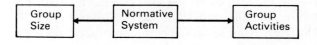

Figure I.2

Then of course the success or otherwise of the activities influences both the size and the normative system. 'Success' can lead to the attraction of new members; 'failure' can lead to losing members. 'Success/failure' in itself, and through membership change, can influence the Normative System (Figure I.3).

In fact, it turns out that (quite often) the fluctuations in activity lead to a Size Regulating Subsystem. Role specifications, absenteeism, joining and leaving all

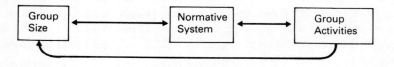

Figure I.3

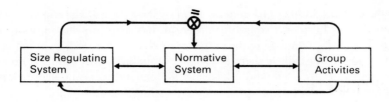

Figure I.4

combine to form a delicate set of balances which match the group size to its activity—and this in turn maintains the Normative System (Figure I.4).

None of this means that stability is guaranteed. Groups can become 'too big or too small'. Activity can be disrupted. The Normative System can disintegrate into conflict. Warring factions are always an implicit danger. Particular danger points for groups are the 'formation period'—the first few weeks or months in the life of a group. Many (probably most) groups do not survive this. Any moment of sudden growth is equally dangerous, as is a situation where group activity is disrupted for any length of time.

The final model draws together all these strands of stability and change; of 'fact', ritual, and politics in a way that—I hope—will be useful and may enable you, the reader, to recast some of your experiences in a new light.

Some final comments. The book will attempt to present the ideas in the way they actually grew. The experience of the Brighton Rents Project preceded the formal account. Both were seen in the light of a strong prejudice in favour of cybernetics and a conviction about the importance of groups in our life. In turn, the conclusions modified the way I (sometimes we) look at my (our) experiences in the groups. The process continues.

In this introduction, I hope I have answered the first question that should arise in the mind of any reader of a book on psychology. What is the author's motivation? This is an area where it is not easy to disentangle prejudice from hypothesis, hypothesis from fact. The rules of evidence are far from clear. But anyone that puts forward ideas that involve poking around in other peoples' lives needs more justification than an 'enquiring mind'!

My personal view is that convivial, non-hierarchical, and non-oppressive forms of social organization can be found all around us. Gramsci was right. But before we generalize, we need to understand. Insufficient time is not an excuse. These chapters are written as a small contribution in that direction.

References

Dickson, David (1974) *Alternative Technology and the Politics of Technical Change*. Glasgow, Fontana.

Appel, K. and Haken, W. (1977) The solution of the Four-Color-Map problem, in *Scientific American* **237**, 4, 108–121.

Beer, S. (1966) *Decision and Control*, London, Wiley.

CHAPTER 1

Paradigms in social psychology

The idea of 'paradigm' in science was introduced by Thomas Kuhn in his famous book *The Structure of Scientific Revolutions*. This is how Kuhn himself defines a paradigm:

> Aristotle's *Physica*, Ptolemy's *Almagest*, Newton's *Principia* and *Opticks*, Franklin's *Electricity*, Lavoisier's *Chemistry*, and *Lyell's* Geology—these and many other works served for a time implicitly to define the legitimate problems and methods of a research field for succeeding generations of practitioners. They were able to do so because they shared two essential characteristics. Their achievement was sufficiently unprecedented to attract an enduring group of adherents away from competing modes of scientific activity. Simultaneously, it was sufficiently open ended to leave all sorts of problems for the redefined group of practitioners to resolve.
>
> (Kuhn, 1970, p. 10)

So a paradigm is recognized as an unprecedented achievement, but leaves 'all sorts of problems' to be resolved. It is also important to notice that a paradigm does not have to be 'true' in any absolute sense. It simply has to 'work'—for a while, at least. In his 'Postscript', Kuhn says that a paradigm is a constellation of beliefs, values, and techniques that are shared by a scientific community. More importantly, it is a set of 'concrete puzzle solutions which, employed as models or examples, can replace explicit rules as a basis for the solution of the remaining puzzles of normal science' (Kuhn, 1970, p. 175).

Social psychology, unlike its close relatives, psychology and sociology, does not have any 'great paradigms'. There is no-one of the stature of Pavlov, or Marx, Weber, or Durkheim. There are no grand theories, like those of Freud and Jung in psychiatry. There is no Keynes and no Mendel, no Einstein and no Darwin. The philosophy of William James is conspicuous by its absence. Nevertheless, there are concrete 'puzzle solutions' that serve as models. In this chapter I shall look at some of the 'puzzle solutions' that influenced me. They all concern the behaviour of people in groups.

A preliminary comment. 'Puzzles' in social psychology, like any other puzzle, can be done again and again. Different variations can be produced on the same theme. Different people can do the 'same' puzzle. In other words, to be a puzzle, a problem has to *recur*—the pattern has to happen over and over again in a similar form. The recurrence of puzzles, the repetition of similar situations, gives rise to a feeling that social psychology is dealing with *objective* data. Just like the natural sciences. Isn't that good! We will return to the question of recurrence and objectivity in Chapter Three, after reviewing some of the main solutions to problems of group behaviour.

Experience in Groups by W R Bion

Bion's *Experiences* were first published in the journal *Human Relations* between 1949 and 1951. They represent one of the first attempts to make sense of the things that happen in small groups. Bion started his work in the rehabilitation wing of a military hospital during the Second World War. At any one time between 300 and 400 men were in for treatment. As far as was possible within the framework of military discipline, the men were allowed to organize themselves into groups within which they set their own objectives. This experiment, which was initiated by John Rickman, was a success and became known as the Northfield Experiment. Rickman drew the following conclusions, which are of great interest as an early—and accurate—attempt to analyse group structure and dynamics.

He remarked that 'good spirit' in groups is as hard to define as 'good health' in the individual—but that the following properties seemed to be asociated with it.

1 Common purpose: it does not seem to matter whether this is fighting an enemy, defending or furthering an ideal, creating a social relationship, or building some physical amenity.
2 Common recognition of the 'boundaries' of the group, and its relationships with other groups.
3 The ability to lose and gain members without disrupting the character of the group. (This 'group ability' will be very important in later chapters.)
4 Freedom from cliques: any subgroups that do form must not exclude other group members.
5 Each individual must be valued by the group.
6 The group must be able to face—and have some way of coping with—discontent.
7 The minimum group size is three. Rickman claims that two people only have 'personal relationships'.

Following this, Bion was invited by the Tavistock Clinic to take therapeutic groups, and the model he developed is largely based on these. Very roughly, it accounts for group activities in the following way.

The group is more than 'the sum of its parts', and has a reality of its own that has very little to do with the individuals in it. The group is omnipresent whether or not it is 'visible'.

no individual, however isolated in time and space, can be regarded as outside a group, or lacking in active manifestations of group psychology, although conditions do not exist that would make it possible to demonstrate it.

(Bion, 1968, p. 132)

A little later, Bion says that gathering people in a room does not *add* anything to the individuals, but *reveals* something that would not otherwise be seen—the group.

According to Bion, the group is as fundamental a part of the individual as the unconscious. Any attempt to explain individual behaviour without either concept is, at best, very partial. Bion elaborates a set of three fundamental forms of activity that have their origins in the group.

The first type of activity is dependence. The group is demanding; it creates a leader from whom it can take succour; all responsibility is heaped on the leader; the group just sits back and waits for him to solve their problems.

The second type of activity is fight/flight. In this state of mind—which Bion surmises is related to a primitive survival instinct—the group unites to attack or run away from a threatening object. In the case of the therapeutic group:

> There will be a feeling that the welfare of the individual does not matter so long as the group continues, and there will be a feeling that any method of dealing with neurosis that is neither fighting neurosis nor running away from the owner of it is either non-existent or directly opposed to the good of the group

(ibid. p. 64)

It is claimed that such a group chooses a leader with strong paranoid perceptions. Since the group finds it difficult to recognize the enemy, the best way out is to choose a leader who can.

The third type of activity is pairing. The group tolerates the formation of couples within it, watches with interest the development of exclusive two-way conversations. Again this is linked to a primitive instinct. The group will tolerate the formation of pairs—although this is not a form of fight/flight—because it supposedly recognizes 'reproduction' is important for group preservation.

These three forms of activity—which are termed 'basic assumptions'—are the manifestations of a group phenomenon which parallels the unconscious in the individual. Basic assumptions are *tacit* assumptions. Individuals behave *as if* they were aware the group was in a state of dependence, fight-flight, or pairing. But the activity is never stated in so many words. The basic assumption 'is a statement that gives meaning to the behaviour of the group as a whole, yet the assumption is not overtly expressed even when it is being acted on' (ibid. p. 94).

The contradiction in the three forms of basic assumption group (which Bion considers to be degenerate rather than truly primitive) is that attempts to realize any of the three assumptions in action are self-negating. Dependence does not lead to succour; fight/flight does not lead to success; pairing defeats the sense of hope which is its purpose. The contradiction is resolved by postulating a fourth type of group that can act on the world: the work group.

The work group meets to 'do' something. The individuals co-operate in an activity or a task. Tasks that are related to reality call for rational methods—the beginning of a scientific approach. This is the stage at which Bion feels the group will be in a position to help its individual members. The work group has reached social maturity.

This four-way model enables Bion to essay explanations of institutions as diverse as the Church (dependence), the Army (fight/flight), and the Aristocracy (pairing). It also enables him to account for complaints made about his groups to the authorities at the Clinic. The problem is seen as one of emotional oscillation. The dependent group needs to believe that their leader is superior in order to be able to help them. He may be believed to be 'a genius'—or less flatteringly, 'mad'. At the same time the group must believe the leader is dependable—that means he must be as they are. In 'reality', these views are contradictory and cannot be held simultaneously. The contradiction is resolved by switching from one view to the other with increasing frequency and increasing intensity of belief. The group becomes unstable as the emotional oscillation becomes less and less comfortable, until, finally

> the group can no longer contain the emotional situation, which therefore spreads with explosive violence to other groups until enough groups have been drawn in to absorb the reaction. In practice in the small group this means impulsion to complain to outside authority, e.g. write to the press, or to a Member of Parliament, or to the authorities of the Clinic. The object of this drawing in of other groups is not, as I at first supposed it to be, revenge on the psychiatrist for discomfort—though that may be there, and damage to the psychiatrist or group may be the result—but to bring in so much inert material in the way of outsiders from the group, who do not share the emotional situation, that the new and much larger group ceases to vibrate. There is no longer the violent and disagreeable mass oscillation.

(ibid. p. 125)

Several aspects of Bion's work stand out as paradigmatic. First, there is the insistence on the reality of the group as such. Group phenomena cannot be reduced to individual actions, nor are they the result of adding up individual actions. On the other hand, the fallacy of the 'superorganism' is avoided. Instead, Bion postulates *group action as such* as an integral part of individual action. The group is within the individual just as much as the individual is in a group. All that an actual group does is provide a field of study in which group-powered actions can be seen for what they are. Some actions only make sense if the individual is seen as a member of a group. Outside that context 'explanations' can still be found, but they are inadequate.

Secondly, there is a striving for objectivity. The categories of fight/flight, dependency, and pairing are seen as universal and observable. There is some difficulty with the observation techniques, which Bion explains and illustrates as the ever present tendency of the analyst to become involved in the 'basic assumptions' of the group. Nevertheless the group and the categories themselves are seen as 'there' and playing a causal role in behaviour. They allow the construction of accounts of group dynamics, such as the one we have just looked at involving 'emotional oscillation'.

Thirdly, there is the systematic use of model and analogy. The basic categories are analogies drawn from theories of primitive and 'herd' behaviour.

Their combination forms a model through which it is possible to explain group behaviour.

In these three respects—group reality; objectivity; explanation by analogy and through models—Bion had a strong influence on small-group research. This influence also led to a mushrooming of therapeutic groups and the appearance of T-groups in other fields.* Here we have to resort to another principle of explanation of human activity.

Any explanation is better than none

Once someone has proposed an explanation, then there is something to talk about. The correctness of the explanation is neither here nor there. Its real function is that of a starting point. T-groups have always had a dual role—research and therapy. As they evolved, the research aspect diminished and the therapy, and 'sensitivity training' aspects were emphasized. In the end T-groups became a highly marketable technique for 'improving management skills' and 'improving industrial relations'. Here the question is no longer a matter of generating theory, but of 'success'. Michael Argyle is one of many to express serious doubts on this score. In answer to the question 'How successful is T-group training in achieving its goals?', he says:

> the situation is very oddly designed from the point of view of learning social skills, since the group is engaged on the very peculiar task of studying itself. There is no reason to expect that the social techniques which are successful here should work in other group situations—they would only work in other T-groups....
> All trainees report that they have been through a very powerful emotional experience, and most feel that they know themselves better, feel more confident, and are able to deal with social situations more effectively. This does not of course show that they have really changed in these ways....
> in some studies there has been an overall decline in effectiveness, possibly due to unskilled trainers, and more serious is the fact that a small proportion of trainees have nervous breakdowns as a result of T-groups. No information is available about precisely how large this small proportion is.
>
> (Argyle 1967)

There is also a more fundamental criticism. The locus of all meaning and truth in the group is the trainer or psychiatrist. Since there is no object of truth apart from the group itself, no tests of truth and falsity that can be applied by anyone other than the trainer, then the trainer has to be right. If the group recognizes this (and seeks to benefit from the trainer's monopoly of insight) then they are dependent. If they challenge this state of affairs, they are manifesting the fight/flight behaviour of the herd. If they try and set up an independent locus of conversation with its own truth values, they are pairing. All obvious responses of the group to its own situation (and in this sense they are basic) are seen as regressive manifestations for the trainer to interpret. This interpretation is of

*Although in the context of 'paradigms' there is a continuity between Bion and T-groups, there are also many differences, and it would be a mistake to equate the two.

course a disruption of the embryonic structure the group is trying to create for itself, and is met with resentment. The resentment is taken as a sign of the correctness of the interpretation, and the trainer's monopoly on truth and structure is re-established. When the group accepts the trainer's account, it is deemed to have reached maturity, and to have become a 'work group'.

The original work by Bion and Rickman (in the military hospital) allowed groups to form around activities—to influence and interact with the world. The move to the clinic sealed the groups in on themselves—a sort of collective sensory deprivation. In these unusual circumstances where all attempts to learn from the trainer or to act autonomously were blocked, it is not surprising that the most frequent responses were prolonged periods of uneasy silence.

In many senses the group environment, and the responses to it, have much in common with the laboratory situations that are usually considered to belong to the other end of the social-science spectrum. 'Generalized and unspecific' responses, 'deliberately ambiguous responses', and a 'special way of going on', may have more to do with the structure of the situation—itself derived from the intentions of the experimenter—than they have to do with the members of the group. Compare Rom Harré's characterization of the usual social psychology laboratory with the T-group setting:

> Experiments take place in special places, often called social-psychological laboratories, where a simplified environment consisting of undecorated walls, plain furnishings, rarely more than two chairs, the mysterious blank face of the one-way mirror, and perhaps the intrusion of the unblinking eye of the television camera. ... But in real life social events occur in highly differentiated environments, rich in sights and sounds, well furnished with symbolic objects, which direct or determine the interpretative procedures and the choice of rule-systems of the actors. The simplified environment of the social-psychological experiment leads inevitably to an unresolvable ambiguity of interpretation. Actors simply do not know which rule-meaning system to draw upon in acting. Every one of their actions is fraught with a kind of uncertainty ... the most generalised and unspecific kind of responses are given, as they would be in the most ambiguous conditions of real life, such as, for example, a meeting between strangers in an undifferentiated public space. Deliberately ambiguous responses are made, so they can later be reinterpreted ... in the absence of an interpreted environment, a social *Umwelt*, no conclusion can be drawn about which of the independent rule-meaning systems individuals have employed. ... There may even be a special way of going on in social-psychological laboratories, knowledge of which may be the final residue of the extraordinary tradition of experiments as a way of investigating social activities. But, as they used to say in the Goon Show, 'I don't wish to know that'.
>
> (Harré, 1979)

It may be that the popularity of T-groups has more to do with hope, and the belief in their effectiveness, more to do with trust than with the science they are claimed to embody. Nevertheless, any explanation is better than none, so it is not sufficient simply to challenge the T-group paradigm. An alternative must be constructed. Explanation, understanding, and change are all legitimate aspirations.

Channels of Communication in Small Groups

This paper, written over 30 years ago, was—and remains—the definitive statement on how people participate in small groups. Everybody knows that, in groups, some people talk more than others. Bales and his colleagues discovered precisely *how much more* some people talk than others. The finding is all the more remarkable because it seems to apply to all groups. See Figure 1.1.

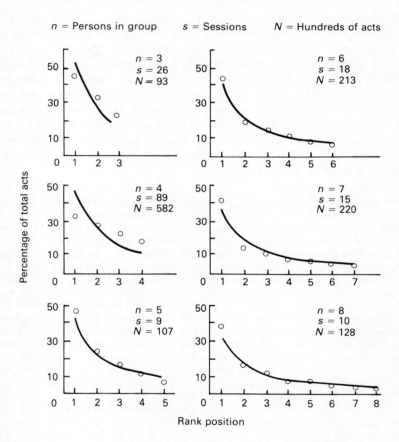

Figure 1.1   The distribution of participation in small groups (Bales *et al.* 1951, p. 46)

Each graph represents a different size of group. Each graph shows the percentage of the time each member spent in talking. In the first graph of a three-person group, the first person spoke for about 45 per cent of the time, the second person for about 32 per cent, and the third person for about 22 per cent of the time. In a six-person group, the percentages are roughly 43, 19, 14, 11, 7 and 6 respectively. In all cases, there is a J-shaped distribution, with a few members doing most of the talking—and this effect becomes more pronounced as the group size increases. The obvious question is 'why?'. To try and answer that, let us look at the original paper, and try to see what was going on.

Robert Bales, one of the main authors, is best known for his development of *Interaction Process Analysis*. This is a set of categories to be used in analysing group interactions at the verbal level. It is based on the idea that verbal contributions divide into two sorts: task-orientated and emotional/expressive. There are various sub-categories within each type. For instance, task-oriented can be divided into 'gives suggestion'; 'gives opinion'; 'asks for information' etc.; and emotional can be divided into positive: 'shows solidarity'; 'releases tension' etc. and negative: 'shows antagonism'; 'disagrees' etc. Once these categories are established groups can be observed in a formal way. Part of the project was obviously to ground the notion of 'role' in the type and number of contributions various people made. The construction of the categories leads immediately to counting, to an attempt to establish a proper metric for small-group studies. This is reflected in one of the opening statements of the paper:

> Various sorts of small problem solving groups were observed with a variety of primary hypotheses in mind. ... The possibility of using the data for the present investigation grew from the fact that a uniform method of investigation was used throughout.

> (Bales *et al.*, 1951, p. 461)

Once this sort of counting had started, the regularity in the differences in participation became clear. Indeed it would have been hard to miss them. The groups were of many different types and sizes. All they had in common was a 'single focus'. In other words, everyone was attending to the same thing with one person talking at a time: 'they did not involve a number of conversations proceeding at the same time, as one finds at a cocktail party or in a hotel lobby'.

Having discovered differential participation, the research team turned to its numerical records to find other regularities connected with it. They reported their findings in the following way:

> (1) Each row (acts directed by one individual to persons other than himself) tends to be ordered so that the cell for the person of the highest basic initiating rank receives the largest number, the cell for the person of the second highest basic initiating rank receives the second largest, and so forth.
>
> (1a) The rank of the total number of acts received by an individual tends to correspond to his basic initiating rank.
>
> (2) Each column (acts received by one individual from persons other than himself) tends to be ordered so that the values correspond to the basic initiating ranks of persons originating the acts.
>
> (2a) The rank of the number of acts directed by an originator to all other specific individuals tends to be ordered to correspond to the basic initiating rank of the originator.
>
> (3) The rank of the number of acts directed by an individual to the group as a whole tends to correspond to his basic initiating rank.

> (ibid. p. 463)

The first thing we notice about the findings is that they are somewhat difficult to understand. The use of a metric led to a very formal way of reporting results—much the sort of way we would expect to find an experiment in the physical sciences reported. In simpler language, it had been discovered that the more someone spoke, the more others spoke to them. Also, the people that spoke most addressed a higher proportion of their remarks to the group as a whole.

The second thing to notice is the huge amount of evidence collected. 'Our sample consists of 171 sessions in which approximately 138,000 acts were observed' (ibid. p. 464). The main concern was to discover, in numerical depth, *what* was going on.

> We believe that the detection of these regularities represents a significant gain in our knowledge about the distribution of communication in small groups, and provides a basis framework of order within which many more detailed analyses of the interaction process may be made.
>
> (ibid. p. 465)

The idea was to take this form of participation as the norm from which to detect, describe, and explain any group whose behaviour was different. Although Bales' categories (Interpersonal Process Analysis) were widely used, this plan underestimated the huge costs of the observations. All groups of interest would have to be continuously monitored. Having discovered what was going on, two main paths were open. One was to try and discover an explanation. The other was to describe the phenomenon even more precisely. By and large, social science followed the second path.

In the following year, Stephan and Mishler (1952) published a paper called 'The distribution of participation in small groups: An exponential approximation'. They demonstrated that the J-curve discovered by the Bales team could be characterized mathematically by an exponential function

$$p_i = ar^{i-1}$$

where: p_i is the estimated percentage for students ranked i;

          r is the ratio of the percentage for any rank to the percentage for the next higher rank;

          a is the estimate for students ranked 1.

Significantly, they also showed that if groups were deliberately distorted—they composed one group out of people that talked a lot and another out of people that hardly talked at all—then the same old J-curve of decreasing participation still appeared.

This process of refinement churned on down the years. The last paper I have come across was published in 1977 by Yung-mei Tsai. This time the groups were United Nations committees of eighteen people representing eighteen nations. The now classic J-curve reappeared, and the original Stephan and Mishler formula accounted for 99 per cent of the variance. Yung-mei Tsai seemed disappointed that the unexplained 1 per cent fell into a regular pattern for which there was no obvious mathematical explanation. (The 'unexplained 1 per cent' was mainly due to the higher ranking participants talking more than the model predicted—something which the Bales team had noticed in the original paper

The question of why this phenomenon appears so universally remains unexplained. The original paper offered the following suggestion:

> ...it can be seen that the top man addresses considerably more remarks to the group as a whole than he addresses to specific individuals. All men of lower basic initiating ranks address more of their remarks to specific individuals (and markedly more to the top man) than to the group as a whole. *This seems to indicate that the top man is acting as a kind of communications centre*, and in this sense is performing a leadership function.
>
> When the amounts each man gives out to the sum of specific individuals is compared to the amounts he receives, a still more suggestive picture is obtained. The top man receives more from particular others in total than he gives out to them specifically. His contributions tend to be addressed more frequently to the group as a whole than to specific persons who address him. All other men, however, tend to receive less from particular others than they give out to them.
>
> (Bales *et al.*, 1951—my emphasis)

If we can get over the unbelievable male chauvinism of this particular passage, we can rephrase the suggestion: the person who speaks most is acting as a kind of communications centre. Some years later, Horvath (1965) offered an alternative explanation. Individuals differ in their reaction times when responding to a conversational pause. The people who speak most have the shortest reaction times.

The 'communications centre' explanation certainly has problems. For instance, in a small group, where everyone can hear quite plainly what is being said, why is a communications centre needed at all. If Jean wants to talk to Lorraine why should she channel her remarks through Doreen. Nevertheless, in a group, this sort of thing does seem to happen—so the explanation needs an explanation. We will return to this particular question in a later chapter. For the moment, the point is that the phenomenon of differential participation is well established and universal. It is paradigmatic in its clarity. It generates puzzles of refinement—how to measure and model that last 1 per cent—and it generates puzzles of explanation. To date there simply is no fully satisfactory explanation.

John James' Model of Size Distribution in Freely Forming Groups

The annual meeting of the American Sociological Society in Denver, 1950, must have been an exciting affair. As well as Bales' talk on the distribution of participation, they heard John James on size distribution. The two papers were then published in the same edition of the *American Sociological Review*. There was, not surprisingly, a strong similarity in the language and manner of approach. Objectivity and formalism—tables of data, and where possible, formulae—were the order of the day. James defined a small human group as one in which:

> ...the members, integrated by direct communication demands, interact functionally and continuously toward the achievement of an end, then the structure resulting from

such interaction is a unitary system of relationships in which the factor of size (number of participants) is one of the determinants of the system. In a word, the size determinant is an integral factor of small group interaction, the fundamental question being the relation of the magnitude of the variable to the range and complexity of the interactory field.

(James, 1951, p. 474)

Stern stuff! What James actually did was to count the number of people in groups, and see how often different sizes of group occurred. Although it is not stated in the paper, James, like Bales, was trying to find out what was going on *before* advancing an explanation for it. He started off with two types of group. On the one hand, he looked at governmental and organizational sub-committees, using reports and minutes, and found that in different areas mean sizes ranged from 4.7 to 7.8. On the other, he made two sets of 'field observations' of people at work and play. He looked at pedestrians, shopping precincts, playgrounds, construction sites, plays, swimming pools, church socials, and many other situations. All in all, his field observations covered 9129 groups. An amazing feat in itself.

The observations in both sets took the form of merely counting group sizes—groups in which the members were in face-to-face interaction as evidenced by the criteria of gesticulation, laughter, smiles, talk, play, or work. Individuals who merely occupied contiguous space were not counted as members of a group.

(ibid. p. 475)

Table 1.1 Frequency distribution of group sizes, by classes of groups

No. in Group	Informal[1]		Stimulated Informal		Work	
x	f	%N	f	%N	f	%N
2	5263	71.07	125	71.02	1104	71.32
3	1496	20.20	38	21.59	357	23.06
4	471	6.36	12	6.82	73	4.72
5	133	1.80	1	0.57	12	0.78
6	41	0.56			2	0.12
7	1	0.01				
	$N=7405$		$N=176$		$N=1548$	

He then tabulated his data, classifying the groups into three kinds (see Table 1.1) and concluded that 'all distributions exhibit the J-curve form'. James goes on to say:

This uniformity suggests that certain conditions, not primarily dependent on age, space, motivation, or social situation, operate to produce the general patterning of group size that was observed. We speculate that ... systems of interaction (groups)

are limited by the number of relationships individuals are able to maintain continuously within a system.

(ibid. p. 476)

In a footnote—on the assumption that there is a paradigm under which 'normal science' is possible—he suggests a consequence

the life of unitary systems characterized by spontaneity may be expressed by the general relation

$$\text{Stability} = \frac{\text{Time}}{\text{Group Size}}$$

(ibid. p. 477)

which would call for further research.

Two years later, James (1953) published a further note in which he showed that the negative binomial (a family of Poisson distributions) was an appropriate model for empirical distributions of small group sizes. Interestingly, the data on sub-committees is dropped, and groups of size 1 (i.e. individuals) are included.

A further 8 years passed before the next paper appeared. This time James collaborated with James Coleman (1961)—using the same data—to produce an explanatory model. They made two basic assumptions: that the probability of any person dropping out of a group was constant, irrespective of the size of the group; that the probability of a group gaining a member was proportional to the number of single persons available. After formalization and substitution in the equations, they generated a truncated Poisson distribution formula, which fitted most of their data rather well. A suggestion was made for further research that would control overall population density. In conclusion they say:

To some, such experiments and the related models for sample processes of interaction may seem trivial. Certainly they add nothing to the richness of our understanding of 'why people behave as they do'. But such a goal of deeper understanding is not the only goal of a science like sociology, and perhaps not even an appropriate one. To be able to *synthesize* individual's actions, to link together our existing understanding of the parts into a system of behaviour is another important goal of sociology.

(Coleman and James, 1961, p. 44)

As far as I know, this particular line of research has not been pursued since. Some people undoubtedly did think it was trivial. I do not—although not for the same reasons given by the authors. More on this later. A more significant reason will have been the sheer cost—not to mention tedium—of collecting all that data. At the moment all that needs saying is that I was impressed by the clarity and simplicity of this study.

Independence and conformity

Solomon Asch's first study—'A minority of one against a unanimous majority'—must count as one of the most important findings in social psychology. The broad question that Asch's work addressed was:

Granting the great power of groups, may we simply conclude that they can induce persons to shift their decisions and convictions in almost any desired direction, that they can prompt us to call true what we yesterday deemed false, that they can make us invest the identical action with the aura of rightness or with the stigma of grotesqueness and malice.

(Asch, 1956, p. 2)

Although the notions of independence and conformity are very general ones, with deep and often contradictory cultural roots in Europe and North America, Asch set up a sequence of highly specific experiments to examine their precise workings. The main experiment appeared, to the people that took part in it, as follows.

You are a student at college. You are between lectures. Another student comes up and asks if you are busy. You say that you are not. He asks if you can spare some time to help in a psychological experiment in visual discrimination. 'Psychological experiment?' 'Visual discrimination?' It could be interesting. You agree. You go with him. You both arrive at the room that's been set aside for the experiment. Other students are waiting outside. There are about seven of them. One you know to speak to. A couple of the other you know by sight. As soon as you arrive, everyone troops into the room. The lecturer—sorry! 'experimenter'—arrives, and you all sit down. You are second from the right in the back row.

The lecturer puts up two cards (Figure 1.2). The first one has a single line on it. The second one has three lines on it. Each one is numbered. The lecturer explains that you have to decide which line on the second card is the same as the line on the first card. That looks easy enough. You settle down a bit. The people in the front row have to give their answers first, then those in the back row, including you. The first two cards are put up. Again the answer is obvious.

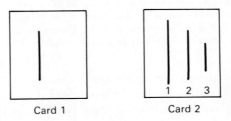

Card 1   Card 2

Figure 1.2

Everyone gives the right answer. The same with the second set of cards. The lecturer is writing down all the answers. The third set of cards are put up. You glance up and see they are fairly short lines, and number 3 is the right answer.

The first person gets it wrong. He thinks the first line—number 1—is the same. The next person gets it wrong too. No-one seems surprised. The lecturer

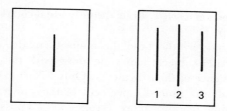

Figure 1.3

just writes the answers down. They are all getting it wrong! Are they seeing something different? Could the first line be right? You screw up your eyes a bit. No—it has to be number 3. Why do they all see it differently? Everybody does. They have all said number 1. It's your turn. What do you say? When it's put like that, it's quite obvious that you would say number 3 because that's the way you see it.

What Asch found was that 17 per cent of his subjects went along with the majority and said number 1. But from then on, the majority continued to give wrong answers to most of the questions, and they gave them unanimously. After twelve 'tests', only 24 per cent of the subjects had 'stuck to their guns' and reported what they saw every time. By the time the majority made its fourth 'mistake' more than half of the people involved were prepared to say what the majority said. This is so remarkable it is worth restating in detail (Table 1.2).

Table 1.2

Number of 'mistakes' made by majority	Proportion of subjects prepared to go along with majority (%)
1	17
2	44
3	50
4	64
5	68
6	70
12	76

What was actually going on? The experiment, of course, was 'fixed'. The students who were already there were in cahoots with the experimenter. They all followed the first person to answer, who in turn read his answers from a card prepared by the experimenter. The object of the experiment was to generate 'a disagreement between a single person and a group concerning a simple and clear matter of *fact*' in which 'the group that disagreed with the individual judged the facts in question *wrongly*, while the individual could not but judge the facts correctly' (ibid. p. 1).

The results were that, by the time the majority made its twelfth wrong judgement, 94 out of 123 subjects had gone along with the majority at least once—against the evidence of their own eyes. Only 24 per cent of the subjects said what they saw all the time. 27 per cent of the subjects yielded to the majority most of the time (eight or more 'errors' out of a possible twelve). The remaining 49 per cent went along with the majority between one and seven times.

Two other results are of interest. Once subjects had yielded to the majority, they continued to yield—whereas the longer they stayed 'independent', the more likely they were to stay independent. The second side effect was the appearance of 'compromise errors'. If the majority judged a very long line to be equal to a very short line, yielding subjects frequently took a middle course, and said the medium-length line was equal to the short line.

Were the subjects a peculiarly spineless lot? All the evidence indicates that they were not. They were all white, male college students, but the 'experimental effect' has been reproduced reliably with lots of other populations. It seems that in this situation, yielding is the most common response. Asch himself tried many variations on the basic situation but the same results always appeared. Thus we may conclude that *what* was observed was a genuine phenomenon.

Two further questions arise. How general is the phenomenon? *Why* does it happen? In several places, Asch expresses doubt about the generality of his results. For instance: 'another interpretation must also be considered a definite possibility, namely, that the consistency observed is specific to the situation studied and may not extend beyond it' (ibid. p. 20).

The question of generality takes several forms. Can the result be reproduced by other experimenters in other places? Here the answer is a definite yes. Can the result be reproduced in similar but different circumstances? Here the answer is also yes. Can the result be seen outside the experimental settings? Here we run into the limitations of social psychological experimentation. The experimental effect is the product of a very unusual situation. Neither the other students nor the experimenter expressed surprise when the subject made a judgement different from their judgement. In fact they all remained totally expressionless throughout. Also, how many of us have ever experienced a straight disagreement over a simple matter of *fact* that cannot be easily resolved? Most disagreements involve opinion, and it is considered legitimate to differ from others in matters of opinion. As Asch says:

> Our procedure produced a failure of consensus where it was least understood and expected, tending to turn disagreement into a more ultimate kind of contradiction. Now consensus, especially on fundamental traits of the surroundings, is the vital prerequisite of social action; to abolish or impair it is to threaten the relations of interdependence which ordinary experience continuously validates.
>
> (ibid. p. 66)

But there is evidence for the Asch conformity effect in folklore. The story of the *King's New Clothes* is the Asch experiment. A unanimous majority announces out loud that it can see the magnificent finery of the king's new robes, and one by one, everyone goes along with it—despite the evidence of their own eyes that the king is stark naked.

Is the effect limited to myth and the social psychology laboratory? In terms of 'Independence and Conformity' I am afraid it is. As was said at the beginning: these notions have deep and often contradictory cultural roots. For instance, the concern with 'conformity' at the time the paper was written must have had its roots in the acquiescence of the German people in the Nazi horrors. How could so many people go along with something they *knew* was wrong? The experiment appears to confirm that it *could* happen, although it has not yet explained why. On the other hand, 'independence' was as much a virtue for the Nazis as it is a fetish with the Americans. The lone hero preserving his integrity in the face of the clamour of the ignorant masses was a favourite fascist theme from *Metropolis* through to Goebbels' 'cultural epics' of 1942–3.

Attempts to generalize the experimental results do so within the framework of 'Independence and conformity', which is reasonable, since this is what the experimenters wanted to examine. Nevertheless it may be that it is the framework that is wrong; the framework that stands in the way of an explanation.

One of the best things about the original Asch paper is the attention given to the explanations of the subjects themselves. Some twenty-five pages are devoted to presentation and explanation of protocols and interview transcripts. It is here that we get a genuine feeling for the nature of the investigation—not in the clear-cut results that are usually quoted. And it is for this reason that it is a great shame that the original paper is now very difficult to get hold of. There is far more to be learned from the things that cannot easily be summarized than from the things that are. Asch himself wanted to *explain* the phenomenon, not just to 'discover' it.

> The task of enquiry in this region is to explore the ways in which group actions become forces in the psychological field of persons, and to describe the forces within persons that co-operate with or resist those induced by the group environment.
>
> (ibid. p. 2)

and

> The pursuit of this problem therefore brings us to the uncharted area of the relations of the person to his own experiences and convictions, and of the relation between these and interpersonal ties. It is in the clarification of these personal-emotional processes that the solution of the present problem lies.
>
> (ibid. p. 52)

But, despite the attempt to remain impartial, there is a clear bias on the part of the experimenters away from the subjects who yielded. Perjorative adjectives are consistently used to describe them and their accounts—'shallow', 'swagger-ing', 'defensive', and so on. This was as nothing to the humiliation experienced, and self-denigration expressed by the subjects who yielded, once the purpose of the experiment had been revealed to them. All this reinforces the aim of generalizing the results within the cultural norms of independent-good and bad-conform.

Perhaps the most striking thing about the interviews is that they do not reveal any great differences between those who yielded and those who did not. Each individual offered their own set of reasons, and although some classification was possible, it was not possible to distinguish—in terms of experience and reasoning—the conformists from the non-conformists.

If we approach the problem from a different framework, a different picture starts to emerge. Let us think of it as a 'problem-solving' situation. The problem is no longer what is *seen* but *how to see* what is there. The first problem is that the problem itself is undefined. The problem might have been to discover why the majority were going wrong. Or—the same problem expressed differently—what was the pattern in the answers given by the majority. If they had got every third question wrong, or if they had always said the longest line was equal to the standard, then their behaviour would have been comprehensible. Strange, but comprehensible.

In fact there was a pattern to the majority responses. There were six lengths of the 'standard' line. With each length of standard line went three 'comparison' lines, only one of which was the same length as the standard line. Whenever the standard line was 2″, 4″, or 10″, the majority answered 'correctly'. Whenever the standard line was 3″, 5″, or 8″, the majority answered 'incorrectly'. Whenever an 'incorrect' answer was required:

> On its first appearance, the majority matched the standard with the comparison line that least deviated from it; when the same lines reappeared, the majority matched the standard line with the line that most deviated from it.
>
> (ibid. p. 7)

The problem sequence of eighteen tests consisted of a repeated set of nine comparisons. In each set of nine comparisons, the tests requiring incorrect answers appeared twice, those requiring correct answers only once. There is enough information in the total sequence to construct an algorithm—quite a complicated one—that would predict the response that the majority would make. This algorithm could not be constructed without full information on at least the first twelve tests, so we are safe in saying that there is no way the innocent members could have detected it. Establishing regularity in difference would have been an important first step in 'solving the problem', but the subjects were denied this outlet. The problem algorithm is sufficiently complex for the experimenters not to trust the majority to remember it. Instead the answers were written down on a card. The first member of the majority read out the answer, and the rest followed him.

This follow-my-leader behaviour was another different kind of regularity. This second regularity seems to have been detected by quite a few of the subjects:

> I actually thought the others were subject to the suggestion of the first one.

> Suppose I told you that your judgements were always right when you disagreed with the group, what would you think?
> —I'd believe it.
> Why?
> —Were the other guys suggested by the first?

> I thought that the ones ahead of me were following the ones ahead of them.

> Frankly, I thought the mob were following the first man.
>
> (ibid. pps. 37, 41, 43, and 48)

The search for an underlying pattern of response would be one way of approaching the undefined problem. This would involve the assumption that everyone *saw* the tests in the same way as the subject. The real problem is then to understand the convention being used by the majority to describe what they saw—and then to decide whether or not to adopt that convention. As one subject expressed it: 'It was like being in a strange country. "When in Rome you do as the Romans do"' (ibid. p.46).

Another way of approaching the undefined problem would be to assume the majority were reporting what they saw and that they were using the same descriptive convention. Our culture provides lots of explanations for this sort of thing. The most obvious one is defective faculties—faulty eyesight. Since A1 vision is itself a convention based on what is normal in a given population, most of the subjects assumed that the majority were seeing normally—and seriously questioned whether their own eyesight was as good as they thought it was. Many considered whether the majority might be defective. 'My first impulse was that maybe they didn't see that one well' (ibid. p. 37).

A second explanation was that either the majority or the subject were suffering from an optical illusion. Many essayed explanations in this area. Some even recreated Berkeley's *Principles of Human Knowledge*:

> Many independent subjects were reluctant to question the accuracy of the majority even when they were confident of their own judgements. (Would you say that the group judged wrongly? 'It's difficult to put it that way: let's say I saw them that way'.)
>
> (Asch, 1956, p.29)

Those achieving independence on this basis seem to have shared more with Berkeley than simply being white male 20-year-old student idealists.

> Berkeley never seriously modified the views thus early arrived at. By the age of twenty or so, he believed he had found the key to a completely satisfactory solution to a vast range of philosophical problems, and he was never conscious of any necessity to qualify this conviction. His surviving correspondence, in fact, shows that in later life

his interest in philosophy was by no means continuous; there is little evidence that he read the philosophical works of his contemporaries, nor did he seek the acquaintance of other philosophers.

(Warnock, 1962)

Idealism was a relatively straightforward solution to the undefined problem in the experimental contradiction. Once 'it seems to be ... ' is substituted for 'it is ... ', there is no more problem and no more need to reflect on the problem. The problem grows increasingly complex as more elements of the experimental world are considered in relation to possible solutions. Was there a trick in the experimental instructions? Is the seating arrangement part of the problem? What does the experimenter *want*? (This seems to have been a major part of the puzzle for many subjects.)

The situation was arranged so that neither the student majority nor the experimenter gave any hint about whether the subject's answers were right or wrong—and thus prevented him from testing any theories about the *meaning* of 'right' and 'wrong' in the 'strange country' of the experiment.

In the event, time was very short, and the subjects had to arrive at quick, arbitrary decisions on the meaning of 'right' and 'wrong'. Since no further information was then given, there was no chance to learn any more about the rules of the game. Even so, there is much evidence of attempts to learn, since about three quarters of the subjects changed their strategy in the course of the experiment.

If we look at the experiment from the perspective of 'problem solving', then the question is not whether the subject is prepared to defy the majority. It is how the subjects defined 'right' and 'wrong'; what evidence they used; and how (and whether) they tried to test their theories. Such questions would extract an entirely different set of relevant responses from the interview transcripts. We are fortunate that there is sufficient interview material for us to be able to raise the question at all.

Asch had discovered a phenomenon that, under strictly defined circumstances, could be reliably reproduced by other experimenters. There was no fully satisfactory explanation of the behaviour of the people that created this 'lawful' regularity. 'Yielders' and 'non-yielders' spoke of having similar experiences, and undergoing similar doubts and suspicions. The formal, statistical, and experimental precision of the experiment, together with the openness of the explanation, allowed successive generations of researchers to create puzzles within the rules. More than this, it created confidence (which I share) that social psychology dealt with definite phenomena, and was consequently a 'real' subject. It was therefore an important paradigm.

The weakness of the paradigm lies in its assumption that 'reality' is physical and object-like; that the phenomena that are discovered are 'there'. We saw a similar assumption in Bion's work and in the presentations of Bales and James. This assumption has created a social psychological 'methodological tradition' which it is very difficult to get round. The methodology owes its strength to its ability to discover phenomena. It is surprisingly weak in the area of explanation.

In our examination of Asch's work we have tried to prize open this weakness a little; to show that the paper was framed in terms of an unproblematic conception of 'right' and 'wrong'. Despite the sensitive reporting of subject's reactions, and the explicit consideration of the theories they developed to try and resolve the situation, Asch comes back to a physicalist conception of the problem facing the subjects. 'He had before him the alternative of adhering openly to his experience and rejecting the majority, or of siding with the majority at the cost of suppressing his direct experience' (ibid. p. 68).

In other words, the subjects were right when they reported what they saw, wrong when they did not. But right and wrong, like truth and falsity, are not given in experience. They are not statements about the world, but statements about statements about the world. From the evidence, it looks as though the subjects were not concerned with the physical world that was given, but with the conventions for making statements about it. It was not right and wrong that was at issue, but 'right' and 'wrong'.

Whyte's Status Hierarchies

William Foote Whyte wrote the classic book *Street Corner Society* which was published in 1943. It was subtitled 'The social structure of an Italian slum'. It demonstrated that every aspect of society has its own definite set of structures and rules. That is the way it is usually taught. Once you get inside the covers, things become less formal. The author becomes Bill Whyte. It is quite clear that he thoroughly enjoyed his research, and that he believed in it—even if, at times, he was not quite sure what he was doing. For me, *that* was the most important *paradigm*. In many ways it was the best definition of 'participant-observation' I have come across. The author includes himself in the account. His description of how to account for himself to the local community is a good example.

> As I began hanging about Cornerville, I found that I needed an explanation for myself and for my study. As long as I was with Doc and vouched for by him, no one asked me who I was or what I was doing. When I circulated in other groups or even among the Nortons without him, it was obvious that they were curious about me.
>
> I began with a rather elaborate explanation. I was studying the social history of Cornerville—but I had a new angle. Instead of working from the past up to the present, I was seeking to get a thorough knowledge of present conditions and then work from present to past. I was quite pleased with this explanation at the time, but nobody else seemed to care for it. I gave the explanation on only two occasions, and each time, when I had finished, there was an awkward silence. No one, myself included, knew what to say.
>
> While this explanation had at least the virtue of covering everything that I might eventually want to do in the district, it was apparently too involved to mean anything to Cornerville people.
>
> I soon found that people were developing their own explanation about me: I was writing a book about Cornerville. This might seem entirely too vague an explanation, and yet it sufficed. I found that my acceptance in the district depended upon the personal relationships I developed far more than upon any explanations I might give. Whether it was a good thing to write a book about Cornerville depended entirely on

people's opinions of me personally. If I was all right, then my project was all right; if I was no good, then no amount of explanation could convince them that the book was a good idea.

(Whyte, 1965, p. 300).

'If I was all right, then the project was all right' just about says it all. I believe we have not yet faced the full implications of that particular 'observation'. For one thing, it means that the subjects of the study participate in the *design* of the research. Inevitably linked to a 'participant-observer' there are a whole number of 'participant-researchers'. To ignore them—or pretend to ignore them—is a recipe for disaster. This is often seen as an empirical problem. How can the researcher be rendered invisible? How can the researcher avoid influencing the subjects? The reverse problem of the subjects influencing the researcher is not often considered in academic circles—probably for very arrogant reasons. Nevertheless, if it were considered, there is no doubt it would be seen as a 'problem'. Whole batteries of techniques for invisibility and deception have been dreamed up. The trouble is that the problem is not empirical. It is a consequence of a methodology that aims at some version of ultimate 'objectivity' in a world where people (thankfully) are not objects. There is a perfectly good way of having an invisible researcher. Do not have a researcher at all.

Fortunately, Whyte was both visible and honest. Many of his findings and suggestions were taken up and developed in social psychology and sociology. They became a series of puzzles for 'normal science'. One splendidly objective finding was the discovery of status hierarchies.

Whyte found that performance in bowling matches was determined by social status and not by talent. Social status is defined thus:

> There were distinctions in rank among the Nortons. Doc, Danny, and Mike held the top positions. They were older than any others except Nutsy. They possessed a greater capacity for social movement. While the followers were restricted to the narrow sphere of one corner, Doc, Danny, and Mike had friends in many other groups and were well known and respected throughout a large part of Cornerville. It was one of their functions to accompany the follower when he had to move outside of his customary social sphere and needed such support. The leadership three were also respected for their intelligence and powers of self-expression. Doc in particular was noted for his skill in argument. On the infrequent occasions when he did become involved, he was usually able to outmaneuver his opponent without humiliating him. I never saw the leadership three exert their authority through physical force, but their past fighting reputations tended to support their positions.
>
> Doc was the leader of the gang. The Nortons had been Doc's gang when they had been boys, and, although the membership had changed, they were still thought to be Doc's gang. The crap game and its social obligations prevented Danny and Mike from spending as much time with the Nortons as did Doc. They were not so intimate with the followers, and they expected him to lead.
>
> Long John was in an anomalous position. Though he was five years younger than Doc, his friendship with the three top men gave him a superior standing. As Doc explained:
>
> It's because we've always catered to Long John. When we go somewhere, we ask Long John to go with us. We come up to him and slap him on the back. We give him so much attention that the rest of the fellows have to respect him.

Nevertheless, he had little authority over the followers. At this time he was accustomed to gamble away his week's earnings in the crap game, and this was thrown up against him.

(ibid. p. 12)

All this looks like a listing of 'objective criteria' for social status. And in a sense it is—because these were the criteria that were used by the Nortons themselves. It is possible to have objective criteria—even objective 'facts' about social life—provided these are underpinned by *subjective agreements*. It is easy to imagine a different context that would reverse the meaning of the criteria listed by Whyte. Mixing with outsiders *could* mean low status. Reckless gambling *could* be part of a high status role.

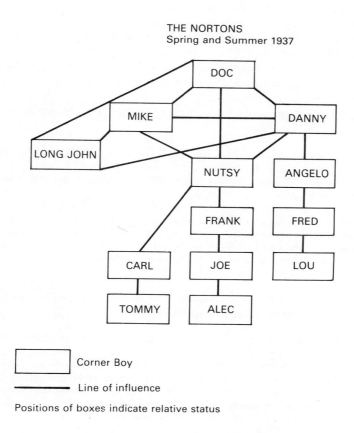

THE NORTONS
Spring and Summer 1937

☐ Corner Boy

▬▬▬ Line of influence

Positions of boxes indicate relative status

Figure 1.4   (From Whyte, 1965, p. 13)

Whyte then matches the status hierarchy (Figure 1.4) against the results of an important in-group bowling contest

The bowlers finished in the following order:

1.	Whyte	6.	Joe
2.	Danny	7.	Mark
3.	Doc	8.	Carl
4.	Long John	9.	Frank
5.	Mike	10.	Alec

(ibid. p. 21)

Although Whyte never did it, this sort of result is very amenable to statistical tests of significance. In this particular case, the correlation of status to bowling result (using Spearman's Rank Correlation Coefficient) is highly significant (0.01)—even without correcting for the non-members Whyte and Mark. If we make this correction, the correlation becomes almost perfect. Whyte contents himself with saying: 'the performances were almost exactly what the leaders expected and the followers feared they would be' (ibid. p. 21).

In keeping with this subjective concept of significance, there is no attempt to establish a 'control group'—which in this case would be an independent measurement of the bowling skill of each individual apart from the group situation. There was, however, good evidence that Frank, Alec, and Joe (as individuals) were excellent bowlers.

Whyte suggests a mechanism that brings bowling performance in line with status:

> There are many mental hazards connected with bowling. In any sport there are critical moments when a player needs the steadiest nerves if he is to 'come through'; but, in those that involve team play and fairly continuous action, the player can sometimes lose himself in the heat of the contest and get by the critical points before he has a chance to 'tighten up'. If he is competing on a five-man team, the bowler must wait a long time for his turn at the alleys, and he has plenty of time to brood over his mistakes. When a man is facing ten pins, he can throw the ball quite casually. But when only one pin remains standing, and his opponents are shouting, 'He can't pick it,' the pressure is on, and there is a tendency to 'tighten up' and lose control.
>
> (ibid. p. 17)

Part of the evidence for this is the commentary made by Doc and Long John on the match results that we have looked at.

> Long John: I only wanted to be sure that Alec or Joe Dodge didn't win. That wouldn't have been right.
> Doc: That's right. We didn't want to make it tough for you, because we all liked you, and the other fellows did too. If somebody had tried to make it tough for you, we would have protected you ... . If Joe Dodge or Alec had been out in front, it would have been different. We would have talked them out of it. We would have made plenty of noise. We would have been really vicious ... .

> I asked Doc what would have happened if Alec or Joe had won.
> They wouldn't have known how to take it. That's why we were out to beat them. If they had won, there would have been a lot of noise. Plenty of arguments. We would have called it lucky—things like that. We would have tried to get them in another match and then ruin them. We would have to put them in their places.
>
> (ibid. p. 21)

On the face of it, this is not very profound. If someone of low status is doing well, his fellows make a lot of noise and put him off. The hierarchy is preserved. It is a fact of everyday life. (In my own experience, I often wondered why there were some people I just could not beat at darts—despite the knowledge that I was better than they were. The converse was not symmetrical. Some people were easy to beat. It was not a problem that they were 'theoretically' better than I.)

With Whyte's work, the fact of everyday life was transformed into a 'fact' of social psychology. The puzzles concerned its generality: how many sports and other activities did it apply to?; how to construct proper control groups?; and so on. The 'facticity' of the result, the relationships between the subjective and objective content, were not questioned. A purified version of the phenomena—its schema—became a model of the sort of thing we should look for.

Erving Goffman's 'Stage' Model of Behaviour

Goffman deals with appearances. The whereabouts of the person—as opposed to the persona—is mysterious. The flavour of this idea is caught in a quote from Simone de Beauvoir:

> Even if each woman dresses in conformity with her status, a game is still being played: artifice, like art, belongs to the realm of the imaginary. It is not only that the girdle, brassiere, hair-dye, make-up disguise body and face; but that the least sophisticated of women, once she is 'dressed', does not present *herself* to observation; she is, like the picture or the statue, or the actor on the stage, an agent through whom is suggested someone not there—that is, the character she represents, but is not. It is this identification with something unreal, fixed, perfect as the hero of a novel, as a portrait or a bust, that gratifies her; she strives to identify herself with this figure and thus to seem to herself to be stabilized, justified in her splendour.
>
> (de Beauvoir, 1953)

The character in the world—the projection from the realm of the imaginary—cannot be treated by the usual rules of science. Even worse, there is ultimately no way of getting at the person behind the mask. Information about others is always inferential, never fully 'factual'. Goffman quotes from W.I. Thomas to make the point:

> It is also highly important for us to realize that we do not as a matter of fact lead our lives, make our decisions, and reach our goals in everyday life either statistically or scientifically. We live by inference. I am, let us say, your guest. You do not know, you cannot determine scientifically, that I will not steal your money or your spoons. But inferentially I will not, and inferentially you have me as a guest.
>
> (Thomas, W.I., 1951, p. 5)

So we never finally and factually *know* about others. Goffman does not go into this as a *problem*. It is simply a *condition* of our knowledge about others. The problem is to give an account of our dealings with others once we know it cannot be 'scientific' in the traditional sense. We need a framework to give an account at all, and Goffman settles for *analogy* rather than 'theory'. The theatre is the basic analogy that runs through all his work.

People give performances. Not just the famous and rich, but quite ordinary people doing quite ordinary things. We have seen de Beauvoir's description of a person becoming a 'woman'. That involved the use of 'costume' and 'props'. Perhaps the simplest example of a performance is taken from Goffman's study of a crofting community. The houses were very dark inside. There was a custom, when visiting, of always being pleasant and pleased to see people. So when a visitor arrived, whatever they were actually thinking or feeling, they would put on a pleasant face as they entered the croft. The crofters, of course, could see out, although the approaching visitor could not see in. They often amused themselves by watching the abrupt change of expression as the visitor reached the threshold. Some visitors knew about this and started their performance early. They put on a glassy-eyed beam as they approached the croft—just in case they were being observed.

Apart from 'costume', 'props', and 'performance', there is the 'stage'. Onstage, convention and expectation are catered for.

> If the bereaved are to be given the impression that the dead one is really in a deep and tranquil sleep, then the undertaker must be able to keep the bereaved from the workroom where the corpses are drained, stuffed, and painted in preparation for their final performance. If a mental hospital staff is to give a good impression of the hospital to those who come to visit their committed kinfolk, then it will be important to be able to bar visitors from the wards, especially the chronic wards, restricting the outsiders to special visiting-rooms where it will be practicable to have relatively nice furnishings and to ensure that all patients are well dressed, well washed, well handled, and relatively well behaved.
>
> (Goffman, 1969, p.116)

And where there is a stage, there is also a backstage:

> Throughout Western society, there tends to be one informal or backstage language of behaviour, and another language of behaviour for occasions when a performance is being presented. The backstage language consists of reciprocal first-naming, co-operative decision making, profanity, open sexual remarks, elaborate griping, smoking, rough informal dress, 'sloppy' sitting and standing posture, use of dialect or sub-standard speech, mumbling and shouting, playful aggressivity and 'kidding', inconsiderateness for the other in minor but potentially symbolic acts, minor physical self-involvements such as humming, whistling, chewing, nibbling, belching, and flatulance. The frontstage behaviour language can be taken as the absence (and in some sense the opposite) of this.
>
> (ibid, p. 129)

For most (non-theatre) performances, the places that are used as 'frontstage' and 'backstage' are not fixed. The whole house may be backstage on a Saturday morning when the kids are playing. In the evening, when the visitors arrive, only the kitchen and bedrooms are backstage.

Two important things stand out about performances, apart from the auxiliary concepts of 'props', 'rehearsals', and so on. Performances are *managed*. The self is presented, it does not simply appear. It is therefore appropriate to study the rules of presentation—and in this there is a complete continuity between ordinary life and social science. People are concerned, implicitly or explicitly, to find out what is going on. Impressions are managed, implicitly or explicitly, to answer that question.

Performances are *staged by teams*. Although Goffman frequently deals with individual selves, and explicitly says: 'Another disclaimer. This book is about the organization of experience—something that an individual actor can take into his mind—and not the organization of society' (Goffman 1976) there is a non-individual dimension to the thought that makes performances essentially *public*. At the first level, it is clear that it is public experiences that are being organized. We are not concerned with the deep crannies of individual motivation, but the framework within which the individual is expressed. At the second level, we have to consider the ontological status of the 'framework'—what sort of reality is it? Goffman's answer is clear.

> When we allow that the individual projects a definition of the situation when he appears before others, we must also see that the others, however passive their role may seem to be, will themselves effectively project a definition of the situation by virtue of their response to the individual and by virtue of any lines of action they initiate to him. Ordinarily the definitions of the situation projected by the several different participants are sufficiently attuned to one another, so that open contradiction will not occur. I do not mean that there will be the kind of consensus that arises when each individual present candidly expresses what he really feels and honestly agrees with the expressed feelings of the others present. This kind of harmony is an optimistic ideal and in any case not necessary for the smooth working of society. Rather, each participant is expected to suppress his immediate heartfelt feelings, conveying a view of the situation which he feels the others will be able to find at least temporarily acceptable. The maintenance of this surface of agreement, this veneer of consensus, is facilitated by each participant concealing his own wants behind statements which assert values to which everyone present feels obliged to give lip service. Further, there is usually a kind of division of definitional labour. Each participant is allowed to establish the tentative official rule regarding matters which are vital to him but not immediately important to others, e.g. the rationalizations and justifications by which he accounts for his past activity. In exchange for this courtesy he remains silent or non-committal on matters important to others but not immediately important to him. We have then a kind of interactional *modus vivendi*. Together the participants contribute to a single over-all definition of the situation which involves not so much a real agreement as to what exists but rather a real agreement as to whose claims concerning what issues will be temporarily honoured.
>
> (Goffman, 1969, p. 20)

And again, more pointedly:

> And now a final comment. In developing the conceptual framework employed in this report, some language of the stage was used. I spoke of performances and audiences; of performances coming off or falling flat; of cues, stage settings, and backstage; of dramaturgical needs, dramaturgical skills, and dramaturgical strategies. Now it should be admitted that this attempt to press a mere analogy so far was in part a rhetoric and a manoeuvre.
>
> And so here the language and mask of the stage will be dropped. Scaffolds, after all, are to build other things with, and should be erected with an eye to taking them down. This report is not concerned with aspects of theatre that creep into everyday life. It is concerned with the structure of social encounters—the structure of those entities in social life that come into being whenever persons come into one another's immediate physical presence. The key factor in this structure is the maintenance of a

single definition of the situation, this definition having to be expressed, and this expression sustained in the face of a multitude of potential disruptions.

(ibid. p. 246)

The maintenance of a single definition of the situation is the work of a group, and it is a public work.

Part of the object of the performance is the maintenance of the public definition of the situation. This account of the formation and maintenance of realities begins to look like science. In *Frame Analysis*, we see the emergence of a large number of 'technical' terms that are not used in everyday conversation. Goffman moves from direct theatrical analogy to a sort of abstract schema of that analogy—the framework of our frameworks. Here the most important concepts are 'primary framework', 'bracketing', and 'keying'.

A 'primary framework' is simply the assumption we make about what is going on. It is a framework because it is an interpretation. It is primary because it is the starting point. There is nothing *more* basic. It may be elaborated or changed or it may become very complicated as we superimpose new frameworks, but it is the starting point. A primary framework is like a gestalt. It enables us to recognize social situations without difficulty. The shop is closed. That is a bus queue. That is a football match. And so on.

'Bracketing' is the way our frameworks slice up reality into chunks we can deal with. When we recognize some situation—like a bus queue—we set it apart from other goings-on. We put brackets round it, give it a beginning and an end, and a position in space. Some brackets enclose very small goings-on: swatting a mosquito; glancing in a shop window. Others can be positively historical in scope: rebuilding the City Centre; campaigning for women's rights within the trades unions. Nevertheless, anything that is bracketed can be recognized.

'Keying' is the activity that changes the contents of the brackets, and the appropriate framework. A hand movement may tell us that someone is not (glancing in a shop window) but (using the reflection to see if their hair is ruffled). Some activities may be inherently ambiguous so that it is difficult to find the right key; others may be deliberately ambiguous or misleading, as when the gasman is a burglar. Other activities may be ambiguous because different people have different keys. The interpretation may be a genuine matter of conflict. Goffman provides a good example:

'This is an important speech,' the barrel-chested welterweight instructor of the Experimental College course in guerrilla warfare explained. 'This is where Carmichael sets a new direction for the Black Power movement—calling on blacks to organize themselves, become nationalistic, almost racist.'

After the speech, recorded at Huey Newton's birthday party rally in Oakland, a panel of 'combat veterans' took the stage and reviewed, historically, the tactics and practice of urban warfare, discussing sabotage, espionage, counter-intelligence and weaponry, with emphasis on the Battle of Algiers.

This unusual college class, a subject of controversy off campus, is being investigated by the state attorney general's office.

'If it is a classroom discussion on guerrilla warfare,' says Charles O'Brien,—chief deputy attorney general here, 'that is one thing; if it is an exercise in guerrilla warfare, if they are training guerrillas, that is quite another thing.'

(Goffman, 1976, p. 68)

In this case the content of the brackets is agreed, but the framework is not. Here a change in framework, a new key, would change the contents of the brackets, although there might be no *new* information about the actual events. We see that sets of events are not just bracketed

(   )

they are also keyed

"   "

and these two symbols provide us with a framework for analysing any social situation whatever:

"(   )"

because we can have as many brackets and keys as we like, in any order we like. Credits usually appear at the end of films and provide the closing bracket. In the Monty Python television series, the credits were followed by the news—which was followed by the news. The newsreader in the second news had to start by explaining that he was 'really' the news. The Python team had keyed their last bracket

(monty python ")"

so that it fouled up all the following brackets. The question of how far we can go with this sort of formalism, and how it could or should be used, is itself a problem. For the moment we may say that recognizing situations by bracketing and keying may be a funny way of putting it, but it is intuitively very much what we do in everyday life. Goffman's 'science' is very close to the fullness of practical life:

> When an individual enters the presence of others, they commonly seek to acquire information about him or to bring into play information about him already possessed. They will be interested in his general socio-economic status, his conception of self, his attitude towards them, his competence, his trustworthiness, etc. Although some of this information seems to be sought almost as an end in itself, there are usually quite practical reasons for acquiring it.

(Goffman, 1969, p. 13)

The paradigmatic aspects I have tried to illustrate are:

The systematic use of analogy. Even the more abstract notions of bracketing and keying are analogies from logic and music. The use of analogy is itself grounded in a conception that social reality is not amenable to the methods of 'normal' physical science because ultimately it is a projection from the realm of the imaginary.

The refusal to deal in any currency but the subjective: 'What is real to people?'

The location of the subjective in the structure of the encounter, in the tacit and explicit agreements between people to maintain a 'single definition of the situation' however fuzzy.

The disregard for the 'scientific' fetish of objectivity as a problem, and the appearance of subjectivity as a condition for, and subject of knowledge, whether practical or scientific. And following directly from this

The conception of subjectivity as social reality, grounded in activities between people that are essentially public.

Themes ...

From the examples that have been cited, two main themes should now be standing out. The first theme is *recurrence*. To be worth naming, a phenomenon has to recur and be recognizable as the same thing. The distribution of size and participation in groups always follows the same pattern. The Asch 'majority effect' can be 'reliably reproduced' by those that wish to do such things. I am sure that fight/flight and so on always appear in Bion groups. Whyte's 'status hierarchies' and Goffman's 'performances' can be widely found in everyday life. When a phenomenon recurs and has been given a name, it appears to be 'out there'. Exactly what it means for a social phenomenon to be objectively 'there' is a matter of *doubt*. This is the second theme.

References

Argyle, M. (1967), *The Psychology of Interpersonal Behaviour*, Harmondsworth, Penguin.

Asch, S.E. (1956), Studies of independence and conformity; a minority of one against a unanimous majority, *Psychological Monographs*, **70**, 9.

Bales, R.F., *et al.* (1951), Channels of communication in small groups, *American Sociological Review*, **16** 461–467.

Bion, W.R. (1968), *Experiences in Groups*, London, Tavistock.

Coleman, J.S. and James, J. (1961), The equilibrium size distribution of freely-forming groups, *Sociometry* **24**, 36–45.

de Beauvoir, S. (1953), *The Second Sex* (translated by H.M. Parshley), London, Cape.

Goffman, E. (1969), *The Presentation of Self in Everyday Life*, Harmondsworth, Penguin.

Goffman, E. (1976), *Frame Analysis*, Harmondsworth, Penguin.

Harré, R. (1979), *Social Being*, Southampton, Camelot Press.

Horvath, W.J.A. (1965), A mathematical model of participation in small group discussions, *Behavioural Science*, **10**, 164–166.

James, J. (1951), A preliminary study of the size determinant in small group interaction, *American Sociological Review*, **16**, 474–477.

James, J. (1953), The distribution of free-forming small group size, *American Sociological Review*, **18**, 569–570.

Kuhn, T.S. (1970), *The Structure of Scientific Revolutions*, International Encyclopedia of Unified Science, London and Chicago, The University of Chicago Press.

Stephan, F.F. and Mishler, E.G. (1952), The distribution of participation in small groups, *American Sociological Review*, **17,** 598–608.

Thomas, W.I. (1951), Contributions of W.I.Thomas to theory and social research in *Social Behaviour and Personality*, Social Science Research Council, New York.

Warnock, G.J. (1962), Introduction, in *The Principles of Human Knowledge*, (G. Berkeley) 7–39, La Salle, Illinois, Open Court.

Whyte, W.F. (1965), *Street Corner Society*, Chicago and London, The University of Chicago Press.

Yung-Mei, Tsai, (1972), Hierarchical structure of participation in natural groups, *Behavioural Science*, **22**, 1, 38–40.

CHAPTER 2

Cybernetic paradigms

In the last chapter we looked at 'objects' that were thought of as being out 'there'. In this chapter we will look at 'systems'. A system is just a constellation of objects—but the emphasis is placed on the nature of the constellation rather than the nature of the object. The spirit behind this kind of explanation is caught by Cartwright and Zander (1969) who distinguished eight distinct traditions of small group research, and went on to say:

> A promising lead, however, has been provided by March and Simon (1958), who have developed several 'maps' which show how the relations among variables reported by different investigators may be combined. These maps make it clear that a fully adequate understanding of the determinants of group life will involve a specification of a network of causal relationships. One of their maps indicates, for example, that the extent to which goals are perceived as shared and the number of individual needs satisfied in the group jointly determine the frequency of interaction in the group, which influences the strength of identification with the group, which in turn affects the extent to which goals are perceived as shared and the number of individual needs satisfied in the group. In other words, there is a circular chain of causal interactions.
>
> The field of group dynamics appears to be ready for rapid progress in the construction of such maps. As attention shifts from isolated causal relations between variables taken two at a time to configurations of relations, a more penetrating understanding of the nature of group life will quickly emerge. And, as a result, the practical value of group dynamics theory will be greatly enhanced, since practitioners must be concerned, not with single relationships, but with the total ramifications that stem from the modification of any particular variable.
>
> (Cartwright and Zander, 1969, p. 30)

That *would* have been a good direction for social psychology to follow. Unfortunately, the causal tradition remained dominant. The identification of 'circular chains' remained a distant ambition. For paradigms about 'what is there' and 'how to get at it' we can remain within social psychology. For paradigms about 'why?' we have to step outside, to sociology, to anthropology, to ethology, and to the other life sciences. If we group these studies by what they have in common, then we have a set of cybernetic paradigms.

Ecological Psychology

This phrase was coined by Roger Barker in a series of undeservedly little known papers and books. Barker and his colleagues were originally concerned with the 'natural distribution' of psychological behaviour. They point out that psychological phenomena are known, but that it is not known how often and where they actually appear in the world. They say:

> This state of affairs is most surprising in view of the situation in the old, prestigeful sciences that psychology so admires, and emulates in other respects. In these sciences, the quest for the phenomena of science as they occur unaltered by the techniques of search and discovery is a central continuing task; ... Handbooks and encyclopedias attest to the success of these efforts. We read, for example, that potassium (K) ranks seventh in order of abundance of elements, and constitutes about 2.59 per cent of the igneous rocks of the earth's crust; that its compounds are widely distributed in the primary rocks, the oceans, the soil, plants, and animals; and that soluble potassium salts are present in all fertile soils (*Encyclopaedia Britannica*, 1962). The fact that there is no equivalent information in the literature of scientific psychology (about playing, about laughing, about talking, about being valued and devalued, about conflict, about failure) confronts psychologists with a monumental incompleted task. This is the task of ecological psychology.

(Barker, 1968, p.145)

Barker also considers the problem that psychologists, by controlling the environment in which they collect their 'data', may be collecting restricted, even artificial 'facts'.

> Take intelligence, for example. Millions of reliable and valid intelligence tests have been administered, scored, and reported. ... These data provide basic information about intellectual functioning within test-score generating systems. ... But this great and successful scientific assault on the problem of intelligence has provided almost no information about the intellectual demands the environments of life make upon people, and how people respond to the 'test items' with which they are confronted in the course of living. The science of psychology provides almost no information about the intelligence of people outside of data-generating systems operated by psychologists.
>
> Or take frustration as another example. Experiments have provided basic information about the consequences for children of frustration, as defined and contrived in the experiments. ... But Fawl, who did *not* contrive frustration for his subjects, but studied it in transducer records of children's everyday behaviour, reported (Fawl, 1963, p. 99)
>
>> 'The results ... were surprising in two respects. First, even with a liberal interpretation of frustration, fewer incidents were detected than we expected ... Second, meaningful relationships could not be found between frustration ... and consequent behaviour such as ... regression ... and other theoretically meaningful behavioural manifestation.'
>
> In other words, frustration was rare in children's days, and when it did occur it did not have the behavioural consequences observed in the laboratory. It appears that the earlier experiments simulated frustration very well as defined and prescribed in theories, but the experiments did not simulate frustration as life prescribes it for children.

(Barker, 1968, p. 144)

The attempt to rise above these problems, and identify 'units' in the 'Stream of Behaviour' (Barker, 1963) soon led to a much more sophisticated concept: *The Behaviour Setting*. In an account of experimental techniques that foreshadows the Harré criticism we considered in the last chapter, we find:

> The view is not uncommon amongst psychologists that the environment of behaviour is a relatively unstructured, passive, probabilistic arena of objects and events upon which man behaves in accordance with the programming he carries about within himself'.

to which Barker counterposes the view that the environment of behaviour is a phenomenon worthy of investigation in itself; that

> the environment is seen to consist of highly structured, improbable arrangements of objects and events which co-erce behaviour in accordance with their own dynamic patterning.
>
> (ibid. p. 4)

This idea is frequently emphasized. 'Studies of ... behaviour settings provide evidence that they are stable, extra-individual units with great co-ercive power over the behaviour that occurs within them' (ibid. p. 17). The argument that underlies this is straightforward.

> 'we made long records of children's behaviour in real-life settings ... *we found that some attributes of behaviour varied less across children within settings than across settings within the days of children.* We found, in short, that we could predict some aspects of children's behaviour more adequately from knowledge of the behaviour characteristics of the drugstores, arithmetic classes, and basketball games they inhabited than from knowledge of the behaviour tendencies of particular children.
>
> (ibid. p. 4—my emphasis)

An important aspect of the idea of behaviour settings is that they cut across traditional scientific boundaries.

> The physical sciences have avoided phenomena with behavior as a component, and the behavioral sciences have avoided phenomena with physical things and conditions as essential elements. So we have sciences of behavior-free objects and events (ponds, glaciers, and lightning flashes), and we have sciences of phenomena without geophysical loci and attributes (organizations, social classes, roles). We lack a science of things and occurrences that have both physical and behavioral attributes. Behavior settings are such phenomena;
>
> (ibid. p. 19)

Barker devoted many pages to the rigorous definition of behaviour settings. Locus, duration, frequency, structure, independence/interdependence, autonomy, coercion, functional positions of inhabitants ('performance zones'), and other things are defined and extensively tested for applicability and observer reliability. For our purposes, the intuitive idea of a behaviour setting— something with both behavioural and physical aspects—is captured in the following passage.

EXAMPLES OF MIDWEST BEHAVIOR SETTINGS

The December 12, 1963, issue of *The Midwest Weekly* contained the following three items:

Midwest County Barracks and Auxiliary, Veterans of WW I, met Nov. 21 in the Legion Hall in Midwest. Fifty-eight members were there to enjoy Thanksgiving festivities. Officers elected will be installed next month. Owing to our regular meeting date being too close to Christmas, we will meet Dec. 19 at 6:30 in the Legion Hall at Midwest. The ladies auxiliary will serve two turkeys. You bring the trimmings and a 25¢ gift and we will have a Merry Christmas party.

On Saturday, Dec. 7, seventeen MHS Latin students and Miss Hoffer attended the Foreign Language Christmas Festival at Ellton State College. They began the day by registering in Albert Taylor Hall, the main building. They practiced Christmas carols in Latin, saw a motion picture in Latin, and listened to tapes of 'interviews on Mt. Olympus'. They attended the Festival in the afternoon and sang their carols along with students of other languages. The program closed with the breaking of the pinata.

Watches—Diamonds
EXPERT REPAIR
Ruttley's Jewelry
Midwest, Kansas

These are glimpses of three behavior settings that occurred in Midwest during the year 1963–64, namely, American Legion World War I Barracks and Auxiliary Meeting and Dinner (of the genotype Dinners with Business Meetings), High School Latin Class Trip to Convention at State College (of the genotype Latin Classes), and Ruttleys Jewelry and Watch Repair Shop (of the genotype Jewelry Stores). The December 12, 1963, issue of *The Midwest Weekly* was in no way an unusual issue; it described the week in Midwest in terms of 106 behavior settings similar to the three above; the settings were of 60 genotypes. In 79 of the 106 behavior setting reports, one or more individuals were identified as participants (usually performers), as in the second and third items above; the other 27 reports describe standing patterns of settings, or fragments of them, without identifying any inhabitant, as in the first news item. In addition to the 106 items about behavior settings within the town, there were two reports of behavior in unspecified settings, 11 reports of out-of-town activities in the behavior settings of other communities, 26 reports of activities within behavior settings of private homes in town, and 14 reports of visits of residents to homes outside of Midwest.

The Midwest Weekly exemplifies the importance of behavior settings in the everyday lives of Midwest residents; settings are, in fact, their most common means of describing the town's behavior and environment. The hybrid, eco-behavioral character of behavior settings appears to present Midwest's inhabitants with no difficulty; nouns that combine milieu and standing behavior pattern are common, e.g., oyster supper, basketball game, turkey dinner, golden gavel ceremony, cake walk, back surgery, gift exchange, livestock auction, auto repair.

(ibid. p. 93)

Repeatable events such as these, with physical *and* behavioural aspects, are good examples of the notion of *ritual* that will be developed in the next chapter. Barker himself explores the dynamics and stability (or otherwise) of behaviour settings in terms of 'circuits' and 'mechanisms'. In the original text examples outweight theory. The behaviour described is often interesting and humorous, full and idiosyncratic. At no point does the effort of formalization dominate a warm and human approach—in many ways this general method of investigation seems to encourage it. Much of this is necessarily lost in the following abbreviated account of some of these 'circuits' and 'mechanisms'.

Goal Circuits. Within a behavior setting there are routes to goals that are satisfying to the inhabitants. A setting exists only so long as it provides its inhabitants with traversable routes to the goals their own unique natures require. In a behavior setting of the genotype Baseball Games, for example, the pitcher may achieve satisfactions by striking out batters, the umpire by earning $25, the concessionaire by selling many hot dogs, and the hometown fans by cheering the team to victory. Unless a sufficient number of the inhabitants of a baseball game are at least minimally satisfied, they will leave the setting, or will not return on another occasion, and the setting will cease.

(ibid. p. 167)

The idea of a goal circuit is fairly self-evident.

Program Circuits. The program of a behavior setting has been defined and discussed previously (see p. 80); it is the schedule of eco-behavioral occurrences that comprise a particular behavior setting. The complete program of a setting is usually stored within the inhabitants of penetration zone 5/6; parts of it are stored within the inhabitants of more peripheral zones. The program is sometimes written out, as in the lesson schedule of a teacher or the agenda and operational guides (e.g., Roberts' Rules of Order) of a business meeting.

Actions along a program circuit are reported in the italicized parts of the following record of Steven Peake, seven years, nine months, within the Yoredale behavior setting Upper Infants Music Class (Barker *et al.*, 1961). The class was assembled for rhythm band in the Cooking and Woodworking room of the school; it was taught by Miss Rutherford. The workbenches were pushed against the wall and the piano brought to the center of the room. The children stood in a semicircle around the piano.

1:52. *Miss Rutherford said, 'All find your places'.*
Steven stood next to Herbert.
Steven exchanged a playful remark with Oran.

Miss Rutherford started to give out the instruments, castanets, triangles, tambourines, drums, and cymbals.

Cymbals were suspended from straps by which they were held.

1:53. *Miss Rutherford handed a cymbal to Steven.*
When all the instruments had been distributed, Miss Rutherford asked that, first of all, they all stop talking.

Steven struck his cymbal lightly with his fist.

The essential features of this circuit are knowledge of the program by one or more inhabitants of the setting and actions by them that control the order of the occurrences that characterize the program.

(ibid. p. 168)

The idea of a programme circuit is particularly important. The notion of 'programme' is of course an analogy—but it goes much further than most analogies in social science. It assumes that there is a coherence to the total situation that can be grasped by the inhabitants, and that this coherence could (in principle) be represented as a series of step-by-step instructions. It also makes a point that is often missed. *The programme for any event need not be contained within any one person.* It could be argued that the programme for any event is only rarely contained within any one person. Let us look at an example.

'Inhabitants of penetration zones 5/6' are defined as 'joint leaders' (zone 5) and 'single leader' (zone 6), and both have 'immediate' authority over the whole setting. Miss Rutherford occupied zone 6 in the example. Zone 1 contains 'onlookers'; zone 2 'audience or invited guest'; zone 3 'member of customer'; and zone 4 'active functionaries'. Miss Rutherford's class of children occupied zone 4—they were active participants in the lesson. They carried at least one essential part of the programme; namely, they had to recognize that Miss Rutherford, not they, carried the main programme. She was instructing and ordering them, not vice versa. Had the children not recognized this there would have been no lesson. Settings become what they are because the parts of the programme carried by different individuals come together to constitute the setting—*but the setting itself contributes to the bringing together of these programmes that constitute it.*

If we use the notion of programme, it does not matter very much how it is embodied. We said earlier that it could in principle be represented as a series of step-by-step instructions. Actually it could *be* a series of step-by-step instructions. It could also be (in part) the physical arrangement of the setting. Instead of asking people to sit in a circle, the chairs are arranged in a circle before they arrive. In terms of the programme, there is no difference. *The physical structure of the setting itself carries part of the programme.* We have all experienced the coercion of settings—'the grass needs cutting again'. It is experienced as if the grass itself contained the message—which is true if it is conceived as a programme carrier. The beneficial effects of being able to encode our intentions into our environment are less obvious. They are usually only conspicuous by their absence—or by the demands they make on us for their maintenance.

We will see in later chapters that the existence of a physical setting that can be used to carry part of the programme makes a lot of difference to groups. Without a specific meeting place they have to do 'work' that would otherwise be turned to developing the group and its activities. Simply getting a meeting together is a considerable effort if the meeting place, time, and date part of the programme cannot be sloughed off into the physical setting itself. There is a qualitative difference between groups that have established a 'habitat' for themselves and those that have not.

Deviation-countering Circuits. This is one of two types of circuits by which a behavior setting is maintained with its routes and goals intact. Deviation-countering circuits are involved within a behavior setting of the genotype Grocery Stores, for example, when the proprietor corrects a clerk's errors in pricing articles, when an employee repairs a broken shelf, when the refrigerators operate and keep their contents cool. Inaccurate employees, broken shelving, and warm refrigerators are grocery store components that destroy and/or block routes to goals (profits, wages, groceries) that various inhabitants achieve; they are deviancies, or inadequacies, that must be dealt with if the program of a grocery store is to be carried out and the inhabitants are to achieve the satisfactions they seek. One way of dealing with inadequacies or deviancies of this kind is to correct or counter them.

Vetoing Circuits. These circuits are identical with deviation-countering circuits except that the behavior setting deviancy is not countered; rather, the deviant component is eliminated. Vetoing circuits are involved when an inaccurate employee is not corrected, but fired; and when a broken shelf is not repaired, but discarded. Action along this circuit is exhibited in the behavior toward Oran of Miss Rutherford at a later point in the record of Steven Peake; the vetoing action is italicized.

2:10. Miss Rutherford commanded, 'Pick up your instruments'.
Oran was acting silly.
   Miss Rutherford said, 'Evidently you do not wish to play in our band, Oran.' She took his cymbal away from him and gave it to Selna Bradley. The string holding her triangle had broken and she was without an instrument. *Miss Rutherford put Oran on the far side of the piano away from the class.*

(ibid. p. 169)

Both deviation-countering and vetoing circuits illustrate how a wide variety of behaviours can be covered by an informative, but very general category.

Barker's notions of the operations of circuits, mechanism, and programme within bounded areas (which together constitute the behaviour setting) have been summarized in some detail because this sort of formalization opens the way for *simulation*(although this was not one of Barker's immediate objectives). Social processes that are represented in these ways can be explored by symbolic 'experiments' on computers or other devices. 'Programme' is a testable analogy. Both consequences and assumptions can be examined. Processes can be compared with actual events and histories. There is a further important consequence of this type of experiment and observation that sets it apart from those we looked at in the last chapter.

It becomes increasingly difficult to confuse the model with the reality

In the social psychology laboratory, the model is embedded in the reality. The aims of the experimenter, the physical set-up, and the behaviour of the subjects are all one. It is easy to assume that the model is what the people are doing. The assumption only starts to come adrift when it is found that every such phenomenon (conformity, participation, etc.) generates a multitude of conflicting explanations. Explanation of the mechanics of the model and explanation of the behaviour of the people are taken to be the same thing. With simulation, the possibilities of such confusions are greatly reduced—not because of any theoretical breakthrough, but simply because it is easier to distinguish the model from the people when you look at them separately.

It is essential to distinguish the 'stream of behaviour' from a stream of symbols. Barker's work is paradigmatic because it achieves this.

Undermanned Behaviour Settings

As a footnote to the paradigmatic aspects of Barker's work, we should look at his concept of the undermanned behaviour setting. This is a notion that will be picked up later when we come to consider the effects of size changes on group life.

Figure 2.1　Vetoing circuits

If we accept that 'a decrease in the number of inhabitants of a behaviour setting ... does not, within limits, change the program or the standing pattern of the setting', then it is obvious that the remaining inhabitants will have to do more to keep the 'setting' going. Barker lists twelve ways in which the inhabitants do more. They engage in more and more varied programme, maintenance, and deviation-countering actions; they are induced to do more; they do more difficult and more important actions more frequently; and 'the inhabitants of undermanned behaviour settings *enter more frequently into the central zones* of behaviour settings' (ibid. p. 192). In other words, it is easier to pass from being an onlooker or a guest to being an active participant in an undermanned than in an 'optimally' or an overmanned setting. More people are chucked out—'vetoed'—in an overmanned setting. Or

> If there are 30 candidates for players in the baseball game, a better game will result with less fuss and bother (less energy devoted to maintenance) if all four-year-olds, mothers, and others who are likely to produce deviant behaviour are vetoed out. The situation is different for behaviour settings with fewer than the optimal number of inhabitants. These settings must make great use of deviation-countering control mechanisms because their inhabitants are functionally too important to be casually eliminated by veto.
>
> (ibid. p. 181)

This concept of over- and undermanned settings will prove valuable when we come to consider various studies on 'group size'.

Psychiatry: Batesons's Double Bind Theory of Schizophrenia

Double Bind theory is of interest here not because it is correct—which it probably is not—but because it locates schizophrenia as a social process in the family, not an individual process in the head.

In essence, the theory says that the identified schizophrenic 'must live in a universe where the sequence of events are such that his unconventional communication habits will be in some sense appropriate' (Bateson, 1956). The 'unconventional communication habits' are statements that seem irrelevant, inappropriate, silly, or mysterious. But the statements are not random. One can sense an underlying logic—an alien logic that confuses rather than clarifies.

> Men die
> Grass dies
> Men are grass

Bateson says that this sort of attempt to formalize schizophrenic logic

> is only a more precise—and therefore valuable—way of saying that a schizophrenic utterance is rich in metaphor. With that generalization we agree. But metaphor is an indispensable tool of thought and expression—a characteristic of all communication, even that of the scientist. The conceptual models of cybernetics and the energy theories of psychoanalysis are, after all, only labelled metaphors. The peculiarity of the schizophrenic is not that he uses metaphors, but that he uses *unlabelled* metaphors.
>
> (ibid.)

By using an unlabelled metaphor, the schizophrenic avoids making any definite statement. It is up to the other person to interpret and give a definite meaning—which can always be denied. The schizophrenic is making use of the magical property of language that allows words to change their meaning. 'I hate you' has no meaning if we do not know the context, the tone of voice, and so on. It could mean (I hate you). It could mean (You are very clever to see the answer so quickly when I have been searching for hours). It could mean (Thank you. I love you). The schizophrenic specializes in removing the cues that tell us what they mean.

In what sort of universe is this communication strategy appropriate? Bateson answers the question clearly. The patient has been subjected by other people (usually the family) to a frequently repeated experience of the double bind. It becomes *habitual* to expect double binds. The ingredients of the double bind are:

> *A primary negative injunction.* This may have either of two forms:(a) 'Do not do so-and-so or I will punish you' or (b) 'If you do not do so-and-so I will punish you'.

> *A secondary injunction conflicting with the first at a more abstract level, and like the first enforced by punishments or signals that threaten survival.* This secondary injunction is more difficult to describe ... is commonly communicated to the child by non-verbal means. Posture, gesture, tone of voice ... may all be used to convey this more abstract message. ... 'Do not see this as a punishment'; 'Do not see me as the punishing agent'; 'Do not submit to my prohibitions'; 'Do not think of what you must not do'.

> *A tertiary negative injunction prohibiting the victim from escaping from the field.* In a formal sense it is perhaps unnecessary to list this injunction as a separate item ... if the double binds are imposed during infancy, escape is naturally impossible. However, it seems that in some cases the escape from the field is made impossible by certain devices which are not purely negative, e.g. capricious promises of love and the like.

> (ibid.)

For example:

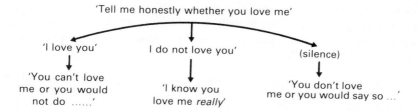

Once the victim has learned to see the world in double-bind patterns, the complete set of injunctions is no longer necessary—any part of it will trigger the schizophrenic response.

Bateson illustrates this process as follows:

> A young man who had fairly well recovered from an acute schizophrenic episode was visited in the hospital by his mother. He was glad to see her, and impulsively put his arm round her shoulders, whereupon she stiffened. He withdrew his arm and she asked, 'Don't you love me any more?' He then blushed, and she said, 'Dear, you must not be so easily embarrassed and afraid of your feelings.' The patient was able to stay with her only a few minutes more and following her departure he assaulted an orderly and was put in the tubs.

> (ibid.)

The problem with double-bind theory, despite the close specification of the communication patterns involved, is operationalization and testing. For instance, Laing modifies the example so that it starts:

As he goes towards her she opens her arms for him to embrace her ...

He responds to her invitation to kiss her, but her posture, freezing, tension, simultaneously tell him not to.

(Laing, 1971, p. 146)

Same story. Different events. *Both* qualify as double binds. Bateson recognized the problem and said:

Our original paper on the double bind contains numerous errors due simply to our having not yet articulately examined the reification problem. We talk in that paper as though a double bind were a something and as though such somethings could be counted.

Of course, that's all nonsense. You cannot count the bats in an inkblot because there are none. And yet a man—if he be 'bat-minded'—may 'see' several.

(Bateson, 1978, p. 242)

For our point of view, we can expand the idea of reification. In earlier sections, we talked of confusion between model and reality, between the 'stream of behaviour' and the stream of symbols. This is one meaning of reification— seeing symbols as things—and it is one to which the experimenter and the psychiatrist seem more prone than the subject and the patient. Like Whyte's 'status hierarchy', a double bind can only be identified with the aid and (in some sense) *the agreement* of the patient. 'Testing' double-bind theory with 'objective methods'—i.e. excluding the patient; finding criteria that can be applied regardless of the patient's viewpoint—is the wrong way to go about it because we are dealing with a strategy not a 'fact'. Strategy only becomes fact when all the parties involved allow it. Explanations about people (as opposed to explanations of models) always have holes in them through which people can duck out if they wish. Bateson concludes his papers on schizophrenia by saying:

severe pain and maladjustment can be induced by putting a mammal in the wrong regarding its rules for making sense of an important relationship with another mammal ... if this pathology can be warded off or resisted, the total experience may promote *creativity*.

(ibid. p. 248)

'in the wrong' and 'creativity' are two essential holes in this thesis. Neither are facts about the world that can be counted until they are defined as such by specific people in specific situations. On the other hand, since it is not possible to exclude such terms from a scientific psychology, we have to be 'bat minded' to get anywhere at all.

Despite this complication, double-bind theory served to change the parameters in the study of mental illness. Possibly for the first time, behaviour was seen as part of an articulate social process with its own dynamic, not at the expense of individual considerations, but as a complement to them.

Anyone watching the transactions which occur between the members of a family containing an identified schizophrenic will perceive immediately that the symptomatic behaviour of the identified patient fits with this environment, and, indeed, promotes in the other members those characteristics which evoke the schizophrenic behaviour ... the family, perhaps gradually, becomes organized (i.e. limits the behaviours of the component individuals) in such a way as to fit the schizophrenia.

(Bateson, 1960a)

Or

I believe this is the essence of the matter, that the schizophrenic family is an organization with great ongoing stability whose dynamics and inner workings are such that each member is continually undergoing the experience of negation of self.

(Bateson, 1960b)

Bateson was aware that his own effort was as much to create paradigms about ways of constructing theories as it was to construct a theory that (accidentally) became a paradigm. Let us leave the last words to him.

A human being in relation with another has very limited control over what happens in that relationship. He is *part* of a two person unit, and the control which any part can have over any whole is strictly limited. ... This gives us a view of the world which is still almost unexplored.

(Bateson, 1960a)

Anthropology: Pigs for the Ancestors.

Every so often groups of Maring-speaking peoples in the highlands of New Guinea uproot a bush called the 'rumbim', stage a festival for neighbouring groups during which many pigs are killed and eaten, and then go to war against other neighbouring groups. Between times, these Maring-speaking groups tend their gardens. Apparently all very simple, if not quite idyllic.

The people themselves give rather complicated accounts of their own activities, often involving various spirits that inhabit the forests in which they make their gardens. Between October 1962 and December 1963, one of these groups, the Tsembaga, found a tall student from Columbia University in their midst. Actually, he was only 5 feet 10 inches, but since the Tsembaga are mostly under 5 feet, he must have seemed tall. This student was called Roy A. Rappaport, and he went on to write a book and several articles. The book was subtitled 'Ritual in the Ecology of a New Guinea People'. Rappaport's story is almost as complicated as the Tsembaga themselves, but his account of the goings-on is rather different from the local one. Tsembaga explanation depends on several hundred years of their own history and experience, whereas Rappaport's rests on a few decades of anthropology, and some years of ecology—the intellectual summit of milennia of imperialism and conquest. Nevertheless, in general, Rappaport recognized the differences, and is at pains not to impose his account on the people themselves. In the edition of *Scientific American* devoted to 'Energy & Power' (September 1971) he even argues that there is much that 'we' should learn from the Tsembaga. The argument runs like this.

In terms of their entire territory the Tsembaga in 1962–1963 were maintaining a population density of 64 per square mile. In terms of all potentially arable land the density was 97 per square mile, and in terms of land that was then or ever had been under cultivation the density was 124 per square mile. Even this figure is below the carrying capacity of the Tsembaga territory; without altering the horticultural regime of keeping 90 per cent of the land fallow the Tsembaga's 1000 best acres might have supported a population of 200 or more to the square mile.

(Rappaport, 1971, p. 118)

This level of population density is equivalent to that achieved(!) by the most advanced industrial countries. The difference is that the Tsembaga do it without any obvious psychological stresses, and *without environmental degradation*. If they were all to disappear in a puff of smoke, the land would show no evidence of their ever having been there. How do they achieve this? They rotate their gardens allowing adequate fallow periods. They actively encourage the return of the forest even in gardens that they are using. And they create gardens that are not susceptible to crop failure:

There is a structural similarity between a swidden garden and a tropical rain forest. In the garden, as in the forest, species are not separated by rows or sections but are intricately intermingled, so that as they mature the garden becomes stratified and the plants make maximum use of surface area and of variations in vertical dimensions. For example, taro and sweet potato tubers mature just below the surface, the cassava root lies deeper, and yams are the deepest of all. A mat of sweet potato leaves covers the soil at ground level. The taro leaves project above this mat; the hibiscus, sugarcane, and *pitpit* stand higher still, and the fronds of the banana spread out above the rest.

The advantages of intermingling the crops are wider than making the best use of a fixed area of land. It

discourages plant specific pests, it allows advantage to be taken of slight variation in garden habitats, it is protective of the thin tropical soil and it achieves a high photosynthetic efficiency.

(ibid. p. 121)

Rappaport contrasts this with the constant need for fossil fuel, fertilizers, pesticides, and other assistance needed by monoculturing major crops in the 'advanced' countries. This type of agriculture creates a permanently immature ecosystem that degrades the environment where the 'normal self-corrective capacity is diminished and eventually destroyed'. He asks 'if a worldwide human organization can persist and elaborate itself indefinitely at the expense of decreasing the stability of its own ecological foundations.'

The level of organization and efficiency in New Guinea is all the more impressive as the Tsembaga have no 'chiefs', no-one to tell them what to do. Their collective activities are all achieved by consensus and unanimity and no coercion is used. Everyone can participate in discussion and decision-making; anyone can initiate collective action. Where is the coordination for all this? Rappaport's answer is that all activities are related and coordinated by *ritual*. He opposes the Homans tradition what maintains ritual does not achieve practical results in the world, and that its 'function' is to give confidence and relieve anxiety. He demonstrates that ritual has at least the following very practical effects:

1. Relationships between people, pigs, and gardens are regulated. This regulation operates directly to protect people from the possible parasitism and competition of their pigs, and indirectly to protect the environment by helping to maintain extensive areas of virgin forest and assuring adequate cultivation–fallow ratios in secondary forest.
2. The slaughter, distribution and consumption of pig is regulated and enhances the value of pork in the diet.
3. The consumption of non-domestic animals is regulated in a way that tends to enhance their value to the population as a whole.
4. The marsupial fauna may be conserved.
5. The redispersal of people over land and the redistribution of land between territorial groups is accomplished.
6. The frequency of warfare is regulated.
7. The severity of inter-group fighting is mitigated.
8. The exchange of goods and personnel between local groups is facilitated.

(Rappaport, 1968, p. 3)

In briefest outline, the situation works like this. As well as gardening, the Tsembaga keep pigs. They only eat these pigs at times of illness or accident. Consequently, the size of the pigs and the size of the herd tends to grow with time. It does not grow as fast as it might, since all the male pigs are castrated, and impregnation of the sows relies on chance contact with wild boars. Nevertheless it grows. The pigs live in houses with the women and are individually owned. They root about in the forest and disused gardens during the day. (This also encourages the return of the forest because they eat the remains of the crops, and generally leave tree seedlings alone.) In the evenings they are fed on a 'substandard' version of the human diet. Since they also eat human faeces, sewage and garbage disposal problems are minimal.

When the pigs become large and numerous, feeding them in the evenings becomes a lot of hard work. Scraps are no longer enough. The pigs also start invading the gardens. When this happens, the gardeners become annoyed, and sometimes kill the offending beast. This can lead to serious quarrels and fighting between neighbours and even neighbouring groups. It certainly leads to discontent and complaint. A sufficiently high level of discontent predisposes members of the Tsembaga to think it is about time for a *kaiko*—the festival in which almost all adult pigs are killed. The *kaiko* itself achieves far more than a reduction in the numbers of pigs and an increase in the size of stomachs. Elaborate ritual surrounds it. Territorial boundaries are marked. Friendly groups are invited to participate. This helps trade and population dispersal by intermarriage. All groups participate in *kaikos*—— with the social contact and excellent nourishment—far more frequently than they hold them themselves. Having established their boundaries and their 'allies', the group holding the festival is now in a position to go to war. As the Tsembaga themselves say: 'Those who come to our *kaiko* will also come to our fights' (ibid. p. 195).

Whatever the rights and wrongs of the warfare (which is highly disapproved by the Australian authorities) it serves to redistribute land in accordance with the agricultural needs of the various groups—more or less. The absence of social stratification means that land is not annexed for its own sake, but only if it is usable and convenient to reach. When the fights are settled one way or another, the *rumbim*—the bush that was uprooted at the beginning of the *kaiko*—is replanted. Because of the complex relations of the Maring with the spirits of their ancestors (to whom the slaughtering of pigs and other rituals are all dedicated) it is impossible to initiate warfare while the *rumbim* is in the ground. Any outstanding scores to be settled must await the next *kaiko*. This delay means that the formerly warring groups have plenty of time to recover. In fact, the worse the defeat, the more time they will get, since there is also a relationship between population density and pig nuisance level that triggers the *kaiko*. The sparser the population, the more scattered the gardens—hence greater number of pigs can be tolerated without becoming a nuisance (ibid. p. 164).

Even this brief sketch should give an idea of the social 'system' in which ritual keeps all the 'key variables' in balance and allows the Tsembaga to survive. People–land, people–pig, and other important ratios must be kept within limits if the people are not to starve or undergo other catastrophic changes. The strength of Rappaport's model is that it shows exactly *how* this is done. As many relevant variables as possible are measured, including rainfall, soil fertility, calorific values of each crop, kilocalories expended per acre in each phase of gardening (clearing underbush; clearing trees; fencing gardens; weeding and burning; placing soil retainers; planting and weeding; etc.), calorific intake of pigs, ecology and composition of primary and secondary forest, composition of wild fauna and flora and their contribution to Tsembaga life, ritual phases and practices, habits of ancestral spirits, trade, marriage forms, decision-making and politics, construction and distribution of dwellings, available tools, and so on. The model relates *precisely* to a complex reality. Nor is there any pretence that the 'system' is stable against all contingencies. Although the Tsembaga were relatively untouched by European influence at the time of the study, the indications were that this influence was on the increase. In 1964, fifteen young men were reported to have been recruited on two-year labour contracts. Even without such events, European-created supplies of salt had changed local trading patterns, and the stone axe was being replaced by steel tools. This last can, of itself, have catastrophic results.*

Nevertheless, within their own context, the Tsembaga form a 'ritually regulated population'. Rappaport's own summary brings out some of the cybernetic concepts used in the model.

> It has been argued in this study that Maring ritual is of great importance in articulating the local and regional subsystems. The timing of the ritual cycle is largely

---

* It is reported in Rogers (1962) that the Yir Yiront—a group of Australian Aborigines—suffered complete social collapse after the introduction of the steel axe. Stone axes had previously been the major, highly valued tool. It was the key to trade with other local groups. It was also the key to social organization. Authority increased with age, and axes were owned by the older members of the group as symbols of their authority, as well as for their usefulness. Steel axes were given to the younger members of the group who ventured to visit the Trading Post. They were, of course, altogether more efficient than the stone axes. Demand for stone axes fell away; trade lapsed; the authority structure of the group collapsed; the group disintegrated.

dependent upon changes in the states of components of the local ecosystem. But the Kaiko, which culminates the ritual cycle, does more than reverse changes that have taken place in this subsystem. During its performance obligations to other local populations are fulfilled, support for future military enterprises is rallied, land from which enemies have earlier been drived is occupied, and the movement of goods and women is stimulated. Completion of the Kaiko permits the local population to initiate warfare again. Conversely, warfare is terminated by the rumbim-planting ritual that prohibits the reinitiation of warfare until the state of the local ecosystem allows the Kaiko to again be staged and completed; participation in the rumbim planting also ratifies the connection of men to local populations to which they were not previously affiliated.

Maring ritual, in short, operates not only as a homeostat—maintaining a number of variables that comprise the total system within ranges of viability—but also as a transducer—'translating' changes in the state of one subsystem into information and energy that can produce changes in the second subsystem. It should be recalled here that the transduction operation of the ritual cycle is such that the participation of local populations in respect to warfare, which is important in the redistribution of land and personnel but is also dangerous, is not continuous. It could therefore be argued that the ritual transducer maintains coherence between subsystems at levels above or below which the perpetuation of the total system might be endangered.

(ibid. p. 229)

Rappaport says that his study is, in part, an exploratory sketch, since some of the variables are not properly quantified (in particular, no values are assigned to the frequency of warfare, or its 'tolerable limits'). Nevertheless, it is sufficiently rigorous to allow experimental simulation as a (partial) test of the postulated systemic relationships (e.g. see Cartledge & Rezac, 1970).

We have said already that simulation makes it more difficult to confuse the model with the reality. Rappaport makes a similar distinction when he contrasts the 'cognized' model of their environment held by the Tsembaga with the 'operational' model he has created.

The cognized model is the model of the environment conceived by the people who act in it. The two models are overlapping, but not identical. While many components of the physical world will be represented in both, the operational model is likely to include material elements, such as disease germs and nitrogen-fixing bacteria, that affect the actors but of which they may not be aware. Conversely, the cognized model may include elements that cannot be shown by empirical means to exist, such as spirits and other supernatural beings.

Some elements peculiar to the cognized model may be isomorphic with elements peculiar to the operational model. The Tsembaga say, for instance, that they are loath to build houses below 3,500 feet because certain spirits that are abroad at night in low areas give one fever. The behavior of these spirits—and the consequences of their behavior—corresponds closely to that of anopheles mosquitoes, which the Tsembaga do not recognize to be carriers of malaria. But elements, and relationships among elements, in the two models need not always be isomorphic or identical. The cognized and operational models may differ in some aspects of their structure as well as in the elements included in each.

This is not to say, of course, that the cognized model is merely a less adequate representation of reality than the operational model. The operational model is an observer's description of selected aspects of the material world. It has a purpose only for the anthropologist. As far as the actors are concerned it has no function. Indeed, it does not exist. The cognized model, while it must be understood by those who entertain it to be a representation of the material and nonmaterial world, has a function for the actors: it guides their action. Since this is the case, we are particularly concerned to discover what the people under study believe to be the functional relationships among the entities that they think are part of their environment, and what they take to be 'signs', indicating changes in these entities or relationships, which demand action on their part; but *the important question concerning the cognized model, since it serves as a guide to action, is not the extent to which it conforms to 'reality'(i.e. is identical with or isomorphic with the operational model), but the extent to which it elicits behavior that is appropriate to the material situation of the actors, and it is against this functional and adaptive criterion that we may assess it.* Maring notions of disease etiology are certainly inaccurate, but the slaughter and consumption of pigs during illness is just as effective when undertaken to strengthen or mollify spirits as it would be if were specifically undertaken to alleviate stress symptoms.

(ibid. p. 238)

As can be seen, Rappaport takes the position (essential to any *actor*) that his operational model is a yardstick against which to measure some aspects of the Tsembaga's cognitive model. It is also clear that his model would be useless to the Tsembaga. Thus we have another example in which the stream of symbols (in this case, two of them) can be distinguished from the 'stream of behaviour'.

It seems that the more articulate, precise, and testable the model becomes, the easier it is to separate it from the reality in question.

Management: A Message from Stafford Beer

Stafford Beer invented the cybernetics of management, and in doing so redefined cybernetics as 'the science of effective organization'. Under the heading *Cybernetics and Freedom*, he writes:

What is cybernetics, that a government should not understand it? It is, as Wiener originally called it twenty-five years ago, 'the science of communication and control in the animal and the machine'. He was pointing, in that second phrase, to laws of complex systems that are invariant to transformations of their fabric. It does not matter whether the system be realized in the flesh or in the metal.

What is cybernetics, that government should need it? It is, as I should prefer to define it today, 'the science of effective organization'. In this definition I am pointing to laws of complex systems that are invariant not only to transformations of their fabric, but also of their *content*. It does not matter whether the system's content is neurophysiological, automotive, social or economic.

This is not to argue that all complex systems are really the same, nor yet that they are all in some way 'analogous'. It is to argue that there are fundamental rules which, disobeyed, lead to instability, or to explosion, or to a failure to learn, adapt and evolve, in *any* complex system. And those pathological states do indeed belong to all complex systems—whatever their fabric, whatever their content—not by analogy, but as a matter of fact.

With cybernetics, we seek to lift the problems of organizational structure out of the ruck of prejudice—by studying them scientifically. People wonder whether to centralize or to decentralize the economy—they are answered by dogmas. People ask whether planning is inimical to freedom—they are answered with doctrines. People demand an end to bureaucracy and muddle—they are answered with a so-called expertise which, from its record, has no effect. If dogma, doctrine and expertise fail to give effective answers, then what criterion of effectiveness shall cybernetics use? My answer to this question is: the criterion of *viability*. Whatever makes a system survival-worthy is necessary to it.

Necessary, yes, one might reply; but surely not also sufficient? The more I consider that criticism, the less I see its force.

(Beer, 1975, p. 425)

When I was first considering theories about how small groups 'work', those words were not written; all that was available to me was *Decision and Control* (Beer, 1966). The ideas that Beer later went on to develop were going through a first formulation. Nevertheless, there is sufficient cohesion in the whole opus to use the later books to illustrate the influential—and paradigmatic—concepts.

The first important concept that runs through everything is 'objectivity'. This is connected with the tradition we examined in the last chapter that saw social reality as 'out there'. But there is a difference. Beer has an *explicit* criterion for the construction of 'reality'. It is not enough that it is given. There is simply too much of 'it' to deal with. As he says in *Decision and Control*: 'The kinds of system under consideration exhibit literally billions of variables. There is no *rigorous* means of knowing which matter.' Reality, for Beer, is not to be dealt with by plucking out variables for individual scrutiny. Instead he looks for signs of discontent, of unhappiness, and then looks to see if the Law of Requisite Variety is being ignored. This involves the identification of a system, and hence of the relevant variables. Thus we arrive at reality through signs made by people and through a model. Beer uses three models, to be exact.

The first model *is* the Law of Requisite Variety.
The second model is 'a basic structural model for any viable system'.
The third model is the one held by people who are supposedly managing the system in which the problem arose in the first place.

Let us look at each of these models in turn.

The law of requisite variety

The Law of Requisite Variety was discovered by Ross Ashby. His account of it in the classic *Introduction to Cybernetics* remains definitive, and the reader who wishes for a deeper understanding should go out and buy the book. A brief summary only will be given here.

Variety itself is defined as 'the number of distinguishable elements in a set'. Thus, if the order of occurrence is ignored, the set

$$c,b,c,a,c,c,a,b,c,b,b,a$$

contains only three distinct elements—a, b, and c. Ashby's technical use of 'variety' is very close to the common sense meaning. How much variety is there in that flock of sheep? Let's see. There are ewes and lambs. Some are black, some are white. So we can have black or white lambs, and black or white ewes. The variety is four: correct. But Ashby also says:'It will be noticed that a set's variety is not an intrinsic property of the set; the observer and their powers of discrimination may have to be specified if the variety is to be well defined' (Ashby, 1956, p. 125). To us, the flock of sheep may have a variety of four. To the shepherd there may be as much variety as there are sheep, since she can distinguish each individual animal.

Once the variety of a set is defined, the Law of Requisite Variety enables us to define *control*. In order to control any system, the controller must have as much variety as the system. Ashby illustrates this with the example of a game with two players, called R and D.

> *Play and outcome.* Let us therefore forget all about regulation and simply suppose that we are watching two players, R and D, who are engaged in a game. We shall follow the fortunes of R, who is attempting to score an a. The rules are as follows. They have before them Table 11/3/1, which can be seen by both:

Table 11/3/1

		R		
		α	β	γ
	1	b	a	c
D	2	a	c	b
	3	c	b	a

> D must play first, by selecting a number, and thus a particular row. R,knowing this number, then selects a Greek letter, and thus a particular column. The italic letter specified by the intersection of the row and column is the **outcome.** If it is an a, R wins; if not, R loses.

(Ashby, 1956, p. 202)

It soon becomes obvious that R *can* always win. If R plays according to the rules:

if D plays 1, then play β.
if D plays 2, then play α
if D plays 3, then play γ

then R *will* always win.

In fact, with this particular table, R can always win whatever the desired outcome. By selecting appropriate rules of play, R could force a, b, or c as the outcome. In this situation R has complete control over the outcomes.

From this 'game' we can also see that if R only had one move (α) he would only be able to get his desired outcome a if D played 2. If D played 1 or 3, the outcome when R played α would be b or c. Thus, at best, R could only control the outcome for one-third of the time. In the first case, R's variety matches D's variety. The control ratio is 3/3 (or equivalently, 1/1, or simply 1). In the second case the ratio of R's variety to D's variety is 1/3. From this, we have a general method for describing 'control'. As Ashby comments:

> The theorum is primarily a statement about possible arrangements in a rectangular table. It says that certain types of arrangement cannot be made. It is thus no more dependent on special properties of machines than is, say, the 'theorum' that four objects can be arranged to form a square while three can not. The law therefore owes nothing to experiment.

(Ashby, 1956, p. 209)

This means that the law, like Euclid's geometry, applies to the world but is not derived from it. It has the appearance of a Kantian *synthetic a priori*. In twentieth-century terms, this is simply a *universal convention*. In our terms, the law is a *model* that enables us to define (and, hopefully, deal with) problems of control. Referring to the 'game' in the example, the Law of Requisite Variety says that only variety in R's moves can force down the variety in the outcomes. More generally, 'only variety can destroy variety'.

When we consider management, this means that *effective* management is only possible where the discrimination—and hence the range of options—open to the manager matches the range of states in the system to be managed. This may sound obvious, but it is amazing how often people try to ignore it and land in a mess.

Using Ashby's law as a basic filter, Beer goes on to define a viable system.

Beer's structural model for any viable system

Full details of the model are given in the companion volumes *Brain of the Firm* and *The Heart of Enterprise*. The model itself is intended to apply to any system: psychological, physiological, ecological, biological, or social. The discussion and presentation centres on social systems and their management. The model itself is *recursive*. This means it applies at each level of analysis, and that all viable systems are contained in and contain viable systems. The hospital is part of a higher system called the National Health Service, but contains sub-systems called wards. The ward itself contains sub-systems called the people in the ward—orderlies, doctors, patients, nurses. All are viable systems in their own right (although some of them, very sick patients and possibly the monolithic Health Service itself may be teetering on the edge of viability—about to blink out of existence). Viability does not mean viability for all time and under all circumstances.

Beer's Model of any viable system involves five levels; policy, intelligence and anticipation, control, co-ordination, and action. The categories, levels, and inter-relationships are derived from a lengthy consideration of Ashby's Law of Requisite Variety. The model itself is very complex, and it would be a mistake to try and simplify 1000 pages of ideas into one section of one chapter.

The point is that the Beer model gives us a general way of describing and analysing organization. If the system can be mapped onto the model, it (probably) conforms to the Law of Requisite Variety. If the system can only be partially mapped onto the model, then the system is trying to violate the law; is in danger; may not survive. We look for the source of the problem (signified by discontent or unhappiness) in the mismatch between the system and the model. This is a very powerful diagnostic method, but it should be noted that the 'system' that is diagnosed is not the 'reality'. It is a construction from the 'reality'. We are mapping a model onto a model, and the lower level reality (the 'system') has been carved out of the billions of variables that *might* matter by the use of the higher-level model. The procedure is fundamentally dialectical. The elegance ultimately lies in self-reference.

The other model

Another well-known consequence of Ashby's law is that any control system must contain a model of the system to be controlled. 'Control' is often considered to be a hard term, and has nasty connotations of someone ordering someone else about. Management is somehow softer and more acceptable. Nevertheless, the object of management is to influence outcomes—control is the intention. Management must therefore have a model of the system to be managed. Beer demonstrates convincingly that—even in the simple terms of the Law of Requisite Variety—the models actually held by management in many specific instances are woefully inadequate. Beer distinguishes models from 'surrogates'—bad models that stand outside almost everyone's 'reality'.

> Every one of us is committed to operate in the world in terms of his conceptual understanding of the world—his model of it, if you will. I respond to my children in a certain way, because my mental files about them include models of how they are—and, please note, how they are likely to respond, which means that I have a predictive model in just the sense described.
>
> Well, the manager of any situation is no less committed to his model of what he manages than any of us. As we see in Figure 1, the model intervenes between the manager and the situation. It must do this; it is a kind of filter intended to cut out noise and enhance perception of meaningful patterns. We may note two things about it immediately.

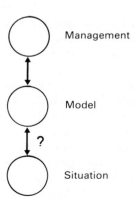

Firstly, the model may be no good. It is more like *us* than external reality, as my drawing tries to show. Think of a city with a traffic problem, which in turn generates a street parking problem. Then city managers have a conceptual model which vividly depicts how people go to work in buildings and leave their cars outside—so that traffic can no longer conveniently pass down the road. The model at once proposes the answer: let the business fraternity take their cars *into* the buildings with them, and then the road will be clear and the traffic can move. Accordingly, the city managers legislated to say that all new buildings must include off-street parking facilities in their design. The result of this policy was that wherever it took effect other people altogether noticed free places in the road—and parked their cars in them. This made the problem worse. There were twice as many cars in the offing. And naturally the total traffic flow increased into the bargain. So then there was some more legislation to *dis*courage the inclusion of parking facilities in new buildings. Unhappily, people do have models which are just as bad as that. They not only give the wrong answers: they oscillate. It happened: in London.

The second point is that you will discover how people often begin to mistake the model for the reality—and start managing the model instead. Let me give you a true instance of this too. The residents of a certain small town got up a petition to ask the railway company to put on a train at three o'clock in the afternoon to take them to the big town. Now the railway company had a model of this line and more than a mental model in this case. They had done an empirical study and had quantified their model. The reply the residents received (this is going to strain your credulity, but I saw the letter) said that the Railway had undertaken a factual survey—and there was no one *waiting* for a train at three o'clock. It happened: in Sussex.

(Beer, 1975, pp. 400 and 401)

In this chapter on Cybernetic Paradigms, we have tried to look at the distinction between the 'stream of Behaviour' (reality in some sense) and the stream of symbols. We have tried to show that the better, more articulate, and more contentful a model becomes, the easier it is to disentangle it from 'reality'. A good model performs an apparently contradictory function. It defines 'reality' but at the same time refuses to be mistaken for it. There is a circularity in action, in being in-the-world, that is creative. Let us look at a very practical example in which one model is superseded by another.

Finding a Metric

One of the basic operational problems of practicability is to determine how relevant measurements are to be obtained. People talk about 'imponderables' as if they were small demons lurking in their offices. And indeed, if one says: 'I must know what is going to happen on the 13th of June next year', then there is no means of knowing, and that is that. But there is no point in asking absurd questions which, in the nature of things, cannot be answered, and setting up a wail about imponderables. A better approach, better because it works, is to invite the scientist to examine the problem situation from every possible slant, re-shuffling it as it were, in search for a commensurable approach. The scientist will look for some critical feature of the situation that is on the face of it measurable, and he will try to find a metric which fits it. Here is an actual example, which brings out both the ingenuity of the scientist and the thought block by which people deny the possibility of measuring anything which *they* regard as imponderable.

There is a narrow channel between Denmark and Sweden which provides the only entrance to the Baltic. The narrowest crossing is between Helsingor (which lovers of Shakespeare usually call Elsinore) in Denmark, and Hälsingborg in Sweden. The

Scandinavians, a particularly civilized people, transport themselves and their goods freely across the Sound. The journey by ferry-boat takes less than half an hour and little fuss is made about such formalities as passports. Now the cross-channel traffic is steadily increasing, and so is the sea-going traffic between the Baltic and the outside world. Thus there is an increasing congestion in this channel and obviously an increasing risk of collision.

The Governments of Denmark and Sweden set up a joint commission to investigate this situation. In particular, there could well be a bridge between the two countries. Consider, said the Commission, the state of affairs when the traffic in both directions has doubled. Needless to say, it is not very difficult to make a statistical forecast of the date when this will occur, nor is it difficult to support the statistical extrapolation by arguments from the plans and intentions of all concerned. Clearly, the risk of collision will be increased, compared with the risk today. The layman might very well imagine that when the traffic is doubled the risk of collision is doubled; on the other hand, he might very well wonder whether this would be true. In any case, it is very likely that the layman will suppose that no conceivable way of computing this risk could be obtained—short of running an experiment, whether in the water or by computer simulation, in which a doubled traffic was allowed to run. But an experiment in the water is clearly impracticable, for it would take an enormous amount of organization and money even if it could be done. And a simulation may well be impracticable too, for the very good reason that collisions depend in the last resort on the failure of human beings standing on ships' bridges to avert them. It is very difficult indeed to say what role will be played by the human element in a situation which no-one has yet experienced.

In these circumstances, the commission very properly sought operational research advice. Professor Arne Jensen, now of the Technical University of Copenhagen, and incidentally the holder of the first so-named Chair of Operational Research in the whole of Europe, was asked to measure the increased risk for a doubled traffic flow. Many people said it could not be done: the research is impracticable; the risk is imponderable.

Jensen had in fact no more idea than anyone else, at the start, of how to set about the task of making this measurement. He talked with the captains of both ferry-boats and ocean-going ships about the problem, and everybody agreed that the risk of collision would be higher, and wagged their heads. This did not take the problem much further. Now Jensen knew that, given a knowledge of the stochastic processes governing the movement of ships, he could in fact calculate the likely number of incidents in which two ships could enter the same arbitrarily sized area of water at the same time. But no-one could tell him how near to each other the ships had to be before they could be said to have embarked irrevocably on a collision course. The practical men, very naturally, said that if the ships missed each other—even by a hair's breadth—then there was no collision; whereas if they did not, there was. But it is quite clear that to compute the probability that two ships simultaneously arrive on an area of water having the size of one ship, would seriously underestimate the chance of a collision. Such a computation would be based on a model in which ships suddenly appeared at a point, whereas in reality we are obviously dealing with an interacting system of some complexity.

So Jensen, still entirely puzzled about the key problem of establishing a metric, decided that as an empirical OR scientist he should at least try to obtain some facts. People were free with opinions, beliefs and prognostications; but the first step should be to make some kind of measure of some kind of event which actually occurred. Accordingly, Jensen made a film of the traffic actually moving about on the Sound. What he filmed was a radar screen on which the movement of ships appeared as it would familiarly appear to ships' masters. The camera recorded the state of the screen at discrete time intervals and not continuously. The resulting film was a correct record of movements except that everything appeared to be happening at about 250 times the proper speed.

Having obtained some basic facts, Jensen did not know what to do next. He did of course study the film, and he observed certain areas in which congestion was characteristically high. But neither he nor experienced colleagues could yet find a means of defining a collision risk. The Professor's next move was therefore to mount his film in a theatre, and to show it to a group of very experienced men. These included six who had been ships' masters themselves, and now held posts in administration on behalf of responsible authorities. One had become an accident inspector, another was the chief of the harbour authority, another was running the ferry-boat service, and there was a representative of the Navy. These experts were asked to collaborate by watching the film, and trying to detect dangerous situations. How near would two boats have to approach each other before a genuine collision risk was involved? In particular, thought Jensen, a conglomeration of six, seven or eight boats, even if they were not right on top of each other, must surely take some sorting out. If the captains, having watched the film, could apply their own experience to it, they might help to suggest the approach to devising the 'risk metric' which was wanted. But unfortunately they could not.

The cybernetic computer in the cranium, however, often tells its owner things which he *cannot* analyse and report about to professors of operational research. Jensen noticed that there were moments of tension among his audience. The experts would catch their breath in unison: there would be a straining forward in the seat; there would occur curtailed exclamations. When he noticed that these incidents were occurring, Jensen had their times recorded. It is emphasized that this was not part of the plan: it was opportunism. For here were some more facts—if only one could make some use of them. In all, forty incidents of this kind were noted down, with the time at which they occurred from the start of the film. After the experts had gone home, Jensen made a careful analysis of the tape recording carrying this fluctuating level of noise, and of the frames on the film corresponding to the forty noisy incidents. It was here that he found his answer.

In sixteen cases everyone agreed that the audience reaction was due to especially high velocities. Since the film was an accelerated version of real life, unusually fast craft looked incredibly dangerous. This left twenty-four incidents for further study. Jensen was looking for a pair of ships which had become dangerously close, in the hope that the threshold of danger could be measured. He was looking for conglomerations of many ships, which might have looked threatening to experienced sailors. He found neither of these things. What he did find, in twenty out of the twenty-four cases, was a clear group of *three* ships: not appallingly close to each other, but still three. He recalled the experts and demonstrated this to them.

The situation suddenly became very clear. The codes of seamanship by which captains navigate their craft are based on a binary logic. If the captain of ship A sights ship B, then he has a set of rules which enable him to decide how to steer in relation to ship B. Since ship B has the same set of rules, it takes complementary action which is consistent, and the ships pass each other safely … each master knows how his own situation will appear to the other master, and how the other master will reply. In other words, both captains are effectively simulating the entire affair in their heads in advance.

Now the situation that arises when a third ship appears on the scene is evidently dangerous. The master of ship A, who is conducting a simulated dialogue with the master of ship B, suddenly has to enter into a similar discourse with the master of ship C. Moreover, the action which the navigational code requires ship A to take in relation to ship B may not be consistent with the action it is supposed to take in relation to ship C. While the master of ship A is worrying about this, the masters of ships B and C are also faced with their versions of the dilemma, and the simulations may well become intolerably difficult. In fact, the difficulty of treating a triadic relationship in terms of a binary logic is notorious among logicians, never mind ships' masters. In practical terms, the human brain boggles at the difficulty of analysing a dynamic triadic situation—even when there is a capability to pass direct information. This is the reason why the search for incidents involving a considerable number of ships went unfulfilled. The mind trained in seamanship, and working to a binary logic, simply cannot encompass the further area of sea and the larger number of ships.

Here then we see the OR scientist grappling with a problem of measurement which appears impracticable, without knowing in advance what he really intends to do, and carrying in his mind ideas which he thinks must be right, but which will actively mislead him unless he keeps his wits about him. Here also, we find the experienced practical man, precluded by that very experience and that very practicality, from understanding precisely what is the difficulty in a situation with which he is trained by long experience to cope in practice. The captains agreed with the analysis when they saw it, but were incapable of making it themselves. Nor, incidentally, is there any obvious solution to the problem now defined. One cannot readily legislate for three-way radio conversations between ferry-boats and ocean-going ships of different nationalities which are within distance of each other for so very short a time. Nor is an OR man likely to propose a solution to a local problem of this kind by demanding that international shipping codes be radically changed. But this was not Jensen's problem. His problem was to calculate the increased risk in a doubled traffic flow.

The answer is now terribly simple. According to empirical analysis of the data, the distribution of ship interactions on the water is Poissonian. That is to say, it has as might be expected a structure characteristic of chance interactions. If the traffic flow doubles, *and the triadic relationship of vessels is the dangerous one*, then the rise in the risk of collision, because of the applicability of Poisson's laws, is $2^3 = 8$. So the risk of collision does not double, but is eightfold in the circumstances proposed.

(Beer, 1966, pp. 531–536)

'Finding a Metric' is a good story. Like all good stories, there is a strong 'hit-and-miss' element, and no guarantee of a happy ending. Nevertheless, it *is* social science. Not because it comes up with an almost-too-neat mathematical formula (the happy ending!), but because a model emerges from a fog of indeterminacy. The three-way risk of collision model was something all the participants could agree on—and having agreed, take action to reduce the risks. Other models might have done just as well. But *only* if they were agreed to represent the problem and the 'reality'. The three-way model was an innovation. It was not contained in the original problem. The agreement on it was a characteristically political decision: once it had been adopted it looked as though there never was any other alternative; without the consensus, no action would have followed. Once the model was adopted, the action on it was (presumably) unproblematic, like filling in a crossword puzzle. Looking backwards. The solution appears 'factual'.

In the next section, other 'factual' results are considered, about ethological systems—the behaviour of animals. There is a parallel. The researchers start with a model—in this case the cybernetic model of simple homeostasis (the keeping of essential variables within predefined limits). The 'political' decision about the appropriateness of the homeostatic model is not part of the story. The innovation had already been made—and agreed—by the time the story starts. However, the perspective made possible by the adoption of the model leads to the discovery of corresponding 'facts'. The blood supply structure in the kangeroo's wrist would not have been 'discovered' if the model had not led to questions about licking and cooling efficiency being seen as important. Other models would have led to the discovery of different 'facts'. Sorting out the puzzles of applying models is part of 'normal science'. But even where 'mere animals' are concerned, there is a note of warning. Agreement has to be reached between the 'scientists' and the living objects of the study. If a 'scientific' ritual is simply imposed on animals (as in most zoos and laboratories) the 'facts' that emerge can be as peculiar and unhelpful as the models that give rise to them. 'Pecking orders' (like Fawl's frustration in children) are easy to find in 'controlled conditions', and pretty hard to find outside them. In the studies cited here, the agreement the ethologists make with the animals is, in the main, simply to leave them alone. Hopefully, this avoids most of the problems of imposition, while at the same time providing a convincing demonstration that the precise models of cybernetics can be applied without degradation of either party to the study.

Ethology

Thermoregulation

Thermoregulation—the problem of temperature control—has long fascinated ethologists and cyberneticians. One evident reason is that 'temperature' is easy to define and measure, unlike other variables like 'communication'. Even so, the elegance of temperature-control models in living systems created a paradigm for models themselves. To illustrate this we will look first at an individual, then at a social thermoregulatory system.

Our individual example is the kangaroo. The kangaroo, if you think about it, needs a highly efficient temperature-control system. It lives its life in a hot desert where the air temperature can rise about 45°C (or 115°F). The direct sunlight—or sunheat—raises the effective temperature much further, and the only shade to be found is under the small and sparse acacia bushes. It was once thought that the kangaroo was a very primitive sort of beast. Although it spent some time sitting in the 'shade', its only other defence against the heat was to lick itself occasionally. Presumably, being primitive, it simply did not mind the discomfort. T.J. Dawson likes both kangaroos and the beautiful country in which they live; since he is also a professor of zoology in New South Wales, he was able to observe them, and arrive at a more satisfactory explanation of their way of life.

Amongst other things, he established that the kangaroo is no more primitive than the domestic cow. Twenty-five-million years of evolution in the isolation of Australia had seen the development of some remarkable adaptive strategies—with much evidence of 'mistakes' (interesting types of kangaroo that are no longer with us) along the way. Hopping turned out to be very efficient in terms of energy conservation—and also very fast when necessary. When Captain

Cook's *Endeavour* arrived in Australia, he was accompanied by one Sir Joseph Banks. With true European panache, Sir Joseph's first move was to set his dogs—greyhounds—on the kangaroos. The kangaroos got away.

Another feature of the kangaroo is that its reproductive cycle is one of the most sophisticated in the world. At any one time, there are three young in 'the pipeline': a young joey at foot; one in the pouch; and another in a sort of suspended animation ('embryonic diapause') in the womb while it waits for the pouch to be vacated. The young-at-foot and the joey in the pouch both suckle, but at different teats—and the two milks in the separate mammary glands are quite different in quality, volume, and composition. This trick has not yet been explained.

How then does the kangaroo regulate its body temperature? On very hot days, it does, quite sensibly, make use of what shade there is—and it uses it efficiently. It does not lie down in the shade, but stands hunched with its tail tucked in—thus presenting the smallest possible surface area to the sun. Its dense red fur provides near-ideal insulation against the heat. It also licks itself, thus losing some heat by evaporation. But this is not a primitive mechanism. As Dawson puts it:

> The kangaroo's licking behaviour was long a puzzle to my colleagues and me because the forelimb area usually licked is small. It seemed that the overall heat dissipation benefit would be doubtful in view of certain possible disadvantages. Probably more in frustration than for any other reason, we undertook a study of the blood supply to the forelimbs ... we found that there was a dense and intricate network of superficial blood vessels in the region the animals usually lick. Further study revealed that during heat stress the blood flow to the region is greatly increased. The forelimb region is thus a site of significant heat transfer. Indeed, by spreading saliva on their forelimbs kangaroos may well be making the most efficient use possible of an overflow of fluid from their respiratory system, the principal site of evaporative heat dissipation in resting animals.
>
> (Dawson, 1977, p. 84)

Kangaroos also lose heat by panting and sweating. The kangaroo pants both while exercising and at rest. Its sweating behaviour—as we should now expect—is more sophisticated. It only sweats when it is exercising. The moment it stops exercising, it stops sweating. Is this just another odd feature of the kangaroo? Other animals, such as horses or men, lose heat by sweating both during and after exercise. It turns out that horses and men are simply less sophisticated than the kangaroo—because they do not need to conserve water so carefully. The kangaroo pants. The result of sweating would be unnecessary loss of water. Evaporation from the skin lowers the surface temperature of the skin, which then absorbs more heat—so yet more water is needed to get rid of it. Panting does not lower the skin temperature, so the cycle is avoided. Even the 'surplus' water created by panting is—as we have seen—used to cool the forepaws.

The kangaroo employs one last strategy.

> Under conditions of heat stress and dehydration ... the kangaroo lowers its temperature overnight, so it can start the next day with its body temperature from

two to four degrees below the normal level.

As a result of these combined adaptations for water economy the minimum water requirements of kangaroos are similar to those of the desert ungulates of Africa. Field studies indicate that arid zone kangaroos turn over only a fourth of the water needed by sheep and wild goats.

(ibid. p. 89)

At this point the kangaroo's thermoregulatory system connects harmoniously with its water-conservation system, its reproductive system, and its locomotive systems. We see that the kangaroo has developed seven distinct methods of temperature control for use under different circumstances (shade, posture, insulating fur, licking, panting, sweating, and night-cooling). The combined systems are both impressive and successful. Despite the dogs and the guns, historical records indicate that there are now more kangaroos in Australia than there were before the Europeans arrived. We are well on the way to having a precise model that explains why.

Social thermoregulation is an almost exact analogy to the individual, physiological temperature control systems. It can be just as precise, and is in many ways even more striking. Here we can demonstrate—at least at the level of insects—that homeostasis can be a property of social systems as well as of biological organisms. The society in question is that of honeybees (*Apis mellifera*). Figure 2.2 shows clearly the way they maintain their temperature at a constant level, regardless of the weather outside.

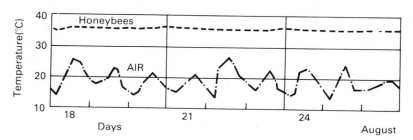

Figure 2.2   The nest temperature maintained by colonies of honeybees in cold air. (Redrawn from Kemper & During, 1967; quoted in Wilson, 1971, p. 307.)

This temperature control is a two-level process. First, an environment (nest) is chosen and modified. All the crevices are sealed except for an entrance hole. Heat and moisture are sealed in. Second, colony members have short-term responses to temperature perturbations. If the nest temperature falls, the bees cluster together, warming each other—the greater the fall, the tighter the cluster. The clustering itself is articulate. The outer zone is composed of several layers of bees sitting quietly with their heads inwards. The bees in the inner zone are more active. They move about restlessly, sip honey, and from time to time shake their abdomens and breathe more rapidly. Thus the central bees generate heat, while the outer bees serve as an insulating shell.

Temperature control on summer days is even more sophisticated. As the nest temperature rises above 30°C, the workers cool the hive by fanning their wings to circulate air over the brood combs and out of the entrance. If the nest temperature exceeds about 34°C, water evaporation is added by a series of elaborate behavioural steps.

The tuning of this social air-conditioning system has been described by Lindauer (1961):

> One might imagine that each bee would set out to collect water as soon as it detects the overheating. This is not so: not just any bee is able to collect water. Only bees that know the terrain and are experienced foragers can perform this task. Furthermore, it is an advantage when bees are divided into water collectors and water sprinklers. So there is a very strict division of labour between the older flying bees, who collect water outside, and the younger hive bees, who distribute it. Indeed, we found a special mode of communication by means of which the water collectors receive instructions from the hive bees about when to start collecting and when to stop.
>
> Let us begin with the simple case. Let us assume that water collecting is still in progress and the foragers are to be informed whether or not there is need for more water. To transmit this information the hive bees make use of *the short moment when they have contact with the collectors*: this is during water delivery at the entrance hole. As long as overheating exists, the homecoming foragers are relieved of their burdens with great greed: three or four bees at once may rush up to a collector and suck from her the extruded water droplet. This storm begging informs the collector bee that there is a pressing need for more water. When the overheating begins to subside, however, the hive bees show less interest in the water collectors. The latter now have to run around the hive themselves, trying to find somewhere a bee that will relieve them of at least part of the water load. The delivery in such cases takes much more time, of course. This rejecting attitude contains the message 'Water needs fulfilled', and the water collecting will thus stop, even though the collectors themselves have not been at the brood nests to experience the changed temperature situation.
>
> This delivery time is in fact an accurate gauge of water demand ... with delivery times up to 60 sec. the collecting is continued industriously. Beyond that, however, the eagerness for collecting decreases rapidly, and when delivery takes longer than 3 min. collecting practically ceases altogether.
>
> A second point is apparent: When delivery times are very short (up to 40 sec.), the water collectors even perform recruiting dances to stimulate hive bees to fly to the water source ... These recruiting dances subside somewhat if the delivery time is longer than 40 sec. and later cease completely.
>
> (Quoted in Wilson, 1971, p. 309)*

Individual and social thermoregulation systems provide a paradigm of precision for explanatory systems. Well-defined variables are related in a quantitative way. But this is not all. In terms of the bees, as Wilson makes clear, the exact biological and genetic mechanisms in individuals that underlie this thermal homeostasis are not known. It is possible to make useful and exact statements about one 'level of resolution' of a social system *without* specifying the micro- and macro-systems that compose and surround it.

* Surprisingly, similar and equally effective temperature control mechanisms have been discovered in *swarming* honeybees (see Heinrich 1981).

Animal Dispersion

Wynne-Edwards' scholarly account of *Animal Dispersion in Relation to Social Behaviour* (1962) draws heavily on the notion of homeostasis. The problem was to explain why animal populations do not 'over-exploit' their food resources. Before considering his solution, we should look at the evolution of the problem.

> On purely theoretical grounds Volterra (1928) reached his well known conclusion that two species, one of which feeds on the other, must undergo perpetual oscillations in numbers, because, he assumed, the predator population would inevitably increase until it overate its food supply, thereafter itself declining in consequence, thus giving the prey a chance to build up its numbers once more and so on in successive cycles.
>
> (Wynne-Edwards, 1962, p. 389)

Taking man's predation on fish as his model, Wynne-Edwards shows that this is a suspect sort of theory. Exploitation above a certain critical level does not lead to a decline in the number of predators. It leads to the extinction of the prey. In real fisheries with diminishing catches, there had been concern over this possibility since the turn of the century, when some species of whale were the first to 'disappear'. The relationship between 'tolerable' levels of fishing and the survival (or otherwise) of the prey was demonstrated experimentally.

> The experiments on fish-populations which particularly concern us were made by Silliman and Gutsell (1958), primarily in order to apply a practical test to the type of mathematical model erected by exponents of the overfishing theory. Four identical aquaria under uniform conditions were stocked with guppies (*Lebistes reticulatus*), two of them being kept as duplicate controls, and the other two as duplicate experimental populations. They were all allowed to develop in the presence of superabundant food until the 40th week, and all increased up to about the same ceiling level so far as the total mass of fish was concerned, of approximately 32 grams in 17 litres of water (*see* fig. 41). This was to be expected: Breder and Coates (1932) had earlier found that two tanks when started with one gravid female and with assorted fish respectively, took only about 20 weeks to reach the same practically constant population of 9 or 10 fish each.
>
> After this equilibrating period, tanks C and D were allowed to continue without interference for 2½ years until the 174th week: during this period the biomass in each case underwent only minor oscillations. Tanks A and B, however, were subjected to 'cropping' at 3-week intervals—three weeks being the average turnover of each generation of guppies under the conditions of the experiment, equivalent to perhaps a year under the usual conditions of a natural fishery.
>
> At first, 25 per cent by weight of the fish were removed every three weeks from A and B. The number of adults and young fell rather sharply, but by week 60 there had been a great new influx of juveniles (guppies are of course viviparous), and a new stable ratio of young to adults was established; the biomass averaged considerably below that of the controls. After week 79 the exploitation rate was reduced to 10 per cent; the biomass now progressively increased, and, though A and B were not quite uniform in this respect, the proportion of juveniles to adults tended to decline again. From week 121-150, exploitation was at the high rate of 50 per cent; the result was a great increase in the proportion of juveniles, and a progressive decline of the whole biomass; rather severe overfishing, in other words, was taking place. Finally, from

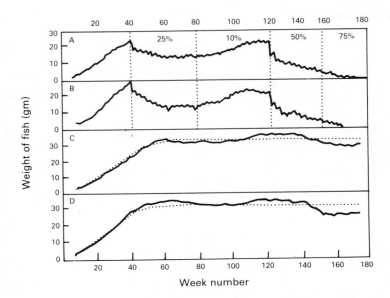

Figure 41   Weekly population weights (biomass) during Silliman and Gutsell's fishing experiment with guppies. A and B are duplicate experimental populations exploited at four different rates in succession (25, 10, 50 and 75 per cent); C and D are duplicate controls. (From Silliman and Gutsell, 1958.)

week 151, the exploitation rate was put up to 75 per cent, and this led more or less swiftly to extinction, and the end of the experiment.

(ibid. pp. 499–502)

Wynne-Edwards took the Silliman and Gutsell result as a general model of exploitation of prey. Although different sorts of prey can obviously tolerate different levels of exploitation, the basic idea is clear. There is not much difference in terms of yield between a 'tolerable' level of fishing, and one that leads to extinction. This is illustrated in Figure 2.3.

In other words, the 'oscillation' theory would not be a balance. It would lead directly to the extinction of the prey, and then to the extinction of the predator. Wynne-Edwards concludes: 'It is impossible to escape the conclusion, therefore, that *something must, in fact, constantly restrain them, while in the midst of plenty, from over-exploiting their prey*' (ibid. p. 7).

The 'something' that restrains them is their ability to control the size of their own populations.

That some such restraint often exists in nature is most easily comprehended, perhaps, in a situation where a population of animals has to depend for a period on a standing crop, which must be made to last out until the season comes round for its renewal or until alternative foods become available. Many small northern birds, for instance, are provisioned ahead for four or five months in the winter by the standing crop of seeds of a few species of trees or herbs, or by a finite stock of overwintering insects. It would be fatal to allow birds to crowd in freely in autumn up to the maximum number that

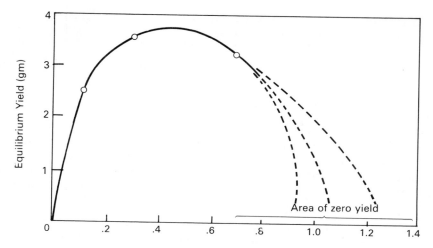

Figure 2.3 Relation between exploitation rate and sustainable yield in the guppy fishing experiments. The optimum point comes about the 35–40 per cent exploitation rate and any rate exceeding about 50 per cent leads to extinction and zero yield. (From Silliman and Gutsell, 1958, in Wynne-Edwards, 1962, p. 503)

could for the moment be supported by the superabundance of food, without regard to later consequences. The optimum population-density, on the contrary, would generally be one that could be carried right through till the spring on the same stock of food, supposing the birds were winter-resident species such as tits *(Parus)*, robins *(Erithacus)* or woodpeckers *(Pici)*. To achieve this optimum it would clearly be necessary to put a limit on the population-density *from the beginning*, while the resource was still untapped.

The need for restraint in the midst of plenty, as it turns out, must apply to all animals whose numbers are ultimately limited by food whether they are predators in the ordinary sense of the word or not. ...

To build up and preserve a favourable balance between population-density and available resources, it would be necessary for the animals to evolve a control system in many respects analogous to the physiological systems that regulate the internal environment of the body and adjust it to meet changing needs. Such systems are said to be homeostatic or self-balancing, and it will be convenient for us to use the same word. Physiological homeostasis has in general been slowly perfected in the course of evolution, and it is thus the highest animals that tend to be most independent of environmental influences, as far as the inward machinery of the body is concerned. Population homeostasis, it may be inferred, would involve adaptations no less complex, and it might therefore be expected that these would similarly tend to reach the greatest efficiency and perfection in the highest groups.

We are going to discover in the concluding chapters of the book that such homeostatic adaptations exist in astonishing profusion and diversity, above all in the two great phyla of arthropods and vertebrates. There we shall find machinery for regulating the reproductive output or recruitment rate of the population in a dozen different ways—by varying the quota of breeders, the number of eggs, the resorption of embryos, survival of the newborn and so on; for accelerating or retarding growth-rate and maturity; for limiting the density of colonisation or settlement of the habitat; for ejecting surplus members of the population, and even for encompassing their deaths in some cases in order to retrieve the correct balance between population-density and resources. Not all types of adaptation have been developed in every group, though examples of parallel evolution are abundant and extraordinarily interesting.

(ibid. pp. 8–9)

The bulk of the book is devoted to the amazing multiplicity of ways in which various insect, bird, and animal species control the size (or in some cases the biomass) of their own populations. Specific mechanisms for doing this are diverse, but all—necessarily—have in common a means of 'estimating' population size, and a means of translating this estimate into 'corrective action'. The estimate of population size is—again necessarily—a *symbol*. This is a matter of great importance because it means that the sheer 'fact' of a given population size does not 'cause' anything. It is the symbol that does the job.

> The reader is already aware that conventions and conventional behaviour, with which we are so pre-eminently concerned, are in the nature of artefacts, more or less widely divorced from the real sanctions by which their observance is ultimately enforced. The more remote they are from absolute reality, the more do they become symbols arbitrarily endowed with a meaning (just as are the conventional signs that make up a printed page); and the more they are likely to differ from ordinary 'real' adaptations by being somewhat bizarre or even extravagant in nature.

(ibid. p. 15)

Instead of 'real competition' we find 'symbolic competition'. In general, fights to the death do not happen. There are social conventions that prevent it. And

> Conventions ... must, by their nature, always be properties of a concerted group, and can never be completely vested in, or discharged by a lone individual in perpetual isolation: their observance has to be re-inforced by the recognition and support of others who are bound by the same convention.

(ibid. p. 132)

Conventions largely determine which, and how many creatures breed, and what happens to those that do not breed—the options range from simple matelessness to forced migration and even 'execution'. The consequence is that chronic individual competition for food is not 'permitted' to arise.

The estimates of population size that trigger or defuse conventions are arrived at in a variety of ways, from the symbolic 'counting posts' of dogs, cats, and bears, to the massing of the total population of many insects, especially those of the winged varieties. Whatever system is used incorporates the two processes necessary for homeostasis:

> an input of information, acting as an indicator of the state of balance or imbalance of the system, that can evoke the appropriate corrective response.

and

> a means of bringing about whatever changes are needed to restore the balance when it is disturbed.

(ibid. p. 13)

Although Wynne-Edwards theories have since been criticized on both general and specific grounds (see, for instance, Wilson, 1975), the importance and scope of his thesis has not been challenged.

In *Animal Dispersion,*we see that even fairly simple cybernetic concepts can unify and render comprehensible many apparently unrelated and diverse social phenomena. We also see, again, that it is possible to deal with social systems and their properties at their own level without necessarily specifying the nature of their micro- and macrosystems.

A last point, but an important one. Wynne-Edwards has keen sense of the *living* nature of his systems that I believe characterizes all good cyberneticians— and distinguishes them from mere 'systems-theorists'. The intellectual tools are necessary, but they are never the whole story. 'Man' often distinguishes himself from 'mere animals'—puts himself at the summit of the evolutionary pyramid— by saying that he *alone* can create and use tools. Wynne-Edwards discovers everywhere symbols and social conventions—'tools'. Even the lowliest of living creatures possess them. We are once more back *in* a living world.

Themes

In the first chapter, we looked at a set of examples drawn from social psychology; conformity, participation, status hierarchy, and so on. All these phenomena were expected to *recur*—to occur over and over again in similar form. From this, there was a common assumption of *objectivity*—of the scientist providing a description of some small part of the world that had independent existence. This in turn encouraged the adoption of methods from the physical sciences (hypothesis, experiment, verification/falsification).

In the second chapter we have looked at cybernetic examples; behaviour settings, double-binds, people-pig mutualism in the Tsembaga, collision-risk shipping models, and so on: there were some outstanding differences between the cybernetic and social psychological approaches. Cybernetics covered unique as well as recurring phenomena; the distinction between the model and the 'reality' was made very clear; the real search was for connectivity and consistency, not for objectivity. This was because of an underlying acceptance that no model can be definitive, or we would not need a model. As Ashby put it:

No electronic model of a cat's brain can possibly be as true as that provided by the brain of another cat; yet what is the *use* of the latter as a model? Its very closeness means that it also presents all the technical features that make the first so difficult. From here on, then, I shall take as a basis the thesis that the first virtue of a model is to be useful.

(Ashby, in Stogdill, 1970, p. 96)

or alternatively:

'The designer's act of selecting one model from many is equivalent to some determining factor fixing an input at a permanent value'(Ashby, 1956, p. 254).

In other words, models are adopted by decision (based on their use in some project in hand) not because they are 'true' (in some absolute sense). This way of looking at models allows cyberneticians to admit, as part of their methodology, several things that social psychologists ignore, or put into the 'unscientific' parts of their books. These are, first, the freedom of subjects to influence the research. Second, that the model originates in a social context in which the intentions of the researchers plays an important role. Third, that there may be terms in the model that have more to do with the decision to select *this* model out of many alternatives than they have to do with 'reality'. Such terms are outside the scope of a physical science methodology because they look to the investigator not to the world for their 'truth'. Taken together these differences mean that the modelling processes at the heart of social science do not fit easily into the 'hypothesis-experiment-verification' framework. They are much more like the situation that Goffman called 'a kind of interactional *modus vivendi* where:

> Together the participants contribute to a single over-all definition of the situation which involves not so much a real agreement as to what exists but rather a real agreement as to whose claims concerning what issues will be temporarily honoured.

The idea of 'honouring claims' rather than 'finding facts' is often thought of as a second-best that will have to do for the moment until something better comes along. Social science will have 'grown up' (i.e. it will look like natural science) when that 'something better' comes along. In the next chapter, it will be argued that the process of 'honouring claims' is the central and essential method of social science.

References

Ashby, W.R. (1956), *An Introduction to Cybernetics*, London, Chapman and Hall.
Barker, R.G. (1963), On the nature of the environment, *J. Soc. Issues*, **19**(4), 17–38.
Barker, R.G. (1968), *Ecological Psychology*, Stanford University Press, Stanford, Calif.
Bateson, G. (1956), Towards a theory of schizophrenia, *Behavioral Science*, **1**, 4.
Bateson, G. (1960a), Minimal requirements for a theory of schizophrenia, *A.M.A. Archives of General Psychiatry*, Vol. 2, pp. 477–491.
Bateson, G. (1960b), The group dynamics of schizophrenia in *Chronic Schizophrenia: Explorations in Theory and Treatment* (Ed. L. Appleby, J.M. Scher, and J. Cumming) The Free Press, Glencoe, Illinois.
Beer, S. (1966), *Decision and Control*, London, John Wiley.
Beer, S. (1975), *Platform for Change*, London, John Wiley.
Beer, S. (1979), *The Heart of Enterprise*, London, John Wiley.
Beer, S. (1981), *Brain of the Firm*, London, John Wiley.
Cartledge, J.W. and Rezac, G.J.(1970), *Simulation of the Tzembega Ritual Cycle*, Dept. of Cybernetics, Brunel University (Xerox).
Cartwright, D. and Zander, A. (1969), *Group Dynamics. Research and Theory*, New York, Row, Petersen.
Dawson, T.J. (1977), Kangaroos, *Scientific American*, **237**, 2, 78–89.
Espejo, R. (1979), *Information and Management: The Cybernetics of a Small Company*, The University of Aston Management Centre, Working Paper No. 125.
Fawl, C.L. (1959), *Disturbances Experienced by Children in their Natural Habitat: a Study in Ecological Psychology*, Doctoral Dissertation, University of Kansas.
Heinrich, B. (1981), The regulation of temperature in the honeybee swarm, *Scientific American*, **244**, 6, 120–129.

Kemper, H. and Dühring, E. (1967),*Die Sozialen Faltenwespen Mitteleuropas*, Berlin, Paul Parey, p. 180.

Laing, R.D. (1971), *Self and Others*, Harmondsworth, Penguin.

Lindauer, M. (1961), *Communication Among Social Bees*, Cambridge, Harvard University Press.

March, J.G. and Simon, H.A. (1958), *Organizations*, London, John Wiley.

Rappaport, R.A. (1968), *Pigs for the Ancestors*, Yale, Yale University Press.

Rappaport, R.A. (1971), The flow of energy in an agricultural society, *Scientific American*,**224**, 116–133.

Rogers, E.M. (1962), *Diffusion of Innovations*, London, Collier-Macmillan.

Stogdill, R.N. (ed.)(1970), *The Process of Model Building*, Ohio State University Press.

Volterra, V. (1928), Variations and fluctuations in the number of individuals in animal species living together (translated by M.E. Wells), *J. Cons. Int. Explor. Mer.* 3.

Wilson, E.O. (1971), *The Insect Societies*, Cambridge, Belknap Press of Harvard.

Wilson, E.O. (1975), *Sociobiology*, Cambridge, Belknap Press of Harvard.

Wynne-Edwards, V.C. (1962), *Animal Dispersion in Relation to Social Behaviour*, Edinburgh, Oliver and Boyd.

CHAPTER 3
Methodology

Introduction

This chapter is devoted to the difference between *politics*, *ritual* and *fact*. It gives the reasons for the approach taken to groups in the rest of the book. The following chapters do not try to analyse the politics of the various groups. This is not the proper subject matter for systems analysis, cybernetics, or any of the other 'social sciences'. Politics—in the broadest possible sense—is indeterminate, and the subject of reflection and innovation. There are simply no handles on which to hang a 'scientific' analysis in the traditional sense.

The proper subject matter of social science is the *ritual* that flows from political intention so that groups (or individuals) can realize their ends and get 'results'. A much firmer distinction than usual is made here between social and natural science. The nub of the matter is that social science gives an account of events that include people, whereas natural science gives accounts of events that exclude people. Social science needs a *different methodology* to natural science. The following pages are an attempt to justify and describe the differing approaches needed to politics (all aspects of personal and collective decision-making), to ritual (repeatable activities undertaken by people to get 'results', and to the 'proper' objects of natural science.

It must be emphasized that this three-level distinction is intended as a rule of thumb. For all I know there could be twenty-seven levels; or 127. The point is that the usual two-way art/science or hard/soft or natural/social distinctions are insufficient. Failure to distinguish political, indeterminate, and creative aspects from agreed methods and rituals leads to a silly social science. Worse than this it can lead to a social science that is both inhumane and dangerous. Any project that tries to deal with people as if they were objects is suspect.

Bearing in mind that the political/ritual/natural distinction is meant to be useful, not absolute or final, let us have a preliminary look at the differences of method and content.

Natural Science

The central concept of natural science is the *experiment*. Of course, any particular experiment, or set of experiments may turn out to be wrong—but they can only be shown to be wrong in the light of other experiments. So the experiment itself remains the central idea. Along with the idea of experiment goes the idea of precise measurement. Natural science is characterized by the use of batteries of measuring instruments—clocks, thermometers, volt-meters, pressure gauges, precise balances, and so on. Other instruments are introduced to bring the objects of investigation into focus so that they can be measured—telescopes, microscopes, oscilloscopes, infra-red photographs, and a host of others. Increasingly sophisticated mathematical methods are used to deal with the numbers that result from all the measurements. Nevertheless, the basic idea of cause and effect remains. The final result may be stated in terms of probabilities and error factors, but the underlying notion is that the experiment itself is repeatable. Given the same set of causes, the same set of effects will follow. Because of this, natural science can generate predictions—and predictions about predictions which are called 'laws'.

Social Science

The central concept of social science is the *simulation*. A simulation is an entirely different sort of animal to an experiment. There are two main differences, one of which is important, and another that is not so important. Let us look at the less important difference first.

Simulation is used when the subject matter is too complicated for experiment. Earlier we quoted Beer (1966) as saying: 'The kinds of system under discussion exhibit literally billions of variables. There is no *rigorous* means of knowing which matter.'

Complexity is the nub of one problem. If the initial set of conditions—'the same set of causes'—cannot be defined, then proper experiments cannot be carried out. Simulation is brought in as a substitute. But simulation, as a method used to deal with complexity, does not make a distinction between natural and social science. Models of aircraft are tested in wind tunnels to generate predictions about the behaviour of real aircraft. Simulation can be a method of natural science.

The second difference is more important. Simulation is used to deal with the objects of social science because causal relationships—and hence experiments—are inappropriate. Behaviour, events, and situations that involve people (or any other beings that can learn), do not depend upon causes, but upon decisions. The situations and events that are being dealt with are not 'out there as a matter of fact'—they are out there 'by permission' as a result of choice and agreement. If the 'permission' is withdrawn, then the events cease. If an event is 'out there by permission' then it has a different sort of status to an event that is 'out there as a matter of fact'. The former event is the one we have chosen to call *'ritual'*. Rituals are recurrent, and are objective and open to inspection, but their basic status is totally different to the 'facts' of natural science. They are, as Goffman so beautifully put it, a projection from the realm of the imaginary.

Simulation does not result in predictions and laws, but in *models*. It can be used to make diagnoses and projections. It can reveal a lot about the *limits* of behaviours and events. It does not make precise predictions about the content of events because it cannot—partly because of the problem of complexity—but mainly because the objects of social science do not have the status on which predictions can be based.

In the construction of models, the central problem is not of scale or measurement, but of relationship, structure, and configuration. The characterization of social science in terms of ritual, simulation, and model will be fully illustrated and argued in the pages that follow. To complete the overview, we should now look at our third category of subject matter—the political.

Political Science

The central concept of political science is *dialogue*. No 'statement' is final or definitive. Everything is open to question. Politics is always an arena of real conflict. Truths are not established by experiment: the subject matter is too complex and lacking in definition. Nor are truths established by simulation: by models of relationship and similarity. Truths are established by the elimination of the other contending parties (Griffiths, 1981).

A political decision is one that sets the framework for a ritual. Once the ritual is established at the social level, then measurement becomes possible at the material level. This includes not only the 'experiments' of natural science, but technologies, factories, and bureaucracies—all forms of organization whose structure and purpose depends on counting and number as well as basic enactment. For instance there is no such thing as a factory whose output cannot be counted. There is no such thing as a factory whose purpose is to have a non-countable output. This is not true of a craft, where the essence is ritual, technique, and enactment. It does not matter in the least if the output of a craft cannot be counted. One masterpiece may be of greater value than hundreds of 'products'. This can never be true of a factory. Similarly, in natural science, a non-replicable, non-measurable 'experiment' is a nonsense.

In Practice, Political, Social, and Natural Science are Inseparable

Once we have made a distinction between the three levels, it is quite easy to see how any activity must involve all three. A scientific activity, especially one in 'natural science' may render the political level partly or wholly invisible. A political activity may lose sight of its material consequences. But a rounded account of either must take into consideration all three forms. To illustrate this, we will give an example from natural, and an example from political science, then we will look again at some of the 'social' paradigms covered in the first two chapters.

The idea of a heliocentric solar system—one in which the earth goes round the sun, rather than vice versa—was first stated in Ancient Greek times by Aristarchos of Samos, yet Galileo (rightly) gets the credit. Why? The immediate answer is that Aristarchos was politically eliminated. As Caianiello (1980) puts it:

> The heliocentric system was not accepted when it was first introduced. At that time, the idea of the sun was connected with the idea of a fire. Fire is something that by its nature tends to go up. Earth is something that tends to go down. So it was an absurdity to suppose that the earth, which is heavy, goes round something which is weightless. By the time Copernicus read Aristarchos and re-invented the idea—with additions that are not at all an improvement—times had changed and it was acceptable.

In other words, the heliocentric system was first postulated in the context of political debate—questions about relations between assumptions. Aristarchos was unable to establish a following—a ritual to pass on his theory in a persuasive form. Without the following, there was no room to seek practical consequences (it was a little early for strict experiment) that would allow the theory to become established.

Copernicus was luckier. He wrote *On the Revolutions of the Heavenly Spheres* in 1543, and the idea was accepted—as a useful technique. It made astronomical calculation easier to 'suppose' that planets went round the sun—but no-one believed that was what actually happened. Once the ritual (the calculating technique) had been established, it only remained for Galileo to step in with a real and measurable consequence. Venus has phases just like the moon—and these are incompatible with non-heliocentric (Ptolemeic) theory. The initial 'political' assumption had generated a ritual, and the ritual had allowed the discovery of a 'fact'.

Of course, the politics were not quite over. There was the little matter of a dispute between Galileo and the Church over that nature of 'proof'—whether nature or the Bible was the final authority (Gingerich 1982). But this time round it was the opposition that was politically eliminated.

In general, we can say that behind every experiment, there is a whole apparatus of ritual. The whole experimental procedure and apparatus are not part of the experiment—nor are they usually subject to experiment. They are agreed and consensual, which, in our terminology means ritual. And behind the ritual is the 'real' debate or conflict. Agreement or disagreement about assumptions that allows the ritual to come into being.

Now let us take a political example. And since politics are contentious let us take a contentious political example. The dispute between the Stalinist and Trotskyist factions in Russia after the Revolution of 1917.

It is well known that Stalin and Trotsky advanced very different theories on almost all topics—foreign policy, industrialization, the collectivization of agriculture, and so on. Although the two started from more or less equivalent 'power bases' (Trotsky had led the Red Army during the Revolution), it was Stalin's ideas that were put into practice. Trotsky and most of his following were politically—which in this case means physically—eliminated. This result (in summary) is often put down to Stalin's 'grip on the bureaucracy'. As it stands, this is an insufficient explanation, although it points in the right direction. It is also generally agreed that Trotsky advocated far deeper and more radical involvement of the working class and the peasantry in decision-making. The 'agreement' on this is controversial. Some categorize it as 'genuinely revolutionary', others as 'ultra-left and objectively counter-revolutionary'.

My belief is that Trotsky made a fundamental and fatal error in constantly maintaining the struggle at the political level. There was a failure to develop organizational forms (rituals) that allowed the political debate and political involvement to be perpetuated *and* was effective in running factories and farms.

Trotsky was not alone with this problem. Nor is it clear, even today, that it is a soluble problem. The pattern of mass popular involvement giving way to bureaucracy and autocracy has been many time repeated—in China, in Cuba, in Vietnam—and the danger signs are beginning to appear even in Nicaragua this year, despite every effort of the Sandinista government. The corollary of autocracy is alienation and disaffection—the beginning of the degeneration of the workers' states.

The problem of the absence of an *effective and democratic* organizational form was highlighted in a speech byRaul Castro. He summarized the ills afflicting the Cuban Economy; the world economic crisis, runaway inflation, low world sugar prices and smut plague on the sugarcane, blue mould disease on the tobacco fields, *and*—to quote the report—

> The President's brother was courageous enough to confess that Cuba's ills could not all be blamed on the U.S. blockade, the crisis of capitalism or the wrath of nature, however often they may have been 'used as pretexts to hide our deficiencies'.

> To the objective factors we have described we must add the presence of indiscipline, lack of control, irresponsibility, complacency, negligence, and 'buddyism' which, in addition to aggravating many problems, prevent others from being solved and generate justified irritation on the part of broad sectors of the population.
> Particularly in agriculture, Sr. Castro charged, many people were working only 4 to 6 hours a day. The norm system was being widely abused, with people fulfilling their norm two or three times over in one day and then knocking off for two days. There was unwillingness to overfulfil norms lest they be increased ...
>
> (*Financial Times*, 22 January 1980)

Here we see quite clearly that socialism has failed to develop an organizational form that works as a way of running factories and farms—and allows the workforce to use their intelligence. Just as in capitalist factories, innovations—especially those that could result in massive increases in productivity—are kept secret from the management. For good reason. The reason that management and workers are not on the same side, and the reason for the reason can be identified with the theories of F.W. Taylor, whose ideas about 'scientific management' have infected socialist and capitalist practice since the turn of the century. Taylor (1906) said of his own methods: 'In my system the workman is told precisely what he is to do and how he is to do it, and any improvement he makes on the instructions given to him is fatal to success.'

Lenin took these ideas on board as an appropriate method for the development of soviet industry, and said of Taylorism:

Like all capitalist progress is a combination of the refined brutality of bourgeois exploitation, and a number of the greatest scientific achievements in the field of analysing mechanical motions during work, the elimination of superfluous and awkward motions, the elaboration of correct methods of work, the introduction of the best system of accounting and control etc., the Soviet Republic must at all costs adapt all that is valuable in the achievement of Science and Technology in this field. The possibility of building socialism depends exactly on our success in combining the Soviet Power and the Soviet Organisation of Industry with the up-to-date achievements of capitalism. We must organize in Russia the study and teaching of the Taylor system, and systematically try it out and adapt it to our ends.

(Lenin, 1965)

The strength of Taylor's paradigm was that it provided an easily understood framework for the organization of industry. A factory was composed, like a machine, of a number of simple components that could only be put together in a limited number of ways. Once it had been put together, problems (defective components) could be removed and replaced without disturbing the rest of the system. In other words, all the political and social aspects were reduced to the measurement concepts of natural science. The wrong ritual has been giving rise to the wrong politics (alienation) ever since. The new politics of socialism—of mass involvement—failed to give rise to a new ritual; failed to give rise to a new way of measuring social effort. From the old ritual flowed the old way of measuring work—and from that came at least some of the old political problems.

Politics—human dialogue—that cannot ground itself in ritual gets defeated, and often eliminated as an option. Trotsky's political defeat had as much to do with this as with any inherent political defects in the ideas.

'Holes'

The idea of a *minimal three-level analysis* of intelligent activity should now be becoming clearer. The problems that arise when fewer distinctions are made can be very serious indeed. Interestingly,the problems arise within the theories and models, not only in practical applications. 'Internally' the problems appear as 'holes' in the theory.

A 'hole' is a concept that cannot be fully defined at the level at which it appears. It represents the appearance of politics *within* science or within ritual. All the key concepts that we discussed in the first two chapter had 'holes' in them. This was easiest to see in Bateson's theory of the Double Bind—because, in the end, Bateson saw it himself.

Double-bind theory describes the way in which one human being manages to put another in the wrong at every turn. Jump through this hoop. Anyone that can not jump through this hoop is a fool. Only fools jump through hoops! It all looked very objective; like a 'fact'. But of course the vicious activities that we recognize so easily as double binds are not 'facts', they are rituals. They are 'there', and they are open to inspection—but their being 'there' depends on agreement, on convention, and (at some point) on decision. Bateson calls this difference the 'reification problem'. In our language, this means confusing a ritual with a fact. Bateson puts the matter very elegantly when he says:

> We talk ... as though a double bind were a something and as though such somethings could be counted.
> Of course, that's all nonsense. You cannot count the bats in an inkblot because there are none. And yet a man—if he be 'bat-minded'—may 'see' several.

Bat-mindedness is not something that can be 'cured' by resorting to better and better measuring techniques. It is not that sort of problem. Which is not to say that rituals cannot be very precisely quantified (Rappaport's work proves that point) but no matter how 'good' the quantification, they remain rituals. Their existence is rooted in politics and in decision. Any 'prediction' is only valid for as long as the ritual maintains the agreement of its participants. (Agreement is used here in the widest possible sense. Any way of going along with a social activity is agreement—giving permission for that activity to exist.)

All the theories and models of social science have 'holes' in them. This is simply because the theories are about people, and the people can decide to act outside the framework of the theory. This has implications for the methodology of social science. We are not trying to specify what people *will* do, but what people *may* do. A model in social science is therefore totally different from a model in natural science.

In natural science, a model has to correspond with 'reality'. In social science, the model may (or may not) be adopted *as* the reality. Whether the model is adopted or not has nothing to do with natural or social science, but with politics in its full sense. Even when a model is adopted, traces of its political origins remain in its concepts as 'holes' through which the politics may re-assert themselves at any moment.

To put it another way, concepts that appear in models, but reflect scientific, investigative, or everyday activity constitute 'holes'. They are not defined by *correspondence* to anything that is 'there', but by *agreement* on a framework—and by the consistency and coherence of that framework. There can be no *test* of such terms within the model, which by definition looks in the wrong direction—towards the world and not towards the scientist. 'Conformity' was a concept that looked to the Asche team for its meaning, not to their experiments for its 'truth'. It remains a central 'hole' in their thesis. If we make the political decision to re-evaluate the whole experiment, then the concept of 'conformity' could be replaced by the concept of 'problem solving and hypothesis formation' (see chapter 1). When we look through the 'problem solving' spectacles, the behaviour of the Asche subjects has to be evaluated in an entirely different way, and we can reach a set of alternative conclusion. Others have suggested reaching different conclusions by replacing 'conformity' with the simpler notion of 'deception'.

Brian Gaines captures the idea of the appearance of the investigative activity in the science (cybernetic, systems, or social) at the most fundamental level when he says:

Definition: A *system* is what is distinguished as a system. At first sight this looks to be a nonstatement. Systems are whatever we like to distinguish as systems. Has anything been said? Is there any possible foundation here for a systems science? I want to answer both these questions affirmatively and show that this definition is full of content and rich in its interpretation.

Let me first answer one obvious objection to the definition above and turn it to my advantage. You may ask, 'What is peculiarly systemic about this definition?' 'Could I not equally well apply it to all other objects I might wish to define?' i.e.,

A *rabbit* is what is distinguished as a rabbit.

'Ah, but,' I shall reply, 'my definition is adequate to define a system but yours is not adequate to define a rabbit'. In this lies the essence of systems theory: that to distinguish some entity as being a system is a necessary and sufficient criterion for its being a system, and this is uniquely true for systems. Whereas to distinguish some entity as being anything else is a necessary criterion to its being that something but not a sufficient one.

(Gaines, 1979)

The existence of systems is not independent of the activity that created them. Choice not 'objectivity' is an irreducible underlying factor.

So far, we have distinguished a minimum of three levels of activity: political, ritual, and natural. At each level there is an appropriate methodology and an appropriate technology: dialogue and conflict, simulation and model, experiment and measurement. We have tried to show how any activity, in practice, involves all three levels, and how each level ultimately relies on all the others for its validity. Politics has to be grounded in ritual and sometimes in measurement—distinctive politics must generate distinctive 'facts'. Politics appears in ritual (in social and even in natural science) as concepts that cannot be defined with reference to the 'world'—as 'holes'.

So much for the theory. What are the consequences?

1 Political options that cannot ground themselves in distinctive ritual (method, organizational form, repeatable activity) will be assimilated or eliminated. Part of the purpose of this book is to look at rituals that might fit the politics of mass participation, that might lead towards 'convivial institutions of the working class that could replace all the useful, but oppressive capitalist functions of management and administration'.

2 Social science should not try to imitate the methods of natural science because they are inappropriate. The job of social science is to produce models of behaviour that can be used. These models play a significant role in constituting reality, they are not just a reflection of it. Consequently, they cannot be 'tested' as if they were 'descriptions'. The models of small group processes that will be produced in later chapters have the appearance of descriptions—and I hope they are 'accurate'. But it must never be forgotten that people can choose to act in other ways. A social model—unlike a model of natural events—is only valid for as long as it has 'permission' to be so.

If the 'by permission' aspect of any model of the behaviour of any living and intelligent being is forgotten—if the model is thought of as a 'fact', and the behaviour as caused, inevitable, and predictable—then the model is headed for a catastrophe. Taylor's system only appears to work because (usually) the workman who is told 'precisely what he is to do and how he is to do it' agrees to understand the instructions. The 'hole' in Taylor's theory is the word 'precisely'. Any set of 'precise' instructions is only 'precise' to the extent that they are understood by the person to whom they are given. Brian Lewis has identified this particular problem clearly in his work on Ordinary Language Algorithms—ways of telling people precisely what to do. Commenting on the problems of turning Acts of Parliament into algorithms, he said:

> If you are too precise, people can evade the law by producing categories that fall outside it. If you are too vague, then it is not clear whether any judge would uphold your regulations. The problem of specificity runs through the whole attempt to algorithmicise any area whatsoever.
>
> (Lewis, in Pask and Robinson, 1980)

In Cuba, people *were* doing 'precisely' what they were told—and that was the problem. 'Precisely' is not a factual concept, but the appearance of politics within the model. It depends for its meaning on tacit or explicit agreement, or on convention. Ultimately it is rooted in dialogue or conflict, not in a reflection of the 'objective' world.

Once 'precisely' is questioned, the idea of an 'instruction', of being 'told what to do', comes into question. Taylor's theory turns into so much morning mist. So it is with all social models.

3 Political science should not try to imitate the methods of social science, because they are inappropriate. Once a political decision has been established, then the mode of organization and activity that carries it out can be the subject of social science. The decision itself, or any challenge to that decision, cannot be collapsed down to that level where simulation and model-building are appropriate methods of analysis. Conversely, a political idea cannot be *disproved* by reference to consequences and actions. Such a disproof takes place at the wrong level. Bad consequences can only invalidate a political idea if their result is disillusion with the idea. But in this case, the invalidation has taken place at the political level, by methods of dialogue or conflict. This slightly abstract point will become clearer when we look at the way the self-validating political ideas of the Brighton Rents Project did change (in chapters 5 and 6) and the way the self-validating ideas of systems theory—which pretended to include politics as their subject matter—were forced to change (later in this chapter).

We will now make some comments on the earlier social and cybernetic paradigms in the light of the crude political/ritual/natural distinction —trying to show that it is a better analytical tool than the simpler two-way (social/natural) split.

Social and Cybernetic Models: Comments

Bion

Bion suggested a four-state, two-level model of group process. The group could be in one of three 'basic assumption' states of Fight/Flight, Dependence, or Pairing—or they could evolve to the state of scientific Work-Group. Movement between the three basic assumption states was 'caused' by tension originating in internal contradictions in each state.

There is nothing wrong with this model—as a model. It is a coherent system in its own right. There is no doubt that its dynamics could be formalized and simulated. We could also construct alternative models. We commented at the time that 'the locus of all meaning and truth in the group is the trainer'. We gave an alternative account of the social process whereby the group switched from one state to another. In our account, all obvious responses of the group to its own situation—attempts to establish a conversational framework and suitable rituals—were interpreted by the trainer as regressive manifestations, and thereby blocked. After each such block, the group tried a different approach. The original model of the group process *excludes* the trainer. The second model includes the trainer. The decision about which model is valid cannot be included within either model (at the level of social science and simulation). It is, fundamentally, a political decision. In the first (Bion) model, politics are excluded—because the only political animal is deemed to be the trainer—who is excluded. In the second model, politics are also excluded. We have included the trainer, but the model only 'works' if the trainer continues to give the ritual explanations that he would give if he believed the first model. If the group chooses to discuss the models then it has stepped outside the framework of models—moved from the social to the political.

Here we see that the political aspects have to do with *redefinition* (and so cannot be modelled) whereas the ritual aspects have to do with *predefinition* (which is the precise condition of modelling).

The political battle going on in Bion's groups was concerned with the ability of the trainer to impose his account on the group members who were in turn trying to impose their account. The issue could not be settled by reference to the inherent validity of any version of the events. If the issue was settled, the dominant version could be realized as ritual, and represented by a model. But the model can never be definitive. Its political content—its 'holes'—always open it to challenge and redefinition.

In commenting on Bion, and on social science in general, we also said 'any explanation is better than none'. This can now be elaborated. Political options depend on the existence of a variety of models, and on tensions and antagonisms between them. Without the models—no matter how rough and ready or unscientific they may be—there can be no real choice. Social science can generate models, but their validation is a political matter. The process of validation itself cannot be included within the model. That is fairly obvious. What is not so obvious is that the model cannot be of the political process from which ultimately the validation must flow. If this project is attempted, then the action is taking place at the level of politics, and not at the level of social science. Bion's activities in his groups were political—involving conflict—until the Work Group was established. At that point an agreed ritual could be created that was not riddled with 'holes'.

Bales

The work of Bales takes natural science as its model, and the ritual and political aspects seem to disappear. It simply appears as 'true' that in groups some people talk more than others, and in a way that can be mathematically predefined—in much the same way that the trajectory of a bullet, given mass and velocity, can be mathematically predefined.

The ritual aspect was that the groups agreed to have a 'single focus'—to attend to the same thing with one person talking at a time. Itself a rather unusual and artificial situation. Then only one aspect of this ritual was dealt with. The convention by which individuals ordered their verbal contributions. This convention was not problematic for the Bales groups. We may surmise that they were more concerned with the content of the discussion and with techniques of expression—conventions that Bales was rather unsuccessful in quantifying. It seems likely that this lack of success had to do with the 'fact' that the task-oriented/socio-emotional role division (amongst others) was still the subject of political negotiation within the group. No one convention surfaced as decisive. Hence no 'scientific' result.

Although Bales did not find it necessary to specify it, it seems that all his groups were *male*. Probably the statistical majority were young (many of them were students), white, male, and North American. In other words, a group that would find it easy to agree on a hierarchical ordering of participation. A common political assumption gives rise to a convention that can be dealt with by social science. A political challenge to the hegemony of this group could also reach down to undermine this form of structured participation—and the scientific results that neatly flow from it. Womens' groups, for instance, often have a deliberate convention of encouraging the least articulate to express themselves—and of consciously rejecting the task-orientated/socio-emotional distinction.

Here we see that even the 'hardest' numerical results in social science finally depend on ritual flowing from political decision. Their truth may be *in* the world, but is is not really of it.

James and Barker

John James and Roger Barker (see chapters 1 and 2) were both concerned with 'naturally' occurring social behaviour. James counted the numbers of people in

'freely-forming groups'. Barker—on the explicit analogy of the natural distribution of the element potassium—set out to discover the 'natural distribution' of
social behaviour, of laughing, playing, talking, being valued and devalued, of
conflict, failure, and so on.

James' work led to the formulation of a mathematical model that predicts the
distribution of group sizes. Barker's work led to a formal account involving the
concept of behaviour setting with its own programme, with its own 'circuitry'
and definite 'mechanisms'. The model allows predictions to be made about
behaviour. For instance, about size changes in 'undermanned or overmanned
groups'. Similarly, in a later chapter, we will produce a formula that predicts
attendance at meetings in informal organizations.

James', Barker's, and (we hope) our prediction all work. The only point at
issue here is the notion of 'prediction'. The model predicts A, and A happens. In
natural science, given lots of other conditions were satisfied, this would count
towards the verification of the model. It is 'prediction' in the strict sense. In
social science, we are only using 'prediction' in a loose sense. The 'fact' of freely
forming groups is based on a large number of social rituals and conventions.
Behaviour settings are rituals, and their programmes are conventions. The
attendance of people at meetings is a ritual and depends on conventions. None
of this is 'factual'. If the 'predictions' work, it is because it is convenient to allow
them to work, or because they flow as consequences from rituals and conventions that it is convenient to allow to work. If the conventions are changed or
challenged (politics!) then the model may no longer work. Its 'permission' may
be withdrawn. In James' original presentation it appeared that freely forming
groups were convention free. They happened in the absence of convention to the
contrary, or they happened whatever the conventions. Therefore they were
'natural' and the subject of strict prediction. The truth is that the 'size
distribution of freely forming groups' is the product of whole layers of
convention (about when and where it is legitimate to approach people, about
the nature of swimming pools, and of tea-breaks on building sites, and so on).
James established that his distribution was the product of many different
combinations of convention. But this is not enough for strict prediction. Because
the result is dependent on convention, it can be changed by political decision, or
as a result of political decision. This would *not* invalidate the model. Conventions and rituals (and their products) are simply not the proper subject matter
for strict prediction. Social predictions are conditional on 'permission'. They
may be very useful. They may enable us to make better plans. But they can
never have the universality and generality that we have the convention of
according to 'natural events'. Not all 'facts' have the same status, and the
methodologies must be tailored accordingly.

Asche, Bateson, and Whyte

Asche's concept of 'conformity' (as we have already pointed out) is not a fact,
but a way of looking at things. The ritual that produces 'conformity' may be a

'fact of the world' (or at least of the laboratory) and therefore measurable. But 'conformity' itself is the conceptualization of a political decision by a participant, and as such is open to political challenge by the subjects or by other participants.

This, incidentally, underscores the point that there is no such thing as an impartial observer/scientist at the level of politics. A claim on the title is an attempt (usually unconscious) to disguise the political content of the initial definition of the situation, and to eliminate the permissive aspects of the situation so that it can legitimately be measured. Goffman's observation that a single definition of the situation is an agreement on whose claims will be temporarily honoured is a healthy corrective to the 'impartiality' position.

Bateson's concept of the double bind is similarly a ritual in which a power struggle is being enacted. Without that *content*, although the *behaviour* might be exactly the same, there would be no double bind. And the content is there by permission of the mutual intentions of the actors (although 'permission' might seem a strange word to use in this context). This is perhaps the classic case where politics can re-emerge from the ritual to invalidate any counting or scientific measurement that has been going on. Nevertheless, we must not forget that the *possibility* of measurement is necessary for social rituals to become established. This is the contradiction that good social science always lives with, and bad social science tries to eliminate.

Whyte's idea of a status hierarchy embodies the identical contradiction. It is factual and measurable while its content is the real interactions and intentions of people. It is a perfectly valid model. Yet its permission may be withdrawn. It is a characteristic of models to be one option amongst many. The decision on which model (?) cannot be made by simple reference to the model. All models and rituals are necessarily subject to *predefinition* but can never escape the essential human freedom to *redefine*. Whyte identified the universality of politics (communality; permission-giving) when he came up with that beautiful line: 'If I was all right, then the project was all right'. Forty years later, social science methodology has still not absorbed the full profundity of that remark.

Rappaport and Beer

In Rappaport's account of the Tsembaga, 'ritual' is the central idea. We see very clearly how the ritual involves the people, but serves as a calculus (or even as a 'mechanism') to regulate the relationship between pigs, people, and gardens; to balance diet against resources; to regulate 'warfare' and minimize the severity of conflict; and to redistribute land. In other words, the ritual gives rise to a metric that is useful.

We also see the difference between Rappaport's *model* of the Tsembaga ritual, and the Tsembaga's own *model* of what is going on. Implicit in this difference is our point that a model is a ritual waiting to be realized. The Tsembaga's own account was integrated with their ritual—and it is doubtful whether they could have accommodated Rappaport's model without disrupting their society.

Rappaport's model is not intended for the Tsembaga. It is intended for us. Not just as readers and anthropologists interested in things far away. It is intended for us as producers of food, as a suggestion for a better way of organizing agriculture. The apparently 'scientific' account of a Maring tribe offers a political challenge to our own social organization, with the option of a 'self-correcting ecosystem' counterposed to our 'permanently immature ecosystem that degrades the environment'.

Thus the model deals with ritual and metric, but, *in itself*, does not deal with politics. This accords with our view that political statements cannot legitimately be made within models. Political statements are statements about the model—its value, applicability, and so on. Although there are certain moves within the ritual for Tsembaga actors that appear to be political—since they are about who initiates, who has a 'right' to what, etc.—they are in fact well-ordered within that society's institutional framework. They are 'moves' rather than challenges. They can be counterposed to the real politics and conflicts that take place without such a framework, or as collisions between frameworks. The relationship between the Australian authorities and the Maring—especially the attempt to suppress 'warfare', the relationship between Western trade-goods and the Maring economy; even Rappaport's own advocacy of 'self-correcting' rather than 'immature ecosystems'—are all political phenomena. They are not subjects of ritual, and models of them would not be models of 'fact' but persuasive attempts by 'one of the contending parties' to have its viewpoint realized.

Beer's story of the problems of sea-traffic between Denmark and Sweden illustrates the same point. It looks very much as though there is a metric that identifies 'facts'. After all, collisions between ships are facts. The statement (using Poisson's laws) that a doubling of traffic results in an eight-fold increase of the probability of collision is precise. Yet, as the story shows, models, rituals, and ultimately choice, are inextricably bound up with these 'facts'. The risk of collision is based on a ritual of two-way communication between ships. A different ritual (say three-way communication) would result in a different risk of collision—a different fact. But (of course) a change in ritual would not invalidate the *model* of two-way communication and its attendant risks. It is simply that the model would not apply. Facts that have people in them do not behave like the 'facts' of natural science.

And it is hardly necessary to add that the choice between models—and hence between rituals—is a political one. It may be informed by the logic of the models, but (as Beer is very well aware) these may not be the prime or the decisive factors in the real decision-making process. Unless social 'problems' are fragmented into their metrical, ritual, and political aspects there is a constant danger of confusion between levels—and of attacking the right problem with the wrong tools. Beer himself distinguishes between models and surrogates. This must be taken as a political distinction. After all, from the point of view of the Railway Company (see chapter 2) there *was* no-one waiting for a train at three o'clock.

Goffman and Wynne-Edwards

Last but not least in our re-examination of paradigms we come to Goffman and Wynne-Edwards. An unlikely pair to put in the same paragraph. Yet compare two quotations that we have used before when they are put side by side.

> When we allow that the individual projects a definition of the situation when he appears before others, we must also see that the others, however passive their role may seem to be, will themselves effectively project a definition of the situation by virtue of their response to the individual and by virtue of any lines of action they initiate to him. Ordinarily the definitions of the situation projected by the several different participants are sufficiently attuned to one another, so that open contradiction will not occur.
>
> (Goffman, 1969)

> Conventions ... must, by their nature, always be properties of a concerted group, and can never be completely vested in, or discharged by a lone individual in perpetual isolation: their observance has to be re-inforced by the recognition and support of others who are bound by the same convention.
>
> (Wynne-Edwards, 1962)

Social organization—whether of people or animals—is a ritual matter. It is somehow 'below' the level of politics. Groups of animals whose social conventions *fail* can be said to be in a state of political crisis. Innovation—or more likely, extinction—will follow. In this context, the idea of 'overpopulation' can be seen as a 'hole' rather than a fact. Overpopulation has to be relative to the ritual that balances resources against population—not to some absolute, ideal population size. If the ritual changes, then the number that defines 'overpopulation' will probably also change.

Goffman's concept of 'keying' and 'bracketing' are very relevant here. It will be remembered that 'bracketing' is a way of dividing reality into chunks, of 'drawing a line' round some sets of events so that they can be distinguished from other sets of events; this is a building site, that is a bus queue. (Bracketed events often have much in common with Barker's Behaviour Settings). 'Keying' on the other hand, changes the contents of the brackets—or changes the way the contents of the brackets are seen.

Although Goffman presents these two concepts in a complex way with many sophisticated examples, 'bracketing' and 'keying' seem to be very basic—even primitive—abilities. It is not uncommon to see animals 'rekeying' situations. Learning processes (whether animal or human) seem to be a series of rekeyings: re-evaluating content in the presence of wider context; or more simply, seeing old things in a new light.

Politics is social rekeying. Bracketing is a way of defining (rather than redefining) content, and connects strongly with our notion of ritual. Brackets enclose things that can be counted, so the ritual can be dealt with scientifically—unless and until it is rekeyed.

Next we will look briefly at available methodologies, and how they mesh with our three-way distinction between phenomena.

Methodologies

Methodologies are simply proper ways of getting at what we believe to be 'there': broad theories on how investigations should take place. In a recent paper, Bjorn Bjerke (1981) identifies the three basic methodologies that can be found in social science—and its area of greatest application, management research. He calls these the *analytical, systems,* and *actors* approaches.

The Analytical Approach is the oldest, and 'co-incides with ways of working within the Natural Sciences'. It assumes that

> there exists a reality which is *objective* in the sense that it is independent of individual human beings. It is the duty of the scientist to explore this reality. This means that scientific knowledge shall follow formal logical judgements and be independent of subjective impressions. Such impressions are regarded as disturbances ...
>
> (Bjerke, 1981, p. 3)

The analytic approach assumes that knowledge is additive—i.e. that knowledge of each part adds up to knowledge of the whole. Its method consists of three stages:

Induction, where general laws are constructed from specific instances;
Deduction, where specific predictions are derived from the general laws;
Verification, where specific predictions are tested by a return to the specific instances (facts).

In our examples, this methodology of prediction and experiment, with its assumption of objectivity, was used by Bion, Bales, James, and Asche. It is the classical methodology of natural science applied to social subject matter.

The Systems Approach is the one which Bjerke observes as dominant in management research. In common with the analytic approach, it believes in an objective reality that can be mapped, but differs in its conception of the nature of that reality.

The relationship between the parts is not additive but synergetic—i.e. the parts interact, and this has effects that must be ascribed to the whole (alternatively, the whole may have properties that could not be deduced from knowledge of the parts.) Other differences are that, (a) the notion of purpose rather than cause is emphasized, (b) equifinality and multifinality are substituted for the condition of *ceteris paribus*. Broadly, *ceteris paribus* means that (in natural science) we make the assumption that, *if all other things remain equal,* then the same effects will follow from the same causes. This assumption is considered necessary for making and testing predictions. In opposition to this the systems notion of multifinality means that a 'cause' may have many alternative 'effects', and the notion of equifinality means that many 'causes' may all have the same 'effect'. In general, this means that (under the systems approach) experience of one situation cannot automatically or directly be used to analyse another.

An important subdivision within the systems approach lies in the distinction between *closed* (or 'mechanical') and *open* (or 'self-organizing') systems. In the closed-system approach, *stability* and the maintenance of structure are emphasized, while interactions with the environment are de-emphasized. In the open-systems approach, *survival* through change of structure, adaptation, or learning, and interaction with the environment, are emphasized. Both schools share the conception that the configuration of the whole is the proper subject matter of systems science—although they differ on the exact meaning of 'whole'. In our examples, Whyte, Barker, the pre-double-bind-revision Bateson, Wynne-Edwards, Rappaport, and Beer all use the systems approach. This coincides with our assertion that the proper subject matter of social science is ritual—but with one major reservation. Ritual is something that may be treated *as if* it were objective. It is not (ultimately) objective. Because of this the counting that goes on in social science is different from the counting that goes on in natural science. For one thing it generates (as the system theorists acknowledge) 'loose' (or 'by permission') predictions; its models do not have to 'correspond with reality'— they only have to be consistent with possible realities. When systems science takes its assumption of objectivity too seriously, the 'whole' usually turns into a 'hole'.

The Actors Approach is Bjerke's third methodological classification. This diverges from the other two in that objectivity is abandoned. Reality is assumed to be a *social construction*. Interest focuses on the actions of important actors within an organization. Where the meanings of the actors overlap, or are shared, the reality is said to be *objectified*. But, this time, since the reality is created by people, it can also be changed or challenged by people.

The basic method of the actors approach is to look at 'the images of reality by which the actors orientate themselves'. Once these meanings have been externalized, explanation becomes possible. An account can be given of the way the images and intentions of different actors relate to one another in a 'continuous dialectic'.

The terminology of the actors approach is strikingly and crucially different from the terminology of the analytic and systems approaches. Acts replace behaviour; meanings replace definition; continuous dialectic replaces 'organization'. The terms naturally flow together. An act implies the creation and negotiation of meaning with other actors. Behaviour implies the passive role of stimulus-receiver and response-giver in a fixed framework (the organization).

Lastly, the actors approach is concerned with the subjective logic (the *intentionality*) of social systems, and does not afford the scientist any special, separate status:

> An observer of social acts can never stand beside or outside what he is studying. It is a dialectical necessity that at the same time as being an observer he is *also* an actor, influencing the organization in which he happens to be at the same time as he is influenced by it.
>
> (ibid. p. 15)

In our examples, Whyte, Goffman, and the post-double-bind-revision Bateson can be said to use an actors approach. Bjerke's definition of the actors approach coincides almost exactly with our concept of political science. It rejects experiment, prediction, predefinition, and any idea of 'special status' for the scientist. It encompasses subjectivity, dialogue, and conflict. Despite all this, there is one major difference. The actors approach has a *tendency* to suck ritual up to the level of politics—and this can lead to serious confusion.

Politics is about indeterminacy—which is why 'decision' plays such a central part. Ritual is about determinacy—which is why it can be usefully analysed as if it were factual. Although politics is always *inherent* in ritual, it is very rarely *manifest*. Therefore to treat ritual as if it were a part of politics is a mistake. If the predefinition of roles and possible actions necessary for ritual is not *actually* under challenge, then ritual can be more fruitfully analysed as system. In logic, it is recognized as desirable to question *each* premise but absurd to try and question *all* premises. Similarly any ritual may be politically challenged (which is the real meaning of political analysis), but it is absurd to try and challenge all ritual. This simply removes the basis on which meaningful(!) politics exists.

Every political decision takes certain 'facts' and certain 'rituals' for granted—and it is inconceivable that it should be otherwise. The analysis of group process that occupies most of this book is an analysis of ritual—an effort to look more closely at the taken-for-granted. The rituals were not under challenge. They were taken-for-granted to the extent of invisibility. Nevertheless, they have consequences and implications that are of political concern. Ritual calls for its own mode of analysis. It is as much a mistake to treat it as if it were always political as it is to treat it as objective fact. Each of the methodologies we have considered is useful at its proper level. The problems arise when a methodology is applied to inappropriate subject matter. The next section illustrates this point in a slightly different way. It shows how each methodology in turn—from the natural through the social and systems to the political—was tried on a particular problem: as the nature of the problem changed, so the appropriate methodology changed.

Successive Methodologies

In a fascinating paper entitled 'Beyond Context', Marc de Mey (1979) considered the development of Pattern Recognition techniques in Artificial Intelligence. The parallel with the methodologies we have considered is quite striking, and suggests that the analysis can be taken a step further. Instead of thinking of each approach as a discrete alternative, de Mey suggests that the approaches should be thought of as successive stages in a problem solving effort. The first (and simplest) step is to apply the methods of natural science. If this fails, the closed system approach is tried. If an account can still not be given, then the open systems approach is applied. If this is not successful we move to a fairly straightforward political approach—and perhaps try to redefine the problem and start again. Not only does de Mey's classification of pattern recognition techniques parallel the methodologies, but their order of succession parallels the development of social science itself.

The sample problem featured in 'Beyond Context' is

THE CAT

These two hand-written words have to be correctly identified by a computer. The first approach is the *monadic*. It is assumed that the 'message' is objectively and factually 'there'. Each component line (hence 'monadic') can be tested against a template held by the computer (experiment) and correctly identified (verification). The assumption is that once each component has been identified, the 'message' is determined. The only real problem is 'noise'—fuzzy letters. If lines can be straightened up, blots removed, small empty spaces closed, letters rotated into a vertical position, and so on, then 'noise' should be eliminated. Again this parallels the way natural science tries to eliminate everything (wind-resistance, friction, temperature differences) except the variables under specific consideration—regardless of whether these variables ever occur in isolation 'in the world'.

Using the monadic method, we end up with either

THE CHT   or   TAE CAT

neither of which seems very satisfactory.

The second approach de Mey identifies is the *structural*, of which he says: 'a *structural* stage considers information units as more complex entities that are to be decomposed into several sub-units arranged in specific ways

(de Mey, 1979).

The structural stage is also called 'feature analysis'. Instead of looking at single lines, it looks for elementary patterns, such as 'bar', 'fork', 'arrow', etc. The signal is then thought to lie in the pattern of relationships between elementary patterns. This is of course our old friend the closed-system approach. The reality is objective—the 'message' is there—and although elements have to be identified, the real task is the discovery of a stable pattern of relationships. The pattern has a significance that cannot be deduced from the parts. The 'system' is self-contained and can be analysed in isolation.

Unfortunately, feature analysis, although more sophisticated, still leaves us with THE CHT or TAE CAT.

The third approach is 'a *contextual* stage where, in addition to an analysis of the structure of complex information units, supplementary information on context is required to disambiguate the meaning of a message'. (ibid).

When the structural stage leaves open several possible interpretations, the only way out is an analysis of context. This is not just an extension of the number of features taken into account. It utilizes a new and higher level of knowledge. Thus, if rules governing the use of consonant-vowel strings in English are taken into account as context, the problematic message must appear as

THE CAT

In general terms, when context is taken into account, we have moved to an open systems methodology. Stability no longer resides in the message (or the fact) which can now be seen in different ways. The problem with the contextual stage—and with open systems analysis—is that context is all too rich in possibility. It can have no well-defined boundary. It can always be enlarged. One can never know if 'enough context' has been covered. For example, it may be that consonant–vowel strings are misleading. We are not talking about small furry animals, but about Government Commissions. Hence,

THE CHT = The Commission for Hydronic Temperature.

This problem of context leads us directly to the last approach, of which de Mey says:

> *The cognitive stage: analysis by synthesis.* The next step, then, is to induce a well defined context by having it supplied somewhat arbitrarily or subjectively by the information processing system itself: *its model of the world*. Recognition is guided by what the system (rightly or wrongly) considers relevant features and relevant context on the basis of its 'world knowledge'. It selects only those features which it knows are to be noticed and it analyses the signal only in so far as it seems necessary in order to check the match between the self generated expectations and the perceived pattern. Nothing can better illustrate this type of synthesis—experienced as analysis!—than proof-reading by an author who, maybe because of his concentration on the content of his text, reads several misprinted words as correct. We use the expression here in a broader sense (Neisser, 1967) to refer to a theory of perception which emphasizes the production of expectations on the basis of a world model to such a degree that intake of input can be seen as almost entirely restricted to a few points of control, and to filling in of parameter values. Within such a view *perception* is, to a large extent, the product of *imagination*, the few points of intake in information only safeguarding it from becoming *illusion* by tying imagination to 'reality'. In familiar scenes much of what we see is what we know should be seen but only few things might be perceived directly.

This fourth stage corresponds to Bjerke's Actors Approach, and to our use of 'political science'. Objective reality gives way to social construction. The idea of an end result—some final truth—gives way to a continuous dialectic. De Mey's account shows how we are forced up through the several methods by successive failures. The succession is not due to the inherent superiority of any method, but to practical necessity. This observation reinforces our initial assertion that, in practice, political, social, and natural science are inseparable. The focus may change depending on how we are getting on with any particular problem. Self-redefining CATs are the essential problem of social and political science. The CAT bit is ritual and social and may even be natural. The choice between CATs and CHTs is political.

In the next section we will look at systems theory, at its relationship to politics, and how various criticisms fit into our three-way breakdown of subject matter and methodology.

Systems Theory: Politics and Critiques

This section will not attempt a review of the enormous volume of literature on systems theory. For the interested reader, seeking a background in the more influential works and journals, a separate reference list is given at the end of this chapter. The task here is simply to show how system theory (both its 'uses and abuses') fits into our general classification of scientific effort.

The first main point is the obvious one that the appearance and growth of systems theory is inextricably linked with the appearance and development of the computer. In the first section of this chapter, we claimed that the subject matter of social science was ritual, and the proper methodology was modelling. We can now add a third ingredient. In order to use a methodology on a subject matter, there has to be an *appropriate technology*. The best medium for model making is the computer. Just as natural science did not really 'take off' until the technology of measuring instruments was available, so social science did not reach 'take-off' point until a modelling technology was available. There were of course excellent models of society, of organisation, of bureaucracy, of the place of the individual in society, and so on. The problem was that many of the models were too general to be of immediate practical value—or where they were made specific, they were too complex to use. The difference between assumption and interpretation was unclear. The models popped in and out of the political arena and were successively transformed without ever really being clarified. The social was practically inseparable from the political. Conversely, there was no way of generating 'facts' that were not immediately challenged. And as we have argued, any science (including political science) needs to be able to generate its 'own' facts. Before the advent of computer modelling, social 'facts' had to be thought of as if they were natural facts. This itself had political consequences that cannot be underestimated. For instance, as Ritchie-Calder (1982) points out, the American Constitution, mainly through the contribution of Jefferson, is based on a theory of political dynamics that owes much to the Newtonian view of the universe. This 'natural' conception of social facts is still very much with us today. 'Holes' are seen as cracks to be papered over, not as avenues of escape, or as an essential part of social models that point to the need for a different sort of methodology and theory. As Thomas Kuhn puts it:

> Assimilating a new sort of fact demands a more than additive adjustment of theory, and until that adjustment is completed—until the scientist has learned to see nature in a different way—the new fact is not quite a scientific fact at all.
>
> (Kuhn, 1970, p. 53)

In our view the new sort of theory must be one in which the model is not conceived as a 'reflection of reality', but as an investigation of consistency, an exploration of political possibility and the limits of action, and as part of the process of the *production* of reality.

The appearance of a new sort of theory is never a neat and tidy business. As Althusser puts it:

> Indispensible theoretical concepts do not magically construct themselves on command when they are needed. The whole history of the beginnings of sciences or of great philosophies shows, on the contrary, that the exact set of new concepts do not

march out on parade in single file; on the contrary, some are long delayed, or march in borrowed clothes before acquiring their proper uniforms—for as long as history fails to provide the tailor and the cloth.

(Althusser, 1970, p. 51)

Social science fits this image nicely. Its concepts mill about on the stage in ill-fitting and borrowed costumes. No-one is entirely sure whether they are watching comedy, drama, or musical. The 'assimilation of a new sort of fact' is demanding a new sort of theory: one that is neither 'factual' or 'political'. Systems theory fancied itself for the part—but has auditioned rather badly, as we shall see in a moment. The new sort of fact has appeared in the absence of, rather than through a new theory. 'Social facts' have become available because an appropriate technology—computing—has become available. There is an analogy with the way natural science grew from a nutrient pool of natural facts:

in the absence of a reason for seeking some particular form of more recondite information, early fact-gathering is usually restricted to the wealth of data that lie ready to hand. The resulting pool of facts contains those accessible to casual observation and experiment together with some of the more esoteric data retrievable from established crafts like medicine, calendar-making, and metallurgy. Because the crafts are one readily accessible source of facts that could not have been casually discovered, technology has often played a vital role in the emergence of new sciences.

(Kuhn, 1970, p. 15)

Social facts, of course, have existed for as long as history—but until recently we were all so busy acting our parts in them that there was no space to stand back, no way of imposing a metric, and no criterion for disentangling the ritual from the political.

Even at the most mundane level, computer use produces 'social facts'. A completed payroll, a set of invoices or transaction accounts, are all social facts. The distribution of income or goods takes place on the basis of ritual, which is itself the embodiment of a political decision (or the partial resolution of a political conflict). At a less mundane level, all the 'facts' of demography, of voting projections, of resource usage models, of epidemiology, of population growth statistics, of economic projections, of formal problem-solving methods and Artificial Intelligence, and so on, are not 'natural' facts. But neither are they 'political' facts although they may have a highly political content. They are models based on laws of consistency and possibility—itself a largely unexplored area (see, for instance, Elster, (1978), for an important discussion of the role of the possible and the counter-factual in social theory). The models are the 'new sort of fact' that demand we learn to 'see nature in a different way'.

System theory made a promising start as a new theory of models—but with a fatal flaw. It mistook the new-found ability to generate and deal with 'social facts' (with ritual) for a new ability to deal with politics. The consequences of this mistake are embedded in its practice and its history. The full flavour of this arrogant project is captured in a short article by Richard Sharpe, which is reproduced here in its entirety. The finer distinctions (and confusions) between natural 'fact', ritual and models, and politics will be considered in the section after next.

SPECIAL REPORT

Explosion of the cult of analysis

There was a time, not so very long ago, when the term 'systems analyst' was less of a job title, more of a slogan. Written in bold characters on the banners of younger managers in the 1960s, it became the rallying point for one of the most profound changes in western management patterns since the Second World War.

At the height of their powers in the mid 1960s, these young managers, who had practical experience of computers, were eagerly tackling the problems of the urban world with a confidence and abandon that, from the problem ridden 1980s, looks like rank naivety.

Today the slogan, like so many others of the period, looks empty. The confidence has gone leaving purely a job title. Just what sparked that process of explosive enthusiasm, and then the collapse into indifference, is part of the history of the computer community in the West.

In the mid 1940s to know how to program a computer you really had to know how the hardware worked, not schematically, but at each cycle of the processor. This first phase of computer installations was built on the notion that computers were really very fast calculators, ideally suited to performing calculations for the mushrooming scientific and technological projects of the early 1950s.

To sustain the thrust of expansion new markets had to be found in commercial applications, a new language had to be designed in Cobol, a new market leader emerge in IBM — and a new job title in systems analysis. The differ-

Managers of the early sixties thought that systems analysis was a dream cure for the world's ills. Richard Sharpe relates the way the dream turned into a violent nightmare

ence between a thorough technical knowledge of the hardware, and the ability to see what types of clerical operations in the corporations of the late 1950s and early 1960s could be computerised became more pronounced.

Clerical systems and management systems had to be analysed before the power of the computer could be unleashed and productivity increased. The old generation of progammers, close to the machine with the detailed knowledge necessary to write machine and assembly level programs, gave way to a new wave of programmers who knew nothing but Cobol, nothing but high level programming.

Many old programmers stayed to fight on the grounds that they could write a much more efficient program in assembler than any new trainee in Cobol. But the new trainee could get the program up and running faster, and had a lower salary, so the older programmer was outflanked. The majority took this defeat as a release from the tedium of programming and switched their attention to new fields of application, analysing as they went along.

Moving rapidly up the management heirarchy this first generation of computer experts virtually swept all before them. It became a symbol of corporate status to install a gleaming new computer on the ground floor where the public could see it through plate glass. The status of the computer expert correspondingly increased because he knew how this new 'electronic brain' worked. While the programmers formed a self-contained elite, systems analysts fanned out over the corporation spreading the word, 'the computer is coming'.

With hind-sight, the methods of systems analysis seem nothing to get very excited about. The analysts stole the clothes of the organisation and methods department and then promptly relegated the o and m people to the backroom, with their status hardly better than that of a time and motion studies officer, clipboard and stopwatch in hand.

Perhaps the most important event in the transformation of systems analysis from a technique into a religion happened in 1961, when Robert S McNamara took up the post as Secretary of Defense in the US, under the new president, John Kennedy.

McNamara came from a corporate management background to his new job — he had been a senior manager in General Motors, at that time the biggest manufacturing operation in the world. Full of the spirit of the new frontier which Kennedy inaugurated, McNamara began to tackle the task of running the largest single management hierarchy, the Pentagon.

Systems analysis found in McNamara a great patron. Jobs for systems analysts were created in abundance as McNamara began to cut into the old management ways of the Pentagon and set about unifying the command, the material and the weapons of the army, navy and air force. The navy had already pioneered the development of computers, it had provided some of the initial funding for Eniac and taken a strong lead in the definition of Cobol.

The Polaris nuclear submarine project, then coming into full production, was almost on schedule and within budget because of the new computer-based project control methods which were later refined into the Project Evaluation and Review Technique (Pert).

Systems analysts were riding high and the computer applications they delivered were the management information and control tools that gave McNamara and his reformers just the edge they needed to cut through the red tape. The analysts supported him in all that he wished to do and he, in turn, supported them.

The very word 'system' began to emerge as the chief buzzword, reflecting a way of looking at each problem and set of circumstances as a whole, an interlocking pattern of events which could, which *would*, break down under rational analysis. No longer 'weapon', now 'weapons systems', no longer just missiles to deliver intercontinental ballistic missiles, now 'missile systems', no longer managers but 'management systems', and so on, throughout McNamara's account of his seven year tenure of office, *The Essence of Security*.

Computers were beginning to bring real benefits to corporate management. At the very least, they were holding in check the explosion of the office population which threatened to absorb the total profits or taxes of every large corporation or government department.

In the 13 years since its formation the Pentagon had mushroomed into a vast and unwieldy bureaucracy, absorbing manpower and money at an ever increasing rate. If the arms programme was to be funded without totally ruining the US then management control had to be reassured, and computerised systems installed.

'In short,' McNamara wrote of this time, 'the new planning system allowed us to achieve a true unification of effort within the Department without having to undergo a drastic upheaval of the entire organisational structure. It would be a shell without

The bloody conflict of the Vietnam war, the bitter social conflict of the US student revolts (right)

substance, however, were it not backed by the full range of analytic support which operations research and other modern management techniques can bring to bear on national security problems.

'To this end we developed highly capable systems analysis staffs within the Office of the Secretary of Defense, the Joint Chiefs of Staff organisations and the military departments. These staffs provided the civilian and military decision-makers of the Department with an order of analytical support far higher than had ever been the case in the past.

'I am convinced that this approach not only leads to far sounder and more objective decisions in the long run but

and riots in the black ghettoes (above right) shattered faith in the analysis 'religion' that people like Robert McNamara founded

yields as well the maximum amount of effective defence we can buy with each defence dollar expended.'

The approach brought results rapidly, releasing more and more money and manpower for the arms race that Kennedy set off in the first year of his presidency, on a totally erroneous estimate of Soviet military power.

But systems analysts were not judging the ends of their actions, only the immediate results. In a few short years, they had penetrated the inner sanctums of power, backed by a powerful patron and confident in their view that the systems approach could solve the unsolvable. could even banish conflict of interest as they systematically allocated

resources.

The big push was not yet over for the system boys. In 1965 two events, both in the US, spread their influence even further. In April 1965 IBM began shipping the System 360, the first unified range of computers with common peripherals. It rapidly made every competitor to IBM an also-ran in the world data processing market. The real expansion of commercial data processing began then and with the new machines went the new confidence in the ability of systems analysts to solve problems that had perplexed management since the mid 1940s.

President Johnson pushed the point home later in the year when he ordered all US Federal Government departments and agencies to adopt McNamara's new planning system's central plan, the Planning-Programming-Budgeting System. Throughout the Federal bureaucracy, anybody who knew how to work the system became an essential recruit as department after department frantically reformed their own management methods to mirror those of the Pentagon.

Systems proliferated all over the place. The National Aeronautics and Space Administration (Nasa) got into its stride fulfilling Kennedy's pledge to put a man on the moon. Thousands of companies supplied systems and sub-systems for rockets, command centres and capsules to Nasa. A new discipline was forced on the suppliers so that they in turn had to appeal increasingly to systems analysts to provide the solution.

The effects were not only felt in production but also urban planning when Johnson launched his Great Society programme in an effort to renew urban America. Where else should the housing authorities, transport planners and urban architects turn but to the systems analysts?

By 1967 things had reached such a point that *Fortune*, the leading monthly magazine of US management, published, without blushes, an article in which it was claimed that systems analysis would 'add a missing ingredient to the quality of American life'.

'The new style of dealing with the future,' wrote Mark Ways in *Fortune*'s January edition, 'offers to millions of living Americans an opportunity far more significant than material progress. . . . That we are now developing a set of more effective methods for shaping the future represents a fundamental advance along a main line of social and individual evolution.'

Ways even believed that the US was fighting a much more moral war in Vietnam because of McNamara's systems. 'That the US still retains its limited-war option is due in no small measure to the confidence that a large part of the public and the White House have in McNamara's system of planning; it is deemed sensitive enough and effective enough to maintain a level of operations in Vietnam calibrated to our limited objectives there, and to changing circumstances.

'True there have been shortages of specific materials and underestimations of cost. Nevertheless, the Vietnam war thus far has been the best calculated military supply effort in twentienth century history.'

Soon after these words were written the tide began to turn. Four events marked the turn, three of them far outside the computer room but all linked directly to the new technology and its disciples. The new religion of systems analysis was soon exposed as the fraud it had become. For the religion claimed to be able to allocate rationally resources between different parts of a system and it approached its task as if conflict did not really exist. But it was commercial, military and social conflicts which tore the confidence out of the whole movement.

The commercial conflict

emerged between users and the big computer suppliers. Promised the earth, users were only able to get the most simple systems up and running. The 'experts' knew all along that this was all that could be done, but more senior management without computer experience had really believed the message pouring out of the publicity machines of the big suppliers. Disillusion set in and accountants began to get some control over data processing budgets.

The military conflict was in Vietnam — the 'limited-war option' was failing to achieve its objectives, however loosely Johnson, and then Nixon, interpreted 'limited'. The term was stretched to include bombing North Vietnam, which, the systems analysts told the Pentagon, could not sustain the battle in the South as long as it was directly under attack. They were proved wrong.

Nixon went so far as to bomb a neutral country, Cambodia, and used the expertise of programmers and systems analysts directly supporting Pentagon computer systems to keep this from all but a few.

The target co-ordinates of all bombing raids were logged into a central system, but when Cambodia targets were logged, a program transposed them into map co-ordinates for a suitable target in Vietnam, so that the official computer-based records system would not reveal the real expansion of the war.

There were two civilian conflicts also. First, massive urban planning projects, inspired by the systems approach, had failed to resolve the conflict between the haves and the have-nots in urban America. Night after night, in the summer of the late '60s, black ghettos burned.

The second civilian conflict erupted on the campus. The systems banner had been taken up by the academics and educational administrators. The 'boom generation', born in 1948, was now entering higher education and the difference between the dream of academic life and the reality of college was just too much.

One of the slogans of the Berkeley, California, students who spearheaded the student movement attacked the sacrosanct attitude towards people by subtly changing the warning note on computer input cards into 'I am a human being; do not fold, bend or mutilate'.

By the beginning of the 1970s the religion was fighting a desperate rearguard action. The final nail was hammered into the coffin during the 1973 slump, as sections within nations and nations themselves did all they could to minimise the impact of the slump.

In the same year Noam Chomsky, a leading linguist who had contributed to the analysis of language and provided fruitful debate for computer scientists, subjected the Pentagon's system analysis approach to a searing attack. The antiseptic quality of decision-making revolted him and other readers of the 'Pentagon Papers', a set of documents leaked by a Federal employee, written by the systems analysts in the Pentagon.

What had once been a 'mainline contribution to evolution' now became just another job title. There are no grand plans in this depression, no systematic attacks on the twin evils of unemployment and inflation. There is just a lot of work for systems analysts to do on individual computer projects which, it is hoped, will build a path out of industrial stagnation.
Richard Sharpe is editor of Computing.

'Explosion of the Cult of Analysis' encapsulates four major criticisms of systems theory, and presents them in an appropriate historical and political context. If we distil them out, the criticisms are:

Systems theory is dehumanizing—the 'antiseptic' quality that revolted Chomsky.

Systems theory does not explain the origins of phenomena—which means that it is ahistorical and apolitical, and encourages such limited perspectives.

The focus on stability, utility, function, and so on, leads to a scientific blindness to alternatives, and lends itself to an ideological justification of the status quo.

Systems theory is untestable—the crucial terms and concepts do not have a clear empirical import.

In the light of the previous comments on methodology, it should be clear that these criticisms are, in general, valid. The methodology of systems theory has been 'overgeneralized'. Its practitioners have attempted to include and explain the proper objects of dialogue and dialectic (politics) *within* system theory. As we have seen, politics is the proper *meta-language* of system theory, but cannot be its object. It is no accident that those who were quickest to see the way systems science was overstepping its limits were working with an 'actor's', a dialectical (often Marxist), or a dialogical approach to social science. In other words, they were already working at the level of politics—and the political assertions in the 'neutral' presentations of system theorists were all too obvious. In the following passage, for instance, Mike Cooley identifies our three levels in order to make precisely the point that, in any given scientific project, all the levels interact; that the systems (or ritual) level is different from, but strongly influenced by the political level.

There is now a growing realisation that science has embodied within it, many of the ideological assumptions of the society which has given rise to it. This in turn has resulted in a questioning of the neutrality of science as at present practised in our society. The debate on this issue is likely to be one of major political significance. The question extends far beyond that of scientific abuses; to the deeper considerations of the nature of the scientific process itself. Science done within a particular social order reflects the norms and ideology of that social order. Science ceases to be seen as autonomous, but instead as part of an interacting system in which internalised ideological assumptions help to determine the very experimental designs and theories of scientists themselves.

It is significant, that those working in the scientific field are themselves beginning to raise these questions. Thus, Professor Silver says that there are risks 'in the scientific method, which may abstract common features away from concrete reality in order to achieve clarity and systematisation of thought. However, within the domain of science itself, no adverse effects arise because the concepts, ideas and principles are all interrelated in a carefully structured matrix of mutually supporting definitions and interpretations of experimental observation. The trouble starts when the same method is applied to situations where the number and complexity of factors is so great that you cannot abstract without doing some damage, and without getting an erroneous result.'

(Cooley, 1980, pp.45–46)

The trouble indeed starts when 'the same method' is applied to complex social situations. What is needed is a method that allows for 'holes' (the possibility of political redefinition) without becoming bewildered (by trying to include the politics) or dogmatic (by pretending that the 'holes' are 'natural facts').

The first specific criticism—dehumanization—is substantiated by Sharpe's historical account of systems analysis. Dehumanization is an obvious—probably inevitable—consequence of confusing levels of subject matter. The sleight of hand involved is not without interest. There is a double definition of what it is to be human: the 'rich' version is reserved for the scientist but denied to the subject. Von Foerster exposed the philosophical absurdity of this 'trick' some years ago in a critique of behaviourist psychologies.

Consider the two conceivable definitions for Memory:
A. An organism's potential awareness of past experiences.
B. An observed change of an organism's response to like sequences of events.

While definition A postulates a faculty (memory-A) in an organism whose inner experience cannot be shared by an outside observer, definition B postulates the same faculty (memory-A) to be operative in the observer only—otherwise he could not have developed the concept of change—but ignores this faculty in the organism under observation, for an observer cannot 'in principle' share the organism's inner experience. From this follows definition B.

It is definition B which is generally believed to be the one which obeys the ground rules of 'The Scientific Method' as if it were impossible to cope scientifically with self-reference, self-description, and self-explanation.

(Von Foerster, 1971)

Systems theory, when it takes organizational behaviour as 'fact' instead of 'ritual' (with a strong subjective component) has used the same double standard. This 'mistake' may be quite deliberate. The project may be to set up a framework that excludes political intervention by those in it. (see Robinson, 1979). *If* the confusion is inadvertent, then 'dehumanization' may be avoided by thinking in terms of 'ritual' and 'action' rather than simple 'behaviour'. It is also as well to remember that people are not part of any systems model—only images of people.

The second criticism—that system theory does not explain the origins of phenomena, and is ahistorical and apolitical—has several facets. It is valid if it is simply the statement that history and politics play an important role in the formulation of models, and the attempt to pretend they do not is palpably false. It is, however, invalid (or misguided) in two important respects.

First, it can lead to a reverse confusion. It avoids the trap of depoliticizing action at the expense of politicizing ritual. Any model should be *internally* apolitical: it is the inappropriate attempts to include politics that lead to the problems.

Secondly, it is a mistake to think that models of the origins of phenomena have any different status to models of function. 'Function' and 'origin' models may be inconsistent with each other (or with other function or origin models) but they are of the same order, and have the same restrictions and limitations. Essentially, they both contain 'holes' that cannot be internally resolved. It is a fairly common fallacy that 'origin' models are the method of a dialectical science. This simply resurrects the confusion of levels that the criticism started with. 'Origin' models (like function models) may be a useful tool for dialectical science—but they are not its method. It is this confusion that leads directly to the weird idea that 'Historical Inevitability' is a truth regardless of the actions and decisions of people—to 'mechanical Marxism'. The only 'historical inevitability' is that the dynamics of ritual (because of the 'by permission' elements or 'holes') are always subject to political redefinition. Marx's basic thesis (system–contradiction–redefinition) is, in my view, consistent with this view of 'inevitability'. We are not dealing with an inevitability of causality or model dynamics, but with the inevitability of a constant movement between predefinition and redefinition. Marx himself had some rather more specific interpretations!

The third criticism—that the focus on stability leads to an ideological justification of the status quo—is similar to the second. It is true that many models mirror and justify the preconceptions of the existing political system. It is true that there is a scarcity of 'dynamic-change' and 'origin' models when compared with 'function' models. But it is not true that models can be 'cleansed' of their political content. And it is not true that 'change' models are inherently more useful or better than 'function' models. Partly because of the complexity of social subject matter (see Beer and Silver earlier), partly because of the indeterminacy of its subjective content, models are always a result of political choice, the 'holes' are permanent reminders of that choice, and the choice between 'change' and 'function' models will depend on the practical problem in hand, not on any inherent superiority of one over the other.

The last criticism—that crucial terms and concepts do not have clear empirical import—can be taken in three ways. First, it is true of much functionalism and many allegedly systemic studies. Unfortunately, it is not confined to them. The waffling theorist is a nuisance in any discipline. Secondly, the criticism may be 'true' about concepts such as 'double-bind' that we have already considered. Here the appearance of such a 'hole' indicates that pure 'empirical import' (correspondence truth) is inappropriate. Other factors are involved in the definition. Thirdly, as Vayda says in the Foreword to Rappaport's (1968) book, such problems are not inherent:

> Paul Collins, for example, has noted a feasible procedure is to specify systems of operationally defined variables which are hypothesised to be maintaining some particular variables within determinable limits (Collins, 1965). Part of the interest of Rappaport's study is that it constitutes a sustained attempt to isolate such systems and to validate hypotheses about their operation through the use of extensive quantitative data in the systemic variables. A way is being shown here for using empirical procedures in functional analysis. Even when Rappaport's data are insufficient for firm conclusions, the implication is not that data cannot be employed for testing the hypotheses but rather that more data need to be collected (*in* Rappaport 1968).

In summary, much of the criticism we have considered cannot be discounted. It can be accounted for (and the problems avoided) if we use a framework of methodological levels. Neither social science nor system science can deal with *real* conflict. It takes place at the wrong level. In the stories about small group processes that follow, there are cases of conflict. An account is given of the process of factionalization that accompanies conflict. It must be stressed that this is an account of the mechanics of conflict, not of the politics in which the conflict originated. Following the methodological distinctions made in this chapter, political accounts must be participatory and partisan. The political accounts included (especially chapter 5) are just that.

Social science can deal with ritual:models and modelling are the appropriate techniques. Ritual takes place within an agreement—and hence the dialogical elements can be temporarily ignored. Ritual places limits on action. It is these limits that this book uses cybernetic methods to try and understand. The conclusions cannot be final, and will necessarily contain 'holes'. Despite this, hopefully, the conclusions will be useful, and will identify steps that have to be reached in order to be passed.

The reader should also note that in dealing with specific groups and group processes, there is a change in terminology. 'Ritual' is a general concept that has been used in describing social science methodology. When the methodology is applied to specific groups, the term 'technique' is used. In general, 'technique' can be equated with 'ritual'. The former is more specific, and, in some cases, several techniques may have to be combined to count as a ritual. Both look like 'fact', but depend crucially on the group's politics (normative structure and content) for their continuing existence.

References

Althusser, L. and Balibar, E. (1970), *Reading Capital* translated by B. Brewster, NLB London.

Beer, S. (1966), *Decision and Control*, Chichester, John Wiley.

Beer, S. (1972), *Brain of the Firm*, London, Allen Lane.

Bjerke, B. (1981), Some comments on methodology in management research, Discussion paper, Dept. Business Admin., University of Lund, Sweden.

Bremermann, H.J. (1962), *Optimization through Evolution and Recombination. Self-Organizing Systems*. Washington, Spartan.

Burrel, G. and Morgan, G. (1979), *Sociological Paradigms and Organisational Analysis*, London, Heinemann.

Caianiello, E. (1980), Commentary, in *Current Scientific Approaches to Decision Making in Complex Systems*. Vol. 1 (eds. G. Pask and M. Robinson) Final Technical Report, System Research Ltd.

Collins, P. (1965), Functional analyses in the symposium 'Man culture, and animals', *Man, Culture and Animals* (eds. A. Leeds and A.P. Vayda), Washington, DC, American Association for the Advancement of Science, 78.

Cooley, M. (1980), *Architect or Bee?*, London, Hand and Brain.

De Mey, M. (1979), Beyond context, in *Proceedings of Problems of Problems of Context*, Amsterdam, 17–19 April, 1979 (eds. G. de Zeeuw, and P. van den Eeden), Amsterdam: V.U. Boekhandel, 349–255.

Elster, J. (1978), *Logic and Society*, Chichester and New York, John Wiley.

Gaines, B.R. (1979), General Systems Research: Quo vadis?, *General Systems*, Yearbook of SGSR (ed. B. Gaines), Louisville, SGSR, 1–11.

108

Gingerich, O. (1982), The Galileo affair, *Scientific American*, **247**, 2.
Glanville, R. (1979), Beyond the boundaries, in *Proc. Soc. General Syst. Research Silver Anniv. Conf.*, London, SGSR.
Goffman, E. (1969), *The Presentation of Self in Everyday Life*, Harmondsworth, Penguin.
Griffiths, P. (1981), Personal communication.
Kuhn, T.S. (1970), *The Structure of Scientific Revolutions*, London and Chicago, University of Chicago Press.
Laing, R.D. and Cooper, D.G. (1964), *Reason and Violence*, London, Tavistock.
Lenin, V.I. (1965), The immediate tasks of the Soviet Government (written 1918), in *Collected Works*, Vol. 27, Moscow.
Lewis, B. (1980), Commentary, in *Current Scientific Approaches to Decision Making in Complex Systems*, Vol. 1 (eds. G. Pask and M. Robinson), Final Technical Report, System Research Ltd.
Neisser, U. (1967), *Cognitive Psychology*, New York, Appleton.
Ritchie-Calder, L. (1982), The Lunar Society of Birmingham, *Scientific American*, **246**, 6.
Robinson, M. (1979), Angus, Bertha, and Conrad: The cybernetics of power, or politics by any other name, in *Proc. Soc. General Syst. Research Silver Anniv. Conf.*, London, SGSR.
Sharpe, R. (1980), Explosion of the cult of analysis, *Computing*, **90**, 8, pp. 20–21.
Taylor, F.W. (1906), *On the Art of Cutting Metals* (3rd Rev Ed.) New York, A.S.M.E (quoted in Cooley, 1980).
Vayda, A.P. (1968), Foreword, in *Pigs for the Ancestors*, (R.A. Rappaport), New Haven and London: Yale University Press, ix–xiii.
Von Foerster, H. (1971), Molecular ethology, in *Molecular Mechanisms of Memory and Learning*, (ed. C. Ungar), New York, Plenum Press.
Wynne-Edwards, V.C. (1962), *Animal Dispersion in relation to Social Behaviour*, Edinburgh, Oliver and Boyd.

System theory, influential books and journals

1948 Weiner, N. *Cybernetics or control and communication in the animal and the machine*, MIT.
1949 Shannon, C.E. and Weaver, W. *The Mathematical Theory of Communication*, Urbana, Chicago, London, University of Illinois Press.
1950 Weiner, N. *The Human Use of Human Beings: Cybernetics and Society*, New York, Avon Books, Houghton-Mifflin Co.
1952 Ashby, W.R. *Design for a Brain*, London, Chapman and Hall.
1956 Ashby, W.R. *An Introduction to Cybernetics*, London, Chapman and Hall.
1965 McCullock, W.S.*Embodiments of Mind*, Cambridge, Mass., MIT.
1967 von Bertalanffy, L. *General Systems Theory. Foundations, Development, Applications*, New York, George Braziller Inc.
1967 Klir, J. and Valach, M. *Cybernetic Modelling*, Iliffe Books, London.
1972 Bateson, G. *Steps to an Ecology of Mind*, New York, Ballantine.
1975 Beer, S. *Platform for Change*, Chichester and New York, John Wiley.
1976 Pask, G. *Conversation Theory*, Amsterdam and New York, Elsevier.
1978 Miller, J.G. *Living Systems*, New York, McGraw-Hill.
1979 Varella, F.G. *Principles of Biological Autonomy*, Oxford and New York, North Holland Press.
1981 Beer, S. Revised Edition of *Brain of the Firm*, Chichester and New York, John Wiley.

International Journal of General Systems
George J. Klir, Editor,
Gordon and Breach Science Publishers, Inc.,
One Park Avenue,
New York, N.Y. 10016.

Behavioral Science
Journal of the Society for General Systems Research,
University of Louisville,
P.O.Box 1055,
Louisville, KY 40201.

International Journal of Man-Machine Studies,
Academic Press Ltd.,
(Dr. Brian Gaines, Editor),
24–28 Oval Road,
London N.W.1.

CHAPTER 4

The development of a model: how do small groups work

'How do small groups work' is a question without a question mark because it is also a statement of assumptions. It excludes a whole number of other ways of looking at groups. It does not raise questions about 'motivation' or about 'attitudes', about 'interpersonal attraction' or about 'leadership qualities'. Nor does it raise questions about typologies of group, about how many there are in each category. It is a question like 'how does a diesel engine work' or 'how does a telephone system work'. It is a question looking for a mechanism. On the face of it, it is a pretty bald and heartless approach. Here we must bear in mind the distinction of levels that was made in the last chapter. We are not trying to account for praxis, for self-realization, for conflict, or even for pleasure. But neither are we ignoring them. They are dialectical considerations that stand above the things that we are looking at. They shape the theories but they are not found in them. An account of a diesel engine does not say what it will be used for. What is important is that it is a diesel engine and not a petrol engine or an electric motor. Its nature places limits on the way it can be used. The same for groups. How they are put together will place limits on what they can be used for, and on what they can achieve.

The assumption above the question is that we are looking for convivial systems—groups where coercion is at a minimum and self activity at a premium. What sort of framework encourages this? That is the political question that is translated into a 'systems' question of how things work. There will be alternative cybernetic accounts—and probably better ones—but we have to make a start somewhere. Here is must be admitted that the notion of levels of science, even the notion of convivial system, were not clear when I started this work. They informed it as an intuition, but they were not explicit. The paradigms were sought out because I liked (some) groups, and wanted to understand them. I wanted them to continue—therefore the natural questions were about existence, about survival, and about viability. I plunged into cybernetics long before I realized it has its own distinct ontology, and that it is always subordinate to dialogue and dialectic. Any naivety or over-generalization in the early versions of the model were usually reflections of this.

How, then, do small groups work?

The starting point was that groups that exist for significant periods of time have recognizable identities. We refer to them by the same name. The membership may change, but the group does not—or so we assert by our everyday use of language. Our ordinary ideas tell us that *if a group stays about the same size and continues to do the same sorts of things, then, even if there has been a considerable change in the membership, it is the same group.* This commonsense description is not too far from a rudimentary cybernetic analysis. The 'identity' of groups involves—at least—two variables, size and activity, staying at about the same level, or staying within limits. If this is the case, then there should be some reason why size and activity do not change drastically—or at least why this is an unusual event. It should be possible to identify regulatory systems that operate on these variables to keep them within limits. The identification of such systems would be a good start in answering the question about how groups work.

The first group I looked at was a crowd of kids in South London. It was particularly interesting to me because it was the same crowd that I had grown up with. The same, that is, except for changes in membership. Most of the people I knew had gone, but there were enough left to be able to find out what was going on without too much trouble. What was going on?

The group met in the cafes, pubs, and clubs near the market place in the town centre. The boundaries were fuzzy, but about sixty people were involved. They all knew the others, and were known to them. On the fringes there were others who knew the group and took part in some of the activity—but they were friends, not members. This was my position when I came back. Counting friends, the group could go up to about 100 people. Ages ranged from 14 or 15 to 24 or so—and there was one amazingly old man of 27.

It took an experienced eye, or a member, to recognize that there was only one group. It was a rare event for everyone to be in the same place at the same time. Usually there were just knots of people here and there. Depending on the day, the time, and what was going on, these subgroups ranged in size from three to fifteen people.

As one would expect, the subgroups grew larger and smaller, exchanged members, dissolved entirely, and so on. They were held together by conversations. People moved from one place to another in these smaller groups.

The group got up to most of the things that kids will. There were frequent parties—and many were gatecrashed. Sex was a prime interest. There was lots of drinking, and the group had been one of the first in the country to discover 'speed' (amphetamine) and marijuana. Lots of rituals and surreptitious trading developed around this. It was a sort of pre-hippy culture of long hair and jeans. Members were thought by the surrounding community to be scruffy and undesirable. In fact, a lot of attention was paid to dress and appearance, and there was a very keen sense of fashion. Although more happened at weekends, and there was an annual migration to the coast, it was very rare to go into town and not find anyone 'around'. Unemployment was common, and easy ways of raising cash were important topics. Working on the 'lump' (casual work for subcontractors on building sites that avoided tax) was one good way. Grants for being a student were another. Many were young enough to be able to live off their parents.

All these things came together as subjects of conversation, and attitude to them was one way of defining group membership. Some people were more talked about than others. Collectively they could called 'leaders'—but this was not a term the group used or would have liked much. There were simply some people that were the first to get into new things. They were often very talkative as well, and moved freely between the subgroups. Their ideas spread, and, often, so did their way of talking, their catch-phrases and grammatical oddities.

There was also an 'old guard'—members that been 'around' longer than others. There were ordinary members and newcomers. There were also people that were tolerated, but were not really part of the group—although from the outside it would have looked like it. They were rich (meaning it was easy to get money out of them), or they had a car, or something else that other members needed. They were made to feel very unwelcome if they turned up without their 'assets'.

Not surprisingly, the activities—and sometimes just the presence—of the group evoked considerable hostility from others in the surrounding community. The attitudes were clearly undesirable, and the activities were often 'delin-quent' if not actually criminal. Occasionally individuals would get caught, and Probation Officers tried to prevent their continued association with the group. There were frequent attempts to deprive the group of its 'habitat'. They would be banned from cafés and pubs. Sometimes the Police or Magistrates would intervene to close a well-established meeting place.

There were forces actively working for the destruction of the group—and there were other forces that made it look as though the group could grow very large very quickly. In the event it simply carried on in much the same way. I wanted to know why— and how.

With the help and sympathy of Professor Gordon Pask, the following explanatory cybernetic model was constructed.

> The group is characterized as a complex homeostatic system in which members are assigned a particular distribution of roles, in which there is a definite communication pattern adhering to conventions which act as the syntax of a 'private language'. In this 'private language' the group gives expression to attitudes and acts which are, on occasion, adopted and effected in reality.

(The role distribution was the different types of member recognized by the group. The communication pattern had to do with the knots of people that we called subgroups—where it was usual for some to talk a lot more than others—and the movement between subgroups. The conventions of the 'private language' were the topics of conversation that the group found interesting. Conversely, there were a whole number of topics and ways of talking that were ruled out or 'discouraged'.)

In order to sustain the flux of discourse, which is part of the homeostatic activity, it is necessary to maintain a critical mass of individuals in close informational proximity. In practice, this amounts to close physical proximity. The magnitude of the critical mass can be stated as the number of subgroups required to perpetuate the conversation, and thus, indirectly, the language.

(To keep the conventions or recurrent topics of conversation going, a minimum number of people and subgroups are necessary. This provides room for stories and gossip to circulate.)

In order to maintain the critical mass of individuals in informational proximity—which in this system amounts to physical proximity—the group needs to maintain occupancy of suitable habitats.

(Pretty self-evident! The group needs places to meet and talk on a regular basis.)

Decay (and other factors) reduce the membership of the group. Social pressure (and other factors) make inroads on the existing habitat.

(Members left as they grew older and assumed job or family responsibilities, or, in some cases, became criminal—they joined new groups with different values. We have already mentioned that the group would get banned from pubs and cafés.)

In addition it is evident that the survival of the group discourse requires a certain influx of variety or novelty. To some extent this variety is supplied in a ritual fashion. If this supply is insufficient, the group may be led to overtly delinquent or criminal acts to maintain the requisite variety.

(The topics of conversation are not self-perpetuating unless they are acted on every now and again. Some of this action was regular—like parties—but boredom could lead to other forms of minor crime, like shoplifting and car theft. Such exceptions and the dangers involved were a good source of stories—and the popularity of the stories made repetitions of the actions more likely.)

Hence it looks as though the stability of the group, or, to use a pertinent piece of jargon, 'its existence as a self-organizing system', depends upon the social analogues of a population density control system of the type mooted by Wynne-Edwards and others in connection with animal populations.

(See the earlier reference to Wynne-Edwards.)

The control system has the primary goal of maintaining (in the face of prevailing circumstances) an adequate balance between the habitat available and the occupancy of this habitat. We would also expect the control system to maintain a balance between conversation (involving symbolic situations) and activity (involving real situations), as well as to reflect the balance or unbalance of these two processes in the group.

(There must be some way of stopping the meeting places becoming over-crowded—they were very limited in number. Just as important, there must be some way of keeping the meeting places occupied. They might be lost to other groups, or the group could disintegrate because members could not 'find' each other often enough, and the group would lose its identity.

Similarly the conversation needs to be kept going to provide a basis for the action, and there has to be enough action to keep the conversation alive.)

> It is our hypothesis that the symbolic conventional structure of the group constitutes the framework *within* which such a population density control system acts, and this framework is of course necessary for it to act.
>
> There is interdependence and interaction between the symbolic conventional structure and the population density control system. Since the conventional structure is a prerequisite for the control system, and since the conventional structure would disintegrate very rapidly if the control system did not function, we are justified both in regarding the existence of the conventional structure in this system as a necessary and sufficient condition of the control system, and the operation of the control system as a sufficient and necessary condition for the existence of the conventional structure. In other words, the total system is reducible to the components of a Cybernetic Model, namely control units of one sort or another. It would not be possible to study either the conventional structure or the functioning of control without regard to its complement.

(The way in which size growth and decay is prevented depends on the conversation—which itself is organized around certain topics. On the other hand, the conversations can only continue in the same form because growth and decay are prevented.)

This cybernetic approach to group process was novel for several reasons. It tackled the question of the 'circular chain of causal interactions', and attempted to create a 'map' or working model of them. It stepped outside the (then) current research tradition by tying value to action, and vice versa, and by showing how both played a vital role in determining group and sub-group sizes, frequency of activity, and appropriate meeting places.

The model itself drew on concepts from outside the social sciences ('homeostasis', 'critical mass', 'population density control system'). This enabled it to steer a sort of fourth way between three dominant traditions—none of which seemed to me to have much future. There was the 'two-variable' tradition—see, for instance, some of the relations discussed later in this chapter under the heading of 'group size'. To say that 'group cohesion' was related to 'democratic leadership', or that 'absenteeism' was related to 'group size' never seemed to me to say enough. There were so many 'ifs and buts', so many other variables lurking in the wings, that any finding would be just as true in reverse. Then there was the 'attitude' tradition, which suffered from the same problem only worse. For example, 'generally speaking, Catholics are prejudiced towards Negroes and orientals, Protestants towards Jews and other working class minority groups, while Jews are prejudiced towards white majority groups' (Argyle, 1958, quoted in Jahoda and Warren, 1966).

How, why, and to what end were the Catholics prejudiced? What about the ones that were not? Was it verbal prejudice—just something they said to the interviewer—or did they practice discrimination? None of these questions seemed answerable while the categories of 'attitude' and 'prejudice' were the dominant abstraction. It always seemed to me that attitudes that were put into action were a very different kettle of fish from 'general attitudes'. Grounded attitudes were meaningful because they were part of the action, and they had to be rooted in small-group processes. General attitudes might be rooted in the newspapers, or in the church, but what did they matter if there were no practice that went with them, or if the practice could not be identified. Retrospectively, one can say that a major problem for attitude research was that it failed to distinguish ritual from politics. It treated competing political positions as if they could be quantified (how prejudiced?), as if there could be an 'impartial observer', and as if the conflict were recurrent, which it was not. The hallmark of a genuine political conflict is its uniqueness, its ability to suddenly change its form, or to be decisively resolved in one way or another. On the other hand, ritual—value-in-practice—was largely ignored.

When there was a concentration on practice, it went too far. The 'case history' approach simply captured too much. It was impossible to tell the wood from the trees. The cybernetic model, on the other hand, had a richness that somehow reflected the complexity of the group itself. It was possible to get a 'feel' for what went on from the bones of the model. At the same time, the process was not lost in the action. The model revealed more than a simple case history by concentrating on general structures that the actors themselves only intuited. Even a slight understanding of these structures would have enhanced the political freedom of the group. The model was not intended to be only descriptive or predictive. It was intended to be a tool that groups could use in the course of their activities and choices.

Unfortunately, it never became possible to test this model in its original context. When the research was finally funded, it was tied to a different geographical area (Sussex), and it was better to work with a new, but more accessible group. This was the Brighton Rents Project. Apart from the money, this had two advantages. The Project was a group of my own contemporaries. I have never trusted outsiders 'studying' groups. Although I had grown up with the South London crowd, age and a large helping of University Education had distanced me from them, and I no longer felt at home with their values. The research would have been more for me than for them—and that left me with a feeling of unease. The second advantage was that the move forced a reappraisal of the original model. How 'portable' was it? How general was it? Which aspects would apply to many groups and which were idiosyncratic to the kids in South London? With hindsight, I am sure that there are many general properties of this group that are not properly understood to this day. My experience was in the very early sixties, and even then I noted (and the Police acted on) the appearance that the group had a potential for explosive growth. In the event—to my pleasure—this was not 'contained', and waves of youth culture have been with us ever since. (There are distinct groups—the boundaries are maintained—but they have the potential for multiplication as well as simple self-reproduction.) Similarly, the organizational structure of shifting knots makes the group very difficult to pin down—from the outside. The riots of the eighties are so resilient because they are based on a similar heterarchical system of value communication that gives rise to action—not on a hierarchical command system that is relatively easy to 'deal with'. The processes of self-organization, and hence identity, are stimulated not eroded by opposition— as Ian Taylor (1971) explained through a superb model that completely anticipated the development of 'soccer hooliganism'.

In terms of the original model, it became necessary to identify and operationalize the key variables.

Major Variables

Human social group

This is of course not a variable in itself but a package of variables. The contents of the package depend on experimental purpose (or whim) rather than on the nature of objects-in-the-world. There have been serious attempts to establish typologies of groups (e.g. Golembiewski, 1962), but these do not seem to have influenced practical research very much. Definitions still range from three strangers behind screens in a social psychology laboratory to fully-fledged subcultures—with little indication of the relationships that might hold between them. The general nature of the sort of group to which our model is intended to apply is as follows.

The groups are 'natural'. They are found in the world rather than in laboratories—the sort of thing that might be mentioned in newspapers rather than created by psychologists. They are 'non-familial'; families may be in groups, but they are so specialized and have so many properties not found in other groups, that they are excluded from the range of this model. They are 'informal'; this means they will not have written constitutions, and the members do not have legal obligations to each other. They do not pay members, nor do they have paid functionaries. Although the model might have implications for work-groups and for organizations with formal structures, these involve many new distinctions and levels of complexity, and in these respects are beyond the scope of the model. They are permeable; members must be able to join or leave at will. They are durable; they should retain an identity over time. This excludes natural 'groupings' such as those studied by Coleman and James (1961) which were casual meetings between people in streets and parks. It also excludes sets of people such as those studied by Newcombe (1961) where there is durable interaction, continuing relations of like and dislike, but where the concept of 'belonging to a group' is missing.

Size

This was defined as the number of people in the group. This commonsense definition later led to problems, and will need refinement.

Although little work had been done on sheer size as an aspect of groups, Shephard (1964) speculates that there is an upper size limit of twenty for informal groups, quoting James (1951) and Bales and Borgatta (1955) as evidence. Studies on the psychological or sociological conditions of joining groups—size increase—were also conspicuous by their absence. My initial 'South London' model had nothing to say about this either. Leaving behaviour and absenteeism—size decrease—had fared a little better. Absenteeism had been related to 'span of control' (Acton Soc., 1953), group size (Hewit and Parfitt, 1953), sociometric structure (Moreno, 1953), frustration and work disruption (Herbst, 1962), and participation and responsibility (Stephan and Mishler, 1952). One very early study (Coch and French, 1948) had found an interesting relationship between the size of the standard deviation from the production norm and absenteeism/quitting behaviour. There were also numerous studies that showed size to be inversely related to 'cohesiveness', participation, and satisfaction (e.g. Gibb, 1951; Hare, 1952; Slater, 1958). The common thread underlying these studies was that size was seen as relating, in some way or other, to normative (including emotive) factors.

Activity and level of activity

Activity is not itself a group variable. Strictly it is a category referring to a set of group variables. This is because the activities of one group may be totally incommensurable with the activites of another. If we want to compare the activities of a discussion group with a work group on a Ford production line, we have to go to a 'second level' measurement. Since the idea of 'high and low levels of activity' have an intuitive meaning for all groups, this would seem to be justified.

In any specific group, the unit of activity has to be specified—preferably in terms consistent with the subjective perceptions of the group members.

Bales (1953) initiated a distinction between task-orientated and socio-emotional activity in small-group research. Only the former will be considered here: it fits better with the groups own idea of activity, and it simplifies the observational requirements. Activity as productivity has traditionally attracted many measures, and been related to many other variables—especially size, 'cohesiveness', and participation. Productivity is usually an ideologically defined measure, and hence an unreliable index of activity. It also assumes formal organizational structures that may well be missing in informal groups, although the consistent way it has been related—like size—to normative factors should be noted.

Symbolic conventional structure

This is best thought of as a set of related symbols, embodying agreements, that define a 'world' and possible actions within that 'world'. Within sociology, it is usually conceptualized in terms of 'norms' and 'roles'—although these terms, like group, tend to be used in many different ways. Attempts at systematization (e.g. Biddle and Thomas, 1969) have not taken any deep roots. Here we will regard the notion of role as a type of norm, following the opinion of Michael Argyle that the two can be collapsed together in small group studies:

> *The shared behaviour* for occupants of a position is sometimes called the *role* for that position, especially when the behaviour is distinct from the behaviour in adjacent positions. This is very similar to the notion of a group norm, and is in fact the same thing if group-membership is classed as a position.
>
> (Argyle, 1957, p. 175)

Another intuitively close idea is that of 'social script' (Jackson, 1978), but we will adhere to 'norm' as the more widely used concept. This will be broken into two aspects: 'Normative Structure' and 'Normative Strength'.

'Normative structures'

These are not, of course, fixed. They can be expected to undergo change with time. However, for the purposes of this model, it will be assumed—given the lengths of the observation periods—that in natural groups *significant* changes do *not* take place. A significant change (almost by definition) would transform the group rather than preserve it. An example would be the change from informal to formal structure. This would be an adaptation (amongst other things) to permanently increased size, not a simple mechanism to restore normal size.

A belief can be designated a part of the normative structure if it is believed by a majority of group members to be held by the majority of group members. It should be noted that this allows for false norms. The group may believe a majority holds a certain view when in fact it does not. The totality of these beliefs is the normative structure.

'Normative strength'

This may be thought of as the power of the normative structure to shape behaviour and action. In terms of the model, it is the ratio of those actually holding a belief to those believed to hold it. Normative strength is represented in the model as a threshold, since its effect is all or nothing. At any point in time an external observer may establish gradual changes in normative strength by interviews. To the group itself, the overthrow of a false norm is instantaneous. At one moment the group believes the majority to hold a given view; suddenly it realises it does not. A new norm is 'revealed'.

For the sake of generalization, it was decided (initially) to stick with these major variables. Others mentioned in the 'South London model'—such as 'habitat', resources, and the role of subgroupings—were omitted. The hypothesis concerning the relationship of each variable to itself was clear. If the group was stable, then size, level of activity, and normative strength should also be stable. A plot of any of them against time should show oscillation around a horizontal mean as shown by Figure 4.1.

The nature of the relationship of each variable to the others was not so clear.

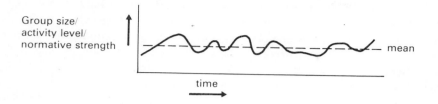

Figure 4.1   Stability as oscillation round a mean

While preparations were made for the major study of the Brighton Rents Project, several smaller 'experimental' studies were carried out on a variety of hypotheses. Most of these turned out to be wrong, and to avoid confusion will not be discussed here. Full details of the studies and the mistakes can be found in Robinson (1977). Two of the studies did cast some light on the problem, and the relevant parts are summarized below.

Preliminary Studies

Despite many reservations about 'artificial' groups, there was convincing evidence that group norms form very quickly even under the most unlikely circumstances—for instance in the Asch groups discussed in chapter 1. Another spectacular demonstration of norm formation was provided —quite accidental-ly—by Stephenson and Fielding (1968). They were conducting experiments on 'behavioural contagion' in small gatherings. Subjects were given boring indi-vidual tasks that had no obvious ending. *They were not allowed to communicate with each other.* It was left to the judgement of the individual to determine when the task was complete, and when to leave. In some gatherings, early- or late-leaving 'stooges' were introduced to see how much they influenced the others. It was found that, once one person had left, the others left more quickly, and in a more clustered fashion than would have been expected had each person been alone. There was 'behavioural contagion'.

The point of interest here is that groups that were retested stuck to their original leaving behaviour regardless of any leads given by stooges. Firm norms had been formed in the absence of any verbal communication, and without any common task. If norm formation were as basic and irrepressible as this, it should be possible to discover something of their role in regulating size even with artificial groups.

Problem-Solving Groups

Part of the Business Studies Course at the Brighton College of Technology was concerned with problem solving and creativity. This afforded a good opportunity to look at the effects of size changes on this activity. The usual methodological procedures were followed to screen out extraneous factors and quantify variables. Satisfaction with the group—as measured by questionnaire—turned out to be a bad way of measuring normative strength. Satisfaction, as expressed, *decreased* with time as the 'novelty' wore off, whereas it was obvious to everyone that adherence to the norms generated by the groups *increased* with time. Similarly, the most marked effect on the very carefully quantified variable 'activity' was also a decrease with time almost regardless of the size changes in the group.

Five groups met for four sessions of one hour each to tackle open-ended problems.

Session 1. Sensitivity training.
Session 2. First problem: 'Design a self-cleaning window'.
Session 3. Second problem: 'Design a thief-proof library'.
Session 4. Assessment of solutions and explanation.

In the first two sessions, each group had either six or seven members. The groups were labelled A,B,C,D, and E. After the second session, two middle-ranking members were transferred from A to C and from B to D. All the groups took common breaks and met in the evening between sessions 3 and 4. There was ample opportunity for the junior managers on the course to assess the members and discuss the performance of all the groups. At the end of session 3, everyone was told to return the next morning to the group of their choice—whichever seemed most attractive to them, or to which they felt they could make the best contribution.

The results were encouraging, and conformed to the prediction that a size increase would be followed by a decrease and vice versa (Table 4.1).

Table 4.1

Group	Initial size	Size after experimental manipulation	Self-determined terminal size
A	7	5	6
B	6	4	6
C	6	8	7
D	7	9	7
E	6	6	6

Most 'shifted' members returned to their original groups. Subsequent discussions put this down to 'group loyalty' and fairly conscious attempts to stabilize interpersonal relationships—both facets of a fairly rapid normative build-up.

Some light was also cast on the question of 'joining behaviour'. In the absence of factors like 'loyalty', which group is most likely to attract new members? Group E reassembled at their room for the last session, but it was then 'found to be locked'. The members were asked to disperse amongst the other groups, and to make their own choice about which group to go to. All the other groups were equally distant. The majority of group E members chose to go to the Group D with the highest 'activity' level. (The measure of activity was based on the number of ideas produced by the group—something that would probably have been reflected in the between session inter-group discussions.) This confirmed an intuitive supposition that high levels of activity would lead to high 'social visibility'—and thus to an increased probability that people would join that group.

Table 4.2

Group	Mean activity level	Number joined from group E
A	206	1
B	192	0
C	240	1
D	275	4

A Crime Simulation Game

This was a further examination of the relationship between size change and activity, and between size change and normative strength and normative structure.

The experiment took place in a social psychology laboratory, and used an 'artificial group' composed of Sussex University undergraduates. Every effort was made to create a situation that was interesting and stimulating. In retrospect I think we succeeded, although at a cost of constantly hovering on the brink of chaos. Seven experimenters were needed to deal with the organization and observation of the activity generated by a flow of fifty subjects.

The initial group of seven subjects were introduced to the laboratory, and given an explanation about the nature of 'criminal subcultures'. They were asked to make-believe that they were such a 'subculture' and that it was their duty to introduce new members to the world of crime. This 'world of crime' was bounded by the laboratory. At one end was a rack of black bags, representing the public, legitimate business, and the various crimes that could be committed. Each bag was labelled with the name of a specific crime, and contained a large number of black and white marbles. A crime was committed by removing a marble from one of the bags. If a white marble was pulled out, the gang had got away with it—and were duly rewarded. The reward took the form of a shower of pennies dropping into the room from a chute in the wall. (This had been specially constructed by the technician as a beautiful parody of a rat-reinforcing food-pellet dispenser, and reminded everyone of the payout chute of a 'one-armed bandit'.) The pleasurable spectacle of the arrival of the cash more than compensated for the rather meagre amounts we could actually afford to pay. On the other hand, if a black marble was pulled out the bag, this meant that the gang had been caught. They were sent to prison—a non-participating penalty area in the corner of the room.

Each crime required a certain number of people to carry it out. This number was written on the bag along with the name of the crime. This meant that the group had to organize themselves before committing a crime. It was not explained to the group that the 'expected reward' in all cases was 1 p per person per crime. Some examples are given in Table 4.3.

Table 4.3

Crime	Number of people required	Actual reward	Success probability	Expected reward per person
Shoplifting	1	1 p	0.95	1 p
Blackmail	1	4 p	0.25	1 p
Murder	2	10 p	0.2	1 p
Kidnapping	6	30 p	0.2	1 p

The group was left to develop its own rationale about which crimes were 'best'. It was also left to the group to decide when to call in new members, and to explain to them the nature of the situation and the rules of the game. After the initial briefing to the first few subjects, no further information was provided by the experimenters.

Since there were some rules that could not be violated without disrupting the experiment (e.g. breaking open the bags, not going to prison, letting the group get too large or too small—above twelve or below four) a red light was provided which came on if a rule of this sort had been broken. No explanation was provided as to *why* it was on, but no crimes were 'rewarded' *while* it was on.

Every so often a white light came on, and a group member would be called out. No further crimes could be committed until they had left. (The people to be removed at any point was determined by a prearranged random schedule held by the experimenters. It had nothing to do with the activities of the group. Again, the group was left to develop its own explanation of why people were 'eliminated'.)

The aim of all this was to leave as many problems and interpretations as possible open for the group to develop its own solutions, discussions, and norms. Only the recurrent reductions in group size were directly controlled by the experimenters.

Records were kept of group size and the times of changes in size; of the activities (in terms of number of 'crimes' per minute), who took part in them, how long they took, when they took place, and whether they were successful or not. The most complex variables to record were normative structure and strength. Norms were identified by a variant on a method developed by Bates and Cloyd (1956). Two observers (placed behind a traditional one-way screen, looking into the laboratory) recorded what appeared to be significant value statements, decisions, and behaviours of the group. Statements on which they both agreed were added to a list. Whenever a member was removed from the group, the updated list was photocopied, and the ex-member asked to fill in a questionnaire about the list. Subjects were asked to place the statements in order of importance; to rate their net importance to the group; to state their own level of agreement/disagreement with the statement; and the number of people in the group that they estimated would agree/disagree with the statement.

The list itself provided a record of normative structure, and of any changes or movement in it. The ratio of personal agreement to perceived group agreement provided an index of normative strength.

The group soon developed its own distinctive method of dealing with the situation. The carefully constructed rationale and detail about 'criminal subcultures' was dropped. Newcomers were only told the bare essentials necessary to operate the money delivering mechanism. Much of the time they were simply left to learn by imitation. This was justified since the group quickly found that it was easier to understand the situation by demonstrating it and by 'trying it out' than it was to describe it. Instead of a standardized explanation, the group developed a norm that legitimized the lack of an explanation:—'You don't know where you stand until you have committed a crime.' This norm persisted through the whole life of the group. Everyone (100 per cent) saw the group as agreeing with it, although in fact only 71 per cent said that they personally agreed with it. There were individual suspicions that there was a clear explanation of the situation, but these were suppressed in favour of 'getting on with it'. *The group evolved a basic strategy of committing as many crimes as possible*—and this can be seen as the key to all the other normative developments. It was also a sensible strategy, given the (unexplained) objective situation. Since the 'reward expectation' per crime per person was objectively equal, total reward could only be increased by increasing the frequency of crimes. The group managed to learn this quite explicitly both as an aim and as a method. Three of the nine basic norms reflected this.

The aim of the game is to get a lot of money quickly.
There is more luck than skill in the game.
The quicker the turnover the greater the profit.

The group's size preferences reflected this strategy (Table 4.4). The most striking thing here is that group members preferred, and perceived each other as preferring, a group size *lower* than the experimental rules permitted. The answer to this, of course, is that the fewer people there were in the group, the

Table 4.4

Preferred group size	Personal preference	Perceived majority preference
1–3	19	18
4–6	13	9
7–9	6	3
10+	6	2
don't know	0	12

Table 4.5

Size of group	4	5	6	7	8+
Mean number of inactive individuals per minute	2.8	3.9	4.4	5.7	6.5

more chance there was to 'get in on the action'. Each member stood to gain more money. This is dramatically illustrated by the way that the number of inactive members rises with group size (Table 4.5).

It should be emphasized that this rise in inactivity was not a function of the experimental conditions, but of the groups own norms. There was no external reason why they should not have chosen to co-operate in activities involving up to eight people. In fact, they consistently gravitated to individual, high-reward crimes, as the Table 4.6 shows.

Table 4.6

Number of participants	Level of reward to individual participants	
	Low (1–2 p)	High (4–5 p)
1	17	27
2	8	18
3	2	12
4+	1	4

There was then no relationship between the size of the group and its level of activity, whether measured as number of 'crimes' or number of participating individuals—nor did the number of 'co-operative crimes' (involving several people) rise with group size. In other words, the group developed a method of tackling the problem that stabilized its activity level—in terms of acts and participants—that was not built into the experimental structure.

Both the normative structure and the level of agreement with it remained constant throughout the life of the group. Norms formed early in the game persisted throughout, and norms detected later were consistent with them. The first ten members expressed a 78 per cent level of agreement with the norm set, and the last ten members a 72 per cent level. (There was a natural tendency for individual levels of agreement with the norms to increase with the length of time that individual had spent in the group, and with the amount of activity they had been involved in).

Thus there was no relationship between group size, normative strength, and level of activity—although the group managed to hold all three at relatively constant levels. This was remarkable considering the totally artificial nature of the group, and the extremely high level of experimental interference. Thirty-eight individuals were removed from the group (according to the random schedule) in less than three hours playing time. This meant that the group experienced a complete changeover of membership more than six times in its short life. The basic strategy—frequent activity by small numbers of people in a small group—persisted throughout.

Towards the end of the session, the group teetered on the brink of a 'catastrophic'* change of strategy. Four members all agreed openly that it was 'OK to try and doublecross newcomers'—thereby innovating on the original theme of criminality. They saw that a consequence of this was that the group size should be large. Since the 'rules of the game' were transmitted by the group itself, the implication was that newcomers could be sent out to take the risks, while the older members sat back and creamed off the rewards. Adoption of this strategy would have changed everything. Preferred group size would have become large. The type of crime chosen, the number of participants, and the way it was organized would have changed. The existing strategy involved a queue as members waited their turn to act. A doublecross strategy would have involved the formation of two subgroups—one active and at risk, the other safe and playing a supervisory role.

This new strategy was not realized. The four 'conspirators' were still involved in operating the old strategy. Two of them were eliminated from the group (by the random schedule) and the other two—no longer a majority— were unable to put the alternative strategy into action when the next lot of newcomers arrived. The idea gradually died out. Nevertheless, this near-event was confirmation for the initial concept of normative structure. A significant change in any one norm would restructure both the other norms and the whole way in which the group functioned. This was compatible with the initial hypothesis that 'the symbolic conventional structure of the group constitutes the framework *within* which the population density control system works'.

*In the sense of Zeeman (1976)

126

Conclusions

From these preliminary studies, it looked as though size, normative strength and structure, and activity were indeed key variables in the maintenance of group 'identity'. Both experimental studies demonstrated the rapid formation of group norms, and of size and activity stabilization around certain levels. Levels of activity and normative strength seemed independent of limited size fluctuations. As yet no general mechanism of size regulation has been uncovered, but there were indications that it was norm dependent. In the Crime Simulation Game, we saw increasing inactivity with increasing size—this would have to be true if activity and size levels were independent of each other. It seems reasonable to suppose that in natural groups increasing inactivity will have significant consequences somewhere. High levels of inactivity might be expected to precede people leaving the group—size decay—or a weakening of normative strength, possibly followed by some 'catastrophic' change in the group's functioning. There were also indications that high levels of activity created a 'social visibility' that encouraged new people to join the group. Fluctuations in the activity level—in natural groups—can therefore be expected to have a 'feedback' effect on group size, depending on how 'outsiders' (in the group's 'environment') see the group. Bearing all this in mind, the schematic model, shown by Figure 4.2, of group functioning was constructed. This schema represents the following relationships:

1 The normative structure is the most important factor, as it influences both size and activity.
2 Normative strength—the ratio of those actually holding a set of beliefs to those believed to hold them—is represented in the model as a threshold. Its effect on the normative structure is all or nothing. Change in the normative structure, if it takes place at all, is not gradual but 'catastrophic', but is preceded by changes in the normative strength. Normative strength is itself influenced by changes in size and activity levels.

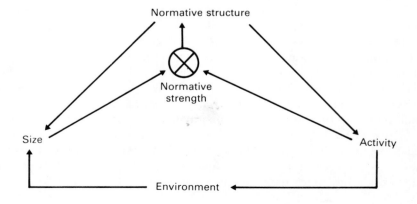

Figure 4.2 A schematic model of group functioning

3 Size level does not influence activity level.

4 Level of activity can indirectly influence size level through the environment. High levels of activity may create 'social visibility' and attract new members.

The next step in the development of the model was to carry out a long-term quantitative study of a natural group: the Brighton Rents Project. The aim, if the group was stable, was to test whether the schematic model provided an adequate general description; to elucidate the processes underlying size increase and decrease; to determine whether any other variables (subgroupings/information and decision making structures/resources/habitat/etc.) were necessary to account for size stability.

All data were recorded in the course of active participation. The volume of data was huge, covering personal diaries, agendas, notes of meetings, leaflets, reports, interview transcripts, and newspaper files. To try and catch the flavour of it all, a dual method of presentation has been adopted. Chapter 5 gives a colourful and partizan history of the Project. Chapter 6 covers the same story as an analytical account of group functioning.

References

Acton Society Trust (1953), *Size and Morale*.

Argyle, M. (1957), *The Scientific Study of Social Behaviour*, London, Methuen.

Argyle, M. (1958), *Religious Behaviour*, London: Routledge, quoted in: Jahoda, M. and Warren, N. (eds.) *Attitudes* Harmondsworth: Penguin.

Bales, R.F.(1953), The equilibrium problem in small groups, *Working Papers in the Theory of Action* (eds. T. Parson, R.F. Bales, and E.A. Shils), Glencoe, Ill., The Free Press, 111–61.

Bales, R.F. and Borgatta, A.F. (1955), Size of group as a factor in the interaction profile, *Small Groups* (eds. A.P. Hare, A.F. Borgatta and R.F. Bales), New York, Knopf.

Bates, A.P. and Cloyd, J.S.(1956), Towards the development of operations for defining group norms and member roles, *Sociometry*, **000**, 00, 000–000.

Biddle, B.J. and Thomas, E.J. (1969), *Role Theory*, New York, John Wiley & Sons.

Coleman, J.S. and James, J. (1961), The equilibrium size distribution of freely forming groups, *Sociometry*, 24.

Coch, L. and French, J.R.P. (1948), Overcoming resistance to change, *Hum. Rel.* **1**, 512–32.

Gibb, J.R. (1951), The effects of group size and threat reduction on creativity in a problem solving group, *Amer. Psychol.* **6.**

Golembiewski, R.T. (1962), *The Small Group*, Chicago and London, University of Chicago Press.

Hare, A.P. (1952), A study of interaction and consensus in different sized groups, *Amer. Sociol. Rev.* **17**.

Herbst, P.G. (1962), *Autonomous Group Functioning*, London, Tavistock.

Hewitt, D. and Parfitt, J. (1953), A note on working morale and size of group, *Occupational Psychol.* **27**.

Jackson, S. (1978), Social context of rape: Social scripts and motivation, *Women's Studies International Quarterly*, 1.

James, J. (1951), A preliminary study of the size determinant in small group interaction, *Amer.Soc. Rev.* **16**.

Moreno, J.L. (1953), *Who Shall Survive*, London: Beacon House.

Newcomb, T. (1961), *The Acquaintance Process*, London: Holt Rinehardt and Winston.

128

Robinson, M.J. (1977), *Thesis*, Brunel University.
Shepherd, C.R. (1964), *Small Groups: Some Sociological Perspectives*, London, Chandler Pub. Co.
Slater, P.E. (1958), Contrasting correlates of group size, *Sociometry*, **21**.
Stephan, F.F. and Mishler, E.G. (1952), The distribution of participation in small groups, *Amer. Sociol. Rev.*
Stephenson, G.M. and Fielding, G.T. (1968), An experimental study of the contagion of leaving behaviour in small gatherings, Dept. Psychology, University of Nottingham (Xerox).
Taylor, I.R. (1971), Soccer consciousness and soccer hooliganism, *Images of Deviance* (ed. S. Cohen), London: Penguin.
Zeeman, E.C. (1976), Catastrophe theory, *Scientific American*, April, 1976.

CHAPTER 5
The Brighton rents project

Introduction

The Brighton Rents Project started in May 1969 and collapsed eight months later, in January 1970. In many ways the Project was not so much an organization as a collision between organizations. A whole number of strands, insignificant in themselves, came together to create a piece of local history—history being something that is remembered by people who were not there. The question 'where did it all start?' does not apply. It started in the middle, with the first public meeting. Nevertheless, the out-of-the-blue success of the first meeting can to some extent be explained, and we will look at the origins of the Project in the next section.

The Rents Project can best be described as an umbrella organization bringing together all those people interested in fighting bad housing conditions and homelessness. It involved tenants, students, workers, professional people, and the homeless themselves. Political currents ranged from liberals and Labour Party members with their roots in 'mainstream' politics to various types of far-left activists. The common platform was to attack bad—in some cases, appalling—housing conditions, of which the most extreme form was homelessness. In the beginning, before the first public meeting, it was thought that bad conditions were the central problem. No-one *knew* that there were homeless people in Brighton. As soon as the Project was launched, the homeless made themselves visible. They were prioritized. Squatting became and remained the central activity of the Project.

Up to 300 people attended the first Public Meeting. The slogan

HOUSES FOR PEOPLE NOT PROFIT

was unanimously adopted. Squatting was suggested and the idea was greeted with universal enthusiasm. A few days later the first, token squat took place, and was a huge success in terms of publicity and morale. A demonstration at the Town Hall on the day of the Mayor's Inauguration consolidated the Project as an organization. Then the real squatting started. First two families, then three, then five and six. Sub-standard council houses near the railway station were taken over. After a while the council started repossession proceedings.

Late June and early July were taken up with courtroom skirmishes. Uncertainty grew with the realization that the houses were difficult to defend legally, and just about impossible to defend physically.

Wykeham Terrace was the answer; it was an empty luxury block of flats owned by the Minstry of Defence. Families could be switched between flats to evade legal action. The block could be defended as a whole. More and more families joined the original six, until fifteen families were finally installed. Defence and the possibility of violent eviction loomed large in everyone's minds. Press stories reflected this. A 'petrol bomb army' awaited bailiffs. The Brighton and Hove Gazette reported 'concern over "private army"'. The police 'warn rents squad'. On the other hand, it was the 'biggest squat of all'; the Rents Tribunal praised the work of the Project members in representing tenants; the local MP backed the Project; homeless families and their supporters were given full page feature coverage in the local press. Events took on a dynamic of their own seemingly beyond the control of Project members. But it was working until...

...until a certain person went bananas and bombed the local army offices. Not that it was anything to do with the Rents Project as such. But the Rents Project caught the backwash and went into retreat. 'De-escalation' became the order of the day. September and October were taken up with trying to regain public sympathy, with fighting court battles, and with a desperate search for 'legitimate' homes for the families. Some families were rehoused and the numbers dwindled. Finally, in late November, in the snow, the last three families were evicted... and were offered refuge in the University.

The Brighton Rents Project tried to recover and re-orientate itself, failed, and disappeared.

What was my involvement in all this? I was a post-graduate student at the University at the time, happily writing a thesis on the nature of human groups. The Rents Project was *not* the subject of my research. I was busy in the Social Psychology laboratory, hidden behind a one-way mirror, poking 'rewards' and 'punishments' down a tin chute, and observing 'coalition formation'. I used to stay up all night wrestling with huge tables of 'experimental results', designing computer simulations, and writing progress reports for my supervisor. In my spare time I dabbled in politics. I went along to a few Rents Project meetings, and carefully stayed in the background. I knew a lot of the people, but I *was* very busy with other things. When the first court case started, it seemed to me that things were not being handled in the best way. I said so. The next thing I knew I had been volunteered to do 'legal liaison'; which I did—after all, it was a limited commitment. But it involved meeting the families, and getting involved with their problems—which were the problems of the Project. Gradually it took up more and more time until the research became the hobby. Then I hit on a good ruse—or something that seemed like a ruse. Tell my supervisor that I was studying the Brighton Rents Project: do a few interviews and some participant-observation. He might not like it but so what? He didn't like cybernetics either. As it turned out, the ruse fooled no-one. I lost my grant and my University

Major dates and events in the story of the Bright Rents Project

May

1	First public meeting. Start of Rents Project.
10	Token squat in *North Place*.
16	Second public meeting. Formation of activity groups (squatting, rents registration, propaganda, fingers-in-pie, pamphlet, and co-ordinating).
20	North Place houses abandoned.
22	*Town Hall Demonstration*: ten arrests

June

7	*Terminus Road*: two houses occupied by families.
14	Terminus Road: third family moves in.
18	Start of legal action for repossession by council.
30	Seven families now occupying houses around Terminus Road.

July

2	Court order against first two families.
19	*Wykeham Terrace*: 'Squatters invade Army in Dawn Swoop'.

August

4	Queen Square houses occupied.
5	Drill Hall occupied.
14	'Biggest Squat of All' claim (fifteen families!)
19	Twin bomb blast rocks Brighton Service Offices.

September

14	'Hippadilly' in London.
26	Drill Hall reoccupied by council.
	Queen Square houses vacated.

October

11	High Court action against Wykeham Terrace squatters starts.

November

13	High Court grants possession order against the squatters.
25	Council offers houses to five families from Wykeham Terrace.

December

January   Last Rents Project press statement.

February

March   Last Rents Project meeting: six people.

place. By that time I did not really care. The Rents Project was *real*. Mainly out of habit, I did do the interviews, and make notes, and keep all the press cuttings. Someday, there might be time to sort it all out. And thanks to Gordon Pask, the Professor of Cybernetics at Brunel University, and later, Celia Bird, Social Sciences editor of John Wiley, someday there was.

The Origins of The Brighton Rents Project

Without trying to give a proper account of Brighton itself, there are some characteristics of the town that form the context of the Rents Project.

First, there is the population structure. Brighton differs from most other towns in having a high number of 'immigrants' from other parts of the country. Many old people retire to Brighton. About 35 per cent of the population are aged 60 and over, whereas in most towns the figure is nearer 25 per cent. Many young people come to Brighton for three- or four-year courses of full-time education, so, at any one time, the resident population is swollen by about 10 000 students. In the summer months there is a huge influx of tourists and holidaymakers. All these factors combine as additional demand on the town's housing resources. Council-house building in Brighton was minimal. Private-sector renting was orientated to more profitable lettings to students and holidaymakers. The prices of private flats and houses were driven up by outside demand, while local wages remained low. Thus house purchase was not an option for most of the working population. With scarcity, overcrowding and sub-standard conditions became more and more common.

Secondly, there were no institutional channels for dealing with the problem. Those suffering at any given time were a minority distributed about the town. They were no-one's particular 'constituency'. Although, contrary to popular belief, industry was the major factor in the Sussex economy, the organized labour movement was very weak. The workforce was mainly ununionized. Thus the 'usual' way in which the problem might have been raised as a problem was lacking.

Discontent with the housing situation was widespread, but unorganized and inarticulate. The problem itself remained invisible to the authorities, and steps to alleviate it were outside their perspective. Also, as is frequently the case in such situations, information on the problem was almost non-existent, or, where available, inadequate and misleading. It was claimed, for example, that there was little discontent with the housing situation because there were very few applications to the Rents Tribunal. More on this in a moment.

Lastly, the student and youth groups in the town were responsive, directly and indirectly, to the upheavals of 1968—the anti-Vietnam-war Movement; the events in France; the rediscovery of popular versions of socialism, and of Marx himself. The ideas of direct action and direct control over our lives were very much on the surface.

On the national scene, homelessness had been brought into focus by the film *Cathy Come Home*, by the increasingly strident factual reports from Shelter, and by Ron Bailey and the East London Squatters in Ilford.

Locally, a section of the Labour Party had set up a working group called the 'Brighton Rents Project' which produced a report: 'Housing and Rents in Brighton'. Amongst other things they pointed out:

> Of the tens of thousands of tenants who really should ask for their rents to be fixed by the Sussex Rents Tribunal, only 314 applied and of these only 215 were in fact registered in the year ending June 30th 1969. And these, believe it or not, are the figures for the whole of Sussex.

The report made an overwhelming case for the lack of applications being due to ignorance and/or fear rather than 'contentment'. The question was how to follow up the Report. Students from the University and Colleges began to meet with the original groups for informal discussions. It was decided to call the public meeting that marked the birth of the Brighton Rents Project.

The First Public Meeting

> 'It was really beyond our wildest dreams in terms of the number of people who turned up. The place was absolutely packed out. We had to get more chairs, then a bloke told us we were breaking the fire regulations. The meeting was electric from the start. People were getting up and talking about their problems.'

> (Gary)

The meeting hall in the Pavilion Buildings was large and not particularly well lit. The meeting was scheduled to start at 7.30 p.m., and by that time the hall was already full. More people kept arriving. The neat lines of seats were soon lost. More chairs filled the aisles. People were standing at the back and sides, and sitting on the platform.

Ken, a member of the original survey group, was in the Chair. The meeting started with a description of some of the worst housing cases that the survey had uncovered, and an explanation of the eight original demands on the leaflet (see Figure 5.1). Then the meeting took on a life of its own, often by-passing the Chair. People vied with each other to give public accounts of the conditions they were living in. They got worse and worse. Maureen made her first appearance at that meeting. She was standing somewhere near the back, and did not speak until the meeting had been going for some time. She was not very tall, and at first all we heard was her voice. Gradually, as she caught everyone's attention, the people in front of her moved aside so that she could be seen.

Maureen had platinum-blonde hair and was smartly dressed in black. No matter how bad things became, she was always careful about her appearance—something that was later to give rise to a particularly fatuous comment from the *Sunday Times* Theatre Critic in his paper. Maureen drew, in graphic detail, a picture of what it was like for a woman with kids in cheap bed-sits. At the meeting she only gave a fraction of her story—and that was bad enough. Afterwards we got a full 'case-history'.

Her story had started eight years before, when she, her husband and child were living with her mother in a council house which had been in the family since it was built. The council told her to leave. She was married, and thus no

demands:

1 register all rents
2 houses fit to live in is a right not just luck
3 open the housing list to everyone
4 stop selling – start building council houses!
5 tenants control over your own home & neighbourhood
6 build homes not luxury flats and offices
7 housing for people's interest not profiteers'
8 public ownership of all land and property

join the campaign for home

Figure 5.1

longer a 'member of her mother's family'. The eviction resulted in Maureen walking the streets with her husband and child—only *ten days* before her second child was due! She went to the Welfare, but was simply told to find accommodation within forty-eight hours or her child would be taken into care. The family spent the next three days sleeping on the beach, then were 'lucky' enough to get a holiday flat (at full peak-season rent) for two weeks after a last-minute cancellation. During the two weeks they found a furnished basement with bedroom, kitchen, and living room. They moved in with the new baby. Things did not go well. The landlady was occupying the living room with her three pekingese dogs, and helped herself to their food. Maureen complained, and was told to keep out of the kitchen and living room altogether— and to emphasize the point the woman struck her child. Eventually, leaving minor horrors out of the story, they found another basement flat—but the property had been condemned, and so they were evicted again. At this point—eight years ago—they made their first application for a council house.

The next basement flat they found turned out to be over-run by rats, bugs, slugs, and cockroaches. The children were poisoned by bug bites, and the family had no alternative but to move out into a bed-sitter—which meant they were now paying rent on two places. When they went back to get their furniture, they discovered it was green and so badly infested they had to leave it behind. They made their second application for a council house.

The next 'flat' was not much better. It was uninhabitable except for one room. There was no bathroom or kitchen. The toilet had no door, and was exposed both to the inside of the house and to the garden. And the floorboards were completely rotten. At this point, under these strains and conditions, Maureen's marriage broke up, and she was left to cope by herself.

After that, she found the two rooms where she had lived since. Again the toilet was exposed. A partition across the front room made two tiny bedrooms for her and (by now) three children. There were fleas and occasional mice. The children had bronchitis from the damp. Maureen had a nervous breakdown.

Last year she went to the council to find out why they had not helped her since she had been on the housing list for seven years. They denied all knowledge of her previous applications, and told her to re-apply—and wait a further three years. None of the private landlords will take a single woman with three children.

Other people had stories similar to Maureen's. Overcrowding and overcharging; rats, fleas, and bugs; damp basements; in a word, squalor. And nothing was being done. Various political groups advanced theoretical perspectives on the problem. The demands on the leaflet, in the context of the experiences that were being talked about, began to seem too abstract and remote. The original slogan

HOUSES FOR PEOPLE NOT PROFIT

was unanimously supported. But everybody wanted to do something.

Squatting had been discussed before the public meeting, but had seemed impracticable.

'Somebody came to one of the Manifesto meetings and said that squatting wasn't on in Brighton because there wasn't a problem of homelessness. It wasn't really homelessness so much as bad conditions. Some social worker said it. Ken as well. But then at the meeting the idea of squatting came up again. The problem of there being no-body homeless seemed to disappear, 'cos there was such a welter of bad conditions that we knew somebody would...

(Gary)

Then

'...the idea of squatting was mooted. There was immediate uproar and everyone clapped... the idea ... this was a thing everyone was in agreement on...'

(Andy)

At this point the first anarchist influence appeared:

'Saul was the person who really hit that meeting... he and I, essentially, together, did the work in the early squatting group.'

(John)

'Saul got up and spoke about Ilford. He got himself situated as being a squatter, you see. A bit later on somebody said "Here is somebody who knows about squatting. He ought to be in on it."'

(Gary)

Squatting was accepted by acclaim. It was decided to investigate and stage a token squat; to picket the next council meeting to call for better housing conditions and the opening of empty houses for the homeless. The demands of the original leaflet were accepted in the same way—without dissent. Although these things were unanimous, the idea of a decision-making mass meeting was new or foreign to many people.

Chris was a radical Labour Party member, a lecturer, and a leading participant in the original survey on housing conditions. He, like everyone else, thought the meeting was very successful, but had some reservations.

'What I thought was going on was simply that there were very big meetings that were badly chaired—not deliberately badly chaired—but unchaired, or only semi-chaired. The people in the room had a consensus to let things emerge, to be as democratic as one possibly could. This seemed to me quite a useful idea as long as the ideas were then processed by a co-ordinating committee. I was worried that this wasn't happening.'

(Chris)

Andy was a quiet student from the University. He was never in the foreground but, as far as I can remember, he did not miss one significant event or meeting in the life of the Project. He had slightly different doubts about the nature of the decision-making.

'I had an idea about political meetings in general—University political meetings in particular, because they were the only ones I'd seen. The line put by people at the first meeting was that we shouldn't have any structure in the Rents Project; that all decisions should be taken by general meetings, and this would not exclude anybody from the decision-making process. I recognized that the people who had already discussed what the Rents Project could, and should do, before the meeting, could in fact control what decisions were taken at the meeting. In other words, the group can support each other by saying "I agree entirely with what Comrade so-and-so has said...." This tends to create an illusion that there is a consensus in the whole meeting. The truth is there may not be... a lot of people are ignorant of what's going on.'

(Andy)

Despite the reservations, many people saw the intentional openness of the meetings as a success, and as a way of conducting politics at a new level. For instance:

'The Public Meetings were very good, inasmuch as they were a forum for people to come and really have a moan—and even try and do something—in a way that just had not been available to them.'

(Mick)

Whatever the exact mechanics of the decision-making, everyone agreed there was a decision to stage a token squat and to demonstrate at the Town Hall.

There were behind the scenes meetings over the next three days. Then on Saturday

SQUATTERS IN TAKEOVER OF EMPTY HOUSE

was the front page headline in the mid-day edition of the local paper, the *Brighton Evening Argus* (Figure 5.2). The headline in the mid-afternoon edition read:

SQUATTERS IN TAKEOVER OF TWO HOUSES

The first action of the Rents Project was underway (Figure 5.3).

The Token Squat in North Place

The technique used to occupy the house in North Place was to become fairly standard. For obvious security reasons, the house was located and investigated by a small number of people—usually not more than half a dozen. The North Place house was scruffy—most empty houses are—but seemed structurally sound and was tolerably dry. There had already been some public concern over the two empty houses which were due for demolition to make way for a car park. They had been vacant for a long time, and were council owned. The group that originally investigated the house then set a date, and all regular members of the Rents Project were informed.

At about six in the morning a few people entered and occupied the house. Immediately this was accomplished, a snowball of phone calls was set in motion. As many members of the Project as possible were rushed in. Within half-an-hour of the first entry, between twenty and fifty people were installed. Describing the scene in my notes, I wrote:

Then the publicity machine swung into operation. The front of the house was draped in banners, posters put in every window, the Press notified, and Public Statements issued.

138

Evening Argus

SPECIAL

Incorporating the
SUSSEX DAILY NEWS

Fivepence

Squatters in takeover of empty house

MICHAEL BURY—"Number 12 is being occupied to expose gross distortions of human priorities. While Mr. and Mrs. X with their three children (one spina bifida) live in a damp flat with no drainage, while five young families with children share one decrepit Victorian house with just one toilet, many sound properties remain empty due to council officialdom."

By DOUGLAS DAVIS

ABOUT 20 members of the Campaign for Homes have occupied an empty Brighton council house at 12 North Place. The occupation will go on all day today.

The occupation has been staged to draw attention to the "appalling scarcity and quality of accommodation and homes in Brighton."

Among the occupiers are two families with their children. The Campaign for Homes was formed by a group called the Brighton Rents Project. The project was started by a group of young Socialists who spent the past year looking into the town's housing problem.

Last Tuesday night, they packed a conference room at the Brighton Royal Pavilion, when they held their first mass meeting.

It was decided at the meeting to take direct action to spotlight the problem and a token occupation of empty council houses was among the suggestions.

NORTH PLACE

Members of the occupation will spend today tidying up the house and painting it. "As far as we can see the houses are in perfectly adequate condition to be lived in," said one of the organisers, Mr. Michael Bury, a student at Sussex University.

This was merely a token occupation. If there were efforts by the authorities to have them removed, they would resist.

"There is no chance of a physical confrontation," he said. "But we would offer passive resistance."

In a pamphlet issued today, the project said that the house had been bought on a compulsory purchase order by Brighton Council four years ago.

Since then, 12 North Place—and the house which they bought next door—had remained empty "despite their good condition and despite the fact that many young families in Brighton are living in squalid flats paying extortionate rents."

"No. 12 is being occupied to expose these gross distortions of human priorities. While Mr. and Mrs. X with their three children (one spina bifida) live in a damp flat with no drainage, while five young families with children share one decrepit Victorian house with just one toilet, many sound properties remain empty due to council officialdom."

Figure 5.2

Evening Argus

Saturday
May 10, 1969

Incorporating the
SUSSEX DAILY NEWS

Fivepence

EXTRA
SPECIAL

Squatters in takeover of two houses

By DOUGLAS DAVIS

JUST one hour after members of the Brighton Rents Project occupied an empty council-owned house in North Place, they moved into a second house next door—also council-owned and empty.

The occupation, which will probably last all day, is a protest "against the appalling scarcity and quality of accommodation and homes in Brighton."

The occupation was organised by the Rents Project after they held their first mass public meeting in Brighton last week, when they packed a conference room at the Brighton Royal Pavilion.

It was started by a group of young Socialists who spent the past year examining the town's housing problem.

Between 9 a.m.—when the occupation started—and 10 a.m., support for the occupation had increased from about 20 people to 60.

At 10.30, a police car drove up to the houses. Doors to both houses were hurriedly closed—and the police drove away.

Meanwhile, the owner of 10 North Place, Mrs. Violet Probert, who is supporting the action, opened her doors for a Press conference.

Council members, who decided to pull the two houses down to make way for a car park, she said, had no idea of the problems of "ordinary working-class people."

"It was an unfair decision made by a small minority behind closed doors," she said.

NORTH PLACE

"Problem families" had been housed in one of the houses for short periods since they were taken over by the corporation, she said.

Two families, who are living in poor housing conditions are among the occupiers.

Also among the occupiers, is Mr. Ray Blackwood the Labour councillors who was defeated at the local elections in the Lewes Road Ward last week.

"Councillors like myself were representing wards in the town where there are a very large number of families in sub-standard houses," he said.

Mr. David Steed, the unsuccessful Communist candidate for St. Peter's Ward, was also present.

Mr. Blackwood said he had been campaigning for better housing for the past 20 years. Today's

Figure 5.3

This was a simplistic view. The order that flowed out of the chaos was something of a miracle. Between twenty and fifty people more or less sums it up. Every room was overflowing with people doing something. Cars came and left: some would arrive full and leave empty; others arrived empty and left full. Some people went and talked to all the neighbours who were all very sympathetic. People came and went all the time, and most of the project members were involved in some way or other. As Mick put it:

> '...you didn't have to be very serious in order to do it. People were just sort of coming and going. You could go for an hour or for a couple of hours. I felt this myself, that I could go home to tea although I was squatting... or technically squatting.'

When things calmed down a bit, a meeting was called to assess the action and decide on the next step. Which was of course where problems arose. An entirely new situation had been created, and there were no rules or procedures for dealing with it. The first part of the 'operation' had a clear procedure (even though it had not been tried before) and it had clear aims. Occupy a house and gain the maximum publicity. By midday this had been achieved. In bold type, on the front page, *The Argus* featured the following statement:

> Number 12 is being occupied to expose gross distortions of human priorities. While Mr. and Mrs. X with their 3 children (one spina bifida) live in a damp flat with no drainage, while five young families with children share one decrepit Victorian house with just one toilet, many sound properties remain empty due to Council officialdom.

But what next? Some saw the meeting as an opportunity for discussion, a way of raising our own level of education on housing. This seemed a good idea, but foundered when no-one actually started the discussion. Besides, there were other, more immediate questions. Several people felt that, having gone this far, we should keep the house. We could turn it into a Housing Advisory Centre. People could come for advice and assistance. It would be a friendly alternative to the official places, and a way of bringing pressure on them. On the other hand, some people felt strongly that there should be a family in.

> 'We didn't know exactly what we were doing. We decided at the end to withdraw while we were in force. And we left on Sunday... I suppose... did we?'
>
> (Gary)

We did not, in fact. Most people did, but others stayed on. They were still there a week later, when the second public meeting took place. This was as large as the first, and elated by the publicity success of the token squat. The overrun of the token squat was a fact, and was not questioned. It was a large step forward since the first meeting. The question was how to carry on the momentum. The decision to picket the next council meeting was re-affirmed. The demand to let all empty council property to the homeless seemed much more realistic now we had *done* something about it.

What about the houses in North Place. Clearly we could not just move out and let them be demolished. Chris suggested a public audit and an injunction to prevent the demolition. No-one was very clear about how to do this, but it seemed the best idea and was accepted. (In the event, the Council moved too quickly, and only direct action was possible.)

The next thing that was raised was organization. 'We ought to have a Constitution.' 'We've got one. Its the leaflet.' The meeting was just too large and impatient for Ken's point to be accepted—a set of demands is not a constitution; but it did not matter, organization emerged.

Retrospectively, I still find it difficult to believe that an obvious—to me—distinction between demands and a constitution was irrelevant. I am tempted to say a compromise was reached, but it was nothing of the sort. It was a quite adequate solution to the problem in hand, which was: How should the Rents Project be organized so all the demands could be pursued?

The activities that everyone agreed on were:

Squatting
Rent Registration
Propaganda
Investigation—who *exactly* was making a profit out of the housing shortage, and
who was helping them.
Pamphleteering—detailed publishing along the lines of the original survey.

So it was natural to form voluntary groups around each of these activities, and this was done. On top of this, there was an obvious need for a co-ordinating committee—although it later turned out that different people had seen this in very different ways. This despite an apparently clear specification. It was to be composed of one person (not necessarily the same person) from each of the other groups, and its function was to avoid duplication of effort and to disseminate information. Lastly, it was agreed that we needed someone to be treasurer. Troy, somewhat reluctantly, accepted the nomination. At this point the meeting effectively ended. Groups formed in various corners of the hall to discuss specific activities. Like the meeting, from this time on, Rents Project history also went in several directions.

There was the 'mainstream' history of the Project, as defined by major events, interviews, and hindsight. Additionally, each subgroup had its own internal history. These are an important part of the story, so we will take them out of sequence, and look at them now, before coming on to the mainstream of events.

The Subgroups of the Brighton Rents Project

The rents registration group

The Rents Registration Group was set up to help people living in furnished and unfurnished accommodation to register their rents, and to back them up in conflicts with landlords. It was the most stable of the subgroups, and lasted longer than the Project itself. In fact, it was not really set up at the second public meeting. It had already been in existence for a year before it was 'set up'.

It was basically the offshoot of the Labour Party that had called itself the 'Brighton Rents Project' and had published the original report. The meeting simply gave it the chance to enlarge its membership a little.

Chris was the group's convenor; he was tall, slim, bespectacled; his manner was serious, and this somehow gave him the appearance of having a slight stoop. He, of all the Rents Registration group members, was most involved with the Project as a whole. His comments—which we will often use—reflected the perspective of his group. As we mentioned earlier, he was a university lecturer.

In terms of its own aims, the group was highly effective. Its methods were simple and direct. Members would go round in twos and threes knocking on doors and enquiring about conditions. Where bad conditions were found, the tenant would be encouraged and assisted to use the Rent Tribunal or Rent Officer machinery to try and improve his or her lot. The group produced a second report on its activities and findings called 'Rents in Brighton'. This speaks for itself:

Goals   'To help any individual tenant to register his rent;
To encourage several tenants of the same landlord to apply simultaneously, thus presenting a united front against any victimization;
To produce complete surveys of selected streets, thus putting individual cases into perspective'. (p. 1)

Typical extracts from case histories:

'Mr. & Mrs. C. of ... Road were paying £5.10/- for a tiny and dirty single room at the top of a house, furnished with one bedstead (no mattress) and one sideboard. With their child they had to share the one bed. The house had one unhygienic toilet shared with 15 other people, and one unusable bathroom...' (p. 3)

'Mr. & Mrs. C. of ... Place have two rooms for which they were paying 6 gns weekly. They share the toilet and bathroom (often out of order) with about 20 other people...' (p. 4)

'Mr. K. lives in the Basement and is bedridden. He is looked after by a lady in her seventies. On the day the landlord's lease ran out he intended to put them out onto the streets. Without a Court Order or proper notice. "I shall just call an ambulance and have them removed".' (p. 5)

The Rent tribunal:

'Mrs. B. complained vehemently at being subjected to indecent exposure, immoral suggestions, and physical maltreatment... the Chairman patiently explained to her that if she did not like the place she was free to leave'. (p. 10)

'Furnished tenants were the least well off. Security of tenure for them is an illusion as they can be evicted with relative ease by the persistent landlord who has no obligation to find them alternative housing'. (p. 9)

The Rent Officer:

'Works on the *totally unreal assumption* that a furnished tenant has deliberately taken accommodation which has furniture sufficient for his needs ... he is actively encouraging slum landlords to 'furnish' their properties with a few bits of junk. In Brighton this abuse is widespread, and hundreds of

landlords thereby evade the controls on unfurnished properties'. (p. 12)
'only a minute percentage of applications come from poorer tenants' (p. 12)
The Local Authorities:

'... Brighton Housing Committee is actually *proud* of having 18,000 enquiries at the Housing Managers Office last year, when it rehoused less than four hundred families'. (p. 14)
'The Chairman of the Housing Committee, himself an estate agent, said boldy enough on Radio Brighton (23rd May 1969), "Every single inch of land in Brighton that goes over to council housing is against any estate agent in the town as he is losing housing that he could deal with, sell, or let."' (p. 14)

Reform:

'We are very pessimistic about the willingness of most local authorities to do anything realistic to solve the housing shortage. Individual pleading, public petitioning, noisy campaigns for reform can be contemptuously disregarded ... even if liberal opinion was united within Brighton Council and outside it, there would be a virtually inexhaustible repertoire of minor reforms which could be conceded without this shortage being substantially effected'. (p. 17)

The report was widely circulated, and concluded with a demand for the abolition of the Rents Tribunal in addition to the points in the original leaflet.

The Rents Registration Group also gained a lot of attention in the local Press (Figure 5.4) in its various appearances at the Rents Tribunal. Naturally, in combination with the squatting, these activities attracted vociferous right-wing opposition—of which 'Victims of the faceless anarchists' is a good example (Figure 5.5). Opposition also took more unpleasant forms:

'And we still get calls in the middle of the night. Always at twenty past two. Perhaps its because this particular landlord we've upset has left his wife. He rings us, and some other rents group people regularly at twenty past two. The effect we've had on a lot of landlords is quite unbelievable. We met this one about three months ago. The trouble we caused him—by explaining their rights to his tenants—has resulted in this kind of attack.'

(Chris)

The activities of the Rents Registration Group were consistent over the nine months of its official existence—especially when it is compared with the other groups. As Chris said: 'We felt the group was getting on very well... that we had the mechanics right.' They registered rents; produced a pamphlet; initiated the demonstration at the Town Hall, and a 'day of action' in a square notorious for its dilapidation and overcrowding; they got good publicity in the local papers. Members were still working on particular cases well after the main Rents Project had disintegrated.

What were the characteristics of this group? First, it was homogeneous. Its members, with one exception, were all members of the Labour Party, were all university educated, and mainly aged between 25 and 35. Chris sometimes identified the Rents Registration Group with the Regency Ward group of the

144

ING ARGUS, Wednesday, September 3, 1969

Tribunal praises member of Rents Project

Cut for tenants

A MEMBER of the Brighton Rents Project was congratulated by the Sussex Rents Tribunal for "so ably" representing the tenants of a house in Bedford Place.

Mr. Chris Baxter appeared on behalf of a 71-year-old woman, Miss E. A. Barrett, with a bedridden middle-aged man to look after, and Mr. W. H. Rowden, a man in his late 60's with an elderly spastic wife, all of whom live in Bedford Place in a house owned by Bedford Properties, Ltd.

Mr. Baxter alleged that the company had allowed another tenant to let the house fall into "an appalling state" so that they could get rid of the tenants and redevelop the property more profitably.

He told the tribunal all the other tenants had already been "illegally evicted," and Mr. Rowden and Miss Barrett had been served with notices to quit which expired in May.

And he claimed that a third tenant of the company, Mr. F. Buechler, was acting on behalf of the company when he threatened to have these remaining tenants removed in an ambulance if they would not leave voluntarily.

'SCANDAL'

Said Mr. Baxter: "Their only crime is to stand in the way of profitable conversion of the house. They could stay there and conversion be carried out one room at a time.

"It is a well-known scandal in this town that middle-class landlords who wish to convert properties let the place run down so they can get a closure order."

When the tribunal chairman, Mr. J. R. W. Alexander, said the landlord was always entitled to eventual possession of his property, Mr. Baxter replied: "I do not see that your remarks are compatible with natural justice.

"Rent tribunals should be given the power to force landlords to bring their properties up to standard."

IMPROVEMENTS

Describing the property, visited by members of the tribunal, Mr. Alexander said: "There is no question that the whole of this house is in a most unsatisfactory condition. Major improvements will be needed and even then it is doubtful whether it would be an economic proposition to make the place habitable."

The Rowdens had a single room on the first floor and paid £3 a week inclusive. They had electric light but no other power at all.

Miss Barrett and the bedridden man she looked after shared the basement flat — two rooms in a condition, said Mr. Alexander, "as near uninhabitable as a place could be." They paid £3 10s. a week.

Describing the whole house, Mr. Alexander said: "It is not a suitable place to live in, but unfortunately in this world there are people who have to live even in these conditions. It is quite clear the rent is excessive."

TRESPASSERS

Representing Bedford Properties, Ltd., Mr. Thomas Field said his clients had owned the house since 1960. Until June this year, when he was forced to leave, Mr. Buechler kept the rent.

Since then no rents had been charged and the company regarded the Rowdens, Miss Barrett and her guest as "trespassers."

The company wished for vacant possession of the property, fully realising that it was in a shocking condition. "My clients are anxious to put it into a good state."

Mr. Field added that the company did not believe the property provided suitable accommodation for tenants like those living there at the moment.

Many of Mr. Baxter's remarks seemed "unnecessary and probably a little fatuous."

FRIENDLY

Mr. Frederick Hamilton, a director of Bedford Properties, Ltd., told the tribunal he regarded the tenants in a friendly way and had made every effort to fix them up with alternative accommodation.

"But the trouble is you cannot find anything at a reasonable rent. The only thing is about £6 a week and they just cannot afford it."

There was no question of throwing them on to the street.

Mr. Alexander commented that they were both "very sad cases" and highlighted an unfortunate situation arising out of social problems which was now "being placed on the backs of the landlords."

He said: "This is a problem for the whole community, not just the individual landlord."

REDUCED

The tribunal reduced the Rowden's rent by £1 to £2 a week and gave them security of tenure until November 28. They reduced Miss Barrett's rent by £1 5s. to £2 5s. and gave her security of tenure until December 1.

At the end of the hearing the tribunal congratulated Mr. Baxter "for so ably representing the tenants."

Figure 5.4

EVENING ARGUS,

Squatters victims of the faceless anarchists

WHILE NO DOUBT the majority of the squatters are unfortunate and misguided victims of the materialistic rat race of society, some are feckless, greedy, selfish queue-jumpers who are being used by utterly ruthless extreme Left-wingers, such as anarchists, Communists and other assorted progressive bandwagon jumpers-on.

They shamelessly exploit young children and unborn babies by using them to blackmail the community into giving them what they are unwilling to work and wait for.

Two of the squatters refer to a four-month pregnant woman who lost her baby after being hit in the stomach by a bailiff. I would ask by what moral right this woman got herself pregnant when she could not provide her child with a decent home and, having got herself into that condition, by what moral right did she and her husband expose their unborn child to such danger by breaking the law and trespassing?

Brighton squatter Mr. M. Chrismas has displayed both courage and a high moral sense in denouncing the lies put out on his behalf, but without his knowledge and permission, by the faceless people behind the Brighton Rents Project.

To the squatters I would put the following questions:

1. Why did they bring children into the world before they had the means to provide a decent home for them?

2. If they cannot find suitable housing in Brighton at a price they can afford, have they looked elsewhere or considered emigration?

3. If they cannot earn enough to house themselves what steps have they taken, or are taking, to improve their educational and other qualifications which would enable them to earn more?

4. Do they expect privilege over those who have planned their families, studied, waited and saved, or moved from their home town in order to provide decent homes?

BUSINESS

One of the Brighton squatters who unsuccessfully defended himself against the people of Brighton in the county court—at the 'tax-payers' expense, naturally—after-wards admitted that he was earning £20 a week but that he could not find accommodation with enough room for his family and with space to enable him to develop his business ideas. So, presumably, the community must provide it, and why not, if they are mug enough to do so?

On at least three occasions the faceless anarchists behind the Brighton Rents Project have plastered their posters all over the town; this "fly" posting is illegal and it is high time someone was prosecuted.

The more these people are appeased the more arrogant and demanding they will become. The pantomime has gone on long enough: it is time law and order were established before real harm and injury are done.   Peter Dally, Rock Street, Brighton.

Figure 5.5

Labour Party, and when I did the mandatory 'thesis' interview with him, he observed:

> ... in the last few weeks, four people who have been out registering rents have joined the Labour Party. People who have been involved in the squatting are much more likely to join I.S* or the Communist Party or R.S.S.F.† I think this kind of split was noticeable at a deeper level....

Secondly, the core membership of the Rents Registration Group—about eight people—remained the same throughout. Thirdly, the activity of the group could be controlled. It did not snowball, or unleash unforeseen consequences. The group could take on as many cases as they felt competent to deal with; they soon developed a good idea of the amount of work involved in each case. At the same time, the work was interesting. Each case was different—and the furious reaction of many landlords was a fruity source of amusement and anecdote. Also, as time went on, enough small victories were chalked up to make it seem worthwhile. In other words, like the Squatting Group, the Rents Registration Group developed its own set of techniques that formed a framework for their collective experiences.

The Pamphlet Group

The Pamphlet Group was set up to collect and publish information on the housing situation—along the lines of the original survey: it failed. The projected pamphlet was finally published by the Rents Registration Group.

Why did the Pamphlet Group fail so quickly? The group decided, in its first meeting, to do a survey on D... Terrace. They would use a proper questionnaire to be designed by Jim—later known as 'Kestionaire Jim H'. The first meeting and survey attempts took in more than twenty people, including Mick and Andy who we have met already: the numbers dwindled. By the fourth meeting it was decided to abandon the survey, because 'the people were in general old, difficult to talk to, and fairly satisfied with their conditions'. And the questionnaire form was not adequate either.

The fifth meeting would have needed to reconsider and redesign the aims and strategies of the group. Instead there was a joint meeting with the Rents Registration Group to plan a survey of B... Square. This was fairly successful, but members of the Pamphlet Group saw that the Rents Registration Group were better at it than they were.

Thus, demoralized by early failure, seeing others do the job better, and losing many (student) members because of the summer vacation, the Pamphlet Group never managed to generate sufficient cohesion to launch a second survey attempt.

After the summer, there was an attempt to revive the group, but this time there were insufficient people to do anything.

---

*The International Socialists, now the Socialist Workers Party
†The Revolutionary Socialist Students Federation, now defunct.

The Fingers-in-the-Pie (Investigation) Group

The Fingers-in-the-Pie Group started out to investigate the financial background to the housing crisis and the vested interests that might be profiting from it. The initial project was to try and find out why car-parking companies had acquired such a large slice of Brighton on apparently give-away terms. As with the North Place houses, demolition of homes was the usual way to create car parks.

The group was half-a-dozen strong, and started thorough and painstaking enquiries, mainly through the local Reference Libraries and Companies House. Quantities of information were gathered on local councillors, JPs, directorships, contracts, government reports, and local rate spending. Despite some fishy connections, the group kept running into dead ends and 'nominee' holdings that went no further. Nothing sensational turned up.

Unlike the Pamphlet Group, which started with a lot of people who gradually fell away, the Fingers-in-the-Pie Group started with fewer people. Some left and others joined. At some points as many as four political viewpoints were represented. When it became obvious that the pile of accumulated paperwork was not very useful, some of the original members drifted away. They were replaced by a faction called the Internationalists—a sort of cultural Maoist splinter group—who saw 'investigation' as a good way to 'intervene'. The 'intervention' did little for the rest of the group. As Jean, the convenor, put it:

'Talk! They had us over a barrel... said we weren't taking the right *line* ... must decide before doing any work.'

After a month of weekly talks, most of the original members had disappeared. The Internationalists went off in search of greener pastures—an Education Group was being set up at the squat. More people joined, including Troy, the Treasurer, and the library research restarted. The group folded at the end of August, after fifteen weeks, without result. There was quite a lot of disillusion.

'As all the groups which were meant to use our information never actually asked for anything, there didn't seem an awful lot of point going on...'

(Jean)

The Propaganda Group

The Propaganda Group was intended to be the 'service sector' of the Rents Project. It should have grouped together people with specific skills, like silk-screening for posters, and access to duplicators and the like. It was the shortest lived of all the subgroups.

It had no independent reason for meeting, only met twice, and failed to establish a regular meeting place. Its members drifted to other subgroups, and, when it was needed, it no longer existed as an entity. The other side of the coin was that the 'specific skills' were usually possessed by members of other subgroups. When publicity was needed, it was easier for the group involved to produce it directly. No-one thought of asking the Propaganda Group—even if they knew where it was or who was in it, which usually they did not.

Other groups and factions

The other groups that were set up at the second public meeting were the Squatting Group and the Co-ordinating Committee, whose histories are part of the mainstream of Rents Project events.

In addition to the 'formal' subgroups, the picture is complicated by a number of political factions—groups that had aims of their own apart from those of the Rents Project.

'The Anarchists'

This was more of a label used by 'non-anarchists' than a consistent political ideology. Anarchists (the term will be used without inverted commas from now on) were interested in action without explanation.

'The more squats the better, so lets stop talking and get on with it.'

(Saul)

Their numbers varied drastically, since there was much to-ing and fro-ing between Brighton and other squats in London. Overall, about ten people identified with this faction.

The Internationalists

These were a sub-sect of Maoism, whose main aim was the glorification of the Cultural Revolution to Project members. They had minimal involvement with action (as we have seen in the case of the Fingers-in-the-Pie Group). They numbered about five people, and were not taken very seriously by the Project. But they did a lot of talking, and could cause meetings to go on for a very long time.

The International Socialists

Forrunners of today's Socialist Workers Party, the International Socialists, were another highly political group. Five of their members were involved in the Project, usually in the most publicized part, since their main concern was to sell their newspaper. According to them, their aim was

to encourage the active participation of the organized working class in the Project.

The Revolutionary Socialist Students Federation

This was a broad grouping of students, formed in the aftermath of the events of 1968. The Federation included the International Socialists, but, as far as the history of the Rents Project goes, it will mean the group of about ten students who supported the ideas of 'direct democracy' and 'direct action' but were not identified with any national political grouping. The 'RSSF' students played a major role in creating the structure and activities of the Rents Project.

The Labour Party 'Left'

A group of about ten people were identified with the Rents Registration Group, and with publicizing the original eight aims of the Project; they played an important role in laying the ground for the original survey, and in the closing phases of the squatting.

'Liberal Humanists'

This is my classification for the set of individuals who were active in the Rents Project out of concern, but who had no special political affiliation. They were dispersed through the various formal sub-groups.

Families

After a while, the squatting families saw themselves as a distinct group, and obviously had special interests and problems in common apart from sheer homelessness. Their views and activities formed an important part of the mainstream history.

The way in which the various sub-groups, individuals, and political currents combined and merged was complicated. An overview is to some extent artificial since it was not held by Project members. The *absence* of an overview reflected genuine conflicts of interest and views within the Project—and this is part of the story too. A schema of relations between groups and individuals is given in chapter 6.

Meanwhile, the occupation of the North Place houses continued.

The Reoccupation of North Place

'The attack on the Town Hall—or the affair round the Town Hall with the arrests and things—and the North Place occupation, were collective actions done by the Rents Project as a whole. Everybody who was in the Rents Project was involved in those activities.'

(John)

The second Public Meeting had finalized the plans for the Town Hall Demonstration, and had decided to try legalistic methods to prevent the demolition of the North Place Houses. The trouble with public decision-making is that it is public. The council moved at a speed that just might have been coincidence.

Less than twelve hours after the decision to apply for an injunction—at 7.30

the next morning—the demolition gang moved into the North Place houses. Four sleepy 'squatters' struggled into consciousness and sent out the alarm. The houses were reoccupied before too much damage had been done.

The same thing happened on Sunday. The demolition men moved in and started ripping tiles off the roof. The inexperienced occupiers were still asleep and had not locked one of the doors. After frantic phoning, about forty people turned up within half an hour. The roof was being demolished in front of our eyes. After a hurried conference we formed a ring round the house. Any tiles thrown down would hit us. The demolition came to a stop. (See Figure 5.6.).

We discussed the situation. Over half the roof was now gone. Rain would cause further damage, and we had no tarpaulins to keep it out. We had already gained much favourable publicity, and, as there was no family to fight for, we decided to vacate the houses. Two days later they were razed to the ground. The site became a car park.

However, the action was generally seen as successful. The destruction had not gone ahead unopposed and unnoticed. And preparations were now in full swing for the Town Hall Demonstration.

The Town Hall Demonstration

Thursday, 22 May was a fine day. The Town Hall is in Brighton's Georgian town centre, close to the seafront. The light breeze and early summer sunshine swelled the numbers who answered the Project's call for a picket. Small knots of people stood around on the grass and pavements close to the Hall. It was nearly in the season for tourists, and anyway, tourists do not lean on placards while they chat. Not that the placards could be read at this stage. Even those slung over shoulders somehow had their faces turned down. Half a dozen policemen were dotted about on odd corners. They had a relaxed 'I-am-here-by-coincidence' look about them.

Everyone had made their preparations for the events of the day. After the first public meeting, Chris, the Rents Registration Group, and other Project members had a weighty Petition. It called on Brighton Council to open all their empty houses to the homeless. More than 2000 signatures had been collected. Chris was carrying this valuable document in a brown briefcase. Hundreds of leaflets had been distributed advertising the picket and petition. Together with the sunshine, these worked to bring out many more people to join those already there. As Jean remarked afterwards 'Cathy and Gary were there—even George Armstrong managed to stir himself for it. It was something everyone could take part in.' The policemen looked marginally less coincidental. We will probably never know what preparations they had made.

One or two councillors went in and out. There was some confusion about who were councillors and who were not. A few slogans were shouted. After a while it did not matter whether those going in were councillors. They were all officials of one sort or another. The crowd continued to build. Around mid-morning a rumour started that it was 'traditional', after the Mayor's Inauguration, for the

Squatters halt the demolition men

— then they join in a game of football

MORE than 50 members of the Brighton Re. Project today stopped workmen from continuing to demolish two houses in North Place which they had occupied for the day last Saturday in protest against corporation houses standing empty.

The campaigners today again occupied one of the houses just-

before demolition men were due to start work.

An hour later, some of the campaigners were playing an impromptu game of football with demolition workers at the rear of the houses. They decided to occupy the house all day, preventing any demolition work being done.

The two houses, both corporation-owned, are being pulled down to make way for a parking site for six cars.

The decision to demonstrate today came after a second packed meeting of the Project in a conference room at the Royal Pavilion last night.

"We hope to explain to the workers that the buildings are fit to live in and persuade them not to pull the houses down," said one member.

But this morning the workers were not persuaded. " If we are told to go back to work we will go on with the demolition," said one of the men.

" We're just going to do what we are supposed to do. But we can't go on if there are still people inside the houses. With things flying around the place someone is bound to get hurt."

MOTION

Yesterday the demolition men began work in one of the houses. Floorboards on the ground floor were taken up and woodwork and furniture were stripped from the other floors.

They had planned to complete the work within three weeks.

Last night's Royal Pavilion meeting passed a motion "deploring the wanton destruction" of the houses and calling the demolition "a serious indictment of a so-called civilised society which puts a basic human requirement like housing on a commercial basis."

The meeting also approved a letter written by two members of the Project, Mr. Chris Baxter and his wife, Val, of Montpelier Villas.

INJUNCTION

The letter, to the council's auditor, asked for an investigation into the demolition of the houses. " We all trust that the council will not proceed with demolition while you carry out your investigation, while the possibility of an injunction against them is being pursued and while public opinion remains deeply unsatisfied by the explanations given so far for the demolition," said the letter.

It added that it might be found on investigation that the cost of restoring the houses was less than the cost of demolition.

"We believe that such demolition could constitute a gross abuse of public funds."

GROUPS

The meeting decided to set up groups to co-ordinate the Project's activities. These groups

Extend a report on the housing problems drawn up by the Project.

Organise a propaganda machine for the Project.

Find out if any councillors have vested interests in housing and find which fingers are in which pies."

Organise the actual squatting activities when the Project decide to move families into empty houses.

Among members with "specialised skills " who applied for the last group are an electrician, a nurse, a builder and a plumber.

The Project also announced an appeal for funds to help with the running of the organisation.

PICKET

They confirmed they would picket Brighton Council meeting next Thursday and hand in a petition demanding that all empty council-owned houses which can be made habitable should be made available for rental.

Brighton's Borough Surveyor, Mr. Noel Patterson, said today of the North Place houses : " We will obviously not be carrying out any demolition which might endanger anyone."

The Deputy Town Clerk, Mr. Tony Blake, said : " If there is any question of prolonged trespass the council would almost certainly want the necessary action taken to gain possession, including proceedings in court."

A police spokesman said : " We are keeping a watch on the situation, but we have had no complaint of criminal conduct. If we do, we will deal with it."

Note : Brighton Housing Committee chairman, Ald. Stanley Theobald, has put the cost of restoring the North Place houses at £2,900 each. Cost of demolition has been estimated at £750.

Pictures show (above) the "squatters" taking over one of the two houses in North Place and (left) putting up a "Build, don't bulldoze" notice.

Figure 5.6

Councillors to march down to the Royal Pavilion for lunch. About 150 people had gathered by this time. The 'tradition' became accepted fact. 'They' were going to find the march very embarrassing. The petition, guarded by Chris and a few others at the back, was largely forgotten. Expectation prevented the crowd from dwindling. Lunchtime came. A few grey and black suits with sober ties left. More followed in ones and twos, some walking towards the sea, others towards the town. Several got into cars and drove away. The semicircle at the centre of the crowd in front of the Town Hall grew smaller. Saul peered into the outcoming faces. Since he had never met any of the councillors, it was unlikely that he would recognize them. Others followed suit. Finally, from his vantage point at the back, Chris saw the Chairman of the Housing Committee push his way out of the crowd and stride off towards the town. He pointed him out to Del, and the word spread. One group rushed after the Chairman. Another group followed, and soon the whole crowd, after a hesitant series of ripples, broke in the same direction.

Police moved quickly to block the main street. Unfortunately, the route to the Chairman's luncheon appointment did not follow the main street; nor did he; nor did the crowd. The police were left standing in the middle of an empty street. Making the best of a bad job, they set of in pursuit of the crowd which was in pursuit of the Chairman who was following his nose—at least thats the way it seemed, for his nose was poked very high in the air. The crowd caught up with the Chairman, and circled him. Placards bobbed to the chant of 'free FREE propertEE'. The Chairman's nose tilted a few degrees higher and carried on. The police improvized and surrounded the crowd, giving the impression the whole thing was a respectable march. Press cameras popped. (See Figure 5.7). The crowd opened before and closed behind the Chairman, keeping him as the permanent centre of the march. His nose, acting both as compass and sundial, refused to discuss rats in dustbins, overcrowding, or the reasons for 2000 empty houses in Brighton. He also refused to discuss the weather. It seems that he did not like it, or his compass was out of order, because very soon he, his turbulent escort, and its blue escort were back in front of the Town Hall steps. He disappeared within. A great cheer went up from the crowd.

After a few minutes self-congratulation, Andy, Chris, and myself went over and sat on the grass. About twenty others followed. Some people went off for something to eat, promising to return. Others just drifted off. All this had been done without any real plan. The next question was what to do in the afternoon.

The plan had been for Chris to present the petition. Getting all the signatures had been hard work, but no-one had thought about how the thing was to be delivered. At two o'clock there were still more than thirty people on the grass. The placards were piled in a heap to one side. The idea was mooted that everyone should go into the meeting. It was an obvious suggestion, and no-one disagreed. The police were not very happy about it when the remanents of a demonstration got up and lurched to the Town Hall steps. They immediately blocked the door and refused entry. Saul tried to push through, mumbling. Ken, from the Rents Registration Group, demanded to see the officer in charge.

THE GUARDIAN

Friday May 23 1969

Demonstrators protesting against housing conditions in Brighton yesterday

Protest ends with 10 arrests

By our own Reporter

Ten people were arrested at Brighton Town Hall yesterday after an attempt to deliver a petition to the council's annual meeting protesting against housing conditions in the town, had ended in the police being called in to clear the public gallery. The charges were obstructing the police and, in one case, assaulting a policeman.

The petition had been organised by the Brighton Rents Project, the organisation which recently installed two homeless families in empty council-owned houses. It had about 2,000 signatures.

After picketing the town hall the protesters—most of them students—went into the gallery. They were twice threatened with expulsion for applauding. Then when Mr C. Baxter, a lecturer at Sussex University tried to present the petition, the mayor adjourned the meeting and asked the police to clear the gallery.

One of the students, Mr Nicholas McGerr, said last night " We sat down and the police carried us out bodily. Some of the girls were screaming and one chap was dragged along by his feet and brought half the flower pots along with him."

Figure 5.7

Why were they keeping the public out of a public meeting? Gradually the matter was resolved. It seemed that members of the public were allowed in, but demonstrations were not. The difference was that members of the public went in one by one. Two policemen formed an inner door frame, reducing the wide entrance to a gap a thin person could get through without turning sideways. Fat people had to wriggle.

The demonstration, now a regularly spaced crocodile of individuals, wound its way up the wide flights of marble stairs, past the lines of geraniums, slit-leaved *Monstera deliciosa*, and other potted, climbing, or flowering exotica— which were regularly imported into the unlikely gloom on days of importance.

The head of the crocodile entered the Public Gallery, weaving its way around the seats. Several of these were already occupied by ladies in straw hats. Heads turned as the main body of the crocodile followed and threw out its coils in all directions. A lady in a blue satin bow turned and glared. The glare crackled over the sound of shuffling feet. The police shuffled too, uncomfortably, adding to the impression of hubbub. The council meeting had already started, but came to a halt as members stared up to see what was happening. A few individuals moved round the chamber. There was a hurried conference and whispering at the Mayoral end of the huge, austere table. Semaphore-like signals were sent up to the Public Gallery. The straw hats, led by the blue satin bow, got up and marched out. The crocodile disintegrated into seats and murmuring. A minute or so later the ladies appeared in the Council Chamber itself. They were provided with a table and jug of water well away from the main meeting, at the bottom of the hall. Having sorted the 'public' into appropriate grades, the meeting resumed.

The matter in hand was the membership of committees. The discussion was centering on the interests of councillors. Andy's mouth dropped open in amazement. Someone had been thrown off the Highways Committee for having an 'interest'. He was now suggesting that the estate agents be removed from other committees—specifically the Corporate Estates Committee and the Housing Committee. There was clapping and cheering from the Gallery. The Mayor warned that he would have the Gallery cleared if the disturbance continued. Then someone else got up and defended having estate agents on the Housing Committee—on the grounds that they *were* interested in housing. Naturally there was uproar from the entire Public Gallery. Over the jeers the Mayor reiterated his intention to have the Gallery cleared if the occupants could not contain themselves. The meeting continued. There were attempts to remove the Chairman from some of the innumerable committees. There were numerous divisions as the Labour Party had really been axed from the committees. Most younger councillors had been excluded too. The younger Councillors thought he should be replaced by someone younger. The Labour Party people thought the Labour Party ought to be included. In obedience to the Mayor, no more jeers or cheers were heard. Instead the Gallery kept going 'SHHHH' very loudly and conspicuously. Decision after decision of the Committee was passed despite the divisions.

Then came the discussion on the Housing Committee. Chris stood up and said 'Mr. Mayor. I beg leave to present a petition from 2000 residents of Brighton....' The Mayor told him to sit down, that he could not accept such a petition, and that it could only be presented through a councillor. There were murmurs from the other councillors. A Labour Party man from the far side of the table stood up and came round. He never reached Chris.

The Mayor spluttered and ordered the police to clear the Gallery. For a moment they looked bemused. Possibly they understood it was acceptable to be there to present a petition. Maureen shouted 'You don't care. You don't care what happens to us....' Others joined in. Downstairs in the Chamber the straw-hatted ladies stood up and filed out. They were followed by one or two grim-faced lady members. Upstairs extra police flooded in and started clearing the Gallery. In the chaos that followed it was difficult for anyone to get an overall view of what was happening. Gary was sitting near the door:

'They tried to clear us all out. We just sat still, and they carried us out. They carried me out and dumped me on the floor. I just sat there, so they picked me up again. I grabbed hold of all the flowers—the trestle they were standing on. This huge bay of flowers came all crashing down. They blamed Tom for that at the trial. Earth and leaves were all over the place. There were lots of people shouting at the Councillors who came out of their entrance to look at what was going on. There were people being herded around them. Old Ken was shouting very angrily. Maureen was still screaming at them. I was carried off and thrown down the stairs. I landed on top of someone, but I can't remember who. Beb picked me up, and told them to piss off and leave me alone. Then Tom came crashing past being pushed and kicked by the fuzz. They started shouting out the numbers of the police. I was shouting 'We know you, number ninety five. We've got your number. Ninety five. Ninety five.' ... and this huge hand grabbed me by the neck and said 'You've got a big mouth, haven't you' and threw me down the next flight of stairs to the ground floor. We were all pushed outside, but we came back and stood on the steps. That Chief, the one with a moustache: 'The situation is this. You're obstructing, and if you don't move we'll arrrest you.' There were people being flung out and then arrested. Somebody picked up Graham, somebody picked up Tom, somebody picked up Ken—all from around where I was standing. I stood there waiting and they pushed me down the steps. They followed us. The police kept moving us on. We had to go right down to the Pavilion Gardens in the end.'

Andy was on the far side of the Gallery, furthest from the door:

'I called out that all the people in our row should link arms. The police came along. They seemed to be quite bemused. As I say, the thing wasn't clear cut. They said 'Come along now. We don't want any trouble. Please go.' We said 'No. We won't go. Why can't we stay here?' We'd linked arms, and they knew they were going to have trouble with us. Unfortunately the other people had just been dragged out one by one. In fact they allowed us to stay. One of the girls became quite hysterical. She said 'Please! Please! We won't make any trouble if you let us stay'—so they let us stay. It wasn't a very militant line to take, but neither of us had been involved in anything like that before. It was quite dramatic.

It had never been brought home to me before that a Mayor could shout 'Clear the Gallery' and police would come pouring in and throw people down the stairs—which is what they were doing. Some guy stuck out his hand and knocked over all the flowers. The lady friends of the councillors had gone out so they didn't have to see it all. So that was that. We stayed quiet—and quite cowed as well—until the end of the Housing Committee business, then we filed out'.

Later, Andy was arrested too:

'When we got outside, everyone else had gone. We stood around, and the police told us to move on. The girls were arguing with them about obstruction. Jane and I started to wander off, then we saw this guy being carried into the van. I turned round and thought "Well! Its not right that he should be the only one arrested. It wouldn't look very good in the papers if there was only one person arrested." I turned to Jane and said "Perhaps we should get arrested too." I wasn't being serious about it, but it so happened that a policeman came up and said "Hey! We've told him three times to move on. Get him." So they got me.'

Later, in court:

'Graham made the best off-the-cuff speech about housing conditions, and why we were demonstrating. I made some short statement about the difference between the council's hysterical attitude towards demonstrators and their cynical indifference to problems....'

Mick commented:

'The arrests really did shock people. It was quite clear they were mass political arrests... I mean, OK, just one or two... but more than ten out of thirty becames a mass arrest. They just grabbed people willy-nilly. They wanted to get rid of these people—stop it there and then. We were on to an explosive thing, dealing with something very touchy like housing. It was quite clear that there was a lot of wheeler-dealing going on underneath. There was a real scandal somewhere.'

The Town Hall Demonstration stood out in everyone's mind as a success. The aim was the presentation of a petition to the council, urging them to open empty council property for renting to the homeless. The presentation was to be backed by a demonstration outside, and a presence inside the Hall to express the urgency of the situation. The whole thing was to be peaceful and pursuasive. No such thing happened. Instead, Project members were violently ejected by the police before the Petition was even read, and ten arrests were made.

Why then was the action seen as a success? First, it was well organized; it had taken a lot of work to get together 2000 signatures. This was mainly done by the people who became the Rents Registration Group. The publicity was good, and there was no shortage of leaflets and posters. Secondly, the demonstration was well attended. Thirdly, it got very wide press coverage, even reaching the nationals. Lastly, and probably most importantly, it shook up a whole lot of different views, and replaced them with a common perspective. After the demonstration, everyone saw things the same way. Before there had been confusion. Bad housing was 'in the nature of things'; a function of the 'ruling class'; a result of government policy; entirely due to grasping landlords; and so on. A different plan of action followed from each viewpoint. The demonstration satisfied all the viewpoints and then unified them. The enemy was identified. A clique of landlords and estate agents on the council were perpetuating the housing shortage for their own profit. They would resort to violence at a moments notice. To an outsider, this view might seem simplistic. The point is that it worked. The enemy was specific people—not an abstraction. Something can be done about specific people. Nor was there any doubt about what should be done. Direct action was the only answer to people who had proved they would not listen to rational argument.

The Town Hall Demonstration, and 22 May, marked the end of the opening phase of the Project. The first twenty days had seen the packed public meetings, the occupation, and the formation of working groups. People began to get to know one another. All these events provided the basis for a common language and history. Certain types of action were 'in'—others were 'out'. The Project was now publicly established on the Brighton scene. Its aims and tactics were clear. The members and supporters stood on one side, the opposition on the other. Squatting was the next step.

Terminus Road

'... when the squat started, originally, there was great emphasis on secrecy, on technical ability, and keeping a large number of people out of the picture. There was emphasis on this because of the enormous secrecy required to find a site and get in, to get the families in, without being busted before you even started.'

(John)

The history of the squatting group very quickly became the history of the Rents Project. History always has several versions, and this one is no exception. We will concentrate on weaving together the various accounts given by individuals with the 'public face' that was projected to the outside world. No attempt is made to represent the viewpoints of the Town Council and other 'authorities'— except where they had a direct bearing on the attitudes or actions of Project members. *This is a partisan history.* On the other hand, with a view to getting at, and learning from the group processes and conflicts, many aspects of the fight against homelessness have been de-emphasized. *This is not a story about homelessness but about the group processes that were actually involved in trying to do something about it.*

As we have seen, the Squatting Group was set up at the second public meeting with a mandate to help homeless families occupy empty council property. Its composition was technical: people with experience of squatting; an electrician; a plumber; a builder; and so on.

The occupation technique they used did not vary very much, and was similar to the one used in North Place. A homeless family would be found and interviewed. The interview served two purposes. The family was informed of the seriousness of the step it would be taking, and we got a chance to assess whether they were the sort of people we could work with. Then an empty council-owned house would be found. It had to be 'open'. Unless a door or window were open there could be a breaking and entering charge. Funnily enough, there never was a house that wasn't 'open' by the time a family arrived. Then, early in the morning, the house would be occupied. The family would be moved in with their furniture; the press notified; the gas and electricity connected.

On 7 June, two families—Mick and Val, John and Sara—were moved into two empty houses in Terminus Road. This squat marked the beginning of a very real transformation of the Project (Figure 5.8).

The crucial factor in this transformation was the acquisition of 'permanent space'. The group had somehow surfaced in the real world—as opposed to the worlds of 'politics' and 'ideas'. Objects in the real world take up space. This event was obscured from me for a long time because the acquisition of 'permanent space' coincided with the primary aim of the group: 'Homes for People not Profit'. Whether the occupied houses were homes, or homes *and*

Squatters move into empty homes

BY DOUGLAS AND HELEN DAVIS

TWO families were moved into two empty council-owned houses in Terminus Road by members of the Brighton Rents Project at 6 a.m. today.

Outside each house was pinned a notice which said: "We've occupied this property, we're in possession of it, we're claiming it and we intend to stay."

"So you want us out? O.K. But make sure you don't break the law in doing so, because if you do we'll lay the information before the local magistrates and if the Crown won't prosecute then we'll apply for a summons and do it ourselves."

Rents Project members refused to give the surnames of the families they moved in.

John, a 37-year-old carpenter and father of two children aged two and seven months, said he and his family had been living in a one-roomed Hove flat for the past three years.

One of the families who moved in today

BABY

They had been on the Hove council house list for the past two years and were told there was a possibility of a council house in July, 1970.

"But I'm expecting another baby and we just couldn't stay in that room," said his wife, Sarah, who is 23. "We've been looking for another flat ever since we moved into the room but not only are the rents too expensive, landlords just won't take children."

The other family are Valerie and Mick, both aged 21, with a six-month-old baby and another on the way.

They were evicted from their Robertson Road flat in Brighton and were then housed in the Welfare Department reception centre in Elm Grove.

Valerie and Mick were separated and had to be in the hostel every night by nine.

Both Terminus Road houses are large and airy and have supplies of gas, electricity and water. No. 24 has a large bathroom and two upstairs bedrooms, and a kitchen and two smaller rooms downstairs.

No. 25 has a bathroom/toilet and three large upstairs rooms, and another three rooms and a kitchen downstairs.

Beds were made in both houses and in one a five-month-old baby was sleeping happily in her new bedroom.

Rents Project members were hard at work scrubbing windows and floors, cleaning stoves and baths and generally making the houses as comfortable as possible.

A nurse, carpenter and electrician were on hand to help care for the children and cope with major repair work.

Ald. Stanley Theobald, chairman of the Brighton Council's

Housing Committee, said of the squatters' action: "We will do nothing until after the weekend. It is a matter for the town clerk.

It depends, then, on what damage has been done to the houses."

On being told that the squatters were probably improving them, Ald. Theobald remarked: "Well, it's nice to see them doing some work for a change."

The chairman of the Welfare Committee, Cr. Constance Nettleton, said the committee had no policy of dealing with squatters. The first meeting of the committee for the municipal year would be held on Monday morning.

In a pamphlet handed out today, members of the Rents Project demanded: that homes be made a right, not a privilege; that homes be produced for people, not profit; and that all housing be publicly-owned

Members of the Brighton Rents Project were busy today making repairs to the occupied houses

Figure 5.8

meeting places, was always ambiguous. The dilemma of family privacy versus group activity was never explicitly recognized, although both notions were used in the conflicts that this created.

The importance of a permanent physical meeting place cannot be underestimated. As social scientists coldly but accurately put it: 'it allows low-cost information exchange'. If a group can only meet at specific times and at specific places (an arrangement which is inevitably inconvenient for many) then it must also spend much of its time on arranging agendas, formal discussion, and scheduling other meetings. Informal discussion is undesirable and time-wasting under these circumstances. Yet it is precisely informal discussion that is essential in the creation of a language and norms necessary for the cohesion and the smooth functioning of the group. In the Rents Project, this 'permanent space' allowed some subgroups to develop faster, and in a different way, to others. A consequence of this was the creation of a new, *actual* leadership.

Those who could spend most time at the site had the most information, and were called on to do the day-to-day decision-making. The actions, and sometimes the intentions, of the 'full-timers' became information as far as the others were concerned. Another general aspect of this was that the interpretations of events by those at the squat tended to become the standard interpretations.

The occupation of the Terminus Road houses had two other consequences. The Project now had a collective responsibility to the squatting families—a constant source of real problems that fell outside the original political intentions of the movement. The permanent occupation of council property established the group as a permanent problem to the local authority: something that could no longer be ignored.

The consquences of its initial aims and beliefs, as materialized in the first squats, almost entirely determined the future of the Project. The first consequence to become obvious was the change in leadership. Remember how Andy noticed that, at open meetings, people who have discussed things beforehand can have a strong influence on the meeting; can create the impression that their views are the consensus. The people he was talking about (broadly) were the Revolutionary Socialist Students Federation members. They had a strong influence, through the open meetings, on the opening phases of the Project and on the initiation of squatting. Now the squatting group took over from this University-based group. They explicitly claimed decision-making autonomy over the squatting. However, squatting was seen as the central aspect of the Project by everyone—including the media and the local authority; its consequences involved far more people than the squatting group itself—so this was more than just a limited claim.

The change in leadership should have made it clear that three major groupings had evolved. As it was it was only half-seen, because the constant statements of 'unity' to the press influenced the way members saw their own activities. The squatting group identified itself with permanent occupancy of the houses—and thus differed from the Squatting Group that was set up by the public meeting. It was anarchist dominated (remember about the inverted commas) and its emphasis was entirely on practice. It evolved the slogans:

Make squatting a mass movement
The more squats the better
Families before politics
Only those involved in action have the right to decide or criticise.

The squatting group was concerned mainly with physical self-defence—barricades and security to thwart any possible attack by bailiffs or other thugs. This concern was easy to justify because squatters in London were being attacked, evicted, and in some cases nastily injured.

The second group was the Revolutionary Socialist Group (RSSF), who were equally concerned with the squat, although not based on it. Its major concern—under the slogan 'Homes for People not Profit'—was to generalize and widen the struggle. It was often active with propaganda. The literature and press statements put out by the Project tended to reflect the views of this grouping. When they did not, there was trouble.

The third major grouping—broadly the Labour Left—organized itself in and around the Rents Registration Group. It was largely detached from squatting activities except at moments of crisis.

Each of these groupings had a different organizational paradigm. The first—the anarchist squatting group—believed in individual action without any check. The second—the RSSF grouping—believed in evolving policies by democratic debate at mass meetings. The decisions would then be binding on everyone. The third—the Labour Left grouping—believed in control by a centralized executive, under general policy lines laid down by the majority.

The second procedure was the one usually followed in practice. When the first was followed it was interpreted (or justified) as being the second. As we have seen, Chris and the Labour Left grouping interpreted the second procedure as a slack version of the third. The three paradigms were, of course, very different. When conflict did arise, there was no generally accepted ground for its resolution.

The first squat had been successful. Two families had homes. The houses had been redecorated and furnished. They were 'guarded'—although there was as yet no sign of any opposition. The press and public opinion was favourable. A week later four more squats took place in rapid succession. Brian and Flo moved into another empty house in Terminus Road on 14 June (Fig. 5.9), followed on the same day by Don and Pat. Maureen was moved in up the road a couple of days later. An artist and his wife squatted themselves in a disused shop just down the road the next day. Steve, his wife, nanny(!), and child moved into adjoining Railway Street. Seven families: fourteen adults; eleven children.

This rapid escalation of the situation came as a shock to the Labour and Revolutionary groups. The first divisions and doubts began to appear.

The Saturday squatters strike again at dawn

BRIGHTON Rents Project squatters took over another empty council-owned house just after dawn today.

Fifteen helpers cleaned the three-bedroomed house in Terminus Street from top to bottom while the new occupiers, who refused to give their surnames, settled in.

Florence and her husband Brian brought with them two of their three children.

She said she and her husband had been married for nine years and never had a home of their own.

For the last five months they had been living in one room in her mother's council house.

LIST

Brian was told by a Brighton council official that the family could not be considered for a council house of their own until they had been on the list for three years.

His wife has tried to get a flat but no landlord will accept the children. She said they wanted to stay in the Terminus Street house permanently.

They intend to apply to the council for a rent book and will put money aside each week.

No action was taken by the council today.

One of the helpers from the Brighton Rent Project said they had quite a few more families lined up to move into other empty council-owned properties in Brighton.

But the project urgently needs more funds and a large van to help with removals, he said.

The house the squatters took over today

Moving in. Young Keith helps with some of the family's possessions

Figure 5.9

'I came in on one squatting discussion. It was in a very overcrowded small room. The atmosphere was very emotional and disorganized. At the time there had been a decision—in principle—that no unmarried or single mothers would be squatted. The only people who would be squatted would be really independent families who could look after themselves, and wouldn't need any support facilities. It struck me at the time that this was odd—there was a clash going on here—because the ethos at the time was to have as many guards as possible. Some people were saying that Maureen should not be squatted. I knew Maureen. I had met her quite a lot canvassing. I came out of the meeting early because I was so staggered by what I'd seen going on. I went round to her house to advise her that there were a lot of disadvantages in being squatted—especially by the kind of people who had been talking. If people came round and said they wanted to squat her, she should be very cool and make sure they talked about all the disadvantages. I went round but she wasn't in. I went back after eleven, but she still wasn't back. So I got up early the next morning and went round to her house at seven o'clock, because it seemed important to me. By then, she had got her furniture on the stairs and was ready to move.

I am afraid my only participation in squatting in the early days was to try and stop Maureen. I don't think my motive, at that time, was that the Project was squatting too many people. A few days later I was saying that this had got to stop: there were too many people being squatted. This wasn't in my mind on that particular night. It was just that the whole thing seemed to me far too chaotic. At the meeting, people were saying we haven't got vans; we haven't got people; the house isn't ready. The more sensible people were saying 'don't go ahead'. The others, who were clearly in the emotional ascendency, were also saying "we are not ready—but we must squat her".'

(Chris)

There were two attempts by those outside the squatting group to regain some sort of control—or at least get their views recognized. These centred on the third public meeting and the subsequent Coordinating Committee meeting.

The third public meeting took place in a church hall. (After the squatting had started, the Pavilion Buildings in the town centre suddenly became 'unavailable'.)

'I remember one meeting presided over by Kestionaire Jim. Saul was sitting over on the left-hand side at the front, his anarchist scarf round his neck, waiting his turn to say something as if he were the Chairman ... don't think the resentment had started too much at that point'

(Jean)

'At one of the public meetings in the church hall, the squatters gave their first report, right! Several of us, including me and Mick, criticized the report. We said it was too short, too terse, didn't tell people anything. Saul just got up and said "Everybody knows there's a squat going on. We need all your help. Thanks." We wanted a bigger discussion. A discussion about the relationships with the families and what squatting was achieving. What its aims were. There were lots of arguments about what was actually happening. Saul and John were upset by this. They took it as a criticism, you see.'

(Gary)

It was decided to call a meeting of the Coordinating Committee and Squatting Group together to try and sort out the differences.

By now the nucleus of the Squatting Group consisted of eleven people, most of whom were living on the squat as guards. There was Nick, Dave, and of course Saul, who were all unemployed. David and Barbara, Caroline, Judy, Nigel, Prof., and Buzz were all students. Tub had just left school. As well as 'guarding', they had done a lot of painting and decorating, and were often very useful to the families as baby-sitters. They felt they should have the greatest say over things because they had done most of the work. This was expressed in their attitude that only 'full-timers' were genuine squatters. Having a lot of time to talk together in relative isolation from the rest of the Project, they developed their own rationale for squatting. Essentially, the aim of squatting was to destroy the laws of private property by simply disregarding them. On this logic, success was seen in terms of ever-increasing numbers of people taking over empty houses. At the Coordinating Committee meeting, Mick got a severe shock when Saul openly declared his aim:

'If someone doesn't like the house they are living in, and there is a better one empty next door, then they will just pack their bags and move in.'

The 'full-timers' also saw the Rents Project as run by a University-based group; it seemed an interference or an irrelevance. They saw no need to inform, let alone discuss with it, any actions they might plan. The atmosphere at the Coordinating Committee meeting was not helped because many Project members had been ignored or taunted when they turned up at the squat.

'You'd go for your guard duty, and they'd make all sorts of sarcastic comments: "Oh! So you've come up at last...', "Where were you when we did the decorating?" and things like that. Not very many people came to do guard duty...I went along a few times, but there was nothing much to do. I just sat around.'

(Gary)

'Several times I tried to do some baby sitting, or guard duty, or whatever it was called. The times I went up, however long for, there was never any need for it, so I came away.'

(Chris)

'I went only once to the first squat at Terminus Road—as a guard. At the time some anarchists turned up with a record player and started playing records. I was a bit pissed off with this because I thought about revolutionary discipline, man, and I thought they were going to turn it into a discotheque...after that, I wasn't involved in anything to do with squatting.'

(Andy)

The meeting took place in the small front room of John and Sara's house. It was not furnished yet, which was fortunate as more than forty people turned up. Despite the initial intention of one representative from each subgroup, the Coordinating Committee had no clear membership apart from Troy, the Treasurer. This was the first bone of contention. Who should be at the meeting, and what powers did it have? The squatting group saw it as a bureaucratic device packed against them, and were having none of it. In many ways they were right. Certainly there was no justification (in terms of the original structure) for the number of people who were there. The Coordinating Committee was ditched—no-one was really sure who belonged to it anyway. It was suggested that a majority vote at the meeting should be binding.

'You are not going to tell us what to do' said Nick. The Rents Project majority over the squatting group was noticeable.

'I'm not having that' said Saul. 'I haven't seen most of these people here before.'

'We're not going to take public responsibility for your lunacy...' (someone from the Rents Registration group).

'The Project was our idea, and we are not going to let you wreck it...'

'In that case why haven't we seen you before?' (Dave)

'What is the Rents Project anyway?...' (Nick)

'We'll squat whoever we like—we've managed so far without your help.'

'Look, let's be sensible...'

And so on.

Finally the meeting reached a compromise agreement. The Rents Project would be informed in advance of any more squats; Project Members would give much greater practical help.

The decision went unheeded by both sides. The Squatting Group carried on squatting.

> 'I went to London for the weekend. When I came back I found that another squat had taken place without informing the Rents Project.'
>
> (John)

Many members of the Rents Project 'left it alone and did something else'. They were discouraged by the taunting and sarcasm—which in turn helped preserve the ethos of the squatting group. By preventing others from doing anything, the Squatting Group also prevented them from acquiring the right (as they defined it) to participate in the decision-making. The three exceptions to this were John, Steve, and myself. All three of us managed, for long periods, to work within the Squatting Group while preserving a major allegiance to the Project as a whole.

Up to this point, I had been, more or less, a bystander. I was certainly one of the people the Squatting Group had never seen before. There were rumours of legal action against the families at the meeting, but no-one was really doing anything about it. I volunteered to help John (who had been 'officially' a member of the Squatting Group from the beginning) with 'legal liaison'. Steve's 'rise to fame' really came with the move to Wykeham Terrace, which comes later. Each of us, at one time or other, became involved in the 'elitist' decision-making of the Squatting Group. John has already explained the need for secrecy when planning a squat—and that was only one step from what those outside the Squatting Group called 'elitism'. On the other hand, none of us really developed the supporting attitudes, but neither were we ever fully received into the Squatting Group. It may be that it was only us that 'half-saw' the emerging divisions. It was a strange situation: we were all in the position of feeling and recognizing, yet bridging and denying differences.

> 'The problem was that the communications system of the Rents Project was never sufficient...when we'd actually put the families in the communication was never sufficient...half the Rents Project were doing nothing, while the other half were sweating their guts out on the squat.'

and

'...after the first squat there was always a division between...well, there was officially a division...I never accepted this division, and I don't think there was. The way it was most obviously termed was a division between the Squatters Group and the Rents Project. I never saw this division as such. That form of expressing it was in fact put by some members of the Squatters Group, and also by some members of the Rents Project.

(John)

At times the division could not be denied.

'The dispute, at one point I remember, crystallized over the hanging of the Rents Project banner along the side of one of the Terminus Road houses. This was ripped down by one of the so-called anarchists...and there was a row about that.'

(John)

It should also be said that the internal processes of the squatting group were not as chaotic as they appeared to some Project members. There was, as we have seen, a well-developed technique for occupation. The occupied houses were restored, maintained, and furnished—all of which was hard work. And, contrary to some opinion, several 'unsuitable' families were not squatted.

'There was a regulation laid down that we would squat no family which had problems other than housing. This crystallized over a case of an old man and an old woman and their son and things—I've forgotten their names—who came round one night. Steve, Saul, and I—we were the crucial people at that time—were dashing round for hours and hours and hours trying to get these people off our hands. He had a hernia. The son was mad and locked up in jail for setting fire to a house. The woman was very old and very ill. Another son was at Cobs Social Club all the time and slept on the beach. If we'd invited him in, we'd have got Cobs Social Club—all the petty criminals, failed criminals essentially, hang out there. Eventually we took them—we felt very bad about this and she was absolutely in floods of tears—to the Welfare people. It was a really bad scene.'

(John)

I personally remember when a family of heroin addicts wanted us to squat them, and there was a great debate. They were pleasant enough people and they were homeless, but if the press found out we'd be crucified. In the end the dilemma was resolved by the squatting families themselves. They wanted to have nothing to do with it—so we did nothing.

But, in the event, the explosion of squatting was not slowed by any internal reconciliation of views. An external brake, legal action, was applied by the Council. The object of this action was not the organized Project, but the families themselves.

The Families

In every case the families made initial contact with the Project. The first families contacted a number we put in the local paper; others contacted us directly at the squat. All were homeless and all had children. The Project put out a booklet with background information on the families—factual illustrations of the housing problem. Here are some extracts from it.

Florence and Brian

...

After their second child, Flo and Brian could no longer live with their parents. They moved to a flat in Hove. This consisted of a small bed-sitting room that measured 7' × 9', a tiny kitchen 6' × 5', and a bathroom and toilet shared by 8 other families, all with children. The flat was really unfit for habitation since the floorboards were rotten and the windows were falling out. The bathroom was next to their bedroom and the geyser frequently blew up. The landlord refused to repair the property. One of their children, Michael, had stayed with Flo's mother because the flat was so small...

(They had a third child and were forced to move back with Flo's parents.)

Although Flo was born and brought up in Brighton, and Brian in Worthing, the Council stated that they would have to live together in Brighton for three years before they could go on the list. They would have to wait a further three or four years before they could even be considered for a house.

Brian earns £13 a week as a bus driver and can only afford £4.10/- a week rent. At this price,* because of the children, no landlord will accept the family.

Comment

...some 7 million families live in this sort of squalid, crowded, or sub-standard conditions. The problem is not simply one of counting the homeless, but of asking 'What constitutes a home?' In Brighton and Hove alone there are several thousand basement flats let at exorbitant rents which would never pass Ministry of Housing standards.

Pat and Donald

In 1966, Pat and Donald moved into O...Villas at £4.15/- a week. There were two bedrooms, which were the only two reasonably dry rooms in the flat. The dining room was soaking wet, and the front room reeked of damp and decay. The kitchen was used despite the damp. They, and their two children were unable to use the bathroom because the floor was dangerous....

The Council refused to help because they had not been on the housing list for three years, and told them to fend for themselves. They tried all the estate agents to no avail. They were discriminated against because they had children. In desperation Pat went to the Welfare people. They could only offer hostel accommodation 18 miles outside Brighton for her and the children, while Donald would have to find somewhere for himself.

...

Eventually Pat could bear it no longer and her mother took them in. Altogether in the house there were four adults besides Pat and her two children. Pat, her mother, and the two children shared one bedroom. There was so little room that Pat had to sleep on the floor on a lilo for a year. Donald had had to move into a bedsitting room in Hove, near his working place. He could only see the children at weekends....

Comment

In Maureen's story we saw that the stresses and strains of eight years were enough to break up her marriage. With Pat and Donald we see similar forces at work....

These experiences show the various ways in which a council can avoid providing homes. It is true that there are not enough council houses AND THE ANSWER IS TO BUILD MORE. The Council has boasted it has built more new council houses than its predecessors. This claim ignores the fact that it has also pulled down more—such as the two in North Place to make room for 6 cars.

---

*All rents quoted are 1969 prices when £20 a week was a good wage.

We have told Maureen's story at the first public meeting. Brief accounts of the misfortunes of Mick and Val, and John and Sara appeared in the newspaper story about the first squat. We were always at pains to emphasize that the families were in no way exceptional. They were ordinary families, and the men had ordinary jobs (bus driver, engineer, salesman, carpenter, etc.).

I think it says quite a lot for the families that the local council and the press did not attack the families as people at any point. They attacked the activity of squatting as a 'prelude to anarchy'. They attacked the squatters as a group for 'trying to jump the housing queue'. They attacked the Rents Project for just about everything. But they never questioned the integrity of the families.

The Reaction of the Authorities to Squatting

After its opening phase, Rents Projects activities were strongly influenced by the actions of outside bodies: the council; the police; the courts; the press; and, later, the Ministry of Defence.

In the early phases of squatting—North Place and Terminus Road—the police took the view that the matter was a dispute to be solved by the civil courts and outside their jurisdiction. We suspected that, unlike the situation at the Town Hall, they simply did not know what to do. There were no precedents. In any event, they did not appear. Only the council and the press were directly involved. The local papers often had hostile editorials, but the reportage was generally sympathetic. The council first used propaganda and threats, then court action. The basic threat was to strike the families off the housing list. This was of dubious legality, and anyway had little effect on the families. The council had already refused to help most of them. The others saw little chance of ever getting to the top of the list. The council's statement after the first court case, in which propaganda and threat are carefully combined with a lack of any specific ways of helping the homeless, is a good example of their attitude. Patience—preferably eternal—was the virtue.

'We had to do this, and the idea is to prevent squatters, some from outside Brighton, trying to jump the housing queue in front of those people who have waited patiently and legally on the housing list. It would not be fair to them.

We all know the sad problems of those who are homeless. We have been working for years and we are doing all we can to help. But if these people are foolish enough to allow themselves to be persuaded to enter and take over empty houses by militant and illegal means, they will be struck off the housing list.

We really have no option. We must protect the people whose plight may be worse than the squatters. If we close our eyes and condone it, this could lead to anarchy.'
(quoted in the *Brighton & Hove Herald*, 4 June 1969)

Court action caused far more problems. The council applied for repossession of the houses, damages, and an injunction to prevent the families squatting in any of their properties. To everyone's relief, the first case was deferred. The Judge said it was not an emergency. This gave us time to sort our way through various legal terms, get to know the solicitor and barrister, and generally find our feet.

On 2 July the case came up again. This time nothing much went on in court at all. It was all worked out between the barristers.

Mr. Dennis Bradley, for the corporation, told the judge these terms had been agreed: 'There would be in both cases judgement for the corporation for £7 damages for trespass and possession in 28 days, with an undertaking that the families would not exchange the premises or go back into them when the 28 days was up'

(Quoted in the *Evening Argus*, 2 July 1969)

The Judge was not very pleased about this agreement: he thought the families had been very generously treated 'considering they just broke into the premises'. John and I were pleased about it. There had been no general injunction against squatting. The £7 damages against Mick and Val, and against John and Sara, seemed a very reasonable 'rent' for nearly two months. On top of that, there had been no court costs to pay. (That had not pleased the Judge either: he made the stuffy remark 'I suppose the taxpayer is the loser'.) All in all, given the Judge was hardly sympathetic (he crops up again later with some more acid remarks), we thought the result was the best that could be done. Others did not: many of the Squatting Group saw it as a major, possibly final, defeat.

'It's all over. It's finished.'
'What's the point carrying on?'

Some wanted to leave there and then.

The families were baffled. Why had it not been *fought*? The barrister had not even tried to defend them, even when the judge was being abusive. Their desperation had not been mentioned. They had been ordered to get out. Why? What were they going to do now? The barrister was no good. They had been let down. Sold out.

This was the first row I had actually been in the middle of. The families were bewildered and angry; with some justification. John and I knew that squatting would involve shifting families around houses—but the families themselves, even if they had been told, had not been prepared for it. For one thing, they *liked* the houses they were in. For many of them it was their first real home.

The Squatting Group were angry because the families were angry. They were also angry because the Rents Project had cocked it up again. They accused us of putting politics before families. We would have been angry because we were being unjustly abused—but all this was going on in the middle of a press conference!

Actually, the row was going on in the back room of John and Sara's house, and the press were in the front room. We took it in turns to talk to the press. Chris explained about the background of the families, then rushed off to the back room to try and pacify them. I gave our [sic!] version of the court case, then rushed back to try and keep the anarchists quiet. Saul loudly announced his intention of going to Cornwall and not coming back. Fortunately for us, only hints of this appeared in print. Mainly they featured our statements.

The Brighton Rents Project will carry on as before, increasing and extending our activity wherever possible. The needs of the homeless and tenants all over Britain are overwhelming, and they cannot be stopped by vicious intimidation by any Council or Government.

(Chris: quoted in the *Brighton & Hove Herald*, 4 July 1969)

We will treat the Council's opposition with the contempt it deserves. We deplore both the outcome of the case and the Council's action in bringing the case. But this will not make any difference at all to our activities. The problem of homeless families isn't going to be solved by messing about in courts—and if they don't tackle this problem, then we will.

(Mike: quoted in the *Evening Argus*, 3 July 1969)

It sounded brave. The truth was that no-one had the slightest idea what to do next.

The Move to Wykeham Terrace

The problem was not going to go away. Two families had been ordered to quit, and court action was imminent against the other four. On present form, the occupation time for any family and a given house was about two months. Probably it would come down to a month once the Council got itself sorted out.

Squatting, as we had done it so far, had a lot of disadvantages. Once it got to court, we could not win. The only real delaying tactic we could think of was to prevent the council finding out the names of the families. If they did not know the names, they would not be able to serve a summons. It would be difficult and disruptive. People had to go shopping, for one thing. On the other hand, *if* it was successful, the council, in its frustration, might resort to strongarm tactics, as had been done in Ilford. None of the homes could be defended against a determined attack. On top of all this, the families were very reluctant to get involved in permanent moves. They wanted, above all, to be able to settle down.

The Squatting Group found the answer. The meeting was so secret that no other members of the Project were even told who was there. The answer was Wykeham Terrace. From the point of view of defence, it was a natural fortress. It was a terraced block of eight flats, standing in its own grounds. It was impressive, and solidly built. It was 'surveyed' and found to be habitable. The 'survey' took place in great secrecy, with much scuttling and lurking, at midnight. Apparently, even then, the Squatting Group was nearly discovered. Someone else was looking round the building with a torch. A caretaker? A Security Guard? The Group dispersed, tip-toeing off down corridors or up dusty spiral staircases, making their own ways out. Buzz ended up in front of the torch, climbed out of the window, found he was two stories up, fell, and broke a leg. Fortunately secrecy was preserved. Wykeham Terrace was pronounced 'the place'.

All the families would be together, and would be able to give each other mutual support. There was even room for more! There was no damp. There was a good chance that writs could be ducked: each flat had a separate front door, so it would be necessary to summons each family individually. But it would be impossible, from the outside, to discover which family was living in which flat—so it would be impossible to summons anyone. If the 'Authorities' resorted to violence, the Terrace could be fortified as a block.

Last, but not least, there was the prestige value of the occupation. The houses in Terminus Road were good, honest, working-class homes. There was nothing wrong with them. But the council called them 'slums'. And they were scattered down the street, not together. Wykeham Terrace was officially termed a 'Luxury Block'. It was in the heart of Brighton. No one could pretend the homeless did not exist if we got in there. This was the substance of the discussion as I pieced it together later. The conclusions were apparent unanimous.

The operation of occupation went brilliantly (although it was to be the last time the occupation technique was used). All members of the Project were involved. The first I heard of it was two days before. I was asked to hire a van on Friday, and have it ready at 6.00 on Saturday morning. But I was given no inkling of where the move was to. Nor was I told, until the night before, that three other vans and six cars were to be involved. Most of the others were similarly ignorant. We all met, with others who had 'key' jobs, on the night before. The reasons for the move were explained. The location was kept secret.

The next morning, Saturday 19 July, fifty people were at work by 6.15. The vans all had numbers and assignments. Loading and unloading bays were chalked on the road. Wykeham Terrace was taken at 6.00. By mid-day the move was more or less complete. Six families* and all their possessions had been moved in the space of six hours.

Wykeham Terrace was owned by the Ministry of Defence. The Evening Argus headlined the event

SQUATTERS INVADE THE ARMY IN DAWN SWOOP

(See Figure 5.10.)

Wykeham Terrace

I returned to Wykeham Terrace that evening to see how things were going. It was like something out of an Albanian novel. I turned right off the main road. The streetlights, the Clock Tower, the late-night shops, and the tourists were all gone. I walked across the broad pavement under the huge dark trees. In the shadows there seemed to be no noise. Below me was Wykeham Terrace. A small watchfire glowed in the centre of the courtyard. The high walls at each end were just touched by the firelight. A uniformed guard—white webbing belt, white helmet, and 3 foot long white nightstick in his hand—moved towards the entrance. A large alsation dog was close by his side. The building was dark

---

*The self-squatted artist and his wife elected to stay with their shop near Terminus Road—and that was the last we heard of them.

behind him. Two or three of the upper windows flickered with candlelight. All the other leaded panes and gothic arches were dark.

The guard turned out to be Steve in fancy dress. The nightstick was a chairleg. The dog belonged to Mick, who was finishing a bottle of beer in one of the barricaded porches. Nine o'clock, and all was well. Steve explained to me that the building was coming up for auction on Wednesday. The owners—the Ministry of Defence—were an unknown quantity. They might try to get their property back before the auction. Or else the new owners might try immediately after the auction. There was certainly no guarantee they would have the patience to go through all the legal processes. Wykeham Terrace was worth a lot of money—Steve estimated £100 000. We must be prepared to defend ourselves.

This logic led to a dramatic escalation of events over the next month. Things went from big to bigger; from fact to fiction, reaching an explosive climax exactly thirty-one days later on 19 August.

I went back the next day to find a flurry of activity. By daylight the Terrace looked seedier. The impression was not helped by large numbers of freshly boarded-up doors and windows. Preparations were being made for a siege. Sitting on the front was Nick. He was poring over a plan showing the proposed defences. Every now and then he would add further detail. It seemed that Steve had given him this task. He showed me the results. I was astounded, to say the least. Most of the Courtyard was to be dug out as a trench. Barbed wire entanglements were to surround it, and fill the basement stairwells. Concrete bollards were to be built in the main gate to stop any vehicles. Petrol bombs and rocks were being carted onto the roof to hurl at any assault team. Unsealed doors were studded with 6 inch nails, points outwards, to stop anyone putting their shoulder to them. New locks, bolts, and drop in locking bars were being fitted. Nick put the last touch to his plan. The yard was to be studded with mines. Chlorate and sugar was supposedly vibration sensitive. I pointed out that vans were needed to move the various families in and out—and that these caused vibration too.

Fortunately, this medieval panoply of siege tactics was never carried out. Barbed wire entanglements are very expensive. No-one actually said the trenches were a bad idea—but no-one volunteered to dig them either.

Uncertainty was the key factor. The families were bewildered, and as yet had no voice of their own. They had agreed to the move because it was obvious that the Terminus Road houses were unsafe. Court action could take them away at any moment. On the other hand, they were not prepared for the Wykeham Terrace frenzy. By and large they tried to ignore it. Inside the flats they dusted and vacuumed, laid carpets, and organized as much comfort and normality as they could. The electricity and gas had been reconnected so the wartime atmosphere of open fires and candles was banished. Putting lampshades over naked lights made the places more homely—even if the front doors were studded with nails.

The students and Labour Party people were caught in the same trap. They

Evening Argus

Incorporating the
SUSSEX DAILY NEWS

Saturday
July 19, 1969

Fivepence

Squatters invade the army in a dawn swoop

delicate
alancing
act as
a family
moves in

By Douglas Davis

SEVEN squatter families — helped by 50 Brighton Rents Project supporters — moved into the former married quarters of the Territorial Army in Wykeham Terrace, about 100 yards from Brighton Clock Tower, early this morning.

The property is owned by the Ministry of Defence and is due to come up for public auction on Wednesday.

There are eight flats in the block, the last one being vacated about a month ago.

The squatter families all moved out of council-owned properties where they had been squatting until today. Among them were two families who had been ordered by a county court judge to quit their properties by July 28.

The other five had all received summonses to appear in the county court on July 30.

Using four vans, squatters and supporters of the Rents Project started moving into the property at about 7 a.m.

WARNING

One of the organisers—a former Sussex University chemistry student—warned today: "We've moved in and we're not going to be moved out."

The ex-student, who gave his name as "Buzz," said supporters of the Rents Project would act as guards for the families and would resist any moves to force the squatters out.

Buzz had been delegated to looking after "publicity" after breaking a leg a short while ago. "I was looking over this property and unfortunately came out of a window too fast," he said.

Among the Rents Project supporters who helped the families move in was an electrician and a plumber, who will be helping to make the flats habitable.

The families have moved into seven of the flats. The remaining flat will be occupied by guards from the Rents Project. "We are not looking for trouble," said Buzz. "We're just taking precautions."

HALF-WAY

He said the Project were hoping that the Government would hand the properties over to the squatters or to the council for use as "some sort of half-way house."

At the entrance to the flats, a notice reading "Private Property" has been altered to "People's Property."

One of the squatters, Mrs. Sarah Byrne, who, with her husband and two-year-old son, among the first squatters to be helped move into an empty council-owned house in Terminus Road by the Rents Project, said that the move had been "a bit unsettling."

PAGE 4: Dad moves in for Ian's birthday.

Figure 5.10

did not really like all the barricades and bolts. More than that they did not like the glee with which they were being put up. But on the other hand, there had been violent evictions in Redbridge. Gangs of thugs had hurled families back onto the streets. So the defences were necessary. Steve, Nick, and the anarchists were simply having a thoroughly good time.

Everyone participated but attitudes were beginning to slip apart. The anarchists dominated the organization of the squat, and said what had to be done—or undone. That was the trouble. As Gary put it,

'They'd say "screw locks on all the doors, and bolts" so I did that. Then you'd go round the next week and they'd all been taken off again and moved somewhere else. And "knock the wall down at the back", which several of us did—only to find it was never used for the purpose it was supposed to be. It was just a mess and we had to clear the rubble out. Things like that. I was trying to pretend I didn't care whether it was going to be useful or not. But it didn't last very long. I soon discovered that I was being quite useless.'

At the squat you were expected to participate and to enjoy it. Failure to do both spelt trouble. Geoff was put off on the first day.

'That day millions of people came down from London. I had a row with somebody as soon as we got there. Some bloke said all the chairs and tables had to be moved. I was sitting on the wall having a little break. This bloke said, "Would you like to come and have a look at the Drill Hall at the back." I said, "No, I wouldn't. I'd like to sit down for a minute." He went off into a big huff. Rumours started to spread that all the people sitting on the wall hadn't done anything.'

Different versions of the story were repeated by almost everyone outside the anarchist faction. The immediate excuse for the frenzy was the impending auction (Figure 5.11). A meeting was called in one of the unoccupied flats. Most groupings were represented, and it was agreed to put out leaflets (Figure 5.12) and stage a demonstration at the auction. No-one dissented. It was the obvious thing to do. Mike wrote the leaflet. Mick got it duplicated. The Students and Labour party group gave it out in the main street.

Steve had other ideas for sabotaging the auction. A quiet word with the Press, and the Rents Project was transformed into a 'petrol bomb army'. (See Figure 5.13.) The auction fell through. The few prospective buyers who turned up failed to bid to the reserve price. Cheers and a shower of leaflets like confetti greeted the announcement (Figure 5.14). Another victory.

This duality of approach ran right through the next month. On the one side, there were 'standard' organizational efforts. Leaflets, meetings, educational groups, playgroups, and crèches all took up a comparatively large amount of effort. They were not particularly successful, either in terms of their own aims, or in terms of publicity. On the other side, with seemingly no effort at all, Steve organized increasingly fantastic publicity stunts. For a whole period, control of the Rents Project seemed to slip entirely into his hands.

Even the anarchists were bewildered at the rapid twists. After the auction fell through, they became increasingly quiescent. The need for barricade-building was gone. They participated in other activities as individuals, not, as at

Figure 5.11

Terminus Road, as a cohesive group. Their rationale for being at Wykeham
Terrace was to act as 'guards'—but the drama and importance of 'being a
guard' had paled. In fact many people came to regard the 'guards' as a positive
nuisance. When asked how the Rents Project could be improved, many families
simply said 'get rid of the dossers'. Within this view, John commented

'The people who aren't here as families do nothing at all. They are willing to air their
violence, but we don't want violence, we want homes. These people are fractured
from society by their various different conditions, and from these conditions develop
ideas that are absolutely way out and not true at all.'

Jean saw the presence of the 'guards' as reflecting badly on the families
themselves:

BRIGHTON SQUATTERS GO TO WAR

(for the homeless)

This morning six families moved into Ministry of Defence
buildings with the help of Brighton Squatters
This building was to have been auctioned
'for Private Speculation'.
It has now been aquired for homeless families.
More than the Ministry of Defence,
more than financial speculators,
Homeless families need these buildings.

4000 children are taken from their parents each year
because there are not enough houses to go round.

ESCALATE THIS WAR FOR THE HOMELESS

AGAINST THE MINISTRY OF DEFENCE
AGAINST PRIVATE SPECULATION

SUPPORT THE SQUATTERS

Figure 5.12

'This strikes me as the main trouble—what's going on at Wykeham Terrace at the moment. Try as you may, those families aren't just like normal families. If they were ordinary families living in that block, and a load of beatniks took over the end flat, they'd be out on their ear. They'd get together and get rid of them. It's a very unnatural situation.'

When it suited one of his schemes, Steve would consult Saul, or Dave, or Nick: when it did not, he would not. The anarchists resented this loss of control. They nicknamed Steve 'the blond bombshell', but they were no longer a cohesive group. There was little they could do about it. The business of finding houses for new families was no longer necessary. There were sufficient empty flats in Wykeham Terrace. Squatting became easy. Apart from 'guarding', the other activity for which they were essential was dissolving.

Evening Argus

EXTRA SPECIAL

Wednesday
July 23, 1969

Incorporating the
SUSSEX DAILY NEWS

Fivepence

'Petrol bomb army' waits for bailiffs

S QUATTERS armed with petrol bombs stood by today ready to fight any attempt to evict them from the old Territorial Army married quarters in Wykeham Terrace, Brighton.

The squatters and their Brighton Rents Project sponsors have barricaded the houses against bailiffs with nails and barbed wire.

The petrol bombs, said a spokesman for the project, "are for use under particular circumstances."

With the help of about 50 supporters of the Brighton Rents Project, seven squatter families occupied the property—about 100 yards from Brighton's Clock Tower—early on Saturday morning.

Guards stand by in "guard houses" quickly built on the roof. They are armed with sticks, stools—and petrol bombs.

An alarm system has also been rigged up in each flat to warn squatters of possible dangers and, to protect each flat, nails have been hammered through the front doors to prevent them being broken down.

Barbed wire has been strung around the entrance to the flats in the basement and around the sides of the properties.

SHOOT

But the public auction of the homes will go ahead· this afternoon—whether or not the squatters and Brighton Rents Project want it, Brighton auctioneers H. D. S. Stiles and Co., who are responsible for the sale, said.

"Unless they shoot us all, they can't stop it," a member of the firm said.

"I should imagine there will be some demonstrations, but this would not affect the auction in the slightest."

A spokesman for the Brighton Rents Project said that there definitely would be demonstrations outside the Old Ship Hotel, where the auction takes place at 3 p.m.

"Basically we're interested in stopping the auction—no matter what," he said.

AUCTION

Yesterday evening, the project sent a telegram to the Minister of Defence urging him to stop the auction and also calling on him to negotiate with the squatters for lawful possession of the property.

Project supporters have also drawn up a leaflet which will be handed out to members of the public today calling for support.

"When you read in the papers of people who tried to stop the auction at the Old Ship Hotel, decide that next time you'll be with them," it says.

The leaflet also condemns the sale of the property "while many

Squatters stand guard on the roof of the old married quarters, armed with staves and petrol bombs.

families iive in appalling conditions and others have no homes at all.

"It is even more scandalous that a Government department should encourage this property speculation and ignore the inhuman conditions suffered by many of this

nation's homeless."

● H. D. S. Stiles and Co. have said completition of the sale of the properties will be delayed until the buyer can have possession. Action through the courts is in hand.

Figure 5.13

14—EVENING ARGUS, Thursday, July 24, 1969

Jubilant squatters hail sale 'victory'

BUT NOW TERRITORIALS MAY TAKE LEGAL ACTION

LEFT: What am I bid? Mr. H. D. S. Stiles opens the auction sale. BELOW: Rent Project supporters handing out leaflets outside the auction room.

BRIGHTON Rents Project squatters last night claimed a victory after houses they are occupying in Wykeham Terrace were withdrawn from an auction sale. Bidding failed to reach the reserve price.

At the close of the auction a Rents Project spokesman said: "It went exactly as we planned. We intended to scare off any prospective buyer."

The houses, Nos. 7 to 12 Wykeham Terrace, are owned by the Ministry of Defence and were formerly used as married quarters for the Territorial Army. Six squatter families moved in last Saturday.

Yesterday's auction, held in the Old Ship Hotel Ballroom, Ship Street, Brighton, by H. D. S. Stiles and Co., lasted only 10 minutes.

Bidding was sluggish. It began at £20,000 and went no further than £25,000. The auctioneer, Mr. H. D. S. Stiles, then said the property would have to be withdrawn.

Lt.-Col. Nigel Ryle, secretary of the South-East Territorial and Auxiliary Volunteer Reserve Association, and Mr. Stiles said later that the property will now be put up for sale by private treaty. They declined to give the reserve price fixed for the auction.

OPPORTUNITY

Mr. Stiles added: "We did not expect the property would be sold today but thought it only fair that people who had spent a lot of time travelling should be given the opportunity to bid."

Lt.-Col. Ryle said solicitors had been instructed to take appropriate legal action against the squatter families.

Before the auction the Rents Project were thought to be planning a large-scale demonstration, but this did not materialise.

Uniformed and plainclothes police were on duty inside and outside the hotel, but little more than a dozen supporters of the Rents Project turned up.

Some found their way into the auction. When Mr. Stiles announced the properties would be withdrawn from the sale they cheered loudly and showered the audience with leaflets.

One jubilant protester said afterwards: "This has proved that action from a small group of working people helped by students can hinder the profiteering property market."

DELIGHTED

Particularly pleased with the result of the sale was Mrs. Maureen Hales, mother of three, who is at present living in one of the houses.

She told a reporter: "I am more than pleased. I am delighted. It is nice to know at least we have a few more weeks without worrying about bailiffs and barricades. It will be marvellous to live in peace, not so much for myself but for the children's sake."

A Rents Project spokesman said this would give them an opportunity to "negotiate with the Ministry of Defence for the use of Wykeham Terrace to alleviate the shortage of low-rent housing in Brighton."

He added that a letter had been sent to the Ministry of Defence, and Mr. Dennis Hobden, Labour M.P. for Kemp Town, was to take up the squatters' case in Parliament.

Black Dwarf will aid Rents Project

A London squatter, 37-year-old Michael Shrapnell, has come to Brighton for three days to drum up local support for the Brighton Rents Project. And to help him do this, he will be selling copies of Black Dwarf, the underground fortnightly newspaper founded by Tariq Ali. "I hope to raise between £30 and £40 for the Brighton squatters," he said. "This money would go towards buying domestic equipment and also to ensure that the squatters don't run low on food for their children."

Figure 5.14

Their resentment took the form of dragging Steve out of bed in the middle of the night and beating him up. They claimed they suspected him of being a police spy. Before the move to the Terrace, several new houses had been earmarked for occupation. But when the Squatting Group returned, the police were there. How did they know? After this incident, a meeting of the families and Project members was called. Those who participated in the attack on Steve were expelled. Everyone agreed that this sort of violence could not be allowed.

Many of the students who had been instrumental in founding the Project were away on vacation at this time. Visits to the Terrace by members of the Rents Registration Group—now by far the most active group away from the squat—became less and less frequent. There was simply very little to do there. Attempts to organize activity on the squat fell to Dave, Jonathan, and myself—apart that is from Steve. As more families came, we put out press statements, leaflets, and tried to initiate playgroups and general cleaning up activities—not with very much success.

As Jonathan put it:

'When I came back, Steve was a very significant person. The necessary keeping alive of the squat was being done by Steve and Mike. I remember going down and having several discussions with them. What worried me was the incredible tenseness and tension and real terror and fear around at that time. Steve was always bombing off on his escapades, even at that time. Going and plastering estate agents with posters, or beating up the Town Council, or having a confrontation with a police officer—when he should have been wearing a police uniform instead, I gather, but that's another matter. He'd go and do something stupid, and Mike and I, essentially, decided that what was needed was a fantastic cooling down of the whole temperature. Any talk about defences should be stopped. Everybody should be given the impression they were safe. Not *actually* safe, but the building of a social life at the squat was more necessary. I wouldn't necessarily say that the attack on the squat seemed unlikely—although I think it was—but the effects of fearing an attack were going to break the squat. It seemed to me that that must stop immediately. Everybody was at everybody else's neck. Nothing had been done except knocking down a few walls since they moved into Wykeham Terrace. I remember a group of us were very important in clearing out the centre and digging out a place to put dustbins. We initiated a sort of policy of clearing the place up, trying to create a crêche—there was a lot of talk about a playgroup for kids. I don't think the failure of this was quite as important as the fact that people did try and do it—the fact that there was a lot of talk about it. And then meetings began again, regular meetings on a regular basis, and there was an attempt to take things into this forum.

What was important at that time was that Steve seemed to be creating great hysterical situations which got us headlines—then we seemed to be responsible for them. We—Mike and I—spent most of our time unravelling hysterical press reports, and issuing counter statements.'

It was the ambiguity of the situation that gave Steve his chance. Would there be an attempt at violent eviction or not? We needed publicity, but when had it gone too far? Were the press distorting the stories, or was Steve doing it deliberately? Whenever we were *with* Steve the statements—and the stories that followed—were reasonable. From 19 July to 19 August, the Rents Project featured in the local papers almost every day. Some of the coverage was

Family of 7 camp out in welfare office

'I have decided to become one of the fighters'

ARGUS NEWS

" YOU see so many mums in Kemp Town with their children in tow, trudging along to the W.R.V.S. to get a few clothes. They've got no fight left in them, they are beaten. Then you see the squatters, who are angry and rebellious, determined to change things. I've seen both sides and I have decided to become one of the fighters."

Georgina Hickman is 26, unmarried and the mother of a two-year-old girl. She receives no maintenance or welfare assistance and earns roughly £11 a week. She pays £4 10s. for a single room in Paston Place, which includes the use of a bathroom, toilet and kitchen shared with five other adults and five children.

After rent, travelling expenses, nursery fees and heating costs, she is left with about £4 for food, clothing and basic necessities.

A few weeks ago Georgina went to a meeting of the Brighton Rents Project and, not for the first time, met people putting up with housing conditions as bad as, and sometimes worse than her own. People who, like herself, are on the Brighton housing list with no prospect of accommodation for years.

But just the fact that they were at the meeting made them different in one vital aspect—they had decided to do something about the housing situation in the town for themselves and for others.

AN OFFSHOOT

Since that meeting a small nucleus of families has been formed to fight bad housing. There is nothing official about their association and they are an offshoot of the Rents Project.

"The students are the backbone," says Georgina. "We need support from people who are not ignorant of legal things. But we feel that the fight for better housing should be mainly by the people who are living permanently in the town."

This small group, as yet unnamed, is hoping that more families will join their struggle. Eventually they want to form a joint bank account, raise joint mortgages to buy old houses, repair and redecorate them.

"Already we have plumbers, decorators, carpenters and various trades people in the group," she says. "We want to form pressure groups to get council co-operation, to work with squatters, to combine with the students, to fight against municipal council priorities, against fear of the profiteers, against fear of landlords and against ignorance of the legal aspects of housing and rents.

THE IMPETUS

"The Rents Project has given us the impetus by helping us to help ourselves," Georgina does not consider her own case to be particularly outstanding. But as mother, father and bread...

THEN THEY DISAPPEAR

A COUPLE and their five young children today squatted in Brighton's Welfare Offices in Princes Street.

They settled down on the floor to a lunch of fish and chips.

...hen officials went out to ...h the interior reception ...ns were locked, but no ...mpt was made to shift the ...ily.

...Mr. Robert Edwards, aged 45, ... Irish-born wife, Josephine, ...d Jacqueline (seven), Leslie ...ve), Stuart (three), Alison ...wo) and Lynn (aged two ...onths) prepared to stay, hop-...g for action.

IN ATTIC

Mr. Edwards this morning applied to Brighton Welfare Department for help.

"I was met with indifference," he said. "They told me they couldn't do anything for us. Now we intend to stay put here until we get some satisfaction. We'll stay overnight if we have to."

But, despite his intended resolution, Mr. Edwards and his family had disappeared when staff returned to the office after lunch.

Said Mr. R. N. Nicol, Director ... Brighton's Welfare Services: "No one actually saw them go. ...at they apparently left of their ...wn accord at about 12.45 p.m."

He added: "I don't have a ...ue where they have gone because ...ey didn't tell anyone."

Mr. Edwards' wife and children ...turned from Ireland yesterday to ...in him. He has a room in an ...ttic at Highcroft Villas, Brighton, ...ut it is not big enough for the ...mily.

Mr. Edwards said he was a ...urse, until recently, employed by ...ove Corporation. He and his ...mily had lived in a council flat ... Hangleton Road, an occupation-...ed tenancy.

ACTION

When he ceased to be employed ...y the corporation a court action ...as brought and he was given 28 ...ays to quit.

"Hove Welfare Department now ...as we are Brighton's responsi-...ility because I have a room in ...righton."

Mr. Edwards said he now earned ...15 15s. clear as a motor store-...nan. He paid £2 5s. for his attic ...oom. The family had not applied ...or social security benefit.

"I am now a Brighton resident, ...nd the way I see it Brighton ...orporation should help us," he ...aid. "If they won't I shall try ...nd contact Brighton Rents ...roject. I have read all about ...ow they help homeless families."

The Rents Project have installed ...amilies in empty corporation-...wned properties in the town.

It's squatting that unites the Leftists

BY DOUGLAS DAVIS

THE BRIGHTON RENTS PROJECT held its first public meeting in a conference room at Brighton's Royal Pavilion on May 6. Since then, through a series of dramatic and headline-catching events, it has managed to keep well in the public eye.

But what is the Brighton Rents Project? How does it function? Who makes it work? These questions tease angry councillors, irate locals who see squatting as part of an internal Communist plot, and even uncommitted moderates.

There are no ready answers to any of these questions and probably the only common denominator is that virtually all the campaign's supporters are " of the Left." It is, in fact, one of the few movements in the town which have been able to capture the committed support of all factions of the Left.

NO LEADER

The project has no leader, no constitution and no members-only supporters. It is because of this loose structure and lack of " hard line " policy that the movement has been able to contain such a width of opinion and ideology.

All supporters agree that everyone should have a decent home and that a roof over one's head is a right and not a privilege. And they all feel that squatting is the most effective way of highlighting the problems of families without homes or living in poor conditions. Beyond that there is little likelihood of unanimous agreement among supporters for a particular line of action.

One supporter, a radical Socialist, would like to see the organisation stimulate tenants to form associations among themselves and control their own homes : "They are the people who should form the Housing Committee," he said. A Marxist-Leninist sees the movement as eventually being absorbed into a wider political organisation and another Marxist-Leninist sees the fight of the Rents Project as a fight by the working classes against the bourgeoisie.

In Brighton, there are about 250 supporters—and probably about 250 reasons why they support the project and where they want to see the movement going.

INTENTIONS

Squatting can highlight the problems of housing, but in itself can solve nothing. So far, the movement has shied away from declaring any long-term intentions. Undoubtedly, this reluctance to look beyond the immediate activities stems from a fear that a clash of political goals could split the campaign into a myriad of squabbling sects.

MR. ROBERT EDWARDS

Figure 5.15

excellent, some good, some bad, and some left us with a distinct feeling of unease.

The most sympathetic stories carried on the tradition established in Terminus Road. They centred on the human plight of homeless families (Figure 5.15)—often in heartrending detail—or they gave prominence to the ideals and claims of the Rents Project. 'Good' stories had more to do with news, but gave our point of view (Figure 5.16).

'Bad' stories were loaded against us. The represented the views of the council, or the courts. They often gave currency to anti-squatting slogans—'Squatting is Jungle Law'; 'Squatters are trying to jump the housing queue'—or highlighted divisions within the Rents Project that we were trying to keep quiet about (Figure 5.17).

The editor of the local paper was distinctly less sympathetic than his journalists. The reviews of both sides of the case usually started with sympathy in small print and ended with condemnation in bold type (Figure 5.18).

But bad stories were to be expected. The most disturbing feature of this month was that, on the ground, nothing much seemed to be happening—yet the stories systematically escalated the scale of things. Those of us at the squat had a growing feeling of disbelief. There was a strange mixture of fact and fiction. It all started with the 'PETROL BOMB ARMY' headline. The next step, taken unilaterally by Steve, was the occupation of the three houses that backed on to the Terrace (Figure 5.19).

On the face of it, it was logical. The empty houses at the back might present a threat. The front of the Terrace was well defended, but empty houses butting onto the back yard were a loophole. It would be easy enough for a gang of unofficial bailiffs to sneak through early one morning. As Steve said, 'They've got to come in from the street now. They won't try anything dirty if they have to do it in public.' He had surveyed the houses on the first day with a couple of anarchists. All by himself he had found two families and moved them in. He *should* have consulted us. On the other hand it was logical. The houses were a threat; the families did need homes—even though there were still empty flats in the Terrace itself.

Then the Drill Hall was 'occupied'. Which is to say that Steve announced to the press that it was occupied. The Drill Hall also belonged to the Ministry of Defence. It had been used for drilling the Territorial Army, and it was huge. Double doors opened onto Queen Square, and were large enough to bring a tank through with space at the top and sides. Inside, the hall measured some 50 metres by 25 metres. At one end there was a large stage that opened into a labyrinth of ante-rooms.

The 'occupation' of the drill hall closed the last gap in the defences. All access to the squat was now through main doors on the streets. We were now a self-contained island. Sneak attack through other buildings was impossible. In addition, the Drill Hall would make an ideal meeting place. It would hold 1000 people easily, so we would no longer have to hire halls for public meetings. The kids could play there during the day. We could start our own cottage industries.

THE SQUATTERS GO TO TOWN

MEMBERS of Brighton Rents Project are seeing a representative of the Society of Labour Lawyers in London today with the aim of forming a deputation to meet Minister of Defence Mr. Denis Healey over their continued occupation of former Territorial Army married quarters in Wykeham Terrace, Brighton.

They are hoping to persuade Mr. Healey—and M.P.s sympathetic to the plight of the homeless—to make the Ministry-owned property available to homeless families.

On Wednesday the squatters claimed a victory when the seven flats at Nos. 7-12 Wykeham Terrace were withdrawn from a local auction because bidding failed to reach the reserve price. Bidding began at £20,000 but stopped at £25,000.

Afterwards, Lt.-Col. Nigel Ryle, secretary of the South-East Territorial and Auxiliary Volunteer Reserve Association, said the houses would be put for sale by private treaty and solicitors had been instructed to take legal action against the squatters.

The day before, Regency Ward Labour Party sent a telegram to Mr. Healey "begging" the withdrawal of the property from auction. Sale of public housing to speculators was indefensible.

The party, who have expressed all-out support for the squatting activities of the Rents Project, are giving £5 to the fighting fund.

Brighton Communist Party have asked Brighton Council whether they intend considering the Minister of Housing's request that all local authorities examine their empty properties with a view to making them immediately available to homeless families.

Following the news that legal proceedings may be taken, Rents Project members barricaded the houses with planks and barbed wire and a group of six "guards," armed with sticks and stools, have been positioned on the roof.

The spokesman said the Rents Project were unhappy about reports that the squatters were armed with petrol bombs. "Our campaign is a peaceful one and we intend to keep it so. We will only retaliate with force if there is any threat to human life."

Yesterday morning police visited the house. Said one Project member: "It was just a straightforward visit. There were no incidents."

Since they moved in at dawn on Saturday, Project members and other helpers have been carrying out improvements to the houses, including redecoration and work on the plumbing.

One of the mothers of the squatter families said: "We put our name on the council housing list eight years ago but they just didn't acknowledge our forms. My children have never had a home and that's why I'm happier than ever to be in a house like this."

Another mother said: "Where we are now you can come in, shut the door and say: 'This is home.' Many people think that the Rents Project are a group of long-haired layabouts but they're definitely not. They're a group of bloody good people."

Brighton's squatter situation is due to be raised in the Commons today by Cr. Dennis Hobden, M.P. for Kemp Town. He has put down a question for Housing Minister Mr. Anthony Greenwood, asking if he will extend to other local councils, including Brighton, his guidance on empty accommodation as already given to London authorities.

He is also asking if the Minister is aware that certain local authorities are erasing from their housing waiting list applicants who have featured in squatters' action, and if he will take steps to end this practice.

Squatters — and children — outside the ex-Territorial Army premises.

Figure 5.16

'JUNGLE LAW'—says judge in squatters' case

No further public meetings of the Project are arranged for the immediate future but the squat... ...n will be holding a party Square Drill Hall which the

leaders to dissociate themselves from the campaign and the International Socialist Group had told their members to squash squatting.

The spokesman mentioned they had had a few more requests for accommodation at the "occupied" properties but they ... now filled almost to capacity ... ly would have to be ... to be on a tem-

HOUSE squatting was described as "jungle law" Judge Harold Brown at Brighton on Friday be awarded Brighton Corporation damages agains families of squatters who occupied empty counc party in Railway Street of the defendants, Mr. Stephe

When he was now a squatter in Arm Prior, told him he was now a squatter in Brighton, the ju property to Railway Street, Brighton, the ju steps soon. Otherwise it will get out of hand It keeps to than someone will have to take ... with their place in the queue jumping ahead. That and can't be tolerated."

He awarded the corporation £26 Prior and his wife was not a ... to pay her rent for the corp Mr. Prior said he was Prior of Brighton and occupation fee, ... Membership of the occupier deal ... 21 years, he ... The judge awarded similar dam ... and Mrs. Donald Ware after ... Ald. Ward, Wykeham Terrace ... of occupier, an empty Terminus ...

by this township it of the rates offic petition. Dennis of the corpo Prior of Brig Brighton Rent said any member need a He had £5 He had b as long the prop they buil 6 and t What R

Squatters rap Rents Project

BRIGHTON squatters, Mr. and Mrs. Michael Chrismas, have attacked Rents Project supporters for "distorting the facts."

Yesterday Mr. Rex Gordo Robertson Road, forme mases, recei...

untrue," said Mr. Chrismas. "I want to issue a denial here and now as well as make a public apology to my former landlord, Mr. Knight.

'FACTS WERE TWISTED'

facts have all been twisted round. I anything like that. It's all lies. I want who wrote it and get them to make an

night has not brought any pressure on o make this statement. ...ived this pamphlet yesterday and came e in good faith. He naturally wanted name."

r Mr. Knight was considering taking the Rents Project over the pamphlet. it now be doing so," he said. "I d...

Council will not rehouse squatters

HOUSING squatters in Brighton who take over either corporation or privately - owned property will not be rehoused by Brighton Housing Committee.

The committee, without opposition, decided on this tough line after a special secret session on squatters at their monthly meeting. Earlier in the day two squatting families had been ordered by a judge to quit empty council-owned houses.

Ald. Stanley Theobald, chairman of the committee, said afterwards: "We intend to put squatting

they ca... ...t get a council house by squatti ...ow will think twice glad action what

The tee housi peop owni the priv peo ton exp

tion services in the town, Cr. Mrs. Gwynneth Ceccotti told him: "While we are spending money ... we could be building ... services of

Squatters to pay damages

TWO squatter families who "too' ordered by Judge H damages for s...

Brighton Corporation houses were County Court, to pay the corporation junction to prevent them returning

'TOO MUCH POLITICS'

...NCTIONS REFUSED

A SPLIT is widening inside Brighton Rents Project over policy and finance. Differences of opinion have grown up principally between leaders of the Project — which has installed 15 home less families in properties in Wykeham Terrace and Queen Square, Brighton — and members of the squatting group.

A member of the squatting group told the Gazette last night: "Many of us have become dissatisfied with the way the Project are using the whole campaign to their own political ends.

"It seems that they have chosen to put politics on a par with their concern for homeless families. The Rents Project want to dictate policy but the squatters want to remain as a self-governing group within the Project.

"As squatters we have looked on the campaign as a libertarian movement but with the emphasis on providing homes for the homeless."

The squatter spokesman said that members of the Communist and Marxist-Leninist parties had had directives from the local

Squatters are dissatisfied

objectives of the movement will be outlined.

● Mr. Andrew Bowden, prospective Conservative Parliamentary candidate for Kemp Town, hit out at the Project over the weekend when he claimed people were being innocent exploited by the Project for political ends. The Project was trying to pretend that it was non-political and that its only platform was to help people in need of houses," he said. ...ame you ...ou were a trespasser. If Brighton Corporation had been

judge added: "I gather he is so dissatisfied with the premises that there is no chance of him going back again."

When the judge awarded £10 damages against Mr. and Mrs. Brian Baker, stated to have occupied a house in Terminus Street, the judge said: "This man wrote to the town clerk saying: 'I have raw money as a squatter. I am writing to you for a rent.' What imper- tinence."

The judge said he would grant no injunction, "because I have no evidence here of any threat."

In the action against Mr. and Mrs. Donald Ware, now of Wykeham Terrace, Mrs. Ware was asked if she was moved into a house in Terminus Road by the Brighton Rents Project. She replied: "Yes."

PROJECT

Mr. Michael Walker (defending) to ked Mrs. Ware where she was living before. When she replied: "With my mother, and my hus- ...and was living in a bedsitter," the judge said: "I am not going to have complete irrelevancies aired in court. What is the relevance of this, Mr. Walker?"

The hearing was adjourned until tomorrow.

Earlier the judge had dis- missed an action for damages and an injunction brought against Mrs. Maureen Nihill, who was alleged to have occupied an empty house in Terminus Road. Mr. Walker: Hardship.

The judge: Perhaps some day some people suffering great hardship will walk into your property. This is preaching anarchy.

Mr. Walker said that rates were levied on the occupier, but there was a considerable amount of case law that rates could not be levied on "tran- sient occupiers." The council were on the one hand taking like some other organisations in the country they could have instructed half-a-dozen men and evicted you physically. In law they would have been guilty under a statute of Richard II, but I don't think any court would impose any sentence for it. There would have been no civil action at all.

"Did you want to be a martyr?"

Figure 5.17

In terms of the deep frustration which drives men and women into desperate action, there is a well of human sympathy for the squatters of the Brighton Rents Project.

Homeless and in need of urgent help, they have seen corporation-owned property standing idle and empty for months, even years, on end.

The provocation offered by such a state of affairs has erupted into the present highly inflammable situation.

But for the squatters now to maintain that they have a lawful right to occupy property in this fashion is a dangerous taunt to the patience of the authorities.

It threatens the security of every law-abiding citizen, and throws a menacing new spotlight on the inadequacy of the present laws protecting private property in this country.

If there is no criminal offence by the squatters in taking over council and Army property, what is to stop them moving into any unattended house?

The anarchy of an Englishman's home being his castle only if he is strong enough to hold on to it cannot be tolerated.

Figure 5.18

And so on and so on. It was a fantastic achievement—or so Steve said. The trouble was that he had not consulted anyone first. All the *reasons* were good. As always, it was logical. The other trouble was that the Drill Hall was not 'occupied' at all. There was no-one in it.

Steve got over this in his press statement. He simply announced that the Drill Hall had been taken over by 300 militant students from Essex University and the LSE. The papers swallowed it hook, line, and sinker. 'SQUATTERS BRING IN STUDENT GUARDS' blared the *Argus*. The *Brighton & Hove Gazette* had 'CONCERN OVER "PRIVATE ARMY"' as its front page lead (Figure 5.20).

This was Tom's reaction:

'I heard of it in the evening. The paper said "Army of Students" or something. I thought I'd go on my own, just to see who it was... if it was bands of people, have a chat, see what the situation was. I saw this thing as—talk about getting out of hand—really escalating. Pitched battles. The Brighton Rents Project being nowhere to be seen, and yet being completely demolished by people who had never heard of it. I'd never been to the Drill Hall. I thought I'd just go and have a look round. I went round the various sort of stairs and corridors. I was looking for people in all those various rooms. I was going round looking, and I heard a radio. I went right up to the top, right up into one of the houses. There was just a family there, only. And that was it. I'd been sitting on a bus waiting to go there, thinking "cor! fantastic!"—so what must the police have thought, if that's what I thought.'

Squatters upset milk race man

TWO SQUATTER FAMILIES — helped by the Brighton Rents Project—occupied an empty corporation-owned office building in Queen Square yesterday — and upset not only corporation officials but the organiser of next year's Milk Race.

BY DOUGLAS AND HELEN DAVIS

The organiser, Mr. M. A. Cumberworth, has rented the ground floor of the office building next door as his headquarters for the race—and there is access from one building to the other.

When Mr. Cumberworth arrived at his office today, he found that the basement door had been ripped off its hinges and some of his property—£800 worth of equipment for the race plus "irreplaceable records"—had been damaged.

MALICIOUS

" It would seem that someone has disturbed Mr. Cumberworth's belongings and caused malicious damage," a corporation spokesman said.

The extent of the damage had not been fully assessed but police were called in this morning and are investigating.

Mr. Cumberworth found a Brighton Rents Project " Campaign for Homes " poster on the front door of the building, and inside the building, on a door, an inscription has been painted : " No milk today. The race went that-away."

DISTURBED

Mr. Cumberworth, who is organising the race for the Milk Marketing Board, is debating whether or not to give up the 12-month lease on the premises.

" This is the world's biggest amateur cycle race," he said. " I am naturally disturbed that someone has broken into the office where I am storing a tremendous amount of equipment."

The spokesman said he did not think the corporation could offer Mr. Cumberworth alternative premises elsewhere in the town.

The properties were bought by the corporation from the Territorial Army about two years ago. They have been empty ever since.

The building backs on to the Wykeham Terrace flats which have been occupied by seven squatter families. The flats belong to the Territorial Army and came up for public auction last month, a few days after they moved in.

LANDLORD

The squatters who moved into the Queen Square property include a 22-year-old mother with three children, aged six, four and eight months. Her sister has also moved in.

The mother, who refused to give her name, said she had previously lived in a flat in Holland Road, Hove, which she had rented from tenants who were supposed to be living there.

" I paid rent to the tenant but it turns out that he never paid the money to the landlord," she said. " I have an up-to-date rent book. " I was taken to court and evicted in March." For a while the family lived with friends, until the friends, in their turn, were evicted.

ILLNESS

The other family who are squatting also come from Hove. The husband is receiving Social Security benefit because of illness and they have two children, aged two and one.

" The assistance is not enough to clear the rent, rates and feed us all," said his wife. "We fell behind on our rent and we were told we would have to get out."

A council spokesman said that " appropriate action " would be taken against the squatters.

Figure 5.19

The police were indeed worried. Three 'leaders' of the Project were summoned to meet the local Chief Superintendent. The 'leaders' were Steve, Buzz, and I—we happened to be around when the Panda car arrived. The interview was civil. We did not actually say there were no students—only that there were not as many as the press had said, and that they were not there to make trouble. He did not actually say that the police would intervene *to defend us* if we were attacked. He had a four o'clock shadow and a plain-clothes officer behind him took notes. He wanted to know our names and addresses: we lied. After the interview, a Panda car took us back to the Terrace. We issued a press statement: he contradicted it. *The Argus* announced 'POLICE WARN RENTS

Concern over 'private army'

Now family of seven join the 'squatters'

BRIGHTON police officers yesterday met leaders of the Brighton Rents Project in a move to cool the situation which is arising from the community of "squatters" and their "protectors" now in the Queen Square vicinity of the town.

The Project have taken over properties in the square and Wykeham Terrace, adjoining it at the rear, for homeless families.

And connecting the two is the empty, corporation-owned Territorial Army drill hall where the "protectors" are now staying. These are mainly students from Essex University, the London School of Economics and from Ilford—scene of a recent major "squat-in."

Brighton Corporation have already stressed that they will rely on court action to evict the "squatters" from the Queen Square houses and the drill hall. But this is likely to be delayed until after the summer recess in mid-September.

The Town Clerk (Mr. W. O. Dodd) said: " The corporation are immediately issuing proceedings for possession and damages." Last week Judge Harold Brown, at Brighton County Court, awarded damages to the corporation against three couples who had previously occupied houses near Brighton railway station.

The town clerk said: " The judge expressed himself very clearly to the squatters on that occasion." Last night a Project spokesman said they would be appealing against Judge Brown's decision.

The corporation bought the drill hall last May for development as a sports centre but the proposal has been shelved for a year. Two of the properties in Queen Square were intended for youth offices and the third house is occupied on the ground floor by the organiser of the national cycling Milk Race.

The corporation were relying on court action to secure the return of their property. If they had chosen to adopt strong-arm tactics to evict "squatters," as was tried at Redbridge, they could have found themselves in a battle with the student " guards " camping in the drill hall.

It was this situation which yesterday led to the meeting between the police and the Project members.

A police spokesman told the Gazette afterwards: " We pointed out that it is the responsibility of police to maintain law and order in the town no matter who calls upon them and said we have no desire to see any disorder in Brighton.

" WE WERE ALARMED BY REPORTS THAT THE PROJECT WERE BUILDING UP A PRIVATE ARMY."

In a statement issued after the meeting the Project leaders said they reiterated that their campaign was not of a violent nature but was directed at solving the chronic housing shortage.

Yesterday, too, the Project leaders claimed that representative from Stiles and Co., the estate agents acting for the Ministry of Defence over the sale of the Wykeham Terrace properties, had tried to enter the building and caused " considerable distress " to women on the premises.

Only one young man was on the forecourt at the time, say the Project.

A spokesman from Stiles and Co. last night refused to comment.

The agents are planning to sell the property — recently withdrawn from an auction because it did not reach the desired price—by private treaty.

The Project are now planning a teach-in on "squatting" to take place in the drill hall. The students already there are expected to be joined by more next week.

They also have plans for providing an adventure playground for Brighton children in the hall, they want to stage plays there and put on dances.

Cr. Danny Sheldon, who is chairman of the council's Corporate Estate Committee responsible for the drill hall and Queen Square houses, this week

called for tougher laws against " squatters."

" I don't think the courts or the public will tolerate this sort of behaviour much longer," he said. " There is no doubt in my mind that legislation will soon have to be introduced to make penalties higher if this sort of thing continues."

● Residents in Wykeham Terrace, next door to the squatters, had another cause for complaint this week. A new discotheque opened opposite their flats in a converted church. Its name: Sloopy's. Residents complained about the noise of people leaving at 2 a.m. Others thought it might bring down the value of their property. The owner, Mr. Charles Casson said: " Brighton is short of decent entertainment and this is decent entertainment."

RENTS PROJECT IN 'KEEP IT COOL' MEETING

A COUPLE with five children who have been trying for the past three years to find somewhere to settle are Brighton's latest "squatters."

The couple, Mr. Robert Edwards and his wife, Josephine, and Jacqueline (aged seven), Lesley (five), Stuart (three), Alison (two) and Lynn (aged two months) called at the Wykeham Terrace " headquarters " of Brighton Rents Project yesterday afternoon, and sighed with relief when they were told by Project supporters that they could be accommodated in the former Territorial Army married quarters.

" Our acceptance of accommodation was like a dream come true," said Mr. Edwards.

Earlier in the day the family had called at Brighton's Welfare Department in Princes Street in search of accommodation. " We were met with indifference," said Mr. Edwards. " The official just wouldn't say anything."

Their visit to the Welfare Offices was the climax of a particularly gruelling week.

Up to the middle of last week, the family had been living in a council flat in Hangleton Road, which Mr. Edwards was given while employed as a nurse by Hove Corporation. He has now left the job and works as a motor parts man at a garage in Kingsway, Hove.

He stayed on at the occupation-tied flat but at the beginning of last month a court action was brought and he and his family were given 28 days to quit.

When possession expired last Wednesday, Mrs. Edwards took

CONTINUED ON BACK PAGE

The Edwards family outside Brighton Welfare Offices yesterday. From left: Mr. Edwards, Alison (two), Stuart (three), Jacqueline (seven), Lesley (five) and Lynn (two months).

Figure 5.20

Police warn rents squad

‹CHIEF SUPT. WILLIAM ROSTRON yesterday summoned three leaders of the Brighton Rents Project to his office and warned them of the dangers of a build-up of a "private army" of squatter supporters.

The private army—believed to consist mainly of students from Essex University and the London School of Economics—are staying in the corporation-owned Territorial Army Drill Hall, next to Wykeham Terrace and Queen Square properties occupied by squatters.

Following the meeting a spokesman for the Rents Project issued a statement claiming that Chief Supt. Rostron had given an assurance that the police force would intervene if any moves were made to evict the squatters without court sanction.

These remarks were strongly denied by Chief Supt. Rostron, who told a reporter last night: "That is not what I said.

"My words have been taken out of context so that they mean something entirely different. We would only intervene if there was a breach of the peace. Our job is to maintain law and order. We

THE DANGERS OF 'PRIVATE ARMY' BUILD-UP

do not want to see people fighting in the streets.

CONCERNED

" I called the leaders to my office because I have become increasingly concerned about the reported build-up of a private army of 'protectors.' I thought it was time we drew the attention of the leaders to the role of the police."

Chief Supt. Rostron added that he had been assured by the Rents Project there was no such build-up taking place.

A spokesman for the Rents Project, at a special Press conference called last night, following the meeting with Chief Supt. Rostron, repeated that their campaign was not violent. It was directed at solving the chronic housing shortage in the town.

Last night a Project spokesman said that they would be appealing against a Brighton County Court order that squatter families should pay Brighton Corporation damages for trespass.

He also said that after a deputation from the Rents Project had

CHIEF SUPT. ROSTRON—a warning

complained to Brighton's Deputy Town Clerk that squatter dustbins were not being emptied, a corporation dustcart visited the properties yesterday and cleared away all the rubbish.

Figure 5.21

SQUAD' (Figure 5.21): Steve shrugged the whole thing off. I did not like the feel of it at all.

That evening we christened the Drill Hall with a party. Social security, homelessness, squatting, dust, damp, and worry all combine to make people look drab. The party gave the families a chance to dress up and enjoy themselves. Don dug out some fairy lights to go with the wine and music. It was fun. Some of us had wanted a meeting to discuss the latest developments. As the evening went on the party seemed a better idea. After all, the families were getting together. A social life was being established. The meeting was put off for a couple of days.

The next day Steve whistled off to the Houses of Parliament. He enlisted the support of our local MP, who gave him a statement of support, and promised to speak at our next public meeting. Steve fixed the date for 19 August, only nine days away (Figure 5.22).

Hobden slams the churches

CR. DENNIS HOBDEN, Labour M.P. for Kemp Town, hit out last night at Brighton's churches for not showing an interest in helping the homeless.

Addressing a 100-strong public meeting of Brighton Rents Project, the ginger group who have organised the occupation by squatters of council-owned buildings, Cr. Hobden said Brighton was faced with

'SELLING OUT TO PROPERTY SPECULATORS'

CR. HOBDEN

an emergency situation. "Yet not a single voice can I find raised by a minister of the church," he declared.

"When are the churches going to speak out? Aren't they concerned with the problem of homelessness in this town?

SILENCE

"Evidently they have learned nothing from 2,000 years of history. Why the deathly silence? Talk about no room at the inn! In Brighton you can't even get near the manger.

"I said there is a deathly silence from the churches. Yet you can hear the jingling of their cash registers as they sell off their sites to the property speculators.

"This is not to help the homeless poor but for personal profit. It is time they pulled themselves together and got to the basis of their own philosophy if they are really concerned with the ordinary people."

Cr. Hobden said that in Brighton affluence existed alongside "the squalor which we all see around our back streets," and he warned: "Unless something positive is done, an ugly situation could emerge."

RUN OUT

He said: "It is not up to the town council to be aloof and ignore the people who have elected them."

Criticising the number of empty council-owned houses in the town, Cr. Hobden said Brighton had virtually run out of building land.

"There has got to be a lot more clearance of the older parts of the town, and multi-storey flats built to take more people. But people must not be cleared out of their homes until demolition is scheduled to begin, and demolition must not begin until the redevelopment scheme can start."

He described as "ludicrous

the number of houses bought by the corporation for redevelopment schemes which had been empty for years because the schemes had still not gone ahead.

Cr. Hobden said his support for the Rents Project group had caused some raised eyebrows, but he "was amazed at the small politicians who had said tut-tut."

It had caused "terrific embarrassment to the Parks Committee," of which he was a member. "But I have declared my support, and I still support the Rents Project," he said.

"My support is not unqualified, but on the other hand the project have held me in suspicion and some of them have called me names.

"But I do believe there is a need for a continuing dialogue between myself and the Rents Project, and I back them in what they have done to draw attention to the problem of homelessness in Brighton."

REGISTER

Cr. Hobden said Brighton Welfare Services Department were not doing their job. He declared: "They have not got the houses, and so they cannot fulfil their obligation."

He referred to the large number of shops in the town with living accommodation above which was not being used, and called for an accommodation register to be launched by the council, with all estate agents contributing.

The meeting was held at the Drill Hall in Queen Square, near the Clock Tower—a building which the Rents Project are occupying.

Members of the group reported that there were now 15 families, with 21 children, "squatting" and that they intend publishing fact sheets on Brighton's housing problem, based on their research.

Listening to Cr. Hobden's speech at a public meeting held by Brighton Rents Project last night

Figure 5.22

This latest news somehow eclipsed the 'Private Army' scare. Since Steve had fixed a date for the meeting, we had to get on with the preparations. Dave prepared a huge banner, and signwrote the Project's name on the Drill Hall doors. Tom did the leaflets. Instead of talking about Steve, we talked in general terms. 'There was a low level of democracy', 'Information was too centralized', 'There was a need for political education'. Gary and Colin offered to set up an Education Group. Its first meeting would be in two days.

The first meeting of the Education Group was also its last. We met at 7.30 in the Drill Hall. Ten people turned up. Gary and Colin were sitting on one of the trestle tables. We were discussing the programme of meetings when Steve rushed in. One local paper—the *Herald*—had always been very critical of the Rents Project. Steve had gone to see them. He had threatened that their journalists would be excluded from all future press conferences unless they gave us a full page to explain our case. Amazingly, they agreed. The only snag was that the copy had to be at their office by 10.00 the next morning. Steve looked round and grinned. 'Well,' he said, 'lets start!' That was the end of the Education Group.

We stayed up all night and wrote the article. Each of us took a separate section. As each piece was finished Dave bashed it out on my old typewriter. At 9.55 the next morning five dishevelled ex-members of the Education Group delivered the copy. The *Herald* printed it all—and proudly announced they were doing so on their front page (Figure 5.24).

Another undoubted success. We were so pleased with the content and layout that we bought several hundred copies of the paper, and used it instead of leaflets at our next meeting. Apart from anything else it was cheaper. This was another step up the ladder. Chris and Ken from the Rents Registration Group came over to congratulate us. Our confidence grew. What was not possible? We had got away with the 'Private Army' stories—they hardly seemed worth quibbling about now; our MP was backing us; we we writing our own stories in the Press. Steve had regained our confidence, even if the *Herald* piece had been another unilateral action. The families were happier and were settling in; each day that passed without a summons increased their feeling of security.

Steve started talking about hiring a plane and showering Westminster with leaflets. He claimed to have a pilot's licence. In the event he contented himself with generating more headlines. He moved more families in—or claimed to have done so. Then he announced that we had the 'biggest squat of all' (Figure 5.25). We were feeling more relaxed now, and got on with our preparations for the public meeting. A local church was being modernized. Dave managed to get hold of 200 old chairs, and several assorted pews for seating. We were busy moving them in on the evening of the meeting when Tom rushed in waving the *Evening Argus*: 'Twin bomb blast rocks Brighton Service Offices' (Figure 5.26). 'Steve!' he said. Finally it had all gone too far.

Decline

Retrospectively, it is clear that the bomb incident marked the turning point of the squat. The bombs probably did more damage to the morale of Project members than they did to the army and navy offices into which they were thrown. Before 19 August, actions had been expansionist and optimistic. Mistakes had been made, silly things done, and some disagreements were sustained, but none of it really mattered. Each problem—like the original court orders—had been overcome by an escalation of the situation. One line of events reached their climax with the 'Anatomy of a Squat' supplement in the *Herald*.

ANATOMY OF A SQUAT

The actions of the Brighton Rents Project have been in the headlines since they began moving squatter families into Corporation-owned houses in June. The Herald has been strongly critical of the group, who in return have claimed that the Press has been biased in its treatment of them. This newspaper has, in fact, published many reports containing accounts of the Project's intentions and objectives. But on this page today, for the first time in any local newspaper, we invite the Project members themselves to present their case, to state their aims, to explain their structure.

BRP IS FOR KEEPS

THE Brighton Rents Project is for keeps. It is not an experiment or a protest movement. Our final aim is a total change in the distribution of housing and the economics of housing.

The B.R.P. is enthusiastic, and make up for lack of money by hard work. We do not employ furniture removers, we move furniture in borrowed vans, even by hand. Our publicity is not paid ads, in newspapers or on television, but real people trying to get homes, word and mouth and handing out leaflets in the street.

The B.R.P. is democratic. All the major decisions are taken in mass meetings and votes. Everyone can speak. Sometimes it is chaos, often it is boring. But everyone is involved. No one is told to do something without knowing why.

The B.R.P. is anxious, it has housed 12 families, and many more are on the waiting list. Until the Council accepts its responsibilities to these families, or is defeated (we shall be putting up candidates for the next elections), we accept full responsibility for these families. We are anxious lest Hitler-style bailiffs swoop and put them out on the street.

We are anxious in case our efforts to defend the families, our barricades and guards, should offend the public.

The B.R.P. is friendly. Everyone is welcome to come and talk with us, to put their point of view. The B.R.P. is open with its problems — coming together, and deciding to do something about it is — a sort of trade union for tenants.

Case history No. 1

ONE year ago Mr and Mrs Warre (then aged two and 12 months) were evicted from their two children. Mr Warre, a 37-year-old engineer, had had a dispute with his landlord and refused to pay the rent. The landlord got a new home then started.

The difficulties they encountered are typical of thousands of young families in a similar situation. Mr Warre took two weeks off work while he visited different flats, looking for a home for his family. In most cases the landlord wasn't interested as soon as he heard that there were two young children.

Living apart

And if he did offer accommodation the rent was far too high. In the meantime Mrs Patricia Warre moved with the children into her mother's house in Brighton, but Mr Warre had to live apart from them in a bed-sitter. Working a very long day, seven days a week, he could hardly see his children at all. "I think my boy had got to the point where as an uncle who visited him once a week, he doesn't think of me as his father," says Mr Warre.

This put a great strain on their marriage, because they just grew further and further apart. Mrs Warre used to go down and visit her husband in his bed-sitter. "It was so cheap." At the end of June the B.R.P. heard about this and could not take any more of this they would squat. They are now happily living in Wykeham-terrace.

QUESTION AND ANSWER ABOUT THE SQUATTERS

Q: But they are jumping the housing queue. . .

A: The housing queue is at least 1,021 families and six years long. Some jump! On the other hand, there are 2,500 empty houses in Brighton. Four times as many empty houses as people on the list. Some of these are against people who own and build huge blocks of luxury flats, then leave them empty to force prices higher. The serious part is that an absolute right to his house. The special right of private, public or an odd structure of it easily guards his empty flats and houses, while ordinary

'We do not want violence'

WE do not want violence. We are very much aware, from the "scare" headlines that have appeared in the papers. We would rather get on with our own business than fight with bailiffs, rather operate a printing press than build barricades. If we are attacked we will fight back, but we will simultaneously dial 999 and hope that the police will do their duty, and maintain (or restore) the peace.

We have contacted the Ministry of Defence, and although they were a little dubious, confirmed to us that we could not afford to buy Wykeham-terrace (after which we must of course follow proper procedure) and go through an M.P. If it turns out that some members of our Labour Government still remember what Socialism is about.

We have also been told by the Council that our proposals are too

the housing problem, both specific and general, will be considered by the Housing committee at their next meeting. We hope that we have now come around for long enough for the Council to take us a little more seriously than they did at first.

Our plans for the future include a play school for the children, a massive better campaign, the formation of a theatre (and perhaps a film) group to give public open-air performances, and a national summer conference on housing.

Above all, we shall ensure that the families now squatting will never again find themselves without a roof, without a home, or separated by force of the circumstances of being born at the "bottom" end of the social ladder.

If the B.R.P. survives in maturity as a political movement it will not be much to the advice, participation, and even the leadership of these families.

In one of the houses in Wykeham-terrace: Sarah, with Justin (two) and Alexandra, who is eight months.

YOU JUDGE

"HAVE the squatters really helped?" This was the question posed in the previous issue. We ask. But helped whom? We haven't helped the landlords, that is sure. Our objective is to establish the Project's view. The Press naturally wish to protect themselves. Their view is that the real answer to the housing problem of the mass of people, to expose the nature of the system directly, and to join with people in solving it.

It is clear which side is responsible for the problem—but the squatters, by no means the landlord wish to protect the problem. . . . "Project members should consider whether their actions were to the best in . . . would bring trade to local businessmen—e.g. the Milk Race)—or for housing people.

Case history No. 3

AN elderly couple, Mr and Mrs Williams, who have been the boarding for nine years, recently approached the B.R.P. They had been living in very bad conditions for a long time. Their flat was very seriously damp, and through the kitchen, the drain stank and overflowed, and the rent

BRP: history and structure

THE beginnings of the B.R.P. can be traced back to the summer of 1968, when an initial survey found that the 1965 Rent Act provisions were virtually unknown to and unused by Brighton tenants. The major user of this Act, designed to protect tenants, was the landlord to force rent increases. The "jungle law"—the Tribunals—which put in such a way that the first one to get his application in the one comes off best.

The initial survey was

The national situation

THE housing situation in the United Kingdom has now become so intolerable that people have, all over the country, cast aside bureaucracy and substituted "direct action" as the only means of getting things done and have found that it is working.

Belfast: At present 15 families are squatting here and as yet no violence has erupted which has any connection with the occupation of council houses.

Ulster: Squatting is not against the law. If it is an offence at all it is a civil, not a criminal offence, between the private landlord and the squatter. The council cannot take action in civil courts.

Case history No. 2

MARGARET is 25 years old. After three years of marriage she separated from her husband because of his alleged adultery. She took the four children, aged two years, and went to live in a furnished room...

No help

At the beginning of 1967 they approached the Housing Manager...

Searched in vain

About a year ago the Williams were informed that they deeply decided that...

Eviction

Both families were evicted—Margaret's family for the £34 rent arrears and asked if she could put her things into store...

Lewisham: The council capitulated and have offered the squatters all the empty houses—rent free.

Manchester: Mrs Mary Jordan moved into an empty N.C.B.-owned house with the help of the N.C.B....

Ilford. An agreement has been reached with R.B.C. which has meant the rehousing of the Fleming and McNiel families and the opening of all empty redevelopment property.

Fulham: Mrs Foster, who was until last Wednesday squatting, was rehoused at the council's instigation.

Brighton: Fifteen families are squatting—more to come.

South Wales: Three families are at present occupying premises that were lying empty and to the likelihood of their being used.

DIVIDED

Squatting has highlighted the sort of unfortunate families the sort of council houses are facing, and are all over the country...

EMPTY

What does this housing problem after from? On the national level it is estimated that...

VIOLENCE

It is against the law to evict squatters without a court order...

Birth

Finally, May 1969, a public meeting was held in the Pavilion. Over 200 people attended...

OBJECTIVE

To come back to our objective. Take the squat in Queenspark...

Groups

Such was the Council's answer to the request of 2,000 people...

Rents Registration Group.

This group has continued the tradition of survey, discussion with tenants about conditions...

Squatting Group.

The occupation of Wykeham-terrace is the first major landmark in the history of the movement...

Finance Committee.

Assistance

OUR 10 DEMANDS

1. That the Council immediately use all their houses (and just those involved with the Housing or Planning Committee) to provide homes for the people of Brighton.

2. That the Council recognise in public that the development and the renovation of unused housing...

Figure 5.24

'Biggest squat of all' claim

WITH 15 squatter families installed in flats in Wykeham Terrace and Queen Square, Brighton, the Brighton Rents Project are now claiming the biggest squat in the country.

They estimate that well over 100 people—squatters, helpers and guards—are now living in properties they have seized from Brighton Council and the Territorial Army over the past six weeks.

The project have claimed to be drawing on support from students at the London School of Economics and Essex University. Many of them, they claim, are employed by Brighton Corporation as waiters, deckchair attendants and kitchen porters.

But a spokesman for the corporation said today there had not been an unusually large number of students applying for jobs.

At present, about 25 were being employed by the corporation, he said. " We have applications for jobs almost every day from students. But this is not unusual for this time of the year."

DEMANDS

Support for the project has been enlisted from Labour M.P. for Kemp Town, Cr. Dennis Hobden, who has agreed to negotiate with the Ministry of Defence, on behalf of the squatters, for permanent occupation of the Wykeham Terrace properties.

The Rents Project themselves have sent a list of demands to Brighton's Town Clerk, Mr. W. O. Dodd, which will be forwarded to the meeting of the Housing Committee next month.

They are demanding the council recognise " in public " that the idea and stimulus for the renovation of unused development property has come from the project.

They are also demanding that:
● The council accept the principle that a house is a basic right of every individual, and that they take all possible steps towards the immediate realisation of this principle in practice;
● All empty private property be rated;
● A representative of the Brighton Tenants' Association be an ex-officio m e m b e r of the Housing Committee with right of veto on all matters concerning council housing;
● No one with commercial vested interests (i.e. estate agents, building contractors) be on the housing or planning committees, except in a purely temporary or advisory capacity;
● A stop is made to all luxury development u n t i l no one remains in need of housing in Brighton;
● The housing list be opened to everyone and that no qualifications be necessary.
● As a gesture of good faith, the council publicly renounce all claims to costs and damages awarded a g a i n s t squatting families, and recognise the public service rendered by these families in bringing the housing problem to the attention of Brighton.

Figure 5.25

Possibilities seemed limitless—'revised' demands had appeared in the 'biggest squat of all' story. Brighton Council had to

recognize in public that the idea and stimulus for the renovation of unused development property has come from the Project.

The other line of events—the semi-fantasies about 'petrol bomb armies'—reached its climax in the bombing. After that the initiative passed increasingly into the hands of the authorities. The Project suffered blow after blow until it finally disintegrated. Tom was right. It was 'Steve!' We knew some hours before the police arrested him. Not that there was any evidence. It was just that he made sure everyone saw the paper. He didn't *say* he had done it. He just made it clear he was very pleased about it—and that he expected to get away with it.

What had actually happened? There were several stories: the most likely is that he had come to see himself as a famous revolutionary. Between arranging the public meeting on his trip to Westminster and the attack, he had roared off to a weekend anarchist camp in Cornwall. His long list of exploits must have been very impressive. He needed something to cap the story. What better than a

Evening Argus

SPECIAL

Tuesday
August 19, 1969

incorporating the
SUSSEX DAILY NEWS

Fivepence

Twin bomb blast rocks Brighton Service offices

By PHIL MOGER

BOMBS exploded in a Brighton street late last night and early today during twin terror raids on the town's Army and Navy Recruiting Offices.

The raids were in the same street—Queens Road—and within hours of each other.

Early today a bomb was hurled against the window of the Navy and Royal Marines Careers Office.

It shattered the window but crashed back on to the pavement sending a sheet of flame roaring up the side of a wall—just yards from where 16 hotel guests were sleeping.

Earlier, a few hundred yards away on the other side of the road another bomb had been poked through the letter box of the Army Careers Office.

Detectives and fingerprint experts were called out in the middle of the night and spent several hours at the scene.

Police searched the pavements and gutters for signs of bomb-making equipment. Both bombs were believed to be crude home-made ones.

From outside the Navy Office police took away a charred length of wire.

Mr. and Mrs. Joseph Killick were in their rooms at the Stafford Hotel, Queen's Road, next to the Navy Office, when the bomb exploded.

Said 61-year-old Mr. Killick, a fireman, of Erith, Kent, " there was a tremendous explosion. Then a great sheet of flame which lit up the room. My wife looked out of the window and saw a great cloud of smoke."

The man in charge, Lt. W. E. Wilson, said: " The front window bay was in an awful mess."

EXPLODE

At the Army Office, Mrs. Irma Watts, 49-year-old wife of R.S.M. George Watts, said: " I looked out of the window and said to George: ' I can see smoke.'

. " I went out of the bedroom— we live in married quarters above the office—and a great cloud of smoke rushed up the stairs. My husband came rushing down to the 'front and we could see the fire in the letter box."

A few hours after the bomb was pushed through the letterbox of the Army Office two men in a mini van pulled up outside, opened the offside door, looked at the building and then roared off.

A police spokesman said: " Two men are in custody assisting us with our inquiries."

Firemen were called to sheet up the front window of the Navy Office. It is believed the explosions are not connected with the Irish troubles.

A tarpaulin covers a gaping hole in the R.N. recruiting office, in Brighton's Queen's Road

Figure 5.26

bomb? The least likely story—one that he told in court—was that he had been a reluctant participant; that he had substituted harmless smoke bombs for the original fire-bombs. Unlikely on two counts: since it was his idea and he organized it, it is difficult to see how he was reluctant;· there was no substitution—fire-bombs were used. His other story was that he was an informer for the Metropolitan Police and the Special Branch. That had a grain of truth to it. Except that most of the information must have been about his own activities, which would make him an agent provocateur, not an informer. It would also explain why he expected to get away with it, and why he did not bother to make a secret of it.

What was established was that Steve had sent two Hell's Angels, on a bright-yellow motor-cycle combination to bomb the army offices at midnight. They made a mess of it, so he sent them back to have a go at the navy offices. Steve had come across the Hell's Angels dossing in the Drill Hall. He said it would be a 'good laugh'. Since there were dozens of police outside the army office by the time the Angels got back and 'had a go' at the navy office (which was just down the road) it is not surprising they were caught almost immediately. Especially on their bright-yellow bike. The next day, in his capacity of police informer, Steve led the police to a further cache of bombs that he had hidden at Shoreham—so they arrested him.

We were rid of Steve, but the mud stuck. Steve had been a leading figure in the Project. There had been earlier headlines about armies and bombs. It was no use saying they were Steve's fault—although we tried.

> It is true that. . the family were helped to squat by the Project and it is deplorable that he abused the protection of the Project by spreading totally false and ludicrous rumours about a private army and by implicating the Project in this bomb incident.
> We feel that as members of the Project we ought to say that the incidents referred to had no connection with any policy or action of the Project. ... We rebut in the strongest terms any attempt to connect the Project with the incident....
>
> (letter in the *Evening Argus*, 21 October 1969)

To no avail. Every time the case came up it was linked with Rents Project both in court and in the press reports. Looking back, it is easy to ask how Steve ever got into the position to do so much damage.

> 'The first time I saw Steve he was done up in a suit, had a car outside, and was smoking the best fags money could buy. Somebody said he was going to be a Labour MP or something. I went away on holiday, came back, and met him on a bus. He was excited, telling me all the fantastic things he'd been doing. He obviously thought of himself as the leader of the Project. He informed me he was a squatter himself. I also heard he had a nanny and was a Company Director... people looking back now can say "Blime! You should have known he was a bit fishy", but you could have said that of dozens of people.'
>
> (Terry)

And of course Terry was right. There was no way we could check up on people. The best we could do was try and make sure no-one unreliable got into responsible positions. As we have seen, that was not entirely successful. It is always a lot easier to see these things afterwards. The most usual reaction of the

Project was to censure people for acting out of line. This was done once or twice, but was never very wholehearted. For one thing, it was a formal action in a situation that was usually informal. Since part of the Project thought it should be formal, and another part—the squatting group—thought it should be informal, the stage was already set for a fight between factions. An attack on a member of a group would be taken as an attack on the whole group. Rather than split the Project, the matter was usually dropped. Another complicating factor was that out-of-line actions—such as the escalation of squatting in Terminus Road or Steve's scare stories—were always in some way justifiable, if only because they were successful.

The other sanction was to expel people from the group entirely. This happened twice. Ironically, one expulsion had been of the people who dragged Steve out of bed in the middle of the night. Their excuse was that he was a police agent.

The day after the bomb incident we held the public meeting in the Drill Hall. The main speaker was the local MP. More than 100 people turned up. Our occupation of the Drill Hall was truly legitimized. We should have been pleased, but we were not. We were too worried. The meeting went well, all our main points were reiterated. 'Hobden slams the Churches' was the way it got reported.

But the real business of the moment, the underlying fears, were dealt with the next night at the Squatting Group meeting. All the families came, and all sections of the Project were represented. We finally reached a consensus that the bombing really had nothing to do with us. As John put it:

> 'We can't be blamed because criminal elements get attached to us, any more than the Mayor of Brighton can be blamed because criminal elements get attached to Brighton.'

The police thought differently. Over the next months virtually every member of the Project they could find was interviewed. Nothing more came of the bomb incident. But several other crimes were discovered (or rediscovered). Buzz paid the penalty for his involvement in the 'petrol bomb army' story: borstal. Other minor charges were laid against other people. Although none of the main actors in the story were finally charged, the interviews were worrying. It now seemed that *some* of the things we had done *might* be crimes. Imagine yourself on the end of this line of questioning.

> 'I am trying to get the idea of this new slant on procedure at meetings, where there is no agenda, there is no chairman, there is no secretary, there are no minutes, a free and easy atmosphere. Quite unlike meetings that I've normally attended. I accept that this sort of meeting takes place, and there is nothing wrong with it—as far as I can see—providing you've all got good memories, *because someone, other than me, is going to ask all these questions.* At some time or other. And whilst you can say to me "I don't remember" or "I can't recall" *someone is going to be far more persistent.*'

Hints that made you worry. Dave was arrested and then not charged. Terry, a shop steward, was visited at his place of work by uniformed police (the Trades Council complained about that). It was quite difficult to carry on 'as usual'. But that's what we all tried to do.

The families were worried too. Nothing much *actually* changed, but a sort of cut-off point between optimism and pessimism had been passed. It's much easier to tolerate present discomfort when you have great expectations of the future. John and I tried to get some self-help activities going.

> 'We initiated an attempt to clear the place up, to start a crèche, get the dustbins organized, and things like this. After about a week or two, we were both going round saying we hadn't really succeeded. Alright, we had done a lot of work, and cleaned the place up, but it just seemed so apparent that it was not in fact penetrating through to the families.'

> (John)

There were (by the way) now ten families in all. It was easy to lose count, especially since one of Steve's 'biggest squat' stories had said there was fifteen. One can only suppose he counted some of the couples involved as guards, since there was always a grain of truth in his stories. There were the six families who had moved from Terminus Road. Steve had helped two more move into the Queen Square houses that consolidated the back of Wykeham Terrace (Figure 5.27). Paul and Libby and their two children took one house, Maggie and her three children moved into the centre house. Later Betty and her husband joined us themselves, taking the last house. Bob, Josephine, and their five children had come to us when they lost their tied house and were refused help by the Welfare Office—which had been another main story in the *Argus*. They took the last empty flat in the Terrace itself.

The lack of communal activity—or its failure to catch on—was reflected in the size of the squatting group meetings. At the large meeting after the Steve fiasco we decided to have bi-weekly meetings to keep a check on things. Twenty turned up for the first one, then eleven, then five. Finally no-one turned up. Then the council indirectly suggested talks. They let it be known through the press that they would 'unofficially' meet people from the Rents Project who gave their right names and addresses. We leapt at the chance.

The local authority, for the first time, had the initiative. Instead of acting we were responding. Over thirty people came to the meeting within twenty-four hours of the offer. The outcome appeared in the *Argus* (Figure 5.28):

'RENTS MEN WELCOME HOUSING CHIEF TALKS'

A recall meeting of some twenty people was held five days later. Chris had written a long document—a further statement of our position—which was discussed and then sent on to the council.

Nothing further was ever heard. The matter gradually faded away. Things seemed to be steadying themselves again. Ten days later a small caucus of Project members met to discuss the situation. After this lull, we all felt that more offensive action was needed. We thought of extending the squatting to take in private landlords. There were lots of empty flats in Sussex Square, the heart of upper class Brighton. That would do nicely for the future, but there was a more immediate prospect. At the end of the month, the Labour Party Conference was to be held in Brighton. This was a propaganda opportunity that

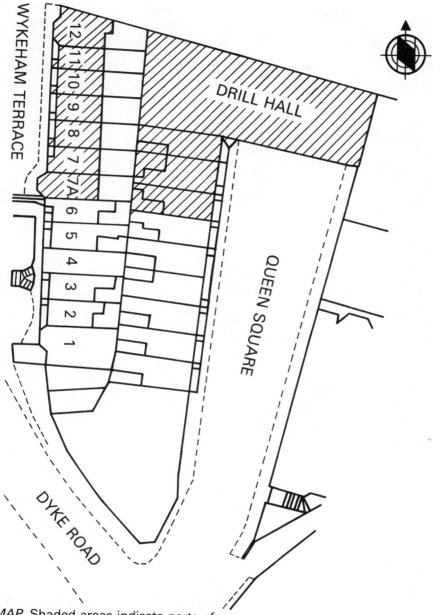

MAP. Shaded areas indicate parts of Wykeham Terrace, Queen Square, and the Drill Hall occupied by the Brighton Rents Project.

Figure 5.27 Shaded areas indicate parts of Wykeham Terrace, Queen Square, and the Drill Hall occupied by the Brighton Rents Project

198

Rents men welcome housing chief talks

A SPOKESMAN for Brighton Rents Project— the ginger group who have organised the occupation by squatters of council-owned property — today welcomed the opportunity of a round-the-table talk with representatives of Brighton Housing Committee.

When the committee met yesterday afternoon they had before them a letter from the Rents Project, signed by Mr. George Armstrong, making a number of demands and asking for a meeting as soon as possible.

The committee decided that chairman Ald. Stanley Theobald and vice-chairman Cr. John Leach should meet leaders of the Rents Project "unofficially."

Ald. Theobald said: "It will not mean that we recognise them as such, but we may be able to clear the air in many respects."

SNEER

Commenting on the committee's decision, a Rents Project spokesman said: "We're delighted. This is just what we've been asking for. I am hopeful now that new areas of negotiation will be opened up.

"The original reaction of the Housing Committee chairman to us was to sneer at 'banner-waving demonstrators.'

"We welcome the change in attitude and the committee's acceptance of the seriousness and usefulness of the Rent Project's activities."

Rents Project members meet tonight to formulate the views they intend putting to the chairman and vice-chairman of the Housing Committee. They were today consulting squatter families and will be largely influenced by

'REGISTER RENTS' PLEA

FIVE HUNDRED tenants in Montpelier Road, Brighton, will soon be getting letters from the Brighton Rents Project urging them to have their rents registered with the Rent Tribunal.

The letters will come from the rent registration group of the project who have spent the past four months interviewing tenants and explaining the workings of the tribunal to them.

A leading member of the group, who has organised the mass posting and is himself a landlord said he has encouraged his tenants to register their rents.

INVITATION

The letter invites tenants who have "any worries or problems" to go to Wykeham Terrace where the Brighton Rents Project and eight squatter

their wishes

It is known that some of the families are becoming fed-up with the uncertainty of their present situation, and security for these families is almost certain to dominate the Rents Project's argument.

DEMANDS

The Rents Project's letter to the committee contained the word "demand" many times. Cr. Mrs. Catherine Vale said: "I object most strongly to the word demand. We are dealing with anarchists. Some of the Rents Project are not even Brighton ratepayers. I don't see what business it is of theirs."

Cr. Mrs. Vale said she had sympathy with the squatter families who were homeless, although it was not necessarily the council's responsibility to house all of them.

"I would meet the squatters, but never in a million years would

families have occupied the former married quarters of the Territorial Army.

"We have helped many families in the area over the last few months who now pay less rent and have security," the letter states.

"Of course, you cannot be thrown out for going to the rent officer or the Rent Tribunal. And in any case, the law is clear —no eviction is legal without a court order. There are severe penalties for illegal eviction."

The letter adds: "When the rent is registered you benefit. And so does any tenant who comes after you. So get it registered now. We will gladly help you for nothing."

The letter also lists some of the rents which have been fixed in Montpelier Road, with details of the flats. Tenants are asked to compare their rent with those already fixed by the tribunal.

I have anything to do with the Rents Project," she said.

Cr. Ronald Shrives declared: "This letter does not merit any kind of answer. It is schoolboy craziness."

But Ald. Theobald said: "I do not see what harm it can do for the vice-chairman and myself to have an unofficial round-table conference with the Rents Project. At least then they will not be able to say we are riding the high horse.

"It strikes me that at present they are completely lacking in knowledge. If we meet them we may be able to enlighten them."

VETO

He was supported by Cr. Peter Best, chairman of the Finance Committee.

Ald. Theobald said one of the letter's demands was for a Brighton Tenants' Association repre-

sentative to sit on the Housing Committee with right of veto on all matters concerning council housing.

"The constitution of housing committees has been decided by Parliament," he commented. "They seem ignorant of this."

The Rents Project also asked the council to recognise in public that the idea and stimulus for the renovation of unused development property came from them. But Ald. Theobald said the Housing Committee had embarked on this scheme long before the Rents Project was heard of.

BASIC

The Rents Project demanded that :

● The council accept their "responsibility" to permanently house the squatter families.

● The council accept the principle that a house is the basic right of every individual and take all possible steps towards its immediate realisation.

● All empty private property be rated.

● A representative of Brighton Tenants' Association be an ex-officio member of the Housing Committee with right of veto on all matters concerning council housing.

● No one with commercial vested interests, such as estate agents and building contractors, be on housing or planning committees except in a purely temporary or advisory capacity (Ald. Theobald is an estate agent).

● A stop be made to all luxury development until no one remains in need of housing in Brighton.

● The housing list be opened to everyone, and that no qualifications be necessary.

● The council publicly renounce, as a gesture of good faith, all claim to costs and damages awarded to them against any squatting families and recognise the public service rendered by these families in bringing the housing problem to the attention of Brighton.

The Rents Project's letter also called upon the Housing Committee to make available complete lists of all council-owned houses, those scheduled for renovation with the estimated costs, slum houses and areas not scheduled for renovation, and other data.

Figure 5.28

we could not miss. We planned a National Housing Rally to coincide with the Conference. There was not a lot of time, and we needed nationally known speakers. We started planning the invitations and posters there and then. The ghost of Steve was fading...

The next day the massive hippie squat in Piccadilly happened (Figure 5.29). A week later they were evicted by an equally massive force of police. That was it. You couldn't pick up a paper that did not see squatting as heroin-ridden degenerates smearing excrement on walls. (I sometimes wonder which agent-provocateur set that one up.) We were all a bit numbed. The families hardly mentioned it. We knew that people must be thinking of us like that, but we did not want to talk about it. The authorities (who are they, in the end?) got

SUNDAY TELEGRAPH

No. 419 September 21, 1969 Price 8d.

Welfare aid to Piccadilly hippies cut

Minister's order

SUNDAY TELEGRAPH REPORTERS

THE Government yesterday stepped in to prevent the hippy squatters at 144 Piccadilly living off Social Security supplementary benefits. Mr. David Ennals, Minister of State, Health and Social Security, said he had given "clear instructions" that "any claim for supplementary benefits for these people are to be refused."

The instructions had been given to the Westminster branch of his Department and to its emergency centre. He referred to the hippies as "squatting exhibitionists who, without rhyme or reason, announced their decision to resist the law."

Speaking at Cheadle, Cheshire, he said the hippies were "anti-social rebels without a cause who had no claim on the compassion of the community."

A spokesman for the Department said: "We believe we will tell at these two offices who these hippies are. They will be required to prove their identity and state their address.

"If we have any doubts we will investigate the address they give and if we find they are from this address they will not get benefits."

Supplementary benefits are non-contributory benefits paid to people without resources of their own. The minimum varies.

Police cordon

Police last night cordoned off the area in an effort to stop more squatters entering the building. Mr. Sid Rawle, self-styled "coordinator" of the London Arts Commune, claimed that "about 900" people were now in occupation.

First signs that the police meant business with their cordon came when a constable sprinted after two girls and a man who broke through the police ranks and dashed for the building. They eluded the constable.

He retired to a chorus of jeers from the squatters, and laughter from crowds of spectators at least 1,000 strong.

A police inspector said: "We would allow people through the cordon if we knew they were living in the house, but we are not going to allow in several hundred more who say that they want to live there."

Missiles thrown

Tin cans and other missiles thrown by the hippies injured several people. Last night a small girl and an icecream salesman received treatment for slight head injuries.

Earlier two policemen had been hit by missiles, including heavy water-filled balls used in a variant of the French game of boule. One of the policemen had to go off duty.

Several scuffles broke out last night as a crowd of hundreds thronged around the house. Police moved in as a small gang of "Skin-heads"—an East End

STREET SCENE: OUTSIDE 144 PICCADILLY

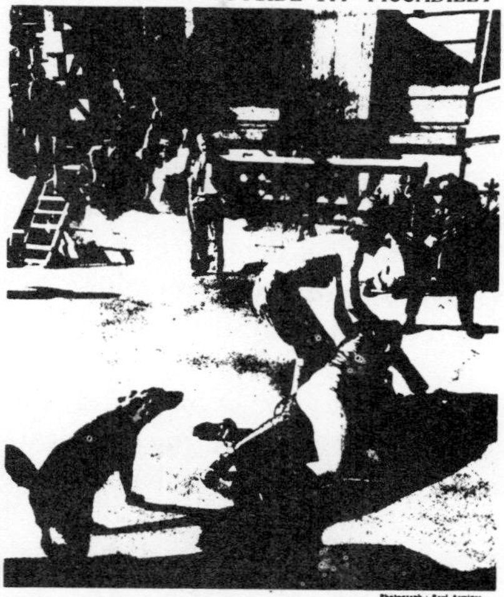

Photograph: Paul Armiger

OUTSIDE 144 Piccadilly yesterday, a shirtless man darts forward to separate two young women rolling on the ground in a furious fight. [Other pictures—Back Page.]

Figure 5.29

something else out of Hippadilly—a brand new legal weapon. The court order that preceded the hippie eviction set the precedent of issuing injunctions against unnamed persons.

To date, our strategy was based on the fact that it was not possible to identify which family was living in which flat—therefore no summonses could be served and no action taken. The Hippadilly precedent removed the basis of our legal security at a stroke.

An emergency meeting was called. Fifty-five people turned up at a few hours notice. We used one of the large rooms above the Drill Hall. Apart from a few hard wooden chairs that were left over from the public meeting, the room was empty of furniture. The atmosphere was fraught with tension and panic. A lot of people were standing up. All sections of the project were there in force, including the families. The meeting was a more or less permanent uproar. Chris and other members of the Rents Registration Group opened. They admitted there was a strong possibility of imminent eviction. They said we should make plans for what would happen afterwards; that we should organize leaflets and demonstrations. The families and the anarchists simply did not want to know. The families wanted to know how they could *avoid* being evicted. They said so loudly. Plans that involved them being on the streets were no good. The anarchists, hammers and clubs in hand, were going to fortify the place. They were going to resist any attempt at eviction, legal or illegal. Individual quarrels and shouting matches broke out everywhere. Violence was not going to help the families. Nor was politics. What do you mean 'politics'? You're the ones that aren't...

The anarchists walked out—their usual move under such circumstances. In the confusion, the families followed. The rest of the meeting broke up. Nothing was decided. In the event, nothing much was done either.

A couple of desultory barricades were placed on the stairs leading up from the Drill Hall, which remained cavernously and stubbornly empty. Footsteps echoed from end to end (whenever there were any). The dossers from Steve's days were gone. All that remained were four or five old cars and vans—relics from the days of optimism and expansion when we had planned to have our own squatting fleet and motor pool for family transport. When this dream faded, Paul and some of his friends started cutting them up for scrap. This was the state of affairs at 6.00 in the morning on Friday 26 September, when a force of thirty council officials, backed by the police, broke open the doors and re-occupied the Drill Hall.

The place *was* a mess, and the local papers made the most of it.

BRIGHTON'S SQUAT-IN SHAMBLES

THE SHAMBLES OF A SQUAT-IN

BACK TO NORMAL AFTER THE SQUATTERS

and so on (Figure 5.30)

It was treated like a mini-version of the Piccadilly affair. Demoralization was rife. On top of all this, our 'National Housing Rally' was scheduled to take place in the Drill Hall in two days time. All the publicity was out. London speakers were coming.

In a last aggressive burst, we issued leaflets saying the rally would take place 'as planned'. This gave the impression that we intended to re-take the Drill Hall. That would give them something to think about. In fact, the ideas was to assemble everyone in Queen Square, use one of the Queen Square houses as a platform for a couple of short speeches, then stage a march through the centre of the town to an alternative hall. That didn't work either. The three families in Queen Square had been terrified by the violent retaking of the Hall. Nothing had actually been done to them but their doors had been pushed open while they were in bed or half-dressed. That was enough. They immediately moved round the corner to Wykeham Terrace where they felt safer. It was impossible to keep up the appearance of occupation once the families were gone. For one thing, the Drill Hall was full of police and council officials. They saw the families go and moved in. There was nothing we could do about it. The Queen Square houses were gone too. The only consolation was that this time we made sure we cleaned up. There was no debris left behind, not even an empty paper

Evening Argus

FRIDAY, SEPTEMBER 26, 1969

Fivepence

Police and council swoop on Drill Hall

BRIGHTON'S SQUAT-IN SHAMBLES

BRIGHTON CORPORATION officials today snatched back the council-owned Drill Hall in Queen Square—a squatters' stronghold since August.

The building fell in a dawn raid by a team of Park Constables led by their chief, Mr. Joseph Morton, a former police inspector at Brighton. Only one squatter was in the drill hall —sleeping in a car.

Shortly afterwards the hall was entered by Brighton police.

And in the building, which was proclaimed a children's playground when taken over, police found half-a-dozen upturned cars and vans.

GARAGE

A quantity of lead was found in the back of one of the vans. Police said it appeared to have been used as a garage for repairing and rebuilding motor vehicles. They found two vans both of which bore the name " D. H. Recoveries."

Two men and a woman were helping police at Brighton's John Street headquarters this afternoon.

The supervisor of the Park police, Mr. J. Morton, said that they met no resistance. They had invaded with the object of " turning out " anyone in occupation of the drill hall.

Mr. Morton added : " All the doors leading to upstairs rooms of the drill hall had been sealed up with 6in. nails and it was necessary to smash down the doors to gain entrance to the upstairs rooms.

" The police were along in case of trouble. They took no part in retaking possession and we have merely asked them here to prevent a breach of the peace."

NO FORCE

Mr. W. O. Dodd, Brighton's Town Clerk, said later " I have no present intention of using force to eject the squatters." He was referring to the families in houses in Queen Square, to which access can be gained from the drill hall.

Mr. Dodd added that a letter was going to the head of the households today pointing out that the corporation cannot allow the taking over of properties.

He said he was attempting to gain a High Court order for repossession but would not disclose when.

Chief Supt. William Rostron was driven to the front entrance of the hall shortly after 9.45 a.m. and was immediately surrounded by angry squatters.

" What right do you have in here ? " one of the squatters asked him. " The same right as you have," he replied.

He told the squatters that four people were in custody. As he stood outside, one of the squatters attempted to pin a notice on the front door of the hall.

Mr. Rostron told him not to be " silly " and the poster was taken away by police.

● The Brighton Rents Project said this afternoon they were

considering taking action against the police, alleging r i o t o u s assembly.

" As far as we're concerned the place was empty and the police

BREAKER'S YARD. This is what police found in the drill hall today

went along and now they're squatting there," said a spokesman for the project.

The shambles they left behind. —See centre pages.

Figure 5.30

bag or old newspaper. 'Squatters leave houses in perfect condition' we said. The paper said nothing.

We still planned to gather our supporters in Queens Square for the rally, but the police took our 'as planned' leaflet seriously. They cordoned off the whole square. All we could do was stand there and direct people across the town to the new hall. They went off in twos and threes. So much for the march. The rally was successful, but the press picked up on our fears. Instead of reporting the speeches, they concentrated on the fact that we ejected a couple of plain-clothed policemen (Figure 5.31).

SQUATTERS' BACKERS THROW OUT THE POLICE

was the way it came over. By this time, the press was the least of our problems. What could we do if they tried a legal eviction? We had never had to face this possibility before. Back in Terminus Road, it would have been possible to simply move. Now we had ten families and more than twenty children to look after. Wykeham Terrace had been a 'last stand'; but we had not expected to lose; we had no plans. All this was in our minds at the rally. We appealed for all those 'prepared to defend the Brighton squatters' to come to a meeting at the Terrace the next night.

The meeting was packed. Again all sections of the Project were there. The subject under discussion was resistence to eviction. For once, the conclusions were unanimous. We did what we decided to do without much variation. For some reason there was a changed atmosphere. People took it in turns to speak, and there were few interruptions.

The first thing that had to be settled was whether to resist any eviction attempt. This had always been on the cards. It was what the guards were for. But we had been thinking of some Redbridge-style strong arm attack. Now the question of resisting a legal eviction came up. The seriousness of such a move became clear to everyone. Yet the idea of resistance was not dismissed out of hand by anyone. We sorted through the strands. 'Can we do it?' It seemed unlikely. How could a handful of families resist a hundred or more highly disciplined police? It just seemed impossible. Then the penalties for making such an attempt would be high. People would be hurt. Some could even be killed. Everyone involved would probably be sent to jail. It just did not seem worth it.

'Should we just leave?' That was impossible too. As one family put it: 'We are not just going to walk out. We've got nowhere to go.' The other reason was that lack of resistance—or anticipated lack of resistance—was not newsworthy. We would get no press coverage; that mattered. Apart from anything else, it was more pressure for rehousing; we needed it. No-one had any doubts that token resistance was the answer. Enough to get press coverage, but not enough to get arrested. Practically, this meant barricades and passive resistance. The families would have to be carried out.

Mixed in with the question of the press was the physical appearance of the place. They must have no more chances to make accusations of filth and wanton

Squatters' backers throw out the police

Police in Bedford Place, Brighton, last night

The meeting was transferred to Bedford Place after police kept Rents Project members from the drill hall

BRIGHTON detectives were last night ejected from a Brighton Rents Project meeting after the organisers picked them out in the audience.

The meeting was originally scheduled to be held in the Drill Hall, in Queen Square, which the Rents Project seized at the beginning of last month but which is now back in the hands of Brighton Corporation, who own it.

The project announced on Saturday that they still intended to hold the meeting there, although they had lost control of the building, but when they arrived last night they found a formidable line of very burly policemen standing guard outside.

So, without attempting to enter, they switched the meeting to a church hall in Bedford Place, which had already been booked in case it was needed. Policemen patrolled Bedford Place.

As Mr. Ian Macdonald, of the United Tenants Action Commit-

PLAIN CLOTHES MEN SPOTTED, TOLD TO GO

tee, from London, the main speaker, got up to address the meeting he remarked: " This place is crawling with fuzz."

A Rents Project official approached two men wearing lounge suits who were sitting towards the rear of the hall and said: " Before we proceed, I must ask you both to leave."

NOT WANTED

One of the pair said he was under the impression it was a public meeting. The official replied: " In law we are entitled to make you leave. We don't want you here."

When the pair still remained seated he warned them: " There is an observer from the National Council for Civil Liberties

standing behind you. I advise you to leave."

EVIDENCE

The two then left. Questioned by reporters, they identified themselves as Brighton C.I.D. officers.

Mr. Richard Moseley, of the National Council for Civil Liberties, said later: " In all, five C.I.D. officers were ejected from the meeting. The Rents Project asked my advice before ejecting them.

" I told them that in law, if a meeting is held in private premises and no admission charged, the organisers are entitled to refuse admission or to ask people to leave and to use such force as is necessary to evict them.

" I have heard that there may be the possibility of serious charges against certain people connected with the Rents Project and I believe the C.I.D. officers may have been there to try and gather evidence for a conspiracy charge."

He added that squatting was unpopular with the public at present and the authorities were anxious to stamp it underfoot while the going was good.

Uniformed police patrolled Bedford Place throughout the evening and police were still standing guard outside the Drill Hall in Queen Square late last night.

But despite the evictions from the meeting Mr. Moseley said he thought two women C.I.D. officers had escaped the net and were present throughout the meeting.

Figure 5.31

damage against us. Practically, the biggest job was getting rid of the rubble at the back that had once been a wall. Poor old Gary had known it was pointless knocking it down all along. But it had to be done. Saturdays (we weren't sure how many we had left) were designated as mass clearing-up days.

What could we do *after* the eviction? At last the problem was faced. There was strong feeling against a re-squat from the families. One by one they made their positions clear. There were different reasons: they would be thrown out again too quickly; they could not keep moving; it would end in violence; the effects on the children; any other place would be a step backwards. There was a custom that, where squatting was concerned, the families always had absolute decision-making power. They were unanimous; no more squats. It still was not clear what we could actually *do*. We set up the Post-Eviction Committee—'PEC' as it became known. Its job was to decide what to do next, and to co-ordinate resistance and support. There were problems about who should be on PEC. The police investigations were getting heavier by the day. The latest threat was a 'Conspiracy to incite to riot' charge after the Queens Square fiasco. The 'as planned' leaflet was the evidence. They were trying to find out who wrote and duplicated it. We decided that PEC membership should be confined to people who were not under hint or threat of being charged. Another of PEC's jobs was rebuilding our tarnished and diminishing public support. Direct approaches were to be made to everyone that might help—the Trades Council; Trades Unions: Labour Parties; Students' Unions at the University and Colleges, and so on.

The meeting was pretty efficient, decision-wise. At the rally we had appealed for anyone prepared to help the squatters. Only one new face appeared. he was about 35 and wore a beard. Near the beginning of the meeting, he suggested that the families should form a private housing society to raise funds to build or buy their own houses. He was exposed to a few 'Oh yes, we've heard all that before,' comments,—then ignored. There was a political argument underlying the rejection of his suggestion. The point was that no-one bothered to make it. Similar suggestions had met similar rejections at previous meetings. Whatever the differences between the Project, the Squatting Group, and the families, we had our own language. The bearded newcomer was not speaking it. He never came back. Everyone else was fairly satisfied with the form and outcome of the meeting.

The next day the summons arrived.

> An affadavit sworn by an enquiry agent said that he visited Wykeham Terrace to find out who was living there. Eight men approached him in a 'threatening manner' and refused the squatters' names. 'In view of their hostile attitude' he left.
> Eventually he got into the block to post notices to quit.
>
> (*Daily Telegraph*, 18 October 1969)

That was it. A few bits of paper pinned to doors, and the eviction process had started. This time it was not an application for an injunction against unnamed persons. Maureen was named as the representative of the families.

We followed our plan. There was an intensification of propaganda on behalf of the families. We cleared up. That wall finally disappeared into a skip and was taken away. A trend began to emerge for the total reorganization of the Project in terms of aims and structure. 'Trend' means that no-one disagreed with the ideas being put forward by the RSSF, IS, and Rents Registration Group. The anarchists were fading away.

Propaganda and Welfare

Wednesday, 1 October.

Press invited to an open day on Friday.

Thursday, 2 October.

A dozen people involved in 'clearing up'.

Friday, 3 October.

The families stage a morning demonstration outside the Labour Party Conference (Figure 5.32).

Sunday, 5 October.

Delegates arrange appeals for help at the Trades Council and University (Figure 5.33).

Wilson regrets he's unable to dine today

THE PRIME MINISTER "regretfully" declined a luncheon invitation from squatters in Brighton today.

It was sent to him by families facing eviction from Wykeham Terrace who wanted to discuss their troubles with Mr. Wilson over lunch.

But Mr. Wilson was too busy today, with the Labour Party conference and with his plans for re-constructing the Government, to oblige them.

Ten homeless families with 20 children have been occupying a group of cottages in Wykeham Terrace since August. Last week

they were served with a writ.

The squatters waited outside the Grand Hotel this morning to try to see Mr. Wilson as he went to the Labour conference. But Mr. Wilson was later than usual and they missed him.

The squatters wanted to

know if he would accept their invitation. Home Secretary Mr. James Callaghan, whom the squatters had also invited, passed them and they shouted: "Callaghan! Callaghan!" and tried to speak to him, but he hurried on.

Figure 5.32

Figure 5.33

Homeless case

TO THE EDITOR

Sir,—Much has been written in the press recently on the subject of homelessness, and also on squatting. Often the impression is given that the homeless are not capable of speaking on their own behalf. As homeless families ourselves we would like to use your columns to correct this impression.

We would like first to record our views on the causes of our homelessness. 1. A Government that is not strong enough to free housing from market fluctuations, and to assert that a house is the right of every family. 2. Although private landlords may not discriminate against coloured people, they are free to, *and do,* discriminate against families with small children, whatever their colour. We are all working (average income £12 per week); the houses and flats here that are not too expensive for us (i.e. over £7 per week) are just not let to families with small children.

3. Our local council has cut its building by 75 per cent over the past few years. With two to five small children each, we cannot wait three to eight years for a council house.

All of us are at present squatting at the address below. This was, in every case, a last resort—there was nowhere else for us to go. We expect to be evicted by the Territorial Army Association (the Ministry of Defence) who are the owners of the property.

In other words, we are to be evicted by the Labour Government for whom, in 1964, we all voted. If we resist eviction we go to prison; if not, our families will be on the streets, or broken up and humiliated in " Welfare " centres. — Yours sincerely,

Mr and Mrs Ware, Mr and Mrs Byrne, Mr and Mrs Baker, Mr and Mrs Chrismas, Mr and Mrs Edwards, Mr and Mrs Thornton, Mrs Nihil, Mrs Martin, Mrs Prior.
7-12 Wykeham Terrace, Brighton,

Figure 5.34

Saturday, 11 October.

More 'clearing up'.

Tuesday, 14 October.

Organization of emergency car, phone, and communication system in case of sudden eviction.

17 October to 5 November.

Several journeys to London by coach and car to gain publicity and defend ourselves in the High Court. It all nearly ended on the Crawley by-pass when the car we were in—an ancient Morris Oxford—had a front wheel blow-out. We survived. Maureen became a celebrity of *The Times* Law Columns. Minor legal history was made. The case got so complicated that the judge called in the Official Solicitor to help him. In the end it went against us. Maureen was told to quit. The other families were given the option of appearing at the High Court and being told to quit, or quitting anyway. Some option!

Saturday, 18 October.

The families express their views in *The Guardian* (Figure 5.34).

Squatter mums and kids in plea for homes

SQUATTER families and their children crowded into the offices of the Brighton Welfare Service Department this morning to demand accommodation if they are evicted from Wykeham Terrace next week.

The families who were moved into Wykeham Terrace by the

Brighton Rents Project during the summer now fear that an eviction order granted in the High Court against one of them, Mrs. Maureen Hales, will affect them all. This notice is due to expire at the weekend.

Eight of the nine families at present living at Wykeham Terrace confronted welfare department officials. Many of the mothers took their babies and toddlers with them.

Each of the families was given a form to fill in and told their case will be considered by the Welfare Services Committee when it next meets on December 1.

Mrs. Josphine Edwards, mother-of-five, said of the possible eviction: " We think it is disgusting with Christmas coming on and we wonder what sort of Christmas our children are going to have."

She described the strain of not knowing when and if the eviction order will be executed: " I think we will all have a nervous break-down before long."

NOTHING

Another of the mothers, Mrs. Patricia Wares, said: " We are all worried to death."

Mr. R. N. Nicol, director of Welfare Services in Brighton, told two of the Rents Project members,

Mike Robinson and Gary Robins, that nothing could be done for the squatters until the committee meets in December.

He was asked to try to arrange a meeting between the welfare departments and housing departments of Brighton and Hove," the Brighton Trades Council, Brighton Rents Project and representatives of the squatter families.

Mr. Nicol replied that he would contact the committee chairman and let the Rents Project know whether a meeting can be held.

Brighton's Welfare Services Committee have decided to consider making preparatory arrangements for housing evicted squatters at their next meeting on December 1. They were asked to call a special meeting for this purpose by the Brighton Labour Party, but decided to discuss the matter at the next full committee meeting.

● Some of the children and parents on steps of the Welfare Office.

Figure 5.35

As the case went on there was an item in the local or national press almost every day. We continued to try and embarrass the council and the government and Ministry of Defence.

Monday, 17 November.
The families and all the children demonstrate at the Brighton Welfare Office (Figure 5.35).
Sunday, 23 November.
Demonstration in Downing Street. Maureen hands in a letter to No. 10, with national press and television coverage.

One demonstration was truly 'staged'. It took place on the opening night of the new University Theatre. The play could not have been better chosen. 'Comrade Jacob' was about the Diggers—an early communist sect who took over land in Surrey after the execution of Charles 1, only to find that Cromwell was a true defender of the old property rights. We took over the stage at the end of the play. Maureen—who was getting to be an excellent public speaker by this time—brought the story bang up to date. It was this that gave Harold Hobson a chance to air his fatuous views in the Theatre Column of the *Sunday Times*

Digging for defeat

THEATRE □ HAROLD HOBSON

As soon as the play was over some young men appeared on the stage, and vainly tried to call the actors back. They looked to be in the last stages of poverty, but they were accompanied by a pretty young woman, very fashionably dressed, who nonchalantly smoked a cigarette, though smoking is not allowed. In his play at Nottingham, "The Demonstration," Mr Caute implied that though students may be right to rebel, they tend to rebel ineptly, and what followed was an example of this. The fashionable lady did not make an appeal on behalf of the apparently impoverished students; on the contrary, the apparently impoverished students made an appeal on behalf of the fashionable lady, who it seems was a squatter about to be evicted.

Now there may be many reasons why a woman, more richly dressed than any woman in the audience, should be allowed to be a squatter. There may be many reasons why she should be allowed to smoke whilst the audience is forbidden to do so. But if such reasons exist, they were not explained to us. The eviction of squatters may be an injustice. But it is not sufficient that injustice should be exposed. It should be seen to be exposed. And it was curious that an evening devoted (apart from those logs) to people who wanted to pay rent should end up with an impassioned appeal for those who do not pay rent at all.

Figure 5.36

Evening Argus

SPECIAL

TUESDAY, NOVEMBER 25, 1969   FIVEPENCE

Brighton to offer temporary homes

COUNCIL ARE TO REHOUSE SQUATTERS

FIVE of the squatter families who are to be evicted from Wykeham Terrace, Brighton, are to be housed in temporary accommodation by the town's Welfare Services Committee.

Acting chairman, Cr. Mrs. Bridie Carroll, said although the committee had no statutory responsibility to house the nine squatters in Territorial Army property in the terrace, they had agreed to give temporary accommodation to five families.

She named the families as Baker, Hales, Martin, Prior and Thornton.

She said: "The accommodation is temporary and it is second-class property we rent from the housing committee. The squat-ters will not be put into proper council houses so we are not putting anyone in front of the council housing queue." The

Housing Committee have refused to rehouse squatters.

In a formal statement yester-day after a two-hour meeting to discuss squatters, Mrs. Carroll said since that since none of the squatter families would have been evicted under "unfore-seen" circumstances, the com-mittee had no statutory duty to rehouse them.

CLEAR

But in view of the concern the committee felt for the children the committee had considered each case on its merits.

She warned, however, that no further cases of squatter fami-lies will be considered by the committee.

HOVE can do nothing to help any of the squatter families. Hove's Town Clerk (Mr. John Stevens) makes this clear in a letter to the Town Clerk of Brighton (Mr. William Dodd).

"My council's policy is to rehouse people who are on their housing list. They are not prepared to accelerate the rehousing of the

families to whom you refer to the detriment of families on the list."

If any were on the list, they would be dealt with in due order. "My council do not know the names of all the families who are alleged to come from Hove. The one family whose name we are aware is not on the waiting list.

"It is observed that your Hous-ing Committee are not accepting responsibility for the families com-ing from Brighton and my council do not understand why they should expect Hove Housing Committee to accept a responsibility they themselves don't acknowledge.

WELCOME

The news that Brighton Welfare Services Committee are to house five families was welcomed today by Mr. Chris Baxter, of Brighton Rents Project, the ginger group which installed the squatters in Wykeham Terrace.

Referring to the standard of housing Brighton was offering, Mr. Baxter said he hoped it was decent housing or it would not be acceptable.

Figure 5.37

(Figure 5.36). Then on Tuesday, 25 November, the breakthrough came (Figure 5.37).

COUNCIL ARE TO REHOUSE SQUATTERS

(Evening Argus headline)

The heading in the later edition was more accurate: 'BRIGHTON REHOUSE SOME SQUATTERS'. The Welfare Committee had decided to rehouse five of the nine families 'temporarily' and 'in sub-standard accommodation'. A couple of days later they added one more family—John and Sara. They said all the families they were going to help had 'lived for some time in Brighton'. The other families were not their responsibility. We took a sour view of this reason. It was not true (although we could not say so very loudly). Some of the families they had decided *not* to help had been in Brighton just as long. They also said they were concerned about the children—yet they were not going to help the family with five children.

Our view was that we had generated a lot of pressure. The council could not allow itself to be seen letting nine families with kids land on the streets; they compromised. They helped the majority to defuse the outcry, but allowed the others to be seen to be ejected with nowhere to go 'as an example'. The so-called 'sub-standard housing' was another example of this. With one exception—was it coincidence that it was Maureen?—the houses were adequate. And it was not the Council's responsibility to keep the families housed. They were still trying to show that 'Squatting does not pay'.

The Re-orientation of the Project

This took place gradually but decisively over the two months following the rally and the project meeting at Wykeham Terrace. It started with a 'caucus' at Chris's house. The brief entry in my dairy said:

> In fact, it was a platform for Chris to attack the anarchists, who were not present. There was agreement that a 'firm line' was needed, but no-one had a clue what it should be. There was also agreement that the Project was, *de facto*, centred on squatting, and this had to be 'sorted out' first.

Then there was a general meeting of the Project on 14 October to which more than a hundred people came. The first thing to note is that, despite the size, it was a 'general' not a 'public' meeting. In fact there were no entrance qualifications, anyone could vote, and the majority of people came because of the immediate danger to the families. In other words, there was no real procedural difference. The change of name was indicative of a change in attitude. Previous meetings had been agitational: aimed at publicity and initiating action on as many fronts as possible. This was organizational: specific actions were needed to defend the families from eviction and ourselves from prosecution.

The first part of the meeting was taken up with a resolution from the Rents Registration Group criticizing the Squatting Group, and calling for reorganization of the Project. Most people would not go along with the criticisms of the Squatting Group (although they might privately agree with them) because it would have split the Project. The call for reorganization was carried overwhelmingly. After this the meeting got down to the business of working out contingency plans for the impending eviction.

This 'general' meeting reflected a significant change in direction, a new 'trend' that we mentioned before. It was the first time a motion had been put that was not just for press consumption. It was the first time an 'introspective' motion had been put—a resolution by the Project on itself, rather than on the council or on planned actions.

Two weeks later, on 28 October, a further meeting decided on the form of the reorganization. Fifty-five people, including most of the activists, were there. People with common views tended to sit together, and it was easy to see how the Project was composed. Nine anarchists occupied the front row to the left of the platform. The front two rows to the right were taken up by thirteen members of the Labour Party—officially the Rents Registration Group. Six Revolutionary Students were behind them near the centre, opposite six members of the International Socialists. Seven representatives from the families ranged themselves along the back, and between them and the platform were about fourteen 'others'.

Two documents were up for discussion. Both had lots of technical detail about organization. There were lots of amendments, some of them pretty linguistic. The anarchists were just not interested, and left in a group right at the beginning. The families drifted off in ones and twos. The field was left clear for the introduction of an executive committee and formal membership. It was decided, with only one vote against, to discontinue squatting and concentrate on the creation of a 'United Tenants' Movement'. PEC was to continue making arrangements for the families during and after the eviction—but was told not to re-squat.

However, winding up squatting and 'changing direction' was easier said than done. It was difficult to back down, and Chris, who had argued strongly against any more squatting, managed to say the opposite when he spoke to the Press (Figure 5.38). The result:

FAMILIES PLAN TO CARRY ON SQUATTING
(*Evening Argus* 15 November 1969)

The End of Squatting

On 13 November, a possession order against the squatters was given in the High Court. By 27 November the council had decided to house six of the families. On 28 November in a snowstorm, the bailiffs moved in to evict the remaining three families. There was very little we could do. The place was surrounded by police. Passive resistance relies on force of numbers, and there were only three families left.

PEC got the Press and a hundred people to Wykeham Terrace by 9.00 in the morning. The families offered no resistance, and were all out by 11.00. Our hopes for national press coverage were dashed. No rumpus—no pictures. Terry kept up a barrage of heckling:

'Aren't you proud. Throwing out women and kids so your bosses can make a profit. Look at that child. How much are you being paid for depriving him of a home?

Your wife and kids are going to be proud of you tonight. But these kids won't have a home...

Hey... are you getting paid by the child...or is it a job lot.'

EVENING ARGUS, Saturday, November 15, 1969.

FAMILIES PLAN TO CARRY ON SQUATTING . . .

THE Wykeham Terrace squatters will resist any attempt to evict them, a spokesman for the Brighton Rents Project said last night. And he hinted that the families had already decided where to squat next if they are evicted.

Mr. Chris Baxter, a member of the Project, told a reporter: "If the Brighton and Hove councils won't provide the families with, somewhere to live, then we shall have to.

"All I can say at present is that the police would wish to try to prevent what has been decided."

A High Court judge decided on Thursday that he had power to make a possession order against only one of the seven squatters. But he gave directions which would enable the owners of the property, the Territorial Auxiliary and Volunteer Reserve Association, to gain eviction orders by

Mr. Baxter said the Project were anticipating that an attempt to evict the squatters would be made a week on Monday.

He added: "I am quite certain that the police will try to prevent the Rents Project from helping the squatters by physically dividing them from the families.

"But these tactics won't work, because the families have plans which they will put into operation whether we are there or not."

HOMELESS

Mr. Baxter said the families would be meeting last night to finalise arrangements. These people were homeless and they have tried to make the local authorities face up to their responsibilities.

"They most certainly don't intend to give up now. But it is still possible that the authorities will see the light and provide welfare accommodation."

Mr. Baxter added that lawyers who had represented the squatters in the High Court were still considering an appeal. "The decision of the court was considered by many to be nothing more than a travesty of justice."

The High Court order

Why I'm a squatter, by an 'ordinary mum'

MRS. MAUREEN HALES says she can't figure out why she and her three children can't have a council house.

"I could understand if I was a beatnik or a hippie, but I'm just an ordinary mother trying to fight for my children.

"But people won't have it. They think we're troublemakers."

Mrs. Hales is the only one of the Wykeham Terrace squatters named in the eviction notices which were fixed to the doors yesterday.

SEPARATED

She is a tired-looking 25-year-old with three children . . . Terena, eight; Lee, seven; and Simon, four. She is separated from her husband and started squatting last June because "I had nothing to lose."

She and her three children had been living in two rooms in Belvedere Terrace for which she paid £4 10s.

"Oh, it was a filthy place; there were rats and no toilet facilities."

She says she would have had to leave there anyway, because she was expecting another baby. But with "all the aggravation" of the squatters' battle, she had a miscarriage.

Mrs. Hales has been taken off the council housing list since she started squatting.

She won't go into a welfare hostel because she would be separated from her children.

At Wykeham Terrace she shares a three-bedroom house with another mother-of-three. She brought her own furniture, including an old-fashioned sewing machine, with her. With its

boarded-over windows the house is not attractive. But it is warm, clean and dry. "It's not such a lot to ask out of

life . . . just a house for these kids before they get older and start pinching things and end up in Juvenile Court."

Mrs. Maureen Hales and two of her children, Simon and Terena

Figure 5.38

214

Some of this got onto the radio, but we did not make any of the national daily papers.

PEC's arrangements went well. Vans got all the furniture away, then we marched, en masse, down to the Welfare Offiice. We stayed there till about 4.00 p.m., demanding houses, arguing with officials, and generally occupying the place. Then the remaining three families were moved to the University.

At this point, the Rents Project as an organization ceased to be involved. There were many quarrels, incidents, and mass meetings of the Students' Union. There was another demonstration at the Welfare Office, and three days continuous picketting of the Town Hall. But this was all arranged by a Steering Committee, elected from a Union Meeting, and using Students' Union resources. Rents Project members were only involved as individuals.

By the end of January, after an intensive search, homes were found for the remaining three families.

The End of the Rents Project

On 5 January 1970 an article appeared in the *Argus* pledging

> even more trouble in the New Year. Our aim is to improve the housing situation in Brighton, and we will continue to fight for that cause.

That was effectively the last that was heard of the Rents Project. The best description of this decay—the Project was never formally wound up—is a bald statement of the frequency of post-eviction meetings, and of the numbers of people that went to them.

18 December.   General Meeting, thirteen people.
 8 January.   Executive Committee Meeting, eight people.
20 January.   Executive Meeting, six people.
22 January.   General Meeting, eight people.

> The last General Meeting of the Project was held on 22 January. Due to bad publicity and a general falling off of support, this meeting was very badly attended. Certain immediate issues need emergency action... There are urgent matters which cannot go forward without the active involvement of Project members. A General Meeting will be held on the 3rd. Feb. This will be the starting point for *action*. Please make sure you come and tell everyone you know about the situation. Our strategy for a United Tenants Movement will be useless unless it is put into effect....

(Newsletter)

27 January.   Executive Meeting, ten people.
 3 February.   General Meeting, fourteen people.
12 February.   Some leafleting, five people.
17 March.   A meeting, six people.

....

....

CHAPTER 6

The Brighton rents project: a formal account

All certainty arises from the comparison of ideas, and from the discovery of such relations as are unalterable, *so long as the ideas continue the same.*

A Treatise of Human Nature, David Hume

The more sharply we focus on any social system, the more complex it becomes. The story of the Rents Project could be told in many different ways, of which the last chapter was only one. The formal account is more general, and loses much of the detail. It tries to say something about group processes that goes *beyond* the detail. First let us remind ourselves of the main features of the organization and history of the Rents Project.

The formal organization of the Project was a set of subgroups that centred on activities and communicated through a co-ordinating committee. All these subgroups followed policies laid down by open meetings of all the members and supporters. The idea of this form of organization is illustrated in Figure 6.1. In practice, the activities of the Rents Project were carried out by two semi-

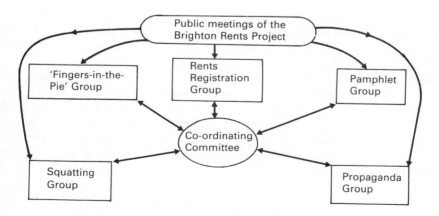

Figure 6.1   Theoretical formal organization of the Rents Project

215

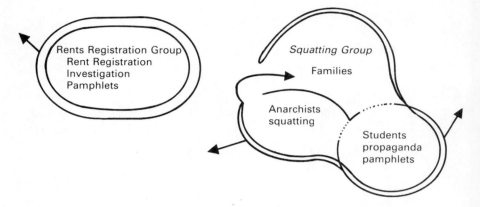

Figure 6.2   Informal organization of the Rents Project

autonomous groupings, and are better represented by the illustration in Figure 6.2. In place of a single, elegant vertebrate, we find two floppy amoebas. The first—the Rents Registration Group—was homogeneous; its members believed the same things. The second—the Squatting Group—was heterogeneous. It was composed of three subgroups (anarchists; families; revolutionary students) with different activities, aims, and beliefs.

The history of the project more or less coincides with the history of the squatting group. The main events are illustrated in Figure 6.3. The history divides into two distinct periods; May to mid-August, and mid-August to December.

The Project was founded in May, and staged a successful demonstration and token squat. In June the first family was squatted. After a period of steady but uneven escalation, fifteen families were squatting by mid-August. During this period, the Project was on the offensive, the authorities on the defensive.

In late August and September there was a series of dramatic reversals. Some of these originated from inside the Project—they were 'its fault' as it were—others originated outside the Project. The bombing followed from the logic of escalation, even though it had little to do with the intentions of individual members. Intensive police investigation and prosecutions followed. On the other hand, the massively publicized hippie squat in Piccadilly—'Hippadilly'—discredited squatting and made it easy for the council to use strong-arm tactics in recovering the Drill Hall. In this period, the Project was on the defensive, the authorities on the offensive. The aim became to defend and rehouse the families. Spreading squatting was forgotten. After the final eviction in November, the Project attempted a re-organization—and collapsed.

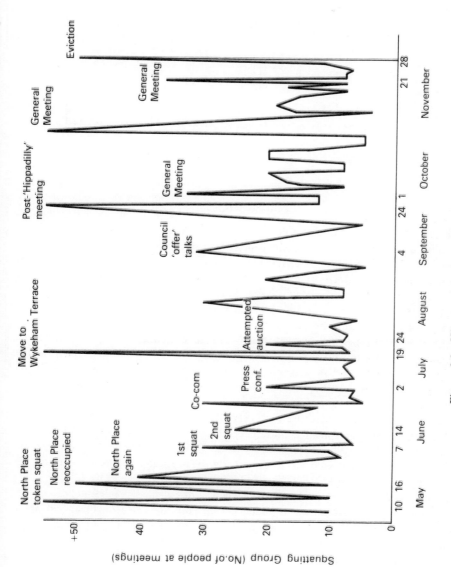

Figure 6.3 History of the Squatting Group

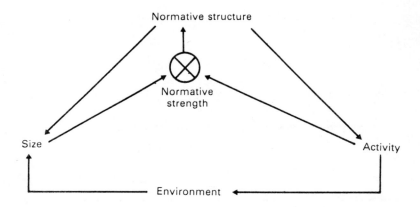

Figure 6.4   A general model for the Brighton Rents Project

The Model

The Rents Project was mapped onto the schematic model developed in chapter 4. The model states that (within limits) size and activity levels are independent—have no effect on each other. The limits of this independence are determined by the normative structure. This means that, within the limits, an increase or decrease in size will have no effect on the level of activity. In this context, it is the 'within limits' that must be stressed. Outside these limits the model—and probably the group—will break down.

Size decay will be precipitated by a 'shortage' of activity. Simply, individuals in the group cannot find enough to do and leave. Size increase will follow from a high level of activity that renders the group socially visible. Simply, someone outside the group (in the 'environment') sees interesting things going on and wants to join in.

It was also expected that a high level of disagreement with any major norm of the group would precipitate a change in the normative structure, and this would change the way in which the entire group functions. This is represented on Figure 6.4 by the crossed circle that leads to 'normative structure'. It means that disagreement builds to a 'threshold' level. Below this level there is no effect on normative structure. Above it there is a sudden massive change.

These processes should account for group stability, as a necessary, if not a sufficient condition. Without them, the group should not be stable, but stability—the continuing existence of the group in roughly the same way—might need more than *just* these processes.

The Rents Project allowed four hypotheses to be tested:

1 There will be no correlation between size*level and activity* level.
2 A low level of activity will be followed by a decrease in size.

* see Note 1, pp. 236–8

3 A high level of activity will be followed by an increase in size.

4 A low level of normative strength* will precipitate a change in normative structure.*

These predictions were made on the assumption that the Brighton Rents Project could be treated as a single group, and that it would be viable in the long term. In the event, neither assumption held. The Project was composed of several distinct groups, and collapsed after an erratic existence of only eight months. Unsurprisingly, the predictions did not hold for the Project as a whole, with the sole exception of 4. The attempt to apply strict predictions to a natural group involved in the full flood of activity led to important changes in the model, and the way it was operationalized. The idea of group size as a head-count had to be changed. The presupposition that it was possible to measure activity in an *informal* group was confirmed. Most important of all, the *subgroups* that survived conformed to the model; those that did not deviated from it. In addition to this, observation of the way people work in groups led to the idea of '*technique*' that goes some way towards solving the sociological 'mind-body' problem. It tells us how normative structure moulds practice, and how practice is embedded in the normative structure. The normative structure is not a check-list of common beliefs, but contains a set of prescriptions for action as its kernel. Without action the whole thing withers away. Another feature of normative structure that emerged was the way in which a common language can disguise a set of entirely different meanings. The disagreement—the decline in normative strength that reaches a threshold and suddenly precipitates a catastrophic change in the whole normative structure—may not be visible to the group members.

The Results

Since the life of the Rents Project resided entirely in the subgroups, predictions 1–3 failed to take account of the real processes at work. There was a strong correlation between size and activity, and none between activity at t and size at $t+1$.† Prediction 4—the way in which the normative structure changes, and the consequences of changing it—was confirmed in a striking way.

The norms of the Rents Project turned out to be wider and more structured than anticipated in theory or by the laboratory tests. Members not only had definite ideas about 'behavioural traits'—the right things to do, but on many other things as well. There was a common characterization of the socio-geographical environment. This can be represented as map of Brighton as seen through the distorting mirror of the group's intentions (see Figure 6.5). There was a common version of the significant events in the group's history, which are the labels on Figure 6.3. There were a set of common intentions that included, pretty explicitly, a description of the nature of society. Together, these

* see Note 1, p. 238
†See Note 2, pp 238–243

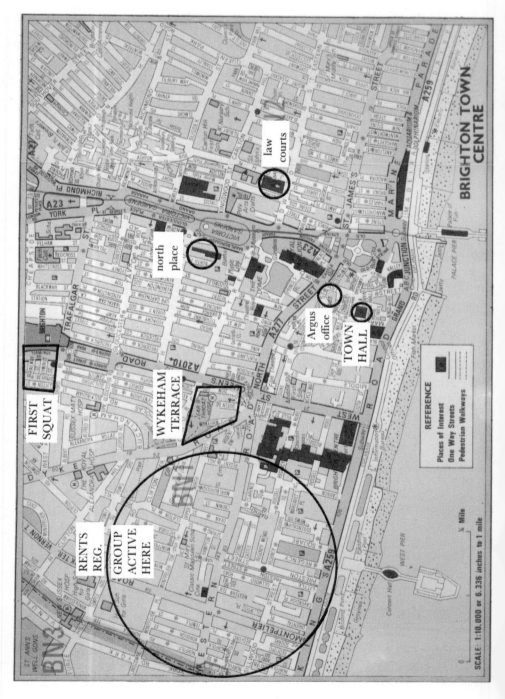

Figure 6.5   Brighton Rents Project's View of the Town

constituted the coherence of the group as a whole—the reason why the Project appeared to be one group rather than a set of factions.

The set of intentions and beliefs common to all project members was derived from discussion, documents, press statements, and over thirty transcribed interviews with Project members and families. Set out as a 'check-list' they appear simplistic. This does not do the group the credit it deserves. The beliefs were the underpinning of practice, and discussed (when they were discussed) in that context rather than as philosophical truths. Ideas that were articulated in many different ways and contexts are listed (in Figure 6.6) as one-line dogmas—and something is necessarily lost in the process.

A striking difference emerged between the norms in a natural group—the Rents Project—and laboratory groups. In natural groups the Bates and Cloyd method of norm identification loses much of its power. The method* was developed to identify norms that were shared by a significant portion of the group, and that were self-conscious. Members not only held the beliefs or sentiments, but were aware that most other members also held them. Conversely, as a diagnostic, the method enables us to identify areas (probably subgroups) where the norms do not hold. Alternatively it enables us to identify in a quantitative way the 'gap' between those that do hold a given belief, and those that are believed to hold it.

In laboratory groups the mean level of agreement with norms can rise to about 75 per cent, while the mean level of perceived agreement can go as high as 90 per cent. In the Rents Project—and I now think in most natural groups—the mean levels of personal and perceived agreement with general norms is indistinguishable from 100 per cent. Everybody agrees and sees others as agreeing. There are two obvious explanations for this.

First, in a natural group with a history there is far more time to interact than in a laboratory situation. Hence members come to be more familiar with each other's views, and are able to reduce the dissonance of conflicting views. This explanation is at best misleading, and in some ways false. It fails to take into account the realities of group process. In the first place, especially in a large group, members do *not* communicate with all other members. In strict terms, the probability of any member (A) communicating with any other member (B) in a group of N members is not $1/N$. People talk a lot with members of their own subgroups and not very much with members of other subgroups. Even within subgroups, it is not talk, but action and the description of action that provides the basis of consensus. 'Technique' plays a structuring role that 'talking' does not, and provides another basis for distinguishing groups from mere aggregates—people who are accidentally thrown together in some situation.

The second explanation is that adherence to—or at least non-disagreement with—the norms of the group constitutes a preliminary 'membership filter'. People who could not speak, or would not learn the language of the group were excluded; two examples follow.

* See Note 1, p. 238, Norms.

GENERAL NORMS OF THE BRIGHTON RENTS
PROJECT

1. Attack the Authorities over bad housing by
   direct action involving the working class.

2. Direct Democracy is the only democracy—belief
   in a system where all people have the power to
   directly decide on all matters that affect them.
   This ideal was not consensual in practice—
   where it often meant subgroup autonomy.

3. Society is ruled by a minority who manipulate
   things for their own benefit. Everyone else suf-
   fers. This is the cause of poverty—which is not
   accidental or the result of laziness.

4. All institutions are suspect. Social services are
   not *meant* to work.

5. Improvements in popular conditions have to be
   forced on Authority. Authority is not amenable
   to rational persuasion.

6. A mass movement is necessary to achieve specific changes, and also desirable in itself.

7. Squatting is good.
   Squatting serves a practical need,
   links students into the community,
   attacks the property owning class,
   creates a mass movement,
   spreads the ideas and practice of socialism.

Figure 6.6

On the night after the 'National Housing Rally' a meeting was called in Wykeham Terrace. Its purpose was to discuss the impending eviction, and what to do about it. Loud appeals had been made for 'ordinary members of the public' to turn up and help; three did. Two of them remained silent. The third, a bearded newcomer, suggested that the families should form a private housing association—raise funds to build or buy their own homes. He was treated to a few 'Oh, yes, we've heard all that before!' comments, then ignored. From the viewpoint of the Project, there were many political arguments underlying this rejection. The point is that no-one bothered to make them. The newcomer was excluded and never came back.

Gary gave an account of the same process as it occurred in the Pamphlet Group: '... a lot of Party members came ... very naive ... very conservative in their view about what could be done ... came and were generally derided by the rest of us. They never came again. Then a new lot came and left'. This process ensured a much higher level of agreement with group norms than would be found in any artificial or short term group.

Differences in the Rents Project emerged *through* the consensus, not outside it. Although the statements themselves were universally accepted, there were profound differences between subgroups in the meaning, interpretation, and emphasis given to key words. 'Direct democracy', 'direct action' and 'working class' were all part of the agreed rhetoric, but had different meanings in the major subgroups. This was the factor that allowed the ideological collision that directly preceded the break-up of the Project.

Each subgroup, in maintaining its own 'techniques' (more about this later), developed specific meanings for the general norms. Although couched in the *same* language, the way in which these subgroup norms were put into practice effectively excluded members of other subgroups. In the same way that the group as a whole operated a 'membership filter', so did each subgroup. The fact that someone from the Rents Registration Group was virtually excluded from meetings of the Squatting Group increased the differential between meanings. For instance, Chris said of the Squatting Group:'Several times I tried to do some baby sitting, or guard duty, or whatever it was called. The times I went up there was no need for it, so I came away.' Chris was excluded by being ignored because he thought and said that squatting (direct action) should be a limited (by whom?) lever to change council policy. The Squatting Group saw their direct actions as the beginning of an (unlimited, spontaneous) *replacement* for council policy. This was almost impossible to discuss since the Squatting Group also developed the idea that those that were around 'full-time' (themselves) should have more say in things than those that were not. The exclusion was backed by a rationale.

This growing gap—the lack of a common language within the common language—led to a collision that centred on one norm: 'direct democracy'. The general meaning within the Project was that public meetings laid down policies that were interpreted in action by the appropriate subgroups. To the Rents Registration Group, this meant that there was a form of central control. To the

Squatting Group, it meant they could act autonomously. In practice, decisions were made by factions, and carried out independently. When there was opposition or conflict between factions, there was no method for settling it in a satisfactory way.

This was not serious when actions were seen as 'successful' by the subgroup that initiated them, or by the Project as a whole. Crises of this sort were experienced on many occasions. The loss of the first court case; the reaction to Steve's scare headlines are two examples. In the first case the anarchists attacked the student grouping who had organized the court defence. The students and the Rents Registration Group saw the verdict as the best outcome given the circumstances. In the case of the scare headlines, the anarchists were pleased with the publicity in itself. Other groupings agreed that publicity was a good thing, but wanted to be more discriminating about it. They thought they should be consulted before, and not after the event.

In neither case were the opponents of the action understood by its proponents. Subgroups were committed to their own techniques. They had insufficient commitment to the Project as a whole to accept majority decisions— especially where there was a hint that these might threaten their techniques.

Under the institutional counter attack of late August and September, the continuing practicability of the technique of squatting was cast into doubt. Dissatisfaction with the current state of affairs reached a peak. The dissatisfaction generalized to cover the techniques that led up to it. The attack that arose out of the discontent centred on one norm only. This was the principle of subgroup autonomy.

The General Meeting of 14 October abolished this principle. It decided on the centralization of the Project through the election of an Executive Committee. The anarchists withdrew. Following this the Executive decided to 'wind up' squatting, and concentrate on the issue of rent rises. The displacement of one central norm led immediately to a total change in the structure and function of the Project.

The Subgroups

The reality of the social structure of the Rents Project lay in the Squatting Group and the Rents Registration Group. Both proved to be viable; both conformed to the predictions about the relation between size and activity; both exemplified the importance of 'technique'. The other subgroups, as can be seen in Table 6.1 and Figures 6.7 and 6.8, faded out rather quickly. Table 6.1 shows the composition of all the formal subgroups of the Project, quantized into the three major event periods.* Figures 6.7 and 6.8 show the size of the formal and informal subgroups over the lifespan of the Project*.

The activity of viable subgroups was independent of their size fluctuations. The general prediction about groups that had been expected to hold for the Project as a whole was true of its components. This is a case where the object of study told the researcher how to organize the research concepts. The concept of the Project

*See Note 3, p. 00.

as a whole was only a reality for the subgroup with which the researcher was most closely associated. But at least there was some agreement on it. Defining group (or subgroup) size as 'the number of people present on any given occasion' did not meet with the approval of group members. It was the simplest operationalization, and highly convenient for statistical purposes. As with so many such measures, it missed the point. It was fortunate that this interpretation was completely falsified by the data—the predictions based on it failed. To the groups themselves, members were members whether they were there or not. Conversely people could be 'there' and definitely not be members.

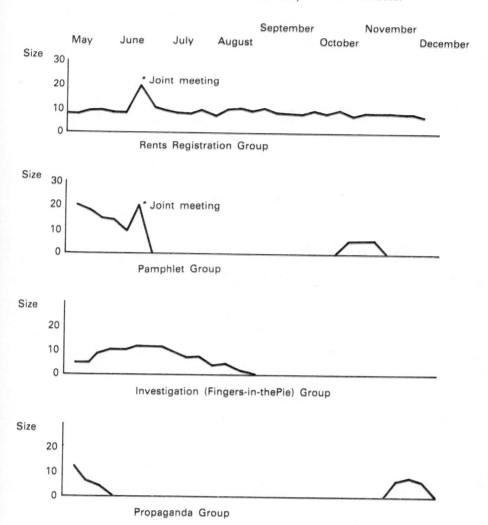

Figure 6.7   Brighton Rents Project: Lifespan and size of formal subgroups. (See Figure 6.3 for Squatting Group)

226

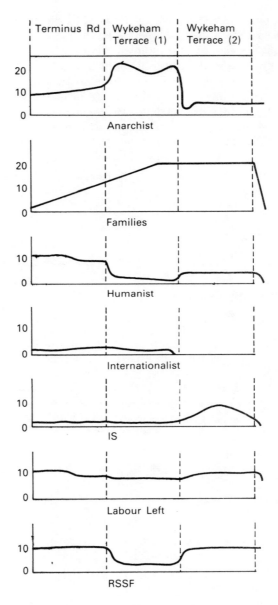

Figure 6.8   Brighton Rents Project: Participation
and size of informal subgroups

This notion of size has to be interpreted (operationalized) in the same way as norms. 'The number of people in a group who are recognized as members by other members of the same group, and who think of themselves as members.' The definition becomes subjective—internal to the group—rather than objective—convenient to the researcher. Under this definition group size becomes harder to measure. You have to *ask* people, rather than *assigning* numbers to them. Nevertheless it meets the intuitive criteria that members can be absent; non-members can be present; and gets over the odd 'fact' that the most common size for all groups will be zero.

Using this group-subjective criterion of size, it was evident that activity was independent of size fluctuation in the Squatting and Rents Registration Groups—see Figures 6.9 and 6.10—although the data was insufficient to test the effects of activity on subsequent size changes.*

Each subgroup developed its own specific norms within the Project as a whole. We have seen that the Squatting Group justified its autonomy under the

Table 6.1

Subgroup	Time					
	Terminus Road (7–6–69 to 19–7–69)		Wykeham Terrace 1 (19–7–69 to 20–8–69)		Wykeham Terrace 2 (20–8–69 to 7–12–69)	
Squatters	Anarchist	12	Anarchist	12	Anarchist	6
	RSSF	1	RSSF	1	RSSF	6
	Family	6	Family	12	Family	12
Rents Registration	Labour Left	8	Labour Left	8	Labour Left	8
	Humanist	2	Humanist	2	Humanist	2
Pamphlet	Labour Left	2				
	Humanist	2				
	Internationalist	1				
	IS	3				
	RSSF	2				
Investigation	Anarchist	1	Internationalist	2		
	Humanist	3	RSSF	2		
	Internationalist	3				
	IS	1				
	RSSF	2				
Propaganda	Anarchist	3				
	Humanist	3				
	RSSF	3				
Coordinating committee	Anarchist	1				
	Family	1				
	Humanist	2				
	RSSF	3				

*See Note 3, p.243

principle that only 'full-timers' were entitled to make decisions. Under this principle only the core members of the Squatting Group *were* eligible to make decisions. In parallel with this we have seen that each subgroup operated its own 'membership filter'—agreement with its norms. In Chris's case (by his own account) we have seen how he was kept out of the Squatting Group. From the point of view of the squatting group, since he was not *in* it, he was not 'full-time', and hence had no right to say what should be done. His attempt to express his views was precisely what invalidated them. Gary's account shows how the Pamphlet Group made a similar rejection of 'outsiders'. However, the most important factor in the stability and viability of subgroups was unity in action and in the description of action. This *single* phenomenon is termed 'technique', and may be defined thus:

'Technique' is the name for a definite and integrated set of procedures that must be carried out for the successful attainment of a specific goal. *

The technique developed by the Squatting Group is described in Chapter 5, that of the Rents Registration Group in chapter 5, pp. 141–6. The Fingers-in-the-Pie Group developed a technique for finding, recording, and filing information, described in chapter 5, p. 147. The Pamphlet, Propaganda, and Coordinating Groups were unable to establish techniques of their own. Techniques were the 'heart' of the subgroup norms. They defined appropriate activity, which then provided the test and touchstone for the validation of more general norms and agreements. This validation had much in common with self-fulfilling prophecies (from an external point of view) but was essential to the cohesion of the group. Techniques as norms also allowed activity to be realized by specifying, as agreements and tradition, appropriate roles. The activity that was the carrying out of the roles confirmed the techniques, validated the more general norm set, and enabled the group to continue to do the same thing again.

Once a technique was established, it was only modified by the intervention of forces external to the group. The techniques of the Rents Registration Group were disrupted by the crisis in the Squatting Group. The crisis of technique in the Squatting Group was caused by the action of the council, government, police, and courts.

From this we may say that, in general, viable groups (here subgroups) have a tendency to develop repeatable techniques, and the repetition of these defined techniques is the regularity of activity.

The role assignment implicit in the techniques defines the limits of necessary group size. 'Necessary', here, should not be confused with 'average' or 'optimum', since the match between roles and persons is never a precise one, and there are obvious advantages in a certain amount of redundancy. Too few people, and the techniques cannot be implimented. Too many people and there may be competition for roles, disagreement, and normative destructuring.

---

* 'Technique' is the practical equivalent of the notion of 'Ritual' developed in chapter 3.

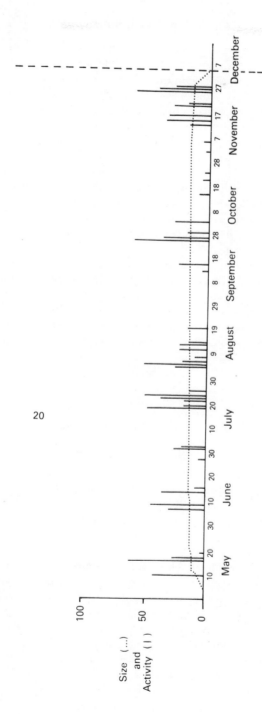

Figure 6.9 Size (subjective) and Activity of the Squatting Group

The Viability of Subgroups

Since some subgroups survived, and others did not, we can begin to draw some distinctions between the two. The criteria for viable subgroups are the development of a *successful* technique (or set of techniques) and homogeneous composition. The first subgroups to disappear (see Figure 6.7) were the Pamphlet, Propaganda, and Coordinating Groups. They developed no techniques, and were heterogeneous in composition (see Table 6.1). The next to disappear was the Fingers-in-the-Pie Group. It developed a rudimentary technique—but one that did not lead to success in terms of its own goals (i.e. public scandal/press coverage). It was also heterogeneous in composition.

The two most successful groups (Squatting and Rent Registration) developed successful techniques *and* were homogeneous in composition. The demise of the Squatting Group was preceded by the abandonment of its established techniques (the result of outside intervention) *and* by a transformation from homogeneity to heterogeneity.

Informal subgroups (see Figure 6.8), with the exception of the families, should also be considered viable. They were, by definition, homogeneous. They were in existence before the Project, and continued to exist after it had collapsed. Unfortunately their techniques fell outside the scope of the study—with the exception of the 'anarchists' and the 'Labour Left' whose techniques coincided with the groups they dominated (Squatting and Rents Registration).

Conclusions

The original model did not apply to the Rents Project as a whole. It did apply to two of its subgroups. The process of application and testing led to modification and elaboration of the model—the 'Mark II' version. This is schematized in Figure 6.11. The model did not apply to the Rents Project because it was not a viable group. It was a collection of groups. The viability of a collection of groups (an organization) can be expected to have different and more complex criteria than simple groups. Part of this will be the viability of the component subgroups. Another part will be the development of norm regulated relationships between the component groups. This did not happen in the Rents Project—the creation of the Coordinating Committee was an attempt to make happen, and the failure of the Coordinating Committee a sign that it did not. The data also suggests that such relationships are more easily built when there is a functional interdependence between the subgroups. The Squatting Group was made up of three interdependent subgroups: anarchists; families; students. These achieved a semi-normalized relationship. There was mutual independence between the Squatting Group and the Rents Registration Group. They did different things in different places at different times. This must have exacerbated the normative divergence that led to the collision that resulted in the restructuring and subsequent collapse of the group.

The aspect of the model that did apply to the Rents Project as a whole was the non-decomposable nature of the normative structure. The idea that a

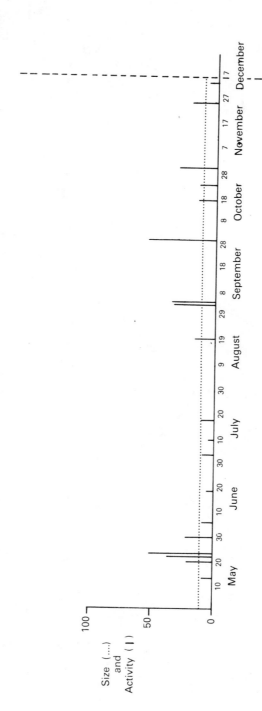

Figure 6.10   Size (subjective) and activity of the Rents Registration Group

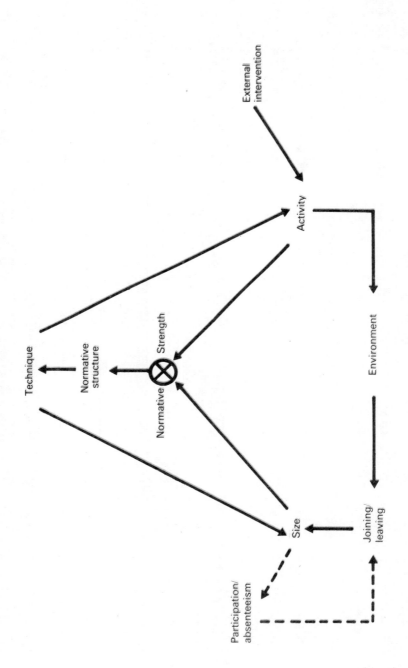

Figure 6.11 A revised general model for the Brighton Rents Project

change in any norm would affect all norms, and that such a change would be sudden. Discontent—arising from lack of activity or the failure or blocking of activity—would collect, as in a transducer, until it reached a threshold. At this point the whole normative structure would be called into question.

The way in which the Rents Project was *not* a group is highlighted in the variable 'activity', even more by the variable 'size'. There was very little common activity between the Rents Registration and Squatting Groups. Only at moments in the first phase of the Project—the Town Hall Demonstration and the Token Squat in North Place—is it reasonable to aggregate the activities of the two groups as *the* activity of the group as a whole. In terms of 'size', even under the original definition, different heads were counted in different places. It takes a strange conceptual scheme (once we have the hindsight) to aggregate the activity of one set of heads with the count on another. Yet this is what a conception of one group and the reality of many groups was demanding. In terms of the later operationalization of the concept 'size'—subjective membership perception of members—it was simply inapplicable to the group as a whole. Following it made clear that there were several groups. From one of the students: 'get rid of the dossers'; from one of the families:'Rents Project? Never heard of them. Dunno who they are'; from one of the anarchists at a Coordinating Committee(!) meeting: 'You are trying to take over, and we're not going to have it. We've never seen you before.' Each subgroup recognized its own members as members. No subgroup recognized members of other sub-groups as members (in any but a token sense) even when they *had* met them. For this reason it was pointless to retest the original hypothesis on the independence of size and activity for the group as a whole using the new operationalization of 'size'. Under the new definition there was, strictly, no group as a whole. This lends weight to the idea that there may be an upper limit to the size of informal groups, somewhere in the region of 10–20 people. Beyond this we are dealing with problems of relations between groups, with problems of organizations.

The model applied to the viable subgroups with a modification and a two part elaboration. The operationalization of size was redefined. Amongst other things, this means that two types of size fluctuation now have to be related to activity. At the outset, size fluctuation was seen as a result of members leaving and new people joining. Now we also have to account for the fluctuation caused by 'absenteeism'—members who have not left, but are not present. The converse of this, and the most usual index, is participation. Analysis of the group 'IREV' in the next chapter will clarify this relation.

The elaboration of the model involves adding the functionally related notions of 'technique' and 'external intervention'. We have said that technique lies at the heart of normative structure. It is the template for the actions through which the structure will be confirmed and reproduced. It is a repeatable plan that provides both regularity and novelty. Techniques can be represented by flow diagrams, as in Figures 6.12 and 6.13, but it must be emphasized that this is a highly artificial format. It misses the strong evaluative component and the

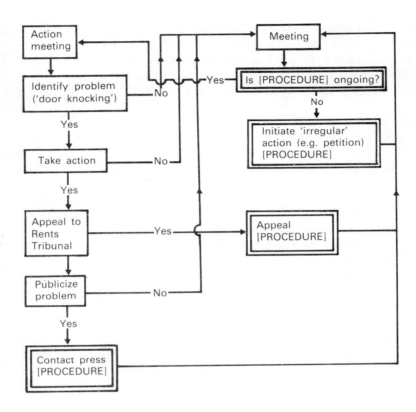

Figure 6.12   [PROCEDURE] means that there was a well-defined technique followed by the group for achieving that particular end

way in which roles are allocated. In groups, techniques rarely exist as an externalized (written down, or otherwise spelt out) and unitary representation. Instead they are distributed over the group members. The plan exists when all the group members are together. Nevertheless, for our purposes, the flow diagram representation is convenient.

The Rents Registration Group followed the technique schematized in Figure 6.12. The basic technique provided regularity, and was itself a source of interest and anecdote (see chapter 5, pp. 141–6. In tandem with this the group would periodically—every six to eight weeks—launch a single burst of activity in another direction. The Town Hall Petition; the joint survey with the Pamphlet group; the publication of Pamphlets, are all examples of this. Its regular activities, its irregular activities, and its size all followed well-defined and bounded patterns. It was the most stable of the subgroups.

The basic activity pattern of the Squatting Group was equally regular, although less predictable in time. It repeated with increasing speed until it was blocked by its own escalating consequences—the counter-offensive by the

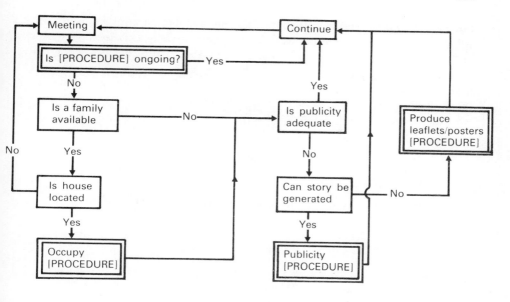

Figure 6.13   Note that this representation of the Squatting Group 'techniques', in the absence of a family, leads to a 'leaflet producing' cycle only — the eventual fate of the group.

Authorities. This reaction can be seen as the response of a larger and more powerful system to a disturbance in *its* stability. After the reaction, propaganda techniques continued to be implemented with some regularity. The rhythm of this activity was determined by the legal and policing systems of society at large, rather than the internal needs of the group. There was also implicit conflict, since propaganda for rehousing was effectively 'desquatting'. In the long term the Squatting Group was not a viable entity—although it did develop many of the charcteristics necessary for viability. It is probably better viewed as a casualty of external forces, rather than a structural failure.

The notion of technique, when combined with that of 'external intervention', casts an interesting sidelight on our ideas of 'organizational conservatism'. It is often implied that organization conservatism is a bad thing. The group, collective, or organization is somehow unable to 'adapt'. Here we see the reality of the situation. Technique (or 'Ritual') is the foundation and the motor for the reproduction of the normative structure—the essence of the group. Radical change in technique implies a complete reshuffle of roles—the way people relate to the group—and of the normative structure. There must be a crisis. Not only this, but the techniques are evolved because they give satisfaction to members as well as being effective. They provide regularity and continuity as well as variety and novelty. In view of this it is not surprising that groups cling to their techniques even when (from the outside) they are clearly becoming inappropriate. Groups that achieve viability do so primarily on the basis of repetition. It

236

takes external intervention (which may take many different forms) to upset this situation. Only when the situation is upset—when there is a crisis—do we hear of 'organizational conservatism' as a term of abuse. Which looks a lot like putting the cart before the horse. Paradoxes usually arise when the aims of a group—its own growth; significant impact on, or change in its own environment—conflict with its need for viability. The problem of growth will be dealt with in the next chapter.

Notes

1 Operationalisation of variables and data reliability

Size

Size of group of the group was measured as the number of people involved in meetings or activities on any given day. Where meetings or other events attracted more than fifty people, the figures are accurate to the nearest ten people. The 'head-count' method involved no problems of accuracy or reliability.

Activity

In line with the considerations in chapter 4, the best measure of activity for the Brighton Rents Project was found to be the number of column inches devoted to the group per day in the *Brighton Evening Argus*. As some activities were reported on the day they took place, others on the following day, data was standardized by eliminating the time lags.

There was a problem of reliability with this measure of activity since news coverage was liable to several types of distortion: 'slack days' on the paper; feature articles; reports on the activities of other groups toward the Rents Project.

An alternative measure of the activity of the Rents Project could be found in the frequency of its publications(leaflets, pamphlets, posters, documents, etc.). Although this measure was more intimately connected with group functioning it had two disadvantages. There was no obvious method of quantification—how can a short, mass-circulation leaflet be compared with a lengthy, but small circulation pamphlet? Publications were infrequent—there were only twenty in the life of the Rents Project. Publication data was therefore used as a check on the reliability of the column-inch data.

To achieve comparability between the two data sets, only those days on which news coverage exceeded 40 column inches were used ($N = 20$) were then plotted against time, which was divided into fortnightly periods. The frequencies were correlated using Spearman's Rank Correlation Test. After correcting for ties, and with a sample greater than 10, this gave a t of 3.98. The null hypothesis was rejected at the 0.005 level—giving a strong indication that the two sets of data were measuring the same thing. A visual comparison of the activity measures is made in Figure 6.14. An alternative measure of activity—the most accurate of all—would have been person-hours spent on group projects. This was too cumbersome and difficult to assess for the Rents Project. A comment is made on an approximation to this measure in Note 2.

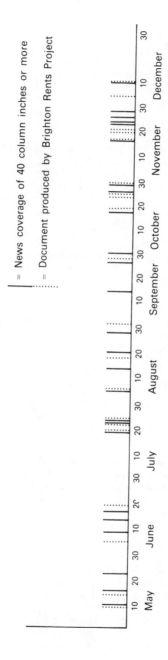

Figure 6.14 Brighton Rents Project: Comparison of activity measures

Norms

The Bates and Cloyd (1956) method of norm measurement was used. This had the following composition:

1 The identification of 'objects' (behaviour traits, people, activities, ideas) about which members of the group may have definite normative sentiments. This is done by the researcher as participant observer.
2 The establishment of the fact that these sentiments are shared by a significant portion of the group.
3 Evidence that members are aware that their attitudes are supported by agreement on the part of other members of the group.

Parts 2 and 3 were established by the use of interviews, questionnaires, and the recording of group discussion and dispute.

There were no problems of reliability when the full method was used. This was, however, time consuming. Only two full surveys wre made. As things turned out (see main text) this did not matter since there was significantly less disagreement over general norms in real life than in laboratory and controlled situations.

2 Size and activity in the Rents Project as a whole

Observation Period

Except where otherwise stated, data is taken for the period 1 May 1969 to 7 December 1969 (221 observations). The latter date was when the group effectively collapsed, although, as a name, it persisted until 7 March 1970.

Significance Level

The null hypothesis is rejected at the 5 per cent throughout.

Size

Size, as operationally defined, ranged from a minimum of 0 to a maximum of 200 with a mean of 13 and standard deviation of 31. Size is plotted against time in Figure 6.15, and the frequency distribution of different sizes is given in Figure 6.16. There was no time trend, and autoregression showed no relation between size on one day and size on the next.

Activity

Activity, as operationally defined, ranged from a minimum of 0 to a maximum of 80 with a mean of 14 and a standard deviation of 20. Activity is plotted against time in Figure 6.17, and the frequency distribution of different activity levels is given in Firgure 6.18.

There was no time trend, but autoregression showed a significant relation between activity on one day and activity on the next. The equation was, however, not helpful in approximating the actual data. It may be surmised that this relationship arose because activity (as 'events') was often prepared for, carried out, then followed up. There was, however, little temporal relation between 'events'.

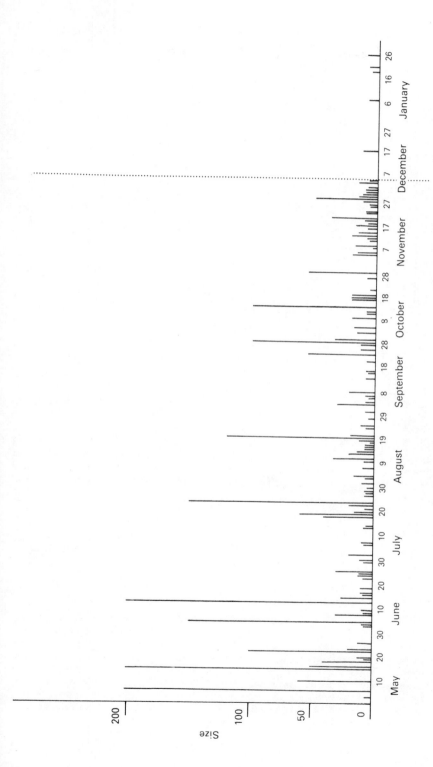

Figure 6.15 Brighton Rents Project: Size against time

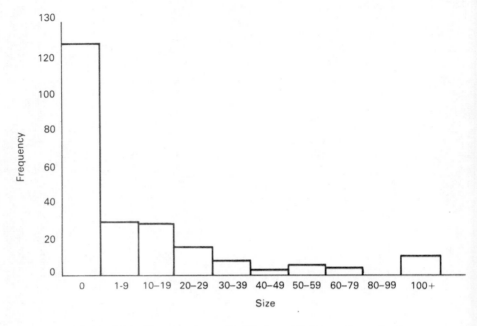

Figure 6.16   Size frequency distribution of Brighton Rents Project

Size and Activity

Against expectation, but in accord with inspection of the data (see Figure 6.19), regression showed a highly significant relation between size and activity. Although a negatively accelerated function would probably fit the data better than a simple straight line, there is no doubt of a direct, positive association between size and activity.

Activity at t and size at t = 1.

Against expectation, there was no relationship, using regression, between high/low levels of activity and subsequent increase/decrease in group size.

The relationship between 'size' and activity

As noted in the main text, the operationalization of 'activity' was satisfactory, that of 'size' unsatisfactory. *Size—as the number of people present at meetings or activities on any given day—was an alternative measure of activity.* As a crude approximation to the fine measure of activity—person-hours spent on any project—the correlation of size and activity confirmed the validity of the column-inch measure of activity. It did not test the relation of 'real' size to activity. Finally this could not be done, since the Rents Project 'sizes' were only amenable to the 'head-count' and not the 'membership subjective' measurements of size. One must conclude that the Rents Project was an aggregate not a group in the true sense.

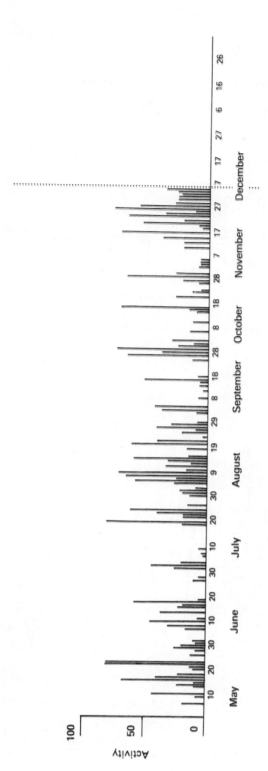

Figure 6.17 Brighton Rents Project: Activity (column inches) against time

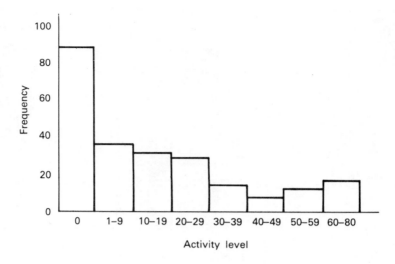

Figure 6.18   Activity level frequency distribution of Brighton Rents Project

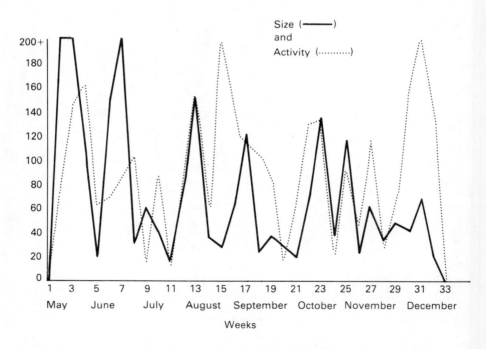

Figure 6.19   Brighton Rents Project: Size and activity against time (weeks)

3 The size and activity of subgroups

The numbers in Table 6.1 represent proportions rather than people, since both absolute numbers and factional representation varied with time.

The numbers in Figure 6.8 also represent proportions—degree of participation rather than absolute, independent size of the factions. No detailed record was kept of the membership and size of the various factions operating the Rents Project. Most of the factions had an existence independently of the Rents Project, and only part of their membership was in the Project.

Figures 6.9 and 6.10 should also be regarded as illustrative, rather than accurate to the last decimal place. The size and activity levels are reconstructed from the data on the group-as-a-whole, not directly measured. Size—the second subjective measure—was derived from attendance figures (the first measure) and *post-hoc* interviews.

No independent record was originally made of subgroup activity levels. News coverage was only an appropriate measure for the Squatting Group, and a partial measure for the Rents Registration Group. It would have been inappropriate in the other cases.

CHAPTER 7

Stability in a Revolutionary Group

'Practice marches ahead of theory.'

The Brighton Rents Project had helped to clarify the model and introduced the important concept of 'technique'. Questions about precise methods of size regulation, and about factors underlying joining and leaving, remained to be answered. We took a two-pronged approach. The first was to build a computer model of the processes to see what assumptions led to the sort of results we had. This will be described in the next chapter. The second was to undertake a further study of a real-life group. This study was again made in the course of active participation, and lasted for three years, from September 1972 to July 1975.

The group, IREV, was chosen from several alternatives because it had the highest level of activity; it met the most frequently; it had been in existence the longest—3½ years at the start of the observation period; it kept detailed records of its own activity and membership; and it was the most homogeneous—thus, according to the previous studies, the most likely to 'survive'.

IREV was the local branch of a revolutionary socialist group, which was itself part of an international federation. This meant that although IREV was organizationally fairly autonomous, it took on a full range of political 'positions' from foreign policy to domestic and local issues. People were usually attracted to the group by one or other of these 'positions', but the group's acceptance of new members depended on their acceptance of the whole set of 'positions'. For instance, someone might be attracted to IREV by its stance on Ireland— 'Troops out now: Self-determination for the Irish people'—but would not be acceptable as a member unless they also accepted its positions on other questions.

A three month 'probationary period' preceded membership, during which intensive discussions took place on the various 'positions' and the theory behind them. As with the Brighton Rents Project, but in a slightly more formal way, this process established common general norms. There was a 'preliminary membership filter'.

244

Despite the national affiliation, the 'language' or general norms, and the 'techniques' governing action were developed within the branch—at the level of the face-to-face group. During the three-year period, there was a complete turnover of membership, but the basic structure, norms, and techniques did not change. Significantly, the size of the group did not change either. This represented a paradox that we will explore later. The aim and intention of the group was to *grow*, but its techniques and its activities needed a degree of stability, which was reflected in an implicit need *not to grow*. The seriousness of this problem for any group bent on expansion cannot be underestimated.

The IREV study enabled the structures underlying joining and leaving, absenteeism and inactivity, to be examined in detail. It also brought to light an interesting and important mechanism of stability that had been known for a long time without its function being realized. This was the 'Early Leaver Phenomenon'.

This chapter will go through each of the variables and relations of the model in turn, gradually building a picture of the formal workings of IREV. For the sake of readability—and for those who want a general picture of how IREV worked—most of the numbers and statistics are included in the notes at the end of the chapter.

Data Sources

All numerical data were obtained from a fairly complete set of minute books, covering the period 20 September 1972 to 30 July 1975. Except where otherwise stated, results are based on 129 'observation weeks'—the minutes of 6 of the 135 weeks covered were lost except for membership details. The minutes were of weekly meetings at which past activities were assessed and future activities planned. Active participation had established their accuracy as records.

The categories of data extracted were determined by the variables and relations of the model, and some of the records (e.g. finances) were not categorized. The minutes were kept in an idiosyncratic way, frequently using obscure initials and abbreviations. Knowledge of the group members and of the events referred to was often necessary to understand them. For this reason, group members and ex-members were asked to help with the coding. Coding was carried out independently, and intercoder reliability was high. Much of the data was factual and unambiguous. (see Note 1, p. 259, for Coding Instructions and Intercoder Reliability.) Where results are said to be statistically significant, this means there is only a 5 per cent chance or less of error.

Group Size

In the three years, size ranged between six and nine members. There were a few weeks when the group reached a low point of five members and a few weeks at an extreme high point of ten members.

Size levels of six or less were quickly followed by an increase—someone joined the group. Size levels of nine or more were quickly followed by a decrease—someone left the group. In other words, size went up and down, but there was no overall tendency for the group to either shrink or grow. The actual size fluctuations can be seen visually in Figure 7.1, and the full details are given in Note 2, p. 260.

As we might expect, absenteeism increased with size. At low size levels, most members turned up for meetings. At high size levels of eight or more, two people (on average) were absent. Apart from the absenteeism, there was also a strong indication that 'inactivity' increased with size. 'Inactivity' was seen when a member turned up to the meeting (so was not absent) but did nothing else. (see Notes 3 and 4, p. 261, for the detail of absenteeism and 'inactivity'.)

Group Activity

Activity was measured as the number of hours members spent on group-related tasks per week. Level of activity ranged from almost nothing (four hours or less in total) to more than twenty hours—with a few high points of more than thirty hours. Although activity, like size, was very variable, there was no overall tendency for activity to increase or decrease. High points were followed by lulls, and lulls were again followed by high points. These fluctuations can be seen in Figure 7.1, and the detail is given in Note 5, p. 262.

More surprisingly—although in line with the predictions of the model—there was no relationship between size and activity. A relatively small size of group could produce high levels of activity; a relatively large group size could produce very low levels of activity. In other words, there was no way of predicting the activity level of the group from a knowledge of its size. (see Note 6, p. 262).

Normative Structure and Normative Strength

There were no crises or failures of technique, and no disruption of the normative structure. Factors that could—from the experience of the Rents Project—be expected to be associated with disruption did not happen. There was no sudden increase or decrease in size, and no external intervention to disrupt activity.

As with the Rents Project, agreement with the normative structure (normative strength) was practically indistinguishable from 100 per cent. In three years, only two instances of disagreement were observed. Both concerned the same topic. In the first instance, Individual 7 expressed a belief in the 'neutrality' of the Chilean Army (during the government of the Unidad Popular of Salvador Allende). He faced the argumentative wrath of the whole group, and the incident was never forgotten. In the second, Individual 10, a new member, expressed a belief in the 'neutrality' of the British Army in Northern Ireland. Discussion of the issue occupied the rest of the meeting. The new member was unable to accept the IREV 'position' and left the group after the next meeting.

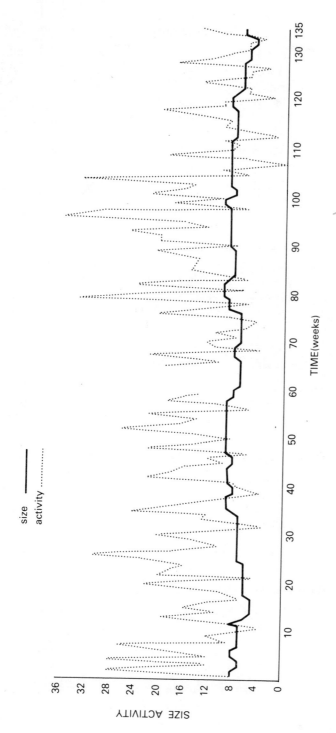

Figure 7.1 IREV: Size and activity against time

Techniques

As predicted by the model (since there were no disruptions to the normative structure), there were no changes in the techniques used by the group.

Technique was formally defined as a definite, integrated, and repeatable set of procedures to be followed in attaining a specific goal. For instance, for IREV, participation in a meeting or demonstration was a technique. It involved listing who was going; evaluating appropriate speeches or slogans; discussing stewarding arrangements; organizing and coordinating transport; instructing new members in appropriate dress and behaviour; etc.

IREV had seven basic techniques (which were derived from twelve categories of activity in the original coding of the minute books). These techniques were as follows.

A1 Participation in meeting or demonstration

This was composed of three activity categories; (a) attend meeting, (b) attend demonstration, and (c) other. The 'other' category had been intended to catch irregular, once-off activities. As these turned out to be the group travelling somewhere to attend something (such as the Annual Conference), 'other' was subsumed under A1.

A2 Preparation for meeting or demonstration

This was composed of three activity categories; (a) call local meeting, (b) produce/distribute leaflets/posters, and (c) prepare for demonstration. All involved propaganda, and attempts to mobilize people outside the group.

A3 Paper Sales

The group sold its newspaper in the local market, and outside local factories, on an irregular basis.

A4 Trade Union Intervention

Group members raised resolutions etc. in local trades unions.

A5 Internal Educational

Extra meetings for members at which theoretical/historical matters were discussed.

A6 Administrative

Actions facilitating the smooth running of the group; phone calls, letter writing, collection of dues, etc.

A7 Visiting Contacts

Visits by members to those interested (or reputed to be interested) in joining the group.

From the behaviour of the Rents Registration group in the Brighton Rents Project, it was anticipated that each IREV technique would have its own measurable rhythm. This could not be proved statistically (see Note 7, p. 263)—but that probably means that statistics are better at detecting trends than patterns or rhythms. Just looking at the frequency at which each technique was used (see Figure 7.2) leaves a strong feeling that each technique *did* have its own rhythm.

How The Normative Structure Determines Size

In previous chapters we have asserted that the normative structure of the group determines its size—but we have not explained how. Using the notion of 'technique', it is now possible to be more specific about this relationship.

First, we need to be clear about what this statement does *not* mean. It does *not* mean that the group members hold a belief about the 'right size' for the group, and that *belief* determines the size. Group members may or may not like the actual size of the group. IREV members were happiest when the size was knocking on its upper limit—but this did nothing to keep it there.

It is the normative *structure* that determines the size *range* of the group. The most important part of the normative structure (for this purpose) is the set of techniques that the group approves and maintains.

The role specifications inherent in the set of techniques serve as a template that determines the limits of group size.

How does this work? In IREV, size usually ranged from six to nine members, while activity usually fell between four and twenty hours per week. If we consider the four extreme cases:

High size/high activity   nine people/twenty hours
High size/low activity   nine people/four hours
Low size/high activity   six people/twenty hours
Low size/low activity   six people/four hours

we can see that in each case there are enough people to carry out the activity without overtaxing themselves—or there is enough activity to give most of the people something to do. (For a more detailed account of the relationship between activity and size, between activity and roles, and for role distribution see Notes 5, 8, and 11.)

This gives us a general way of specifying the functional size limits for any group. *The lower size limit* is the minimum number of members capable of filling the maximum number of roles specified by any technique. *The upper size limit* is

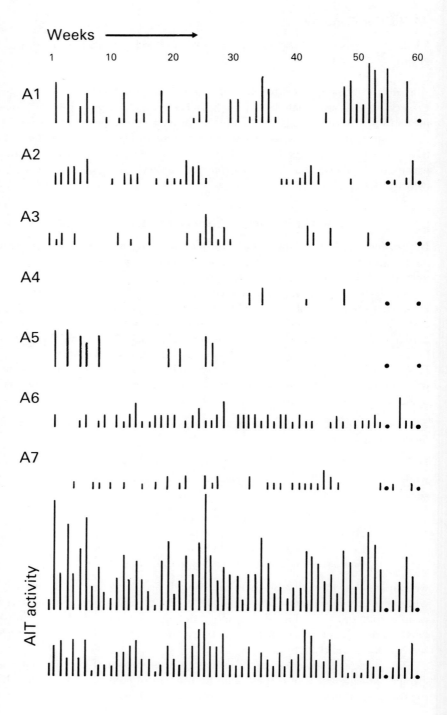

Figure 7.2 IREV techniques and activity against time. (A1 to A7 on a 0–20 scale; activity on a 0–40 scale; weeks 60–65 missing.)

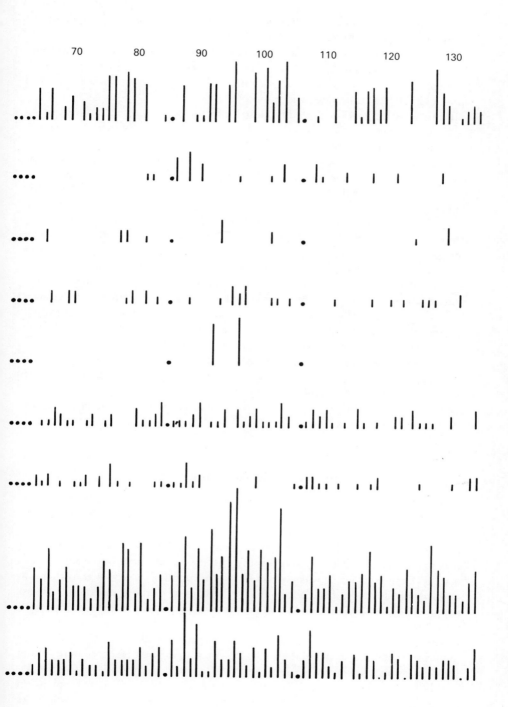

the maximum number of members capable of being absorbed by the maximum number of roles specified by any technique.

This specification of size range is not very startling—when you come to think about it. But it is unusual—I have never come across a case—for groups to look at their own size in this light. There is often a discussion about *desirable* size, but functional size is rarely a consideration.

From the specification of the functional size limits, we can see that any *normal* activity (i.e. one that the group has done before, and for which they have a 'technique') can be achieved from any level of size from within the *normal* range.

In the case of IREV, there was an interesting indication that problems may have been arising at the extreme ends of the size range. Inactivity was higher than might be expected when the group was down to five members—possibly indicating inability to fill roles, and the beginnings of paralysis.(see Note 4, p. 261. Similarly, absenteeism was lower than expected when the group went up to ten members (see Note 3, p. 261). Demand for activity was getting higher than the group could satisfy. If a size decrease had not happened rather quickly, this could have led to discontent and to a crisis in the normative structure.

In considering the relationship between technique-determined roles, activity, and group size, it should be remembered that activity is not equally distributed between group members. IREV members were not equally active. There was a minimum activity level of about two hours a week. Few fell below this, although several were well above it (see Note 11, p. 265). There was also some evidence of role stabilization—certain members concentrated on certain tasks or techniques. This was only surprising to the extent that the group consciously tried to rotate roles (for ideological reasons). They had some success in this aim, witnessed by the fact that role stabilization was not more pronounced. (Again, see Note 11 for details.)

Norms of Leaving and Joining the Group

Group members gave explanations about why they joined or left, but it seemed that these were norm-governed or 'conventional'. More could be discovered by looking at the group process itself.

Both the group itself (its aim was to grow!) and the writer attempted to find reasons for people leaving and joining the group. Reasons for joining were usually expressed as 'I was attracted by the politics' which was rather too uniform not to be 'normal'. Reasons for leaving were more intractable. Most people just 'dropped out' and, while expressing 'sympathy' for the group, were unwilling to give any further reasons. This again seemed 'normal' because it was frequent, and because those who did it had seen others do the same. The obvious exception (Individual 10 who left after an explicit disagreement on the Irish question, mentioned earlier) had only been in the group for two weeks, and had not witnessed such behaviour. This compares well with Stephenson and Fielding's findings (discussed in chapter 4) on behavioural contagion. As an aside—it also makes me wonder how many supposedly subjective reports are in fact 'normal'!

Some members (about 30 per cent) came in from, or left to go to other parts of the country, and thus did not need 'subjective' reasons. Explanation—in the sense of anticipating whether people would join or leave—could be found in the group process better than in the verbal accounts of individuals.

Leaving behaviour

The IREV study was intended to clarify the relations between leaving, joining, absenteeism, and inactivity. It was anticipated that high size, absenteeism, and inactivity would all be associated with leaving. High size was, as we have seen, associated with leaving (or size decrease). Inactivity was associated with high size, and with leaving (more on this later).

Against expectation, absenteeism was associated with *not-leaving* (see Note 3, p.261). This was noteworthy, since high absenteeism *was* associated with high size, which in turn *was* associated with leaving. It seems that absenteeism reduced the *effective* size of the group, thus reducing inactivity, and consequently reducing leaving. It may also be speculated that absenteeism protected the group from over-frequent leaving, by giving 'disgruntled' members time to recover. There is no doubt that 'over-frequent leaving'—a very fast rate of membership turnover—could have had very disruptive effects on the normative structure. Absenteeism—to some extent—protected the group against this. Leaving was associated with high size, inactivity, and *low* levels of absenteeism.

Individual leaving behaviour

To clarify the processes underlying leaving, the 'histories' of individual members were examined. It was found that the individuals most likely to leave the group had the lowest levels of involvement (i.e. the highest levels of inactivity) and had been in the group for the shortest time.

The in-group histories of individual members were constructed from two sets of information: the length of time each member spent in the group; each member's 'level of involvement'—which was defined as the number of hours spent on group activity each week. These 'quantitative histories' are given in Figure 7.3.

The vertical bars in Figure 7.4 show when someone left the group, and how long they had been in it. It is easy to see that members were highly likely to leave in their first ten weeks, likely to leave within a year, and unlikely to leave after they had been in the group for a year or more.

The level of involvement of those that left—when they left—was also very low. Eighteen out of twenty leavers were putting in a below-average number of hours per week. More detail about leaving behaviour is given in Note 9—but the important result is that: *the individuals most likely to leave have the lowest level of involvement, and have been in the group for the shortest time.*

254

Figure 7.3 Level of involvement of individual IREV members against time. (Each individual on a 0–10 scale.)

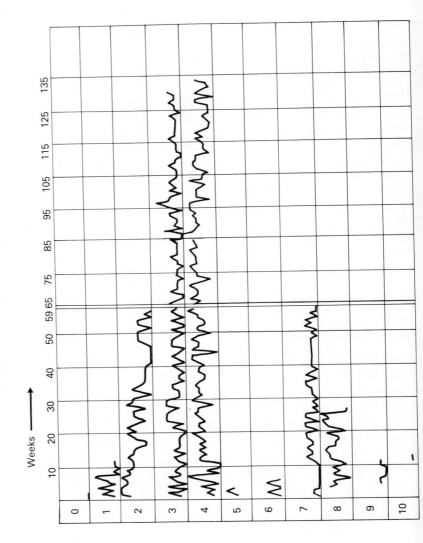

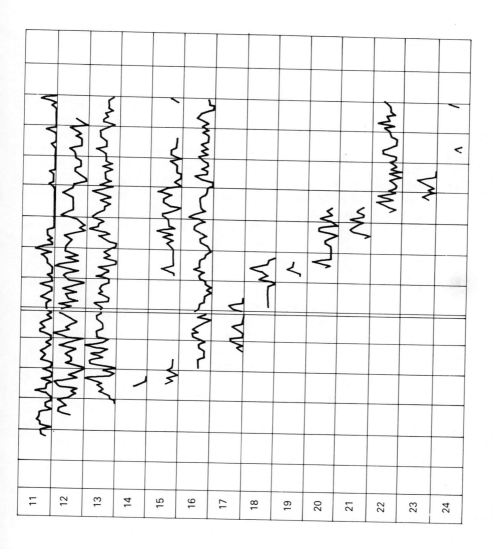

256

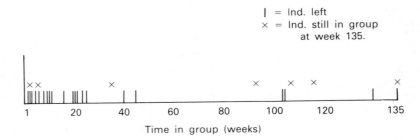

Figure 7.4   Leaving and time spent in group

This can be illustrated by using this criterion to select the three people most likely to leave at each point where someone *did* leave. Despite the random element that some people left to go to other parts of the country—and thus had little personal choice in the matter—the correct individual was chosen in sixteen out of the twenty cases (see Table 7.1). The importance of *early leaving* will be highlighted by the computer simulations, and will be discussed in the next chapter.

Joining Behaviour

In chapter 6, it was anticipated that high levels of activity would make the group 'socially visible'—and new members would join. IREV confirmed this in a striking way. Statistical analysis (see Note 10, p. 265) showed an *increase of two members in the month following an activity peak*, each time there was an activity peak. This was clearly a matter of importance for the group, not just something of statistical significance.

It is also interesting that size increases following activity peaks occurred despite the 'preliminary membership filter' that we mentioned at the beginning of this chapter. This 'filter' served to dampen or reduce the joining rate. It was obvious (when you were there) that the 'entrance requirements' were much stricter when the group was larger.

To Summarize

IREV was a stable group in terms of size, activity, normative structure, and technique. Size fluctuated within limits around an equilibrium point of 7.5 members—despite complete changes of membership, and the group's express intention of growing larger. The independence of size and activity meant that any technique could be actualized at any size level. 'Extreme' size levels that might, given time, have endangered techniques proved to be very transient. The set of techniques did not change in three years, and had their own definite rhythms that, taken together, determined the overall activity levels. Although

Table 7.1 IREV: Predictions of individual leaving behaviour

Week	Who left	First Prediction	Second Prediction	Third Prediction	Number in group
2	0	<u>0</u>*	—	—	8
6	6	7	9	<u>6</u>	8
12	9	10	<u>9</u>	—	8
12	1	10	3	<u>1</u>	7
13	10	<u>10</u>	—	—	6
28	8	11	<u>8</u>	—	7
38	14	<u>14</u>	—	—	9
44	15	2	<u>15</u>	—	9
58	2	17	<u>2</u>	—	9
60	7	17	11	<u>7</u>	8
69	17	<u>17</u>	—	—	8
82	19	15	18	11	10
83	18	<u>18</u>	—	—	9
100	21	3	11	22	10
100	20	3	11	22	9
112	23	<u>23</u>	—	—	9
121	24	11	<u>24</u>	—	9
122	15	11	22	<u>15</u>	8
131	3	11	22	16	6
128	12	11	16	<u>12</u>	7
	20	6	5	5	
			16		

*Underlined number indicates correct prediction.

techniques determined the ranges of size and activity, it was also clear that they depended on size and activity staying within those ranges.

The mechanisms underlying size increase and decrease were clarified. Size increased following high levels of activity. There was also some evidence that size increases were partially choked off at high size levels by the 'preliminary membership filter'. I had the strong impression that 'entrance requirements'— the requisite level of agreement with the group's norms and values—became stricter as the group increased in size (although this was not quantitatively demonstrated).

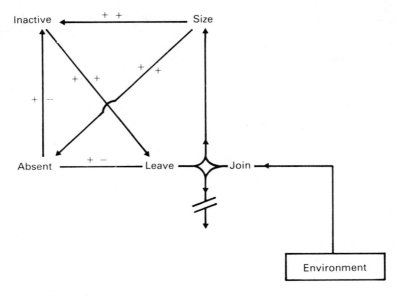

Figure 7.5 IREV: Schematised size regulating subsystem. (++ indicates a positive association — increase leads to increase; +− indicates a negative association — increase leads to decrease.)

Size decreases were associated with high levels of size and inactivity, but with low levels of absenteeism. The specific individuals who left were the least active, newest members. The probability of leaving decreased with length of time spent in the group. Established members tended to have established roles, and were therefore less likely to be inactive. It was speculated that this safeguarded existing techniques. Members who had been in the group longest had been 'selected' for their preferences for, and ability to carry out existing techniques. New, inexperienced members would be most likely to innovate—but were also most likely to leave. Absenteeism seemed to act as an additional buffer, by reducing *effective* group size, reducing inactivity, and therefore reducing the probability that someone would leave—thus protecting the group from the disruptive effects of overfrequent leaving. These relationships were added to the model outlined in chapter 6, and are schematized in Figure 7.5, as the size regulating subsystem of the group.

No structural crisis or failure of technique was observed. We may speculate as to why not. No external intervention deprived the group of any of its techniques. In the Brighton Rents Project such deprivation had led to a large number of inactive individuals, the development of hostile factions, inability to actualize other techniques, inability to attract new members, and an exodus of old members. The group fell below its functional minimum and collapsed. In IREV the smooth operation of the size regulating subsystem prevented the appearance of large numbers of inactive individuals, and (probably) the development of factions that might have changed the techniques. It may be that crises were avoided as well as simply not appearing. The continuity of IREV and the disappearance of the Rents Project underlines the point. The irony remains that IREV's intention was to grow.

Notes

1 Coding instructions and intercoder reliability

The information in the minute books was transferred onto standard coding sheets—one sheet for each week. The minute books yielded two types of data.

1 Data which was regularly and unambiguously recorded: size of group; attendance and absence records for each member at each meeting; and specific activities undertaken.

Specific activities raised a slight technical problem in that minutes might be premature or retrospective. In other words, activities might be recorded before or after they were carried out. A careful watch was kept for these items during coding. It is possible that some activities were mentioned but not carried out, or that some were carried out without being mentioned. Active participation had established that the minutes were reasonably accurate, and the following coding rules were introduced:

(a) Only activities mentioned in the minutes are to be coded.
(b) All activities mentioned are to be coded, except

(i) if it is specifically said that they were not carried out
(ii) if a specific activity is assigned to a member in more than one successive set of minutes—where it will be assumed that the act was carried out on the last occasion it was mention.

2 Data requiring some reconstructive effort by the group members who did the coding, and depending on their familiarity with events. Data of this type was: which (and how many) members carried out which activities; how long each member spent on group activities per week. Even on these matters, the minutes were about 80 per cent specific. Where the minutes were not specific, the coder's memories, experience of the time taken by various tasks, and the coding rules, reduced the discrepancies between coders to very narrow levels.

An ex-member encoded the entire data set—a task which took eight two-hour sessions. As a check on the accuracy of the coding, another group member agreed to encode 25 sets of minutes chosen at random from the total of 135 sets. The most difficult data item to encode was the number of hours each individual spent in group activity per week. The correlation coefficient of the twenty-five sets of code sheets for this item was 0.91. On an easier item—the number of activities undertaken per week irrespective of individuals—the correlation coefficient was 0.93. The significance levels (t tests) of both were well in excess of 0.001, and inter-judge reliability was taken to be high.

On the twenty-five 'test' items there were only two gross discrepancies in scores. When the minutes for these two weeks were consulted, it was clear that the discrepancies were due to carelessness, and agreement was reached. The writer then checked the full encoded data set against the minutes. Nine further 'errors' came to light, of which only two were due to ambiguity in the minutes themselves. These errors were corrected, and the resulting data set used as the base for an analysis of IREV.

2 IREV: Size and size changes

As predicted by the model, group size oscillated around a (technique determined) mean, without any empirically significant tendency to increase or decrease.

Size was defined as the number of members in the group in any week. In line with previous findings, 'member' was defined as someone who was recognized as a member by other members. In the case of IREV, this meant someone who appeared under the heading 'present' or 'absent' in the minute book.

Size ranged from 5 to 10 members, with a mean of 7.8 and a standard deviation of 1.2. The total number of weeks spent at each size level is given in Table 7.2. There was no empirically significant tendency for IREV to increase or decrease in size with the passage of time. This can be seen visually in Table 7.2.

Table 7.2 IREV size distribution

Size	Number of weeks
5	6
6	11
7	34
8	29
9	45
10	5

Size oscillation meant that size should be inversely related to itself. In other words, an above-average size level should be followed by a lower size level; a below-average size level should be followed by a higher size level. This was confirmed by a regression of size at $t = 1$ on size t at a statistical significance level well above that required. The constant was 0.83 and the increment 0.89—which meant, for instance, that a size of 5 should be followed by an increase to 5.28, and a size of 10 should be followed by a decrease to 9.75. The point at which it was equiprobable that joining and leaving would take place was 7.55.

The actual size transformations that took place are given in Figure 7.6.

		Size at $t+1$					
		5	6	7	8	9	10
	5	4	1	1	0	0	0
Size at t	6	2	8	1	0	0	0
	7	0	1	27	4	1	0
	8	0	1	5	17	6	0
	9	0	0	0	6	37	2
	10	0	0	0	1	1	3

Figure 7.6   IREV size transformations

Size and Time—A Qualification

It has just been said that there was no empirically significant tendency for IREV to increase or decrease with the passage of time. This has to be qualified.

Regression of size on time gave a t^2 significance level in excess of 0.01. The constant was 7.3 and the increment 0.0078. This meant that one person would be gained every 2½ *years*. Starting with 7.3 people, the group would take 6½ years to exceed its upper bound of 10. Thus, although the time trend was statistically significant it was concluded that the group was, for all practical purposes, stable with respect to time.

3 Size and absenteeism

It was expected that absenteeism would increase with size, and this was confirmed at the requisite level of significance.

Table 7.3 Absenteeism and group size

Size of group	5	6	7	8	9	10
Mean weekly level of absenteeism	0.5	1.2	1.5	1.8	2.1	1.2

χ^2 probability of H_o = 0.1

Absenteeism and Leaving

It was expected that absenteeism would be associated with leaving. In other words, high absenteeism would be associated with a subsequent decrease in group size. The opposite turned out to be true. *Low* absenteeism was associated with leaving.

Size was regressed on absenteeism in the previous week. Low absenteeism was associated with leaving at a very high significance level ($t^2 = 0.001$).

4 Size and inactivity

It was expected that the number of inactive individuals would increase with size. There were indications that this was the case, but it was not confirmed at the requisite level of significance.

'Inactivity' was defined as the number of people who attended the weekly meeting, but did nothing else (Table 7.4).

Table 7.4 Inactivity and group size

Size of group	5	6	7	8	9	10
Mean weekly level of inactivity	1.5	0.7	1.9	2.3	2.6	3.4

χ^2 probability of H_o = 0.01

5 Activity

As predicted by the model, activity oscillated around a mean without any significant tendency to increase or decrease.

Three alternative measures of activity were investigated. These were:

1 The number of hours spent by group members per week on group tasks.
2 The number of active individuals per week.
3 The number of roles filled per week.

The correlation coefficient for activity (hours) and activity (individuals) was 0.83; that between activity (hours) and activity (roles) was 0.92, both giving t^2 values so high as to approach certainty. The relationship between the measures as given by regression was straightforward. Approximately:

activity (hours) = 3.5 × activity (individuals)
activity (hours) = 2 × activity (roles).

It was concluded that the three measures were, for our purposes, interchangeable. Activity (hours) was used as the main measure of activity for IREV.

Activity ranged from 0 to 36, with a mean of 13.3 and a standard deviation of 7.2. The total number of weeks at each activity level is given in Table 7.5.

As anticipated, there was no significant relationship (by regression) between activity and time. This can be seen visually in Figure 7.1.

Table 7.5 IREV activity distribution

Activity level	Number of weeks
0 – 4	12
5 – 9	30
10 – 14	39
15 – 19	20
20 – 24	17
25 – 29	5
30+	4

6 Size and activity

As predicted by the model, there was no significant relationship between size and activity.

Although the null hypothesis was accepted, visual inspection of the data left a trace of doubt that high size might be related to high activity. Since this result is important for the final model and counterintuitive, it was decided to carry out a further regression analysis.

There was in fact a slight positive correlation, reaching the t^2 5 per cent level of significance, although the correlation coefficient was only 0.15. The regression constant was 6.7 and the increment 1.2. In the group size range of five to ten members, this accounted for an increase of six units of activity from the smallest to the largest size. Since the level of activity ranged from 0 to 36, with a mean of 13.3 and a standard deviation of 7.2, it was felt that, although size might have some small effect

Size	0–4	5–9	10–14	15–19	20–24	25–29	30–36
5	1	2	2	1	0	0	0
6	0	3	3	3	2	0	0
7	5	8	12	3	3	2	1
8	3	5	10	4	5	1	0
9	3	12	11	8	5	2	3
10	0	1	1	1	2	0	0

Activity

χ^2 probability of $H_o = 0.9$

Figure 7.6   IREV size and activity

on activity, this could safely be ignored from the point of view of overall group stability.

7 Techniques and activity

It was anticipated that each technique would have its own measurable rhythm, and that the total activity pattern would be decomposable into these rhythms. This expectation was prompted by the behaviour of the Rents Registration Group of the Brighton Rents Project. Visual inspection of the frequency and level of actualization of each technique in Figure 7.2 leaves a strong feeling that each technique has its own definite rhythm. However, these rhythms were not definable numerically using methods that were available. There was no significant autocorrelation up to a lag of twenty weeks. Also—as expected, there was no significant time trend (with the exception of A2 which showed a slight decline).

Nevertheless, in this case, visual evidence was felt to be sufficient confirmation that each technique had a 'normal' behaviour, and that the oscillations in total activity were a reflection of this.

8 Techniques and size

In previous chapters we asserted that group size was the subject of certain norms, and was therefore influenced by the normative structure. Using the notion of 'technique', we are now in a position to be more specific on this relationship.

The role specifications inherent in the set of techniques serve as a template that determines the limits of group size.

Functionally, these limits may be defined in the following way.

The lower size limit is the minimum number of members capable of filling the maximum number of roles specified by any technique. The upper size limit is the maximum number of members capable of being absorbed by the maximum number of roles specified by any technique.

From this it follows that any *normal* activity may be achieved from any level of size within the *normal* range. This is the relationship that allows size and activity to fluctuate independently. This relationship between size and technique held for IREV during the three-year observation period.

We established earlier that the actual size range of IREV was between 5 and 10 members with a mean of 7.8 and a standard deviation of 1.2. From this we can say that the usual size range was between six and nine members. We also established that the mean activity level was 13.3 hours per week, and the mean number of roles was approximately half this. In fact, the mean number of roles was 6.4 with a standard deviation of 3.6. Thus the maximum likely number of roles is 10, and the minimum likely size is 6—giving an average of 1.4 roles per person. In fact the mean number of active individuals was 3.9 with a standard deviation of 1.7—and thus the maximum likely number of active individuals was 5.6. Since each active individual filled (on average) two roles, it is clear that the maximum number of roles can be filled by the minimum number of members ($5 \times 2 = 10$), and that the maximum number of members could be absorbed by the maximum number of roles ($10 \times 1 = 10$).

It should also be noted that the use of the notions of mean and standard deviation—while providing a general picture of the relationship between technique and size—does not imply that roles were equally distributed. They were not. There was evidence of a specific type of activity distribution and for some role-stabilization, which we will deal with later.

9 Leaving behaviour and individual IREV members

The records of each individual's activity while in the group suggested three hypotheses that might explain leaving.

1   Leaving was a simple function of time spent in the group. A χ^2 test was performed on the length of time each individual spent in the group, and the null hypothesis (leaving was independent of time in group) was rejected ($\chi^2 < 0.01$). Inspection of data (see Figure 7.4) showed that members were highly likely to leave in their first ten weeks and very likely to leave within a year. If members stayed in the group for more than a year, they were then not likely to leave until their third year, if then.

2   Leaving was a function of a low level of involvement. A χ^2 test was performed on leaving and involvement, and the null hypothesis was rejected.

3   Individual levels of involvement declined with time, and leaving was the terminal point of this process. Regressions ($N=17$) *showed clearly that in general individual levels of involvement showed no time trend. The exceptions were Individuals 2 and 11, whose involvement declined with time.*

Hypotheses 1 and 2 were combined to give the following statement:

the individuals most likely to leave the group have the lowest level of involvement, and have been in the group for the shortest time.

Level of involvement

	Below average	Above average
No. left	18	2

χ^2 less than 0.001

Figure 7.7   Leaving and involvement

10 Joining behaviour

In chapter 6, it was anticipated that high levels of activity would render the group 'socially visible', and new members would join. In IREV this was confirmed at the requisite level of significance.

We have also seen that there was a 'preliminary membership filter' that served to dampen the joining rate. The exact mechanics and function of this will be discussed in a later chapter.

Although it was anticipated that joining would be associated with high levels of activity, it was not clear whether this effect would be subject to a time lag. Three ways in which activity could effect subsequent size levels were therefore examined.

1 Activity against size in the following week.
2 Mean activity over four weeks against size in the following week.
3 Maximum activity level in a four-week period against size in the following week.

Regression showed all three measures of activity to have a significant effect on joining. The 'most significant' measure was maximum activity level. This gave a correlation coefficient of 0.32 and a t^2 significance level in excess of 0.001. The constant was 6.6 and the increment 0.06 of the maximum activity level. This predicted an increase of two members soon after the maximum activity level of thirty-six was reached, each time it was reached. This was clearly a matter of importance for the group, as well as being statistically significant.

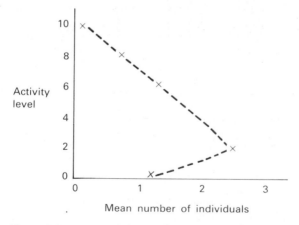

Figure 7.8   Distribution of activity among group members

11 The distribution of activity among group members and role stabilization

IREV members, as might be expected, were not equally active, although there was a minimum activity level and few members fell below this. There was also some evidence of role stabilization—certain members concentrated on certain tasks or techniques—which was only surprising to the extent that the group consciously tried

Role

Member

Role	1	2	3	4	5	6	7	8	9	10	11	12	13	14	15	16	17	18	19	20	21	22	23	24
A1	3	19	34	60	2	1	8	7	–	–	9	49	52	1	14	34	4	2	3	9	7	20	1	2
A2	1	20	8	24	2	1	2	10	1	–	1	7	6	–	4	7	–	–	–	1	–	3	1	–
A3	–	7	6	10	2	–	–	4	–	–	–	10	4	–	2	3	–	2	–	1	1	2	–	–
A4	–	–	2	1	–	–	1	–	–	–	–	15	19	–	–	–	–	1	–	–	–	3	–	–
A5	5	8	5	10	1	3	–	8	–	–	–	3	1	–	1	1	–	–	–	1	1	–	–	–
A6	–	20	6	76	–	–	–	10	–	–	7	11	17	1	7	7	–	–	–	1	–	3	1	1
A7	–	5	–	29	–	1	3	3	–	–	9	17	9	–	3	5	–	–	–	–	–	5	–	–
No Role	6	21	74	19	–	2	45	4	6	2	88	27	27	2	33	39	15	13	3	11	4	12	8	3

Figure 7.9 Role stabilization in IREV. (Outlined cells indicate some degree of role concentration)

to distribute roles equally. They had some success with this aim, witnessed by the fact that role stabilization was not more pronounced.

The average mumber of individuals at each activity level (measured in hours per week) is given in Figure 7.8. The distribution is interesting in its difference from the usual J-curve of decreasing verbal participation (discussed in chapter 1). Instead of tailing away, with the largest number of people at the point of least participation, the IREV curve of activity distribution has a cut-off point. The highest number of people are found at a low level of activity (two hours per week), but very few members fall below this.

Some roles associated with techniques tended to be concentrated on individuals (A2, A4, A6, and A7), while others were undertaken by all members in proportion to the time they had been in the group (A1, A3, and A5). Details are given in Figure 7.9.

CHAPTER 8

A computer model of group behaviour

It seems to me that this purely pragmatic reason for using a model is fundamental, even if it is less pretentious than some of the more 'philosophical' reasons. Take for instance the idea that a good model has a deeper 'truth'—to what does this idea lead us? No electronic model of a cat's brain can possibly be as true as that provided by the brain of another cat; yet what is the *use* of the latter as a model? Its very closeness means that it also presents all the technical features that make the first so difficult. From here on, I shall take as a basis the thesis that the first virtue of a model is to be useful

(Ross Ashby)

GROUP-1 is a simulation model intended to account for the various processes we have identified so far. It does several things. It puts together all the assumptions we have made about groups into a working package, and enables us to see if they fit together and produce group-like behaviour. It tell us whether we have made *enough* assumptions, or whether something is missing—in which case the behaviour of the model will be 'insufficiently' group-like. It tells us if the assumptions we have made are *clear*. If they are not clear, this soon becomes obvious when it comes to writing the computer program. In other words, modelling tells us if our assumptions are consistent, sufficient, and clear.

The GROUP-1 model is a projection. Its usefulness does not lie in trying to *predict* what will happen to any given group, but in trying to discover the *limits* of group behaviour: the conditions that are necessary for action to take place, not which actions will take place. Another way of looking at this (Roberts and Robinson, 1980) is to say that a model specifies one way of doing things—to which people may choose to conform. The model alone cannot specify the choice.

One way—particularly relevant to this chapter—in which this distinction emerges is termed 'the problem of validation'. How do we know whether or not the model is 'right'? It is usually assumed that models can be 'validated' in the same sort of ways that theories in physics or chemistry can be validated. Even where this has not, or seemingly cannot be done, the methodology of the physical sciences is still thought to be appropriate. It is a target to aim at, even when it cannot be reached for the moment. Despite this ambition, attempts to specify validation procedures have not been very successful.

> Validation is the determination of how adequately the simulation reflects those aspects of the real world it has been designed to model. The need for validation, and its logic and procedures, have received a great deal of attention from scholars since simulation studies were first begun. Despite this history, generally agreed on criteria have not yet been developed. There has not evolved a single set of rules and tests which, if satisfied, results in a simulation that is uniformly regarded as valid.
>
> (Lehman, 1977, p. 15)

Our position is that the search for this sort of validation is mistaken. The type of model that we are dealing with exists at the level of systems science, not at the level of natural science. Natural science notions of validation and prediction are inappropriate. This does not mean that we are all at sea, or that there is no way of finding out whether one model is better than another—simply that the sort of 'test' used is different. Perhaps the best-known simulation work that has been done is Forrester's studies on ecological catastrophes (see Forrester, 1971). Using a set of assumptions about population growth, economic development, and the availability of raw materials, he produced a horrifying set of projections that showed spaceship earth was set on a course for disaster. If the standard of living was maintained, the population pressures became intolerable. If population pressure was reduced, all the raw materials would be consumed—and so on. It is interesting that Forrester also recognized his work was concerned with limits—in this case the limits of growth. Both his assumptions and his methods have been severely criticized, but the debate has not revolved around the 'problem of validation'. In one sense it is all too obvious how such 'prophecies' would be validated—so it is not the most pertinent question.

Frijda (1967) argues that the criterion for a 'good' simulation is the correspondence between the program and the natural processes that are being modelled. Although this advice is accepted in the construction of the GROUP-1 program, it rather begs the question of validation. The assumed processes are as much in question as the way of representing them in a program. Lehman follows Abelson (1968) in suggesting the best method of validation would be a version of The Turing Test. This is a formalization of an intuitive method of validation adopted by many users of simulations. Does the behaviour of the model 'look like' the behaviour of the 'real thing'?

Turing Test Validation

It is important to notice that Turing Test validations rest entirely on consensus truth, not, as does validation in the natural sciences, on correspondence truth. We will return to this point.

The Turing Test itself is named after its inventor, Alan Turing, who virtually invented the theory of computing, but was hounded to a premature death before the existence of a movement to defend gay rights. The test (Turing 1963) was invented in the context of the early debate on machine 'intelligence'. 'Will computers ever be able to think?' was the question that taxed the first cyberneticians as they built their prototypes with soldering irons from old post-office relays and vacuum tubes. The resulting clicking, whirring, and overheated artefacts did not look much like specimens of intelligent life. Much has changed since then, but the powerful IBM giants of the eighties still do not look like people—and of course they still do not meet Turing's criterion of intelligence. Turing's point was that intelligence could not be identified with the physical embodiment of the intelligent being. His test has a further (in my view) supreme merit—it can be applied in the absence of any agreed definition of intelligence. If it relied on some specific definition of 'intelligence', it would soon be outdated. Worse than that, it would be essentially inappropriate. 'Intelligence' is a dialectical or conversational concept. Defining it and placing it at the level of natural or systems science simply results in a 'hole' in the theory.

Turing avoided the problem of defining intelligence by taking the point of view that human beings *are* intelligent, and that they can *recognize* other human beings who are also intelligent. An intelligent machine (if machine is the right word) would be one that was *recognized* to be intelligent by a human being. If the machine were intelligent, then it could also be *mistaken* for a human being. Since large metal boxes with wires hanging out would not be mistaken for human beings, Turing placed a wall between the person and the machine. The person on one side of the wall would not be told whether the 'object' on the other side was a person or a machine. (The original version was also complicated by guessing games about the sex of the 'person' behind the wall). Communication was only allowed via a teletype. Within these conditions, the person could ask any questions, or hold any conversation with the 'object' on the other side of the wall. If the person could not tell whether they were conversing with another human being or a machine (and they were in fact talking to a 'machine'), then that machine would have passed the Turing Test. It would be intelligent, and would have to be treated as such—no matter what it looked like.

The Turing Test can be modified—in two stages—to provide a criterion for the validity of simulations. The first modification serves to define the 'ultimate' simulation, as the original served to define an intelligent machine. If, by means of symbolic communication and interrogation *only*, we are unable to detect a difference between the simulation and its object, the simulation is perfect. As Ashby pointed out, the best model of a cat's brain is another cat's brain—and we can add—or something that is indistinguishable from a cat's brain.

The second modification brings us down to earth a little. If by symbolic communication and interrogation alone we cannot distinguish between the simulation and its object *in the relevant respects*, then the simulation is 'valid'. This criterion allows us to *use* statistical (or any other) techniques, but it is important to notice that it is not *based* on statistical techniques. In other words, although we will always use some definable way or other to judge how the simulation or its object lives up to our expectations, the process of judging is not tied to any specific set of correspondences. We are dealing with consensual truth. The validity of a simulation is tied to our interaction with it (which is related to Ashby's idea of the usefulness of the model), not to the absolute relations that hold between the model and the reality.

The test criterion for the GROUP-1 simulation model was simply whether its behaviour, in the relevant respects, looked like—and so could be mistaken for—the behavior of a natural group.

The GROUP-1 Model

The GROUP-1 model was written in FORTRAN IV (for convenience rather than preference) and run on the ICL 1900 Series computer at Brunel University between 1976 and 1977. To keep the program and the model as clear as possible, all the simplifying assumptions recommended by William Morris were used. Where possible:

> variables were made into constants
> total number of variables was minimised
> linear relations were used
> strong assumptions and restrictions were used
> randomness was suppressed

> (Morris, quoted in Stodgill 1970, p. 91)

It was necessary to use random numbers. These were input from cards not generated within the program. This meant that any given run could be precisely recreated.

The variables used in the GROUP-1 model were as follows.

Date or week number

This was represented in the simulation as *cycle number*. Each cycle represented one week. At the end of each cycle, a summary of activity, preferences, group size etc., was printed out.

Group size

As with natural groups, *size* was the number of people in the group. The simplifying assumption that everyone in the group was a member of the group was introduced—the criterion 'being recognized as a member by other members' was not simulated. Since everyone in the simulated group took part in its decision process, this was a sufficient representation of 'being recognized as a member'.

All runs started with a group of eight members—the average size of IREV and of a Rents Project subgroup. The simulated group collapsed if all its members left. Runs were also terminated if the size rose above thirty—this was considered to be a sufficiently large size increase to change the nature and the structure of the group.

Absenteeism

This was an optional variable in the simulation, and was not used in every run.

When it was used, randomly selected individuals would be prefixed with '88', which meant that they were not available for any activity in that cycle. Absent individuals 'experienced' a slow decline in their level of commitment, which was reduced by one point for each 'week' of absence.

Inactivity

As in the natural groups, this was the number of members who were in the group, but did not 'do' anything in any given 'week'.

Activity

This was the number of group members who took part in group activities in any given 'week'.

Joined

This was the number of members who joined the group in the course of any given 'week'.

Left

This was the number of members who left the group in the course of any given 'week'.

Group member

For each run there was a pool of ninety-nine 'individuals', some of whom were designated as group members. Individuals joined the group—became members—from the pool. Members returned to the pool when they left the group. Only group members effected the results, although all individuals in the pool had 'preferences' and a 'level of commitment' which would be activated if they joined the group.

Preferences

Each individual had an ordered set of preferences about group activities. Since the number of activities was set at eight for every run, each individual had a first, a second, and so on down to an eighth preference. For the sake of simplicity in the program, it was assumed that individuals did not feel an equal preference for any two activities, but could always say they preferred one to another. Preferences could, however, change.

Level of commitment

Each individual had a 'level of commitment'—termed 'LOC' in the simulation. This level of commitment was defined as the number of hours that individual was prepared to spend per 'week' on group activity. From the observation of IREV, the maximum level of commitment—'MAXLOC'—for any individual was set at ten; the minimum level of commitment—'MINLOC'—for any individual was set at two. Individuals whose level of commitment fell below MINLOC 'left' the group. Individual's levels of commitment varied between these limits according to their preferences and group activity. How this was arranged will be described later.

Acts

As we mentioned under preferences, the number of possible acts—the range of activities open to the group—was fixed at eight throughout. From the experience of natural groups, this was felt to provide a realistic range of options. In the simulation, an act, *per se*, was the analogy of a 'technique' for natural groups. It existed as an idea whether or not it was realized. If it was realized then it required a certain number of people, and a certain amount of activity (hours to be put in) before it was completed.

Two conditions were tried. In the first, there was a range of acts of increasing complexity, demanding both more people and more time. In the second, all acts were equivalent in terms of people and time.

Table 8.1 GROUP-1 act requirements

	Condition 1		Condition 2	
Act	Minimum number of people	Minimum amount of time (aggregate LOC)	Minimum number of people	Minimum amount of time (aggregate LOC)
1	1	5	3	15
2	2	10	3	15
3	3	15	3	15
4	4	20	3	15
5	5	25	3	15
6	6	30	3	15
7	7	35	3	15
8	8	40	3	15

Preference Set

In the natural groups we have looked at, activities were selected by complex processes of discussion and evaluation. A full simulation of this process was out of the question. It is beyond current computing techniques—and anyway would require a methodology at the level of a dialectical science. Nevertheless, the process can be modelled in a simple way at the level of systems science. Certain simple assumptions were made about preferences, and a set of rules for combining preferences to arrive at a decision. Individual preferences were not explored in the natural groups, and this was deliberate. It was felt that 'preferences' like 'attitudes' and 'personalities' were not objective, but 'conversational' realities (see 'Mystic Numbers' in Pask, Glanville, and Robinson, 1980).

The simulated decision process was based on an n-person elaboration of two-person game theoretic payoff matrices (see von Neumann and Morgenstern, 1953; Shubik, 1964; Howard, 1971). As a general comment, we can say that 'games' are an interesting way of exploring social realities—especially when those realities are to some degree ritualized—but they should not be mistaken for a *representation* of that reality. It is from this point of view that we use the 'preferences' in the simulation of decision-making. They are a gross, but useful simplification.

In looking at natural groups we said that normative structure was the set of beliefs that were common to group members and perceived to be so. The term 'structure' rather than 'set' was used to indicate that the beliefs were interrelated. A change in one would probably precipitate a change in the others. In the simulation, the idea of normative structure was left out. The rationale for this was as follows. In a natural group the function of general norms is to provide a conversational context in which to make decisions about specific activities, and to provide a 'preliminary membership filter'—to make sure people did not get into the group who had little in common with it. In the simulation the set of techniques was predetermined (as Acts 1–8) and therefore did not need a 'conversational context'. Also matters were arranged so that all the individuals in the pool outside the group—its environment—had preferences that were compatible with those of the group. Their preferences referred to the same set of techniques, even if the ordering was different. A membership filter was unnecessary.

'Techniques' were, as we have said, identified with Acts in the simulation. 'Normative strength' could be defined as the rate of change of the sub-set of Acts selected for realization. (This rate of change would reflect consensus or division in the preference set.)

The preference set itself was simply that matrix of preferences of all individuals for each specific act. The preference set was represented in the form illustrated by Table 8.2. Here we see that Individual 1 prefers Act 6 to all the others, with a second choice of Act 2, a third choice of Act 7, and so on. Individual 2 prefers Act 8 to all the others, with a second choice of Act 7—and so on. The initial preferences of each individual were set at random.

The preference set formulation is one way of exploring the idea of normative structure, not a representation of it. It is particularly useful for the way it steers between two extreme views on the nature of 'norms' themselves. The idea that

Table 8.2 A GROUP-1 preference set

Individual	Act 1	Act 2	Act 3	Act 4	Act 5	Act 6	Act 7	Act 8
1	6	2	4	8	5	1	3	7
2	6	4	8	5	3	7	2	1
3	5	2	3	8	1	7	4	6
4	8	4	2	1	6	3	5	7
5	4	1	6	7	3	5	8	2
6	5	1	6	7	4	8	3	2
7	2	7	6	3	1	2	8	5
8	7	5	3	8	1	2	4	6

norms are 'things' over and above individual beliefs is often counterposed to the alternative that norms are nothing but individual beliefs.

The first 'norms-as-things-in-themselves' view is rejected as a simple category mistake. Norms do not exist independently of people any more than 'Oxford University' exists independently of its constituent colleges (see Ryle, 1949). On the other hand, the Gullahorns' (1972) thesis that

> social system behaviour can be explained in terms of psychological processes, and that no principles beyond those necessary to explain individual behaviour are required.

> (in Guetzkow, Kotler and Schultz, 1972, p. 181)

is also rejected. First, it can be pointed out that the impact of *ordered* collective behaviour (including expressed preferences) on an individual is entirely different from the effect of unordered encounters. Secondly, unless the principles necessary to explain individual behaviour include combinatorial principles, nothing much will be explained about collective behaviour. Norms *are* composed of individual behaviours, but the matter does not end there. Norms, as ordered behaviours, then have a strong influence on individual behaviour. In terms of the model, preference set—the combinatorial representation of individual preferences—is taken as a basis of a decision process and of action. This brings us to the dynamics of the simulation.

The Decision Process (Subroutine VOTE)

The natural groups were 'democratic' in the sense of Lippitt and White (1958); the choice of activity was determined in discussion that took account of individual preferences—choice was not the autocratic responsibility of any one member. An algorithm was developed to reflect this process of discussion. The following simplifying assumptions were used.

No individual can participate in more than one activity.
Each individual will be assigned an activity.

Each activity must receive a minimum number of choices to be selected (without this condition, each individual would have been assigned to their most preferred activity). See Table 8.1 for the numbers of choices required by each activity.

No activity may be carried out more than once per cycle (simulated 'week').

The first preference of each individual was assumed to be their choice of activity. If an activity received a sufficient number of first choices (specified in Table 8.1 as 'minimum number of people'), it is carried out. If no 'decision' is made on first choices, then second choices are included, and so on. To illustrate this from the preference set in Table 8.2, we assume Condition 2—each activity needs a minimum of three choices in order to be carried out. We see immediately that Act 5 will be chosen as it receives three first choices. Act 2 will also be chosen as it receives two first and one second choice. Individual 1 must be content with second choice, since the first choice of Act 6 is not shared at the first or second level of preference. Individuals 7 and 8, whose second choice it was, have already opted for Act 5. The remaining two individuals (2 and 4) must now join in with Act 2 or 5, or do nothing. Even if they could agree on a third activity, they would need a third individual before they could carry it out—and the others are all committed. Individual 2 will join Act 5 (the third preference), and Individual 4 will join Act 2 (the fourth preference).

After the Decisions ... (Subroutines DISILLUSION, LEAVE, and ACTION)

In the natural groups, after decisions, actions were carried out, members' levels of commitment (the amount of time they were prepared to put in) varied, and sometimes people left the group. These processes were simulated and the following simplifications introduced.

Changes in level of commitment were determined by the group's choice of activities and the individual's preferences.

Members could only leave the group at one point in the cycle.

DISILLUSION

After Act(s) had been SELECTED by VOTE, all INDS (members) were scanned to see if their allocated Act matched their first preference. Where the allocated Act did not match the first preference, that IND's level of commitment (LOC) was reduced by a constant factor (DIVLOC). After initial tests DIVLOC was set at 0.5 (i.e. members, level of commitment was halved each time each time they took part in an activity that was not their first choice). If an IND was ABSENT (and thus could not obtain first preference of Act) their LOC was reduced by 1.

LEAVE

After DISILLUSION, all INDS were scanned to see if their level of commitment (LOC) had fallen below a minimum level (MINLOC=2). If it had fallen below this level, the IND left the group.

ACTION

In natural groups, the factor that decided whether chosen actions were carried out or not was the effort members were prepared to put in—in relation to the effort needed to complete the action. This was simulated by aggregating the levels of commitment (SUMLOC) of the INDS allocated to the Act.

If SUMLOC was less than the Act requirements, the LOC of the most committed individuals was *increased* by the reverse of DIVLOC (i.e. multiplied by 2) to a maximum of 10, until a match between SUMLOC and the Act requirement was obtained.

If SUMLOC was greater than the Act requirement, the LOC of the least committed individuals was *decreased* by DIVLOC until a match was obtained.

When SUMLOC matched the Act requirement, the Act was COMPLETED. If SUMLOC remained below the Act requirement after the individual LOC increases, the Act was NOT COMPLETED.

After the Actions ... (Subroutines DISSONANCE and JOIN)

In natural groups, successful actions tended to be repeated, and unsuccessful actions tended to be dropped. If there was a high level of successful action, new members tended to be attracted to the group. This was simulated in the following way.

DISSONANCE

After ACTION, the preference orders of individuals were changed.

If an Act was COMPLETED, the INDS to whom it had been allocated increased their preference for it by one point. For example, IND 4 prefers Act 4 to Act 2 (at preference levels 2 and 3 respectively) but takes part in Act 2 which is COMPLETED. Act 2 then moves up to preference level 2, and Act 4 moves down to preference level 3.

If an Act was NOT COMPLETED, the INDS to whom it had been allocated decreased their preference for it by one point.

JOIN

The rate at which new members joined the group was determined by the variable ENTER. Several conditions were tried.

ENTER was set at 0.5, 0.4, 0.2, and 0.125.

The number of new members was determined by the number of individuals involved in completed actions (ICOMP × ENTER).

The number of new members was determined by the number of individuals involved in completed actions and their mean level of commitment. In this condition ENTER was set to equal (SUMLOC/ICOMP) −1)/10.

Alternatively, new members could be added by a predetermined (fixed or random) schedule.

After Each Cycle ... (Subroutine DISPLAY)

After each cycle, subroutine DISPLAY printed out the details of the state of the 'group', as illustrated in Figure 8.1.

The program terminated if the group rose above size thirty or fell to nothing; if the pool of available individuals became exhausted (i.e. the group had a throughput of ninety-nine members); or when fifty cycles had been completed.

The GROUP-1 program is given in Appendix 1.

GROUP-1 Simulation Results

The GROUP-1 program generated six characteristic profiles, each of which was associated with a particular combination of initial conditions.

Significant initial conditions

Joining rate

This could be:

1 low and tied to group activity;
2 low, tied to group activity, and supplemented by the random or regular addition of new members (actually or on average one new member every three cycles);
3 high and tied to group activity.

When the joining rate was tied to group activity, it did not make any detectable difference whether activity was measured by the number of active individuals or a combination of number of active individuals and mean level of commitment.

Level of initial preference matching.

This could be:

1 high;
2 low.

STATE OF SIMULATION BEFORE CYCLE 2

NO. OF PEOPLE IN GROUP 10   2 PEOPLE JOINED AND 0 LEFT

NO. OF COMPLETED ACTIVITIES   2
NO. OF INDS WHO COMPLETE ACTS 7
TOTAL LOC IS 44
AVERAGE LOC IS 4

DETAILED DATA ON ACTIVITIES

ACT	SELECTED	COMPLETED
1	0	0
2	1	1
3	0	0
4	0	1
5	1	0
6	0	0
7	0	0
8	0	0

DETAILED DATA ON INDIVIDUALS

IND.	LOC.	FIX.	ACT.1	ACT.2	ACT.3	ACT.4	ACT.5	ACT.6	ACT.7	ACT.8
1	3	2	6	1	4	8	5	2	3	7
2	3	5	6	4	8	5	2	7	3	1
3	5	5	5	2	3	8	1	7	4	6
4	3	2	8	3	2	1	6	4	5	7
5	5	2	4	1	6	7	3	5	8	2
6	5	2	5	1	6	7	4	8	3	2
7	5	5	2	7	3	3	1	2	8	5
8	885	5	7	5	6	8	1	2	4	6
9	5	0	3	8	6	2	5	1	4	7
10	5	0	7	2	6	1	8	5	3	4

Figure 8.1 Printout by DISPLAY of the state of the simulated group

It is obvious that the initial degree of match between members' preferences could be very varied. Each member has more than 40 000 *possible* preference orderings, and a group of 8 members has (approximately) 7^{36} possible preference sets. Since 'preferences' were a simulation fiction—in 'real life', preferences do not seem to be distinct or clearly ordered—it seemed appropriate to make an intuitive rather than a mathematical distinction between 'high' and 'low' preference matches.

'High' matches were preference sets in which several (four or more) members achieved their first choice of activity. 'Low' matches were preference sets in which few or no members achieved their first choice of activity. Table 8.2 shows a highly matched preference set: five of the eight members achieve their first choice of activity.

Average level of commitment of new members

This could be:
1 high
2 random—thus, in the long run tending to an average of 5.

The level of commitment (index of the hours members were prepared to put into group activity per week) of new members was either set at random (in the range 0–10) or fixed at a constant level for each new member. Low constant levels were not tried. They seemed bound to lead to a speedy collapse of the group. 'High' and 'random' were thus the initial alternatives.

Absenteeism

The program part that allowed absenteeism was optional.

Activity conditions

There were two activity conditions as specified in Table 8.1. In the first condition the numbers of individuals required to carry out an activity increased; in the second condition the numbers remained constant at three individuals per act.

Neither condition made any difference to the stability or otherwise of simulated groups, although in the first condition activities requiring smaller numbers of people were consistently selected.

Disillusionment

Levels of commitment halved when members were not allocated their first choice of activity.

Initial tests showed that very high or very low values of DIVLOC resulted in explosive growth or speedy collapse, and such values were not used. Small variations around the 0.5 level made no difference.

Any

'Any' signifies that the characteristic profile under discussion was only effected by the initial conditions specified, and variations in other conditions made no difference.

Resilience against disruption

Two tests were made to examine the resilience of 'stable' groups—those which did not 'explode' or 'collapse' as a result of the simulated internal processes, but looked as though they would carry on indefinitely.

The first test reflected the blocking of an activity by an external agency. This was simulated by raising the requirements of all the SELECTED Acts to impossibly high levels. The second test reflected the appearance of disruptive individuals in the group. This was simulated by introducing 'new members' with matching preferences, but zero commitment (LOC)—these encouraged specific choices of Act, then disrupted them by leaving. Both tests were applied in mid-run, on re-runs of 'groups' that had proved to be stable.

GROUP-1 as 'Rigid'

Initial conditions: either (a) low joining rate, (b) high preference match, (c) any; or (d) high joining rate, (e) low preference match, (f) any. The 'rigid' profile was usually obtained under conditions (a)–(c), and sometimes under (d)–(f). A typical rigid profile is illustrated in Figure 8.2.

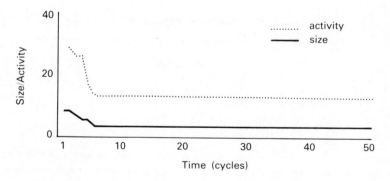

Figure 8.2 GROUP-1 as 'rigid'

Here we see that initial member loss is followed by complete stability—'ossification' might be a better word here. A very small number of people do exactly the same thing week after week. The possibilities for change exist but are never actualized. Change would have to be brought about by an external shock. No-one joins; no-one leaves. Simulated rigid groups were not stable against blocks on activity or disruptive individuals, but collapsed in the face of either.

Comment

Rigid groups were first thought to be a trivial simulation outcome, since the research was concerned with stability in relation to membership change. However, there seem to be natural groups of this type—and it is a reasonable result that the processes that create highly changeable groups can also produce static or rigid groups.

GROUP-1 as 'Stable'

Initial conditions: (a) low joining rate, plus regular addition of new members, (b) high preference match, (c) randomized new member commitment. The 'stable' profile was often (but not always) obtained under conditions (a)–(c). A typical stable profile is illustrated in Figure 8.3.

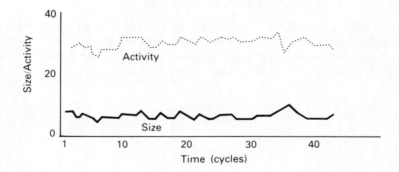

Figure 8.3   GROUP-1 as 'stable'

Here we see that stability is achieved despite a high turnover of membership. Both size and activity oscillate irregularly around their means—without any time trend. (The means in the sample run were (size) 6.7 and (activity) 30.5). Although in most runs size and activity were not statistically independent, all levels of activity could be (and most were) achieved from all size levels. The *condition* of the independence of size and activity could therefore be said to be met.

Simulated stable groups were resilient against disruption, recovering quickly from occasional 'blocks' and 'disruptive individuals'. 'Groups' with stable profiles could tolerate up to three successive blocks before they were disrupted.

Comment

Many of the runs that produced stable profiles were very similar to the historical data on IREV. The size/activity graphs for GROUP-1 (Figure 8.3) and IREV (Figure 7.1) were very similar. The size distribution of the GROUP-1 sample run also compares well with the IREV size distribution (see Tables 8.3 and 7.2).

Table 8.3 GROUP-1 and IREV size distributions

Size	Number of cycles (GROUP-1)	Number of weeks (IREV)
5	1	6
6	19	11
7	13	34
8	6	29
9	1	45
10	1	5

In the sample run, the GROUP-1 and IREV activity distributions differ in range. IREV varied between 0 and 36; GROUP-1 between 26 and 34. This was probably a consequence of the simplifying assumptions: activities were either carried out consistently or dropped; there was no facility for 'rotating' activities, as seemed to be the case with IREV.

Perhaps the most interesting result from the sample run was the distribution of time members spent in the group. This is shown in Figure 8.4 and compares very well with the IREV distribution shown in Figure 7.4.

This sort of distribution of time-in-group-before-leaving not only compared well with the IREV profile: it appeared to be a general condition of stability in all runs. This allows us to elaborate on the empirical finding in the last chapter that: 'the individuals most likely to leave the group have the lowest level of involvement, and have been in the group for the shortest time'.

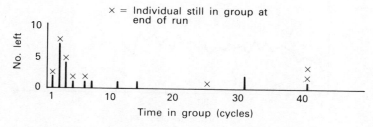

Figure 8.4   GROUP-1 ('stable') leaving and time-in-group

Examination of the simulated processes shows that there is good reason for this. If the probability of leaving were equal for all members, then the random preferences of newcomers would have a destructuring effect on the preference set—which in natural groups would be the normative structure. No sets of individuals would be in the group long enough for interaction to structure their preferences along similar lines. 'Techniques'—and with them the group—would tend to collapse. (This was confirmed in simulation runs of unstable groups.)

Conversely, if new members have the highest probability of leaving, then the older members have time to develop consistent collective preferences—which provide the basis for stable patterns of activity on which the normative structure and the survival of the group depend.

The exact correlates of leaving, and the effects of various types of new member on the group, will be examined in a later section. At this point we can say that the 'early leaver phenomenon'—which has been known for a long time—is connected with group stability, not, as has often been thought, with its opposite.

GROUP-1 as 'Stable–Unstable'

Initial conditions: (a) high joining rate, (b) high preference match, (c) randomized new member commitment. The 'stable–unstable' profile was often obtained under conditions (a)–(c). A typical stable–unstable profile is illustrated in Figure 8.5.

Here we see that the run is characterized as 'stable' because both size and activity tended towards their means without time trend. This profile was also

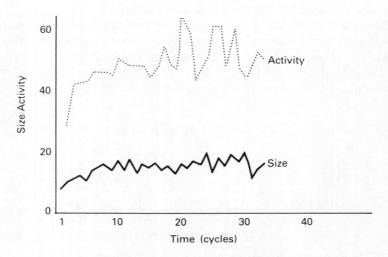

Figure 8.5   GROUP-1 as 'stable–unstable'

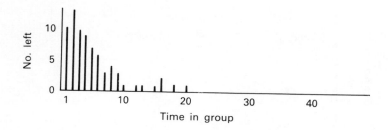

Figure 8.6   GROUP-1 ('stable–unstable') leaving and time-in-group

'unstable' since there was great variability in the activities chosen, and there was a very high turnover of members. It could be said that all members were early leavers (see Figure 8.6).

The apparent stability arose because the preference set, instead of stabilizing or being 'destructured', switched easily from one condition to another. This is the sort of effect that would have been expected had a facility for 'rotating' activities been built in to the model—only it would have happened without the massive early leaving. As it was, the switching mechanism originated in the high joining rate. New members entered in 'groups' which would achieve an independent agreement on activity. These new-member-groups were analogous to 'cliques'. They would initiate their own activity without reference to, or interference from older members. Older members, in any case, were rapidly displaced by non-clique new members, who either annexed their roles, or disrupted their activity by joining in, then leaving. The new cliques were themselves quickly disrupted and replaced.

Comment

The only 'natural' interpretation that can be given to this result is the use of a clubroom, where both activities and people can change with great speed. In fact, the lack of continuity of both persons and activities preclude one from calling this condition of GROUP-1 a group in any ordinary sense of that word. It is included in the result as it illustrates the role of a subgroup (or 'clique') in the initiation of new techniques.

GROUP-1 as 'Unstable–Collapse'

Initial conditions: (a) low preference match, (b) any. The 'unstable–collapse' profile was usually obtained from condition (a) alone, no matter what the joining rate or level of new member commitment. (Occasionally a 'rigid' profile would be generated.) The typical 'unstable–collapse' run illustrated in Figure 8.7 occurred despite a rather high joining rate.

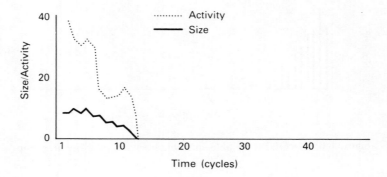

Figure 8.7   GROUP-1 as 'unstable–collapse'

Here we see that despite an initial flash of activity and the attraction of a few new members, both size and activity rapidly fall away to nothing. The group collapses.

Comment

These runs are interpreted as 'groups that never get off the ground'. The lack of any real initial preference match meant that activities could be started but commitment fell. Activities were not completed, and success did not feed back to help create a basic normative structure. Having little in common, the members left, and the group disintegrated.

This result parallels the disappearance of many of the subgroups of the Brighton Rents Project. It seems to be a rather common fate of natural groups in their early stages.

GROUP-1 as 'Unstable–Explosive'

Initial conditions: (a) high joining rate, (b) high preference match, (c) any. The 'unstable–explosive' profile (along with 'stable–unstable' profiles) was often obtained under conditions (a)–(c). A typical unstable–explosive run is illustrated in Figure 8.8.

Here we see geometrical increases in both size and activity.

Comment

No interpretation is given of this effect for two reasons. It is not clear that there is a 'natural' equivalent. The consequences of the 'explosion' could not be fully explored by the simulation. The 'group' reached its size limit or exhausted the pool of new members (and thus terminated the run) before it ran into the limits of possible activity. Had the run continued, and activity limits been reached, we

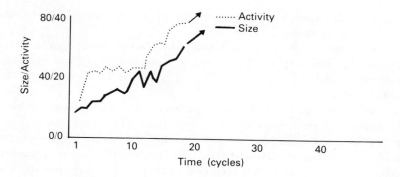

Figure 8.8   GROUP-1 as 'unstable–explosive'

may speculate that an 'unstable–explosive–collapse' profile would have re-sulted.

GROUP-1 as 'Unstable–Explosive–Collapse'

Initial conditions: (a) high joining rate, (b) high preference match, (c) high new member commitment, (d) absenteeism allowed. The 'unstable–explosive–collapse' profile often resulted from conditions (a)–(d), and is illustrated in Figure 8.9.

Here we see an initial size explosion from eight to twenty members in ten cycles. Activity also increases to a high level—in terms of the number of active individuals—but there is no corresponding increase in the *number* of activities.

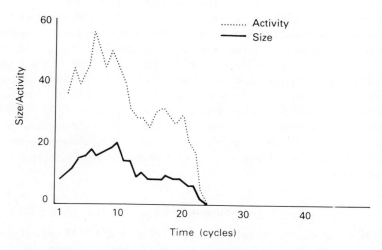

Figure 8.9   GROUP-1 as 'unstable–explosive–collapse'

288

The 'allowed' absenteeism, and the high level of commitment of new members depress the leaving rate.

The size increase comes to a sudden halt when nine members leave simultaneously. This happened as a result of an overall decline in levels of commitment, which in turn resulted from a surfeit of members for each available activity.

The sudden exodus left sufficient older members—with consistent preferences—to restructure the activity at a lower level. (The leaving-and-time-in-group distribution showed some similarity to that of a 'stable' group—compare Figure 8.10 with Figures 8.9 and 8.6). For a while the group appeared to restabilize around a size of ten members. The influx of new members was reduced, but the high levels of commitment of those that did join was sufficient to displace the remaining older members. The preference set became destructured and the 'group' collapsed.

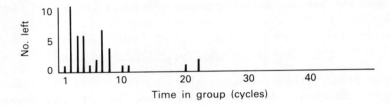

Figure 8.10   GROUP-1 ('unstable–explosive–collapse') leaving and time-in-group

Comment

These runs provide a parallel to the historical data on the Brighton Rents Project, and we can look for similarities in process. The Rents Project had a high joining rate and a limited number of activities, especially if we look at the main subgroup, the Squatting Group. An external block on activity—action by the council and the police— meant that there was not 'enough' activity to go round. There was strong evidence of disillusion—or decline in the level of commitment—and this preceded a factional walkout by a whole subgroup. There was a temporary stabilization at a new level of activity, which was initiated by older members. However, the increasing influence of the Rents Registration Group (who were 'newcomers' from the point of view of the Squatting Group), and their attempted re-orientation of the Project, meant that no activity was possible. There was a rapid decline in membership and the group collapsed.

Summary

The GROUP-1 model was created to try and see if the model of natural groups was consistent, sufficient, and clear. It helped provide interpretations of, and parallels to natural group behaviour. It was especially useful in examining unstable situations: unstable groups are on the point of disappearing, and are therefore particularly difficult to find and 'observe' in practice.

The basic rules of the simulation were as follows:

The group decided on its activities democratically, according to the preferences of its members.

The level of commitment of members who cannot participate in their most preferred activity decreases—but may increase again, or decrease even further, depending on the number of people involved in the activity, and the number of 'person-hours' needed to complete it.

An activity is successfully completed if the aggregate level of commitment of the members undertaking it matches the person-hours needed to complete it.

Members who participate in a successful activity increase their preference for it, while those who participate in unsuccessful activities decrease their preference for them.

Members with a very low level of commitment leave the group.

New members join the group according to a random schedule that can be modified by the experimenter or linked to the level of activity of the group.

It should be noted that the psychological assumptions in the simulation are minimal. People put less effort into things they did not want to do in the first place; they prefer things that work to things that do not.

The simulations generated six characteristic profiles—two of which resembled the historical profiles of The Brighton Rents Project and IREV. The detail of the simulation results—and the general processes suggested—will be discussed in the next chapter, where we will bring them together with the results of the 'natural' group studies. For the moment we will only note the main points that emerged.

1 In terms of the number of possible 'profiles', or group-histories, stability is rather rare.
2 The simulation identified joining rate and the maintenance of a 'reservoir' of older members as the most important factors underlying stability, change, or instability.
3 The ability to reject new members—which appeared as the 'early leaver phenomenon'—was highlighted as an important condition of stability.
4 The simulation construct 'preference set' worked well as a simplification of the inherently conversational 'normative structure', and provided some insights into the ways normative structures may be maintained or fragmented.
5 The independence of size and activity (within limits) as a condition of stability was supported.
6 The idea of a direct, strong connection between level of activity ('social visibility') and joining rate was cast into doubt. The most stable profiles were generated on the basis of a constant joining rate assumption. It may be that other factors (such as 'absenteeism' which were insufficiently explored by the model) are needed to explain this relationship.

References

Abelson, R.P. (1968), Simulation of social behaviour, in *The Handbook of Social Psychology*, Vol. 2, *Research Methods* (eds G. Lindzey and E. Aronson), Reading, Mass: Addison-Wesley.

Forrester, J.W.)1971), *World Dynamics*, Wright Allen Press.

Frijda, N.H. (1967), The problems of computer simulation, *Behavioural Science*, 12, pp. 59–67. (also in *Computer Simulation of Human Behavior*, (eds J.M. Dutton and W.H. Starbuck), New York, John Wiley, 1971.

Guetzkow, H., Kotler, P., and Schultz, R.L. (1972), *Simulation in the Social and Administrative Sciences*, London, Prentice-Hall.

Howard, N. (1971), *Paradoxes of Rationality: Theory of Metagames and Political Behavior*, Cambridge, Mass: MIT Press.

Lehman, R.S. (1977), *Computer Simulation and Modeling*, New York, London, John Wiley.

Lippitt, R. and White, R.K. (1958), An experimental study of leadership and group life, *Readings in Social Psychology*, (eds Maccoby, Newcombe, and Hartley), London, Holt.

Pask, G., Glanville, R., and Robinson, M. (1980), *Calculator Saturnalia*, London, Wildwood.

Roberts, C. and Robinson, M. (1980), The ILSA effect: a special theory of violence, *Progress in Cybernetics and Systems Research*, vols 8–11, Washington, DC: Hemisphere.

Ryle, G. (1949), *The Concept of Mind*, London, Hutchinson.

Shubik, M. (ed.) (1964), *Game Theory and Related Approaches to Social Behaviour*, London, John Wiley.

Stogdill, R.M. (ed.) (1970), *The Process of Model Building*, Ohio State University Press.

Turing, A.M. (1963), *Computing machinery and intelligence*, in *Computers and Thought* (eds E.A. Feigenbaum, and J. Feldman), New York, McGraw Hill.

Von Neumann, J. and Morgernstern, O. (1953), *Theory of Games and Economic Behaviour*, Princeton: Princeton University Press (first published 1944).

CHAPTER 9

How groups work: a general model

In the course of this book we have looked at several groups that hung together because their members wanted it that way. There was no compulsion, and no threat of not getting paid if people did not turn up. The groups were natural, not only because they were 'real', but because their members found their own ways of relating to each other, and decided their own aims, actions, and objectives. Natural groups are like natural children—they come into being without interference from the church or the state. They depend only on the way people want to organize themselves. But this process has *limits*. Self-organization—communication and collective action—has its own needs. Sometimes these clash with the intentions of group members, or even the intention of the whole group. One of the main aims of this book has been to identify some of these *limits*. This does not mean that the limits of natural groups are forever fixed—only that they need to be identified before they can be transcended. In the last section we will look at some ways of going beyond the limits we have uncovered. How we set about 'going beyond' them is a matter of dialectical or conversational science. *What* we want to 'go beyond' can be described in terms of systems science. Accordingly, we will first look at our general model of how groups work; which processes recur; what are the connectivities; which aspects of group life appear to be 'objectively given'. Then we will go on to explore some of the meanings—some plans that might be made after we have taken the model into account.

A Cybernetic General Model of How Groups Work

From chapter 4 on we have seen how the model developed, how it was refined and modified. Now we will try to draw together all the strands into an overall picture that is schematically presented in Figure 9.1.

For clarity, we will split the description of the model into three stages. First we will consider the range of 'stable states' which has two main aspects; the normative system and the size-regulating subsystem. Then we will consider the range of 'unstable states' and their relationship to growth and development.

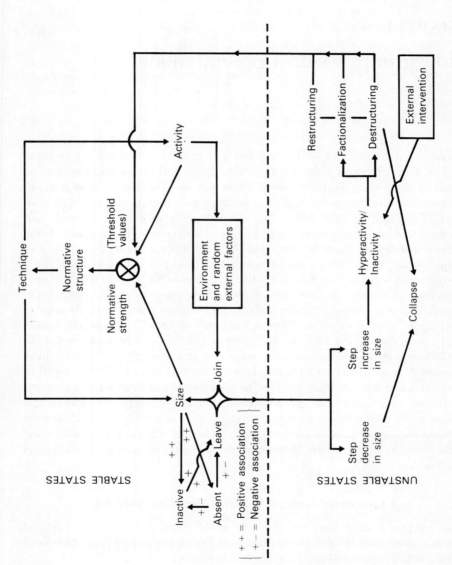

Figure 9.1

The Normative System

The normative system is that part of the model abstracted in Figure 9.2, taking in normative structure and strength, technique, size and activity.

The first thing to note is that 'normative structure' is both the key to, and the major 'hole' in the model. It is that part of the model that can be investigated, but never fully captured by systems science. It is the level where living people appear, make agreements, and experience conflict. The level where we can think about the model without being determined by it: the level at which we can create alternatives. That said, we can now—for the sake of thinking about it—consider normative structure 'as if' it were an object of science.

Normative structure is simply the set of beliefs, values, and descriptions held in common by group members; the agreements underlying, and the context surrounding their conversations. It is a 'big' idea, even when we are talking about small groups, and can be pictured in several ways.

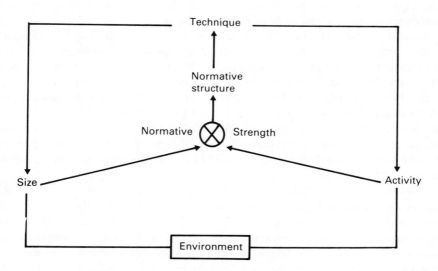

Figure 9.2   The normative system of a group

Normative structures are sets of 'conventions' which, as we said in chapter 2,

> must, by their nature, always be properties of a concerted group, and can never be completely vested in, or discharged by a lone individual in perpetual isolation: their observance has to be reinforced by the recognition and support of others who are bound by the same convention.

Alternatively—to use Goffman's description from the first chapter:

> We have then a kind of interactional *modus vivendi*. Together the participants contribute to a single over-all definition of the situation which involves not so much a

real agreement as to what exists but rather a real agreement as to whose claims concerning what issues will be temporarily honoured.

Normative structures cannot be reduced to individual beliefs but are founded on them. In the simulation these notions were preserved in vastly simplified form when 'preference set' was taken as the basis of decision process. The possible actions open to any group member (the 'outcomes') depended on the combined view ('preferences') of all group members.

The function of, and the way in which normative structure is maintained has much in common with the logic of a self-fulfilling prophecy. Things happen because they are expected to happen—and the expectation is justified by the happening. Normative structure, the total set of beliefs and intentions, gives rise to a set of ways of doing things, called 'techniques'. The resulting technique-governed activity maintains the normative strength—the aggregate level of agreement with the normative structure—and thus maintains the normative structure itself. The group sets out to 'confirm' not to 'falsify' its beliefs. One consequence of this, to be illustrated later, is that the impetus for change in a stable group usually comes from outside the group.

Considering the Brighton Rents Project in chapter 6, we said: 'in general, viable groups have a tendency to develop repeatable techniques, and the repetition of these defined techniques is the regularity of activity'. We saw regular activities, and regular patterns of activity, in the viable subgroups of the Rents Project, in IREV, and in the 'stable' profiles of the GROUP-1 simulation. We also saw that this regularity was derived from techniques originating in the normative structure—and that the success of these techniques confirmed and supported the normative structure. Failure of technique, and its consequences for normative strength and structure, will be covered in the section on 'unstable states'.

The idea has been stressed here that stable groups are characterized by the ability to produce regular patterns of activity. Some may say that the idea has been overstressed. If this is so, it is in reaction to other studies that have concentrated on more eye-catching processes, and largely overlooked the obvious. It is, after all, mainly by their regular activities that groups are recognized. These may not be the most inherently exciting events, but they are basic to an understanding of the sorts of drama we saw in the Rents Project.

When patterns of activity are represented by periodic (e.g. weekly) quantities of activity (e.g. person-hours), the range of group activity can be determined. The numerical values of this range will differ for different groups—but activity levels that fall outside this range mean that the group is becoming unstable. Its techniques are threatened.

Following through the left-hand side of the diagram of the normative system, we may repeat the findings from IREV in general form:

The role specifications inherent in the set of techniques serve as the template that determines the limits of group size.
Functionally, these limits may be described in the following way.
The lower size limit is the minimum number of members capable of filling the

maximum number of roles specified by any technique.

The upper size limit is the maximum number of members capable of being absorbed by the maximum number of roles specified by any technique.

From this it follows that any *normal* activity may be achieved from any level of size within the *normal* range. This is the relationship that allows size and activity to fluctuate independently.

The functional independence of size and activity was shown to be a 'fact' about viable natural groups (where it was statistically confirmed). The GROUP-1 simulation results supported the hypothesis that the independence of size and activity is also a *condition* of group stability.

The question now arises: since members are free to join and leave the group at will, how is it that size remains within its *normal* range?

The Size-Regulating Subsystem

In stable groups, size fluctuates within limits, and the joining and leaving rates are approximately matched. Figures 9.3 and 9.4 show the size and numbers of people who joined and left for IREV and a 'stable' GROUP-1 run. On the gross phenomenon, the match between the natural and simulated group is very close. We now have to explain why.

At the end of chapter 7, following the IREV study, we sketched a size-regulating subsystem, which is reproduced here as Figure 9.5. We also made the following comments

> Size increased following high levels of activity. There was also some evidence that size increases were partially choked off at high size levels by the 'preliminary membership filter'.
> ...
> Size decreases (i.e. members leaving the group) were associated with high levels of size and inactivity, but with low levels of absenteeism. The probability of leaving decreased with length of time spent in the group ... Absenteeism seemed to act as an additional buffer, by reducing *effective* group size, reducing inactivity, and therefore reducing the probability that someone would leave.

Although the idea of a 'preliminary membership filter'—which can be thought of as 'entrance requirements' that become stricter as group size increases—has only been informally explored in these studies, the idea itself is amply supported by the work of Roger Barker and his associates on 'overmanned' and 'under-manned' behaviour settings (cited in chapter 2).

We can now draw these points together into a general model, and postulate a *triple-size regulation mechanism*.

The 'leaving' regulator

It is pretty obvious that group size is reduced if members leave. It is not so obvious that the probability of leaving increases as a linear function of group size—as was shown with IREV.

The broad mechanism underlying this is as follows. The available activity

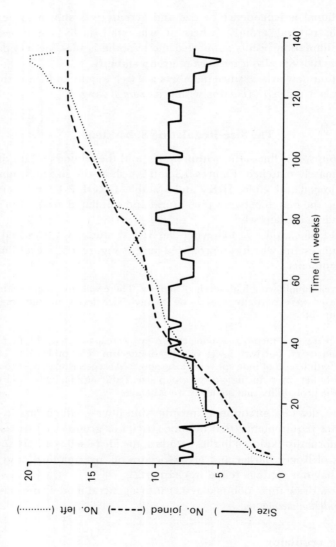

Figure 9.3 IREV joining and leaving rates; resultant sizes

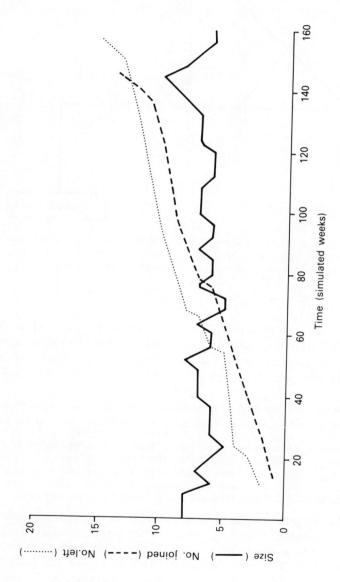

Figure 9.4 GROUP-1 simulation ('stable' run) joining and leaving rates; resultant sizes. ('Cycles' multiplied up to give 'simulated weeks' for visual comparison.)

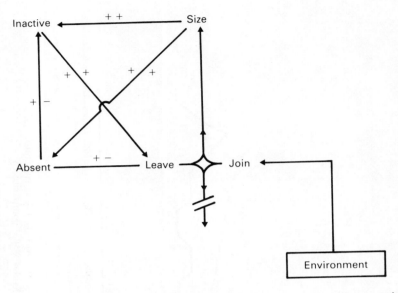

Figure 9.5   The size-regulating subsystem of a group. (++ A positive association; increase leads to increase and decrease leads to decrease. −− A negative association; increase leads to decrease and decrease leads to increase)

does not increase with size, since it is determined by techniques and the cycle of techniques. Therefore, as size increases, less activity becomes available to members. The group becomes less rewarding. The probability of leaving increases. The group tends to return to its *normal*—approximately average—size.

But this mechanism *alone*—as was anticipated in IREV, and demonstrated in the simulations—will severely disrupt the normative structure. As we said:

> If the probability of leaving were equal for all members, then the random preferences of newcomers would have a destructuring effect on the preference set—which in natural groups would be the normative structure. No sets of individuals would be in the group long enough for interaction to structure their preferences along similar lines. 'Techniques'—and with them the group—would tend to collapse.

We noted that in practice, the activity available to less active members was reduced more than the activity available to more active members. Less active members tend to be newer members, and thus newer members have a greater propensity to leave. This was shown for IREV in Figure 7.5; for a 'stable' simulation run in Figure 8.4; and the general form of 'early leaving' is represented by Figure 9.6.

The 'early leaver phenomenon' simply means that the last members to join are the most likely to leave—conversely, the longer members stay in the group, the less likely it is that they will leave. The advantages of this arrangement are that, in

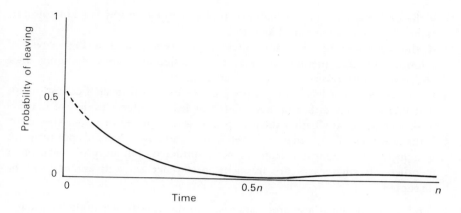

Figure 9.6 The general form of the early leaver phenomenon. *n* is the time spent in the group by its longest serving member. The dotted section of the curve represents the effect of the 'preliminary membership filter' — people that leave before they join by being denied (or denying themselves) entry. The slight rise in the probability of leaving as *n* is approached was only informally supportd in the studies, and is not a strict statistical extrapolation. It seems in line with everyday experience. The precise slope of the curve will of course depend on the specific group under examination

Roger Barker's terms, the storage of the proper 'program' (see chapter 2), which takes time and experience to establish, is not disrupted. In our terms, it means that those members with operational knowledge of techniques are the least likely to leave. These are also the members whose preferences have come to show a 'deep' similarity through interaction over time—and who are therefore more important in maintaining the normative structure.

The mechanism underlying the early-leaver phenomenon may be conceptualized in terms of 'role specialization'—those with specific roles hang on to them, and are therefore less affected by changes in overall activity levels. IREV showed some evidence of this 'role specialization'. Alternatively, the mechanism may be thought of in terms of Barker's 'program', 'penetration zones', and explained by conventions. If the 'program' (in our terms, set of techniques) of a group is mainly stored by the inhabitants of the'central zone'—and it takes a long time, and much experience, to reach this zone—then again activity is more easily available to older members. In other words, there is a time-related convention governing the distribution of activity.

If we accept the assumptions of the GROUP-1 model, then a more detailed explanation becomes possible. In the simulations, 'stable' conditions were most frequently achieved when new members entered at a randomly disturbed constant rate, and had randomly distributed levels of commitment—very much the sort of situation that groups encounter in real life. GROUP-1 allowed four typical cases of new entry to be described.

1 If the new member has mismatched preferences and a low level of commitment, that member is very likely to leave.
2 If the new member has mismatched preferences and a high level of commitment, that member is likely to be assimilated after changing their preferences and lowering their level of commitment.
3 If the new member has matched preferences and a low level of commitment, that member may either be assimilated or leave—after a period of inactivity—depending on whether the group is near to its lower or upper size limit.
4 If the new member has matched preferences and a high level of commitment, that member is almost certain to be assimilated, but may displace older members. If such cases are frequent, preference set and activity can be disrupted.

In 'stable' conditions, these processes result in the appearance of the characteristic 'early leaver' pattern. The processes underlying other types of leaving pattern force out—or prevent the establishment of—older members. This causes variability in the preference set and instability in the group.

In summary, the leaving regulator encourages members to leave the group as high size levels are reached. It works because there are limits on available activity, which apply more to new members than old—and new members are therefore the most likely to leave.

The 'absenteeism' regulator

Figure 9.5 shows that size is positively related to inactivity, to absenteeism, and to leaving, *but* that absenteeism is negatively related to both inactivity and to leaving. In other words, absenteeism has a *damping* effect on inactivity and on leaving.

Operation of the absenteeism size regulator was seen in the Squatting and Rents Registration Groups of the Brighton Rents Project and was quantified for IREV, although it was only reproduced with partial success in the GROUP-1 simulation. In general, the proportion of absent members rose faster than the size of the group.

It seems reasonable to suppose that absenteeism has the same 'causes' as inactivity and leaving, but provides a useful alternative to them. Members are, so to speak, 'put in reserve' against a time when the group is 'short' of members. As we said in chapter 7, when pointing out that absenteeism was associated with *not-leaving*:

> It seems that absenteeism reduced the *effective* size of the group, thus reducing inactivity, and consequently reducing leaving. It may also be speculated that absenteeism protected the group from over-frequent leaving, by giving 'disgruntled' members time to recover. There is no doubt that 'over-frequent leaving'—a very fast rate of membership turnover—could have had very disruptive effects on the normative structure.* Absenteeism, to some extent, protected the group against this.

*These effects *were* demonstrated by the GROUP-1 simulations.

In summary, absenteeism provides an alternative to leaving in the size-regulation process. Some consequences of developing either regulator at the expense of the other will be explored in the section on growth and instability.

The 'preliminary membership filter'

So far we have given two descriptions of a 'preliminary membership filter'. In chapter 6 we said: 'People who could not speak, or would not learn the language of the group, were excluded'. Earlier in this chapter, with reference to Barker's 'undermanned' and 'overmanned' settings, we said that "entrance requirements" become stricter as group size increases'.

Examples of the exclusion process were cited for the Rents Project as a whole, and for the Squatting and Pamphlet groups, and it was also seen more explicitly in the IREV 'probationary period'.

The importance of the preliminary membership filter is that it *functions to regulate size by acting on the joining rate* rather than acting directly on size, as do the leaving and absenteeism regulators. Before considering this third regulator, we should look at our findings on joining rates.

Joining rates were first considered in Chapter 4, when we advanced the idea that: 'Level of activity can indirectly influence size level through the environment. High levels of activity may create "social visibility" and attract new members.' This was confirmed for IREV, where it was found that the maximum activity level over a four-week period was a good indicator of whether an increase in size would happen in the following week. However, the *time-lag* between the maximum activity level and the subsequent size increase was indeterminate. In the GROUP-1 simulations, we found that stable profiles were usually generated when the joining rate was randomized or constant. Joining rates that were directly tied to activity levels resulted in unstable profiles. No-one joined when the 'group' most needed new members—causing 'rigidity' or 'collapse'. Lots of people joined when they were least needed—causing size explosions and instability.

These two results are not inconsistent. The indeterminacy of the timelag can be considered as a partial randomization of the joining rate for IREV. In the unstable simulation profiles there was a strong, direct connection between activity level and joining rate—which probably overstated the relationship between the two. The 'stable' simulation profiles were usually achieved under conditions of a randomized or constant joining rate, incremented by a *low* size increase after high levels of activity. This seems a reasonable and realistic compromise between the assumptions of a constant and an activity determined joining rate.

The possibility that high activity levels are connected, even weakly, to high joining rates points to the need for a third type of size-regulation mechanism that we have called the 'preliminary membership filter'. If 'entry requirements' are imposed, tightened at high size levels, and relaxed at low size levels, then much of the instability we saw in the simulations would be much harder to generate. If social visibility *is* a factor affecting joining rate, then this third mechanism reduces the fluctuations towards a randomly disturbed constant rate that can be dealt with by the other two regulators, absenteeism and leaving.

On the other hand, if activity levels and joining rate are assumed to be unconnected, the membership filter still has a place. By excluding 'mismatched' new members, it safeguards the normative structure, minimizes the need for leaving, and maximizes the amount of activity available to existing members. It can also be regarded as a special and limiting case of early leaving.

Unstable States

The GROUP-1 simulation was especially useful in identifying unstable states, since these are unpredictable and difficult to observe in natural groups. Several 'danger points' were identified.

Formation

When a group first forms, there is a good chance that individual preference profiles will be radically dissimilar, even where first choices are the same. Unless the average level of commitment is very high, any upset or failure leads to the termination of activity, failure to agree on an alternative, or the enactment of an 'unsatisfactory' alternative, the dissolution of emergent norms, and the collapse of the group.

This outcome was a common simulation result (preference orders for 'individuals' were assigned at random) and was also seen in three of the seven subgroups of the Brighton Rents Project. The Pamphlet and Propaganda Groups and the Coordinating Committee never agreed on aims, techniques, or activities, and disintegrated after a few meetings. Mapped onto our general model, this simply means that the core of stability—the normative structure—failed to gell.

Formation is the most 'dangerous' stage in a group's life. It may well be that the vast majority of informal groups do not survive for more than a few weeks. Those that do are not 'safe'. Unlike the honeybees of chapter 2, groups do not maintain a precise homeostasis. There is sufficient uncertainty in the process to guarantee a crisis at some point in the group's history.

Influx of new members(i)

If the entry of new members was *tied to the activity level* of the group, even with a random time-lag, the group almost always became unstable. This could take two forms.

In the first, the group crystallized its activities below the level of social visibility. *No* new members were attracted. This meant that, although the group might continue for some time, any member loss would result in serious disruption of activity, which would be followed by loss of commitment and disintegration. A group with a 'rigid' profile may not be a very stable group: its continued existence owes as much to luck as anything else.

In the second case, high activity levels resulted in rapid growth to well above 'normal' size bounds. High activity, and hence further growth, would be maintained with a very low average level of commitment. Inactivity would grow rapidly. Whole subgroups would suddenly drop out. Since they had been in the group for some time, these subgroups would have influenced the preference structure—and the activity pattern—in their own direction. Their disappearance disrupted activity. The low level of commitment of the remaining members was usually insufficient to continue the activity, or to tolerate the process of normative restructuring. More inactivity was followed by unreplaced member loss, and usually by disintegration. This was the process underlying the 'unstable-explosive-collapse' GROUP-1 profile imaged in Figure 8.12. It was also very similar to the history of the Rents Project Squatting Group, although the latter had the additional hazard of an externally imposed block on its activities. The instability created by a direct connection between joining rate and activity levels demonstrates the need for a 'preliminary membership filter'—although this was not part of the simulation. As we said earlier: 'If "entry requirements" are imposed, tightened at high size levels, and relaxed at low size levels, then instability is much harder to generate.'

Influx of new members(ii)

Even when new member entry was not tied to activity levels, two disruptive cases could happen.

There could be a *sudden influx* of new members, or a constant influx of new members with a very high level of commitment. Both these events had the effect of changing the established preference structure towards the preferences of the new members. Usually this resulted in a new pattern of activity—and older members left after being deprived of their 'favourite' activity. The 'stable-unstable' profile was the best illustration of activity switches caused by influxes of new members. Normative restructuring and drastic activity and membership changes mean that *the formation danger point is repeated*. It is almost certain that the deeper preferences of the new members, and the preferences of new members and old members, will be dissimilar. Compromise activities are initiated that are unsatisfying to everyone. Inactivity, loss of commitment, and disintegration follow.

The Rents Registration Group of the Rents Project managed to reject an influx of new members from the Pamphlet Group—and survived. Sometimes the simulated groups recovered from such an influx after restructuring their preferences and activities—but a constant influx of highly committed individuals would cause successive crises, terminated only by the collapse of the group.

Activity blocks originating outside the group

Both the natural and the simulated 'stable' groups were resilient in the face of occasional activity disruption. Neither could tolerate prolonged blocks on their major activities. In natural groups, such blocks can arise from many causes: lack of finance; competition for resources; deliberate intervention by an external agency, and so on. In the simulated groups, blocks were created simply by raising the 'person-hour' requirements of major activities to impossible levels. In all cases the reorientation of the normative structure required to establish a new activity pattern was so drastic that members became inactive and left long before it could be achieved.

In the simulated groups, where variables could be manipulated easily, crises were easy to achieve. The majority of runs ended, or could be made to end in disintegration. In natural groups, even with longitudinal studies, crises were rather rare. None were seen in IREV. Only one—albeit terminal—occurred in the Rents Project. An interesting 'near-crisis' was observed in one of the short-term experimental groups. Since disruption of the normative structure can be identified with instability, it is worth reviewing these events.

In the Brighton Rents Project, we saw a crisis created by growth and by an activity block. The response—a change in one central norm—was quickly followed by the collapse of the group as a whole. It will be recalled that the Project functioned as a set of co-operating subgroups. Decisions on which technique to actualize, and how often, were the prerogative of each subgroup. The Squatting Group had developed a refined and regular pattern of activity—which was suddenly blocked by the local authority and the police. This provoked a crisis in the subgroup—members were deprived of activity. The Project as a whole attempted to reorientate itself. In the process absenteeism was suddenly reduced, and the squatting group was 'merged' with a lot of people it did not recognize as its members. Decision-making was centralized in an Executive Committee—and the norm of subgroup autonomy was annulled. Many members—especially those from the Squatting Group—refused to accept the changes. Faction fighting and argument further disrupted the Project as a whole. The Rents Registration Group—previously the most stable—was drawn into the process. Inactivity increased to the point where old activities could no longer be carried out, and new ones could not be got off the ground. Both techniques and normative structure failed. The Project collapsed.

In the Crime Simulation Game (described in chapter 4) there was no block on activity. Instead we saw how a group of new members formed a faction that aimed to introduce a new and different technique—which would have resulted in changes in both 'normal size and normal activity'. From a strategy of equal reward in a co-operative small group, members teetered on the brink of changing to a strategy of exploitation in a large group. At one point (on the normative strength measure) the exploitative faction were in a majority. In terms of the perceived normative structure, they did not realize this. Size decrease eliminated some members of the faction (which had come into being at a rather high size level) and involvement in activity prevented the others from pursuing the new aim, and talking about it with others. The cooperative norm recovered. Two things were clear. A change in this central norm would have changed all the norms, and resulted in an entirely different *modus operandi*. The general model was foreshadowed in what actually happened. An influx of new members at a high size level created a faction—which was then eliminated by increasing participation in old activities as size decreased.

From this, we may say that all four major forms of instability operate on and through the normative structure. The normative structure itself forms a whole.

An attempt to change any central norm will affect the entire normative structure and thus creates a last danger point. This may be related to, or independent of the four danger points we have already identified. A central norm is defined as one that is embodied as a technique. Given the methodological equation between technique and 'ritual', we can say that the four danger points identify different mechanisms for disrupting group rituals.

In General

The main variables, size, activity, normative strength and structure, inactivity and absenteeism, leaving and joining; the main regulators, normative structure itself, leaving, absenteeism, and membership filter; and the main causes of instability, formation, influx of new members, activity blocks, and central norm changes, are all drawn together, as a picture, in Figure 9.1.

'In general' we can say that the normative structure and techniques of any group are maintained by the success of the activities that they prescribe. Conversely, two types of event threaten the normative structure. Size levels above 'normal' tend to create an inactive subgroup that is not satisfied by 'normal' activity. The ensuing division of opinion may become public: a gradual decline in normative strength is suddenly catapulted up into the normative structure. Significant changes in functioning—usually collapse— follow. Similar effects occur if activity is blocked by an external agency. Thus we see that when group identity is maintained, normal size, normal activity, and normative structure are inextricably linked.

Summarizing, we can say that if a group survives its formative period, it is likely to become stable. Once this has happened, change, whether it takes the form of growth, restructuring, or collapse, tends to follow from external factors: member influx or activity blocks. Stability, once established, feeds on itself. Our general cybernetic model shows that joining and leaving rates are governed by mechanisms fired by deviations from 'normal size'—but that stability and survival are rarer and more precarious than we might have thought!

Beyond the Model

So far we have considered a set of structural processes that are usually 'invisible' to members of groups. It is a long way from obvious that 'leaving' and 'absenteeism' are regulators. 'Normal size' is not an idea that is taken into account when groups are laying plans for the future. *All these things should be taken into account.* They will not go away simply because we choose to ignore them. Let us look at some simple consequences: lots of new members may not be a cause for rejoicing; absenteeism and leaving may not be something we should worry about.

It is also true that many groups are pleased by new members, and seriously worried by absenteeism. Whether the worry is justified or not depends whether anything can be done about it. Learning the lessons of the general model, it seems that something can be done—but that something is not always obvious.

What are the established 'techniques' or 'rituals' of the group? What things do we do well and like doing? What would really happen if 'absenteeism' was reduced, and everyone wanted to be active? Is there a way of getting round 'normal' size limits without creating factions? What would happen if factions did appear? Is there any precedent for living with differences without blowing the group apart—or letting the hidden processes do their work so the group simply stays the same and can never develop? Can all this be planned without treating people as 'objects'—without losing the meaning of what we are trying to do and how we relate to each other? I believe it can. There is plenty of room for the development of informal groups into organizations—even institutions—that are humanly satisfying without losing the richness of direct informal communication; without sacrificing the fundamental process of simply talking to people. Not only is there room for such organizations, there is a need for them. The need will not be satisfied without conscious effort. Let us look at some consequences of our model in terms of growth strategies.

We said of IREV:

> The aim and intention of the group was to *grow*, but its techniques and activities needed a degree of stability, which was reflected in an implicit need *not to grow*. The seriousness of this problem ... cannot be underestimated.

What could be done?

The triple size-regulation mechanism, together with reflection of the forms of 'instability', indicates several distinct growth strategies.

Organizations concerned with the development of an activist base—a committed membership—sometimes impose a schizmatic requirement on their branches. Units of a certain size must be split into two new branches. This is an appropriate strategy, although we are now in a good position to see that the exact point at which branches are split should depend on an analysis of their particular activities. It is unlikely that several groups will have the same desirable splitting points. Setting an absolute number, and ignoring the particular needs of each individual group, would be a mistake. On the other hand, if splitting is agreed as a general strategy, overall growth can be maintained *and* the stability requirements of each group or branch can continue to be met.

In the absence of, or sometimes despite an overall organization, schizm in the traditional sense—irreconcilable factionalization—is a common consequence of growth beyond 'normal' limits. Schizm, intentional or not, corresponds with the model and with experience. The notion of steady, linear, growth held by many group organizers, including those in IREV, does not correspond to the model—and I know of no case where it has worked in practice. Growth in activist organizations is a discontinuous and a risky matter.

A second and more common growth phenomenon is the development of the absenteeism size regulator. This was not well represented in the simulations, although they indicated one danger. A sudden decrease in absenteeism, once it has become established, causes instability. In the 'unstable–explosive–collapse' simulation profile, and in the Rents Project, a sudden decrease in absenteeism caused a size explosion that precipitated the collapse of the group.

In developmental terms, we can expect emphasis on the absenteeism regulator to lead to *very large groups with a small active nucleus*. This option was not explored in the book since it was not a path taken by the Rents Project or by IREV. There is a second reason. When this work was started it was not obvious (why should it have been?) that groups based on absenteeism were *groups* in our sense and not 'organizations'. Since then indications have appeared that this developmental variant is very common. Around twenty informal observations have been made of clubs, community groups, cooperatives, trade union branches, and branches of established political parties. It seems that these can all be thought of as groups in the sense in which we have been using the term. Broadly speaking, large increases in membership can be tolerated if they do not disturb the *effective size of the active group*. Beyond a certain level, absenteeism rises exponentially with size. The exact nature of the exponential function has not yet been determined, but the following formula has been found to work well in predicting attendance at meetings for 'groups' in the 60–800 size range.

$$A = R + \sqrt{M}$$

where: A is attendance; R is the number of formal roles; M is the total membership.

Example 1

A cooperative employed around 170 workers. Eighteen had formal roles—these were defined as job specifications that included administrative or coordinating functions, and included the shop stewards. The formula predicted attendance at the annual General Meeting as

$$18 + \sqrt{170},$$

$$\text{or } 18 + 13 = 31.$$

In fact thirty-two people turned up.

Example 2

A community group had a membership of forty on a 'one person from each house' basis. There were three roles: chairman, secretary, treasurer. The group held open more-or-less-monthly meetings. The formula predicted an attendance of

$$3 + \sqrt{40},$$

$$\text{or } 3 + 6.3 = 9.$$

There were on average eight people at meetings.

Here we see that absolute but nominal group size makes very little difference to the turnout. The number of roles (which we have seen is related to activity) is much more important. A group of 10 with 5 roles would expect an attendance of 8; a group of 100 with 5 roles would expect an attendance of 15; a group of 800 with 5 roles would still only expect just over 30 people at its meetings.

It should be stressed that this formula only works for normal meetings in normal times. If there is a crisis of any sort, absenteeism can be drastically reduced. Also, although we have explored the mechanisms underlying size stability, the mechanisms and reasons underlying this exponential increase in absenteeism are not clear. The formula works, and results in the maintenance of 'normal size' despite apparently large increases in membership. It is *functional*— although again it may contradict the expressed intentions of group members— and probably functions on the basis of the role requirements underlying techniques which place severe limits on available activity: probably!

The existence of groups based on the absenteeism regulator—groups which appear large, but are 'really' small—again shows that simple growth may not result in increased activity. Something more is needed. Here we come back to a crucial question that arises from the model—to which the model may provide part of the answer: are large convivial organizations possible?

All the way through the book we have been dealing with convivial *groups*. In the very first line we quoted Gramsci as saying that 'the social life of the working class is rich in institutions ... . The assumption was that these institutions could become instruments of social administration without losing their democratic character. We have looked at some small examples of working-class institutions, of the way in which people organize themselves, and at some *limits* of this form of organization. We chose to look at small groups because these are the ones in which the individual is directly involved in the exercise of social power. In larger groups, even where these are 'institutions of the working class', power is concentrated. The individual usually has little say in the policies and activities. In considering the problems of growth, and the operations of the various regulators, leaving, absenteeism, membership filters, and so on, we begin to see why this happens. Survival depends on the maintenance of 'technique' which in turn depends on limits on size and activity. Large-scale growth involves splitting—the formation of several groups—or a massive increase in absenteeism, a form of non-involvement. In the first case there are immediate problems of coordination. In the second, influence is confined to a small minority of the membership. Either way individuals and groupings find themselves further and further from the sources of decision, and from the *effective* ability to influence decision.

The point can be made that in many cases this is no bad thing. From the point of view of the individual, this is often an entirely satisfactory state of affairs. Very few people want to be bothered with 'administration' when things are going well. They have more interesting things to do. They probably belong to various groups of one sort or another (something that was not included in the model) and will put their main effort into the one that is most rewarding. This extra-model consideration may explain why the absenteeism regulator is so common.

If the Trade Union is doing a good job in maintaining your standard of living, why go to branch meetings? If your sports club committee maintains the pavilion, the bar, and the field, why interfere? Things are going perfectly well without you. It is quite ridiculous to expect everyone to become deeply involved in everything. From the point of view of the group, this is also a satisfactory state of affairs. Absenteeism and leaving mean that the techniques are not upset, factionalization is unlikely, and survival is not threatened. Distance from decision-making is only a problem when things go wrong. The first lesson of large convivial groups is that they must not insist on hyperactivity, on total involvement, on the part of the membership. It will not work and it is pointless. People have better things to do unless there is a real role for them.

What happens when things do go wrong, when there is a crisis and when there is conflict? We saw a key mechanism at work in the Brighton Rents Project. The common language—the overall normative structure—has different *meanings* for different subgroups. The diverse meanings can co-exist quite happily unless they are brought together into a common plan of action. If there is no attempt to create a joint technique, there is no problem. But if there is such an attempt, then the conflict is revealed.

In the Rents Project, two subgroups had placed entirely different meanings on the agreed idea of direct democracy. This presented no problem when the Squatting Group and the Rents Registration Group went their own ways. Under conditions of crisis, when they tried to work out a joint plan, they found there was no common ground. The resulting conflict tore the group apart.

The emergence of conflict from consensus, and the disintegration of agreement into violence seems to be a very common phenomenon. Many if not most cases of real conflict can be traced back to hidden differences of intention within a 'common language'. This applies both at the interpersonal level, and at the level of relations between groups or subgroups (see Roberts and Robinson, 1979 and 1980). The root cause of this is usually that the different participants intend different actions and different consequences. Given the importance of 'technique' to groups, it is easy to see that *if groups use the same language to communicate with each other and to underpin their own activity, that language can have a different meaning to each of its users.* This is a major problem when we come to consider the integration of groups into an organization. There are various ways of getting round this problem—none of them very satisfactory.

Before looking at some ways that convivial organizations could be made to 'work', we should be clear about the meaning of conflict. There is a very influential school of thought that is searching for universal methods of conflict resolution, and for ways of demonstrating that 'ultimately' we all have a common interest. Much of the interest in game theory—especially the work centering on the Prisoner's Dilemma problem (e.g. Howard, 1971)—is an attempt to show that there are 'rational solutions' to all conflicts. In chapter 3, we quoted Richard Sharpe's account of 'systems analysis': 'the religion claimed to be able to allocate rationally resources between different parts of a system and it approached its task as if conflict did not really exist'. This is the same thing. If 'ultimately' we have a common interest, then conflict does not 'really' exist. As Sharpe acidly remarks, 'it was commercial, military, and social conflicts which tore the confidence out of the whole movement'. Our position on this is simple. Many conflicts are real. Real conflict is solved by the elimination of one of the contending parties. The belief in universal or quasi-universal methods of conflict resolution by rational means reflects a confusion between systems and dialectical sciences. Real conflict is simply beyond the scope of systems science, because it violates the consensus on which it is based. The conflict is precisely about what the system is or will be.

Any large organization is one solution to the problem of how to fuse groups together. The last chapter in a book on small groups is not the place to review the whole, huge literature on the sociology of organizations. We can make a few polemical comments.

The problem of fusing groups and individuals together is the problem of management. In order to try and make this fusion, management has to *stand outside* most of the groups. When management stands outside the groups it is supposed to manage—even though the organization has a 'common language' or a normative structure—the meanings to the management and to the group itself will be different. This difference is a constant source of potential conflict, although most of the time this will be hidden. In most cases the difference in meaning is the result of a real conflict of interest.

Hierarchical organization in all its forms is primarily a response to this problem. It attempts to remove decision-making from the lower levels and concentrate it at the apex of the pyramid. It denies the meanings of all groups other than itself, the management. The consequences—alienation, conflict, violence—are all around us.

We observed at the beginning that convivial, non-hierarchical, non-oppressive groups are all around us. We investigated their structure and limits. We ended with the question of whether convivial *organization* was possible.

The step from small group to large organization may seem too big a jump. It looks like the daft attempts to explain human problem solving in terms of maze-running rats. But there is a difference that makes a difference. Human organization is founded on the way in which we communicate with each other—hierarchical structures are one way of dealing with the problems generated by the limitations of this communication. They are like an evolutionary specialization. We cannot expect convivial organization to evolve out of hierarchical organization. Instead, we should look to the basic processes in convivial groups to see if their *rituals* can evolve or be developed in a *different* direction. They can: at some moments in history, and in some cooperatives, they have been.

Provided direct communication and its limitations are understood to be the material basis of organization, utopian follies can be avoided. Workers' control, direct democracy, direct involvement in the exercise of social power, all become possible. For some time now we have been engaged in the project of transforming the material basis of communication. Convivial organization *could* be one consequence. The alternative is even more dizzying hierarchical specialization, even greater concentrations of power and coercive ability, finally resulting in the 'mutual destruction of the contending classes'.

GROUP-1 program listing in FORTRAN

The program listing reproduced here is the one which approximated, in output, to the history of the Brighton Rents Project. Special features are the high level of commitment (LOC) of newcomers (INEXT) and a high joining rate. A sample printout (Cycle 2) is presented at Figure 8.3 in chapter 8.

```
FORTRAN COMPILATION BY #XFIV MK 3A     DATE  11/01/77   TIME  10/43/43


0000          LIST(LP)
0001          PROGRAM (GROUP 1)
0002          COMPRESS INTEGER AND LOGICAL
0003          INPUT 1 = CR0
0004          OUTPUT 2 = LP 0
0005          END


0006          MASTER GROUP
0007          INTEGER ACT(8,6),AZ,B,C
0008          COMMON // IND(99,11),I(30),IZ,ACT,AZ,MINLOC,MAXLOC,
0009         1LEFT,JOINED,ICOMP,INEXT,DIVLOC,ENTER,ICYCLE,NSTORE(50,5)
0010          READ(1,10) ((IND(J,K),K=1,11),J=1,99),IZ,ACT,AZ,MINLOC,MAXLOC,
0011         1MCYCLE,ICYCLE,NCYCLF,ENTER,DIVLOC
0012       10 FORMAT(114410,2F0.0)
```

```
0013       DO 7 J=1,99
0014       IND(J,2) = 5
0015     7 CONTINUE
0016       NRUN = 0
0017       JOINED = 0
0018       LEFT = 0
0019     9 DO 1 J=1,IZ
0020       I(J) = IND(J,1)
0021     1 CONTINUE
0022       INEXT = IZ+1
0023       NRUN = NRUN + 1
0024 C RUN IS THE SET OF CYCLES FOR WHICH A COMPLETE DATA RECORD IS MADE
0025       WRITE(2,20)
0026    20 FORMAT(30H1 GROUP (1) INITIAL PARAMETERS)
0027       WRITE(2,30) NRUN,ICYCLE
0028    30 FORMAT (9H RUN NO.,I3,17HSTARTING AT CYCLE,I3 )

0029 C PRINTS RUN AND CYCLE NUMBERS
0030       WRITE (2,40)
0031    40 FORMAT(90H0                              TIME NEEDED TO
0032      1   MIN.NO. OF PEOPLE        )
0033       WRITE(2,50)
0034    50 FORMAT(60H NAME                         COMPLETE ACT
0035      1 REQUIRED IF ACTIVITY       )
0036       WRITE (2,60)
0037    60 FORMAT(90H OF ACT                       (SAME UNITS AS LOC)
0038      1    IS TO BE UNDERTAKEN      )
0039       DO 2 B=1,AZ
0040       WRITE(2,70) (ACT(B,C),C=1,3)
0041    70 FORMAT(7X,I3,27X,I3,27X,I3)
0042     2 CONTINUE
0043 C PRINTS LIST OF ACTIVITIES AND THEIR PRECONDITIONS
0044       WRITE(2,80) IZ
0045    80 FORMAT(35H0NO. OF INDIVIDUALS IN GROUP (IZ) =,I4)
0046       WRITE (2,90) MAXLOC
0047    90 FORMAT(57H MAXIMUM LEVEL OF COMMITTMENT (LOC) PER PERSON (MAXLOC)
```

```
0049          WRITE(2,100) MINLOC
0050   100    FORMAT(56H MINIMUM LOC BELOW WHICH INDS LEAVE THE GROUP (MINLOC) =
0051          1,I3)
0052          WRITE (2,110) DIVLOC
0053   110    FORMAT (85H IF AN IND. DOES NOT JOIN IN HIS MOST PREFERRED ACT, HI
0054          1S LOC IS REDUCED BY (DIVLOC) =,F2.2)
0055          WRITE(2,120)ENTER
0056   120    FORMAT(86H NEW INDS JOIN AS A PROPORTION OF THE NO. OF INDS INVOLV
0057          1ED IN SUCCESSFUL ACTS (ENTER)=,F2.2 )
0058   C  PRINTS OTHER PARAMETERS
0059          GOTO 99
0060   99     DO 3 ICYCLE = MCYCLF,NCYCLE
0061   C  SETS THE GROUP PROCESS A LIMIT OF 50 CYCLES
0062          CALL DISPLAY
0063          IF (INEXT=100)0,89,0
0064          IF(IZ=2)89,39,0
0065   C  ENDS IF POOL OF PEOPLE IS EXHAUSTED
0066   79     CALL VOTE
0067          CALL DISILLUSION
0068          CALL LEAVE
0069          IF(IZ)0,89,0
0070   C  ENDS IF EVERYONE HAS LEFT THE GROUP
0071          CALL ACTION
0072          CALL DISSONANCE
0073          CALL JOIN
0074          IF(IZ=30) 0,89,89
0075   C  ENDS IF GROUP SIZE GOES OVER LIMIT
0076   3      CONTINUE
0077   89     CALL SUMMARY
0078          END
```

END OF SEGMENT, LENGTH   212, NAME GROUP

```
0079        SUBROUTINE DISPLAY
0080        INTEGER ACT(8,6),AZ,AVLOC
0081        COMMON //IND(99,11),I(30),IZ,ACT,AZ,IDUM(2),LEFT,JOINED,ICOMP,
0082       1JDUM,DUM(2),ICYCLE,NSTORE(50,5)
0083        WRITE(2,1) ICYCLE
0084      1 FORMAT (34H1 STATE OF SIMULATION BEFORE CYCLE,I5)
0085        WRITE(2,2)IZ

0086      2 FORMAT (23HONO. OF PEOPLE IN GROUP,I5)
0087        WRITE(2,3) JOINED,LEFT
0088      3 FORMAT(30X,I3,2X,17HPEOPLE JOINED AND,I3,2X,4HLEFT)
0089        N=0
0090        DO 100 J=1,AZ
0091        IF (ACT(J,5)-1) 100,0,100
0092        N=N+1
0093    100 CONTINUE
0094  C ADDS NO. OF COMPLETED ACTIVITIES
0095        WRITE(2,5)N
0096      5 FORMAT(28H NO. OF COMPLETED ACTIVITIES,I4)
0097        WRITE(2,6) ICOMP
0098      6 FORMAT(29H NO OF INDS WHO COMPLETE ACTS,I4)
0099        K=0
0100        DO 101 J=1,IZ
0101        IF (IND(I(J),2)-880) 20,20,0
0102        K = K + IND(I(J),2)-880
0103  C DEAS WITH INACTIVE INDIVIDUA S
0104        GOTO 101
0105     20 K = K + IND (I(J),2)
0106    101 CONTINUE
0107  C 'K' GIVES TOTAL LOC OF THE GROUP
```

```
0108          WRITE(2,14) K
0109      14 FORMAT(13H TOTAL LOC IS,I4)
0110         NSTORE(ICYCLE,5) = K
0111         AVLOC = K/IZ
0112    C THEN THE AVERAGE LOC
0113         WRITE (2,7) AVLOC
0114       7 FORMAT(15H AVERAGE LOC IS,I4)
0115         WRITE(2,8)
0116       8 FORMAT(28HODETAILED DATA ON ACTIVITIES)
0117         WRITE(2,9)
0118       9 FORMAT(4HOACT,3X,8HSELECTED,3X,9HCOMPLETED)
0119         DO 102 K=1,AZ
0120         WRITE (2,10) ACT(K,1),ACT(K,4),ACT(K,5)
0121      10 FORMAT(I4,4X,I4,7X,I4)
0122     102 CONTINUE
0123         WRITE(2,11)
0124      11 FORMAT(31H0   DETAILED DATA ON INDIVIDUALS)
0125         WRITE(2,12)
0126      12 FORMAT(73HOIND.   LOC.   FIX.   ACT.1   ACT.2   ACT.3   ACT.4   ACT.5   AC
0127        1T.6   ACT.7   ACT.8)
0128         DO 103 J = 1,IZ
0129         WRITE(2,13)(IND(I(J),K),K=1,11)
0130      13 FORMAT (I4,3I6,7I7)
0131     103 CONTINUE
0132         J=ICYCLE
0133         NSTORE(J,1)=IZ
0134         NSTORE(J,2)=ITURN
0135         NSTORE(J,3)=N
0136         NSTORE(J,4)=ICOMP
0137    C UPDATES OVERALL DATA RECORD
0138         RETURN
0139         END
```

END OF SEGMENT, LENGTH 205, NAME DISPLAY

318

```
0140        SUBROUTINE VOTE
0141        INTEGER ACT(8,6),AZ,B,H,UA,X,Y
0142        DIMENSION II(30)
0143        COMMON IND(99,11),I(30),IZ,ACT,AZ
0144        DO 4 B=1,AZ
0145        ACT(B,4)=0
0146        ACT(B,5)=0
0147      4 CONTINUE
0148 C SETS ACTIVITY SELECTION AND COMPLETION COUNTERS TO ZERO
0149        DO 5 J=1,IZ
0150        IND(I(J),3)=0
0151 C CANCELS EVERY INDS PREVIOUS ACTIVITY SELECTIONS
0152        II(J) = I(J)
0153 C SETS UP VECTOR II OF ALL INDS WHO HAVE NOT DECIDED ON THEIR NEXT ACTIVITY
0154      5 CONTINUE
0155        IIZ = IZ
0156 C IIZ IS NO. OF PEOPLE IN VECTOR II
0157        DO 50 U=1,AZ
0158 C 'U' IS THE LEVEL OF PREFERENCE UNDER CONSIDERATION
0159        IF(IIZ) 51,51,0
0160 C IF ALL INDS HAVE DECIDED ON THEIR ACTIVITY, THEN VOTE IS COMPLETED
0161     33 Y=U
0162 C 'Y' IS A COUNTER FOR POSSIBLE ACTIVITIES AT THE CURRENT PREFERENCE LEVEL
0163        DO 7 K=4,AZ+3
0164        X=0
0165 C 'X' COUNTS THE NO. OF PREFS. FOR EACH ACTIVITY
0166        DO 6 J=1,IIZ
0167        IF(IND(II(J),K)-U)0,0,6
0168        X=X+1
0169      6 CONTINUE
0170 C IF AT LEAST AS MANY PEOPLE U-PREFER AN ACTIVITY AS ARE NEEDED TO CARRY IT OUT,
0171 C THEN THAT ACTIVITY IS ......
0172        IF(X-ACT(K-3,3)) 7,0,0
0173        ACT(K-3,4) = 2
0174 C MARKED AS POSSIBLY SELECTED AND ......
0175        Y=Y+1
0176 C THE POSSIBLE ACTIVITIES COUNTER RAISED BY ONE
0177      7 CONTINUE
```

```
0178        IF(Y-1)40,20,10
0179  C  THE NEXT STEP DEPENDS ON THE NUMBER OF POSSIBLE ACTIBITIES.
0180  C  IF SEVERAL ACTS ARE POBBIBLE, ONE IS SELECTED AS THE MOST PREFERRED BY
0181  C  THE FOLLOWING PROCESS....:'
0182  C  WHICH ACT HAS THE HIGHEST NO. OF FIRST CHOICES?  IF NONE, OR MORE THAN ONE,
0183  C  WHICH ACT HAS THE HIGHEST NO. OF FIRST AND SECOND CHOICES....ETC....
0184
0185        10 DO 16 UA = 1,U
0186  C  'UA' SHADOWS 'U' AS PREFERENCE LEVEL INDICATOR
0187        X=0
0188
0189           MAXSUM = 0
0190           DO 14 B=1,AZ
0191           ACT(B,6) = 0
0192  C  CLEARS COL.6 IN ACTIVITY MATRIX FOR PREFERENCE COUNTING
0193           IF (ACT(B,4)-2) 14,0,14
0194  C  IF AN ACT IS POSSIBLE....:'....
0195           DO 12 J=1,IIZ
0196           IF (UA = IND(II(J),B+3))12,0,0
0197           ACT(B,6) = ACT(B,6) + 1
0198        12 CONTINUE
0199  C  SUM T8E INDS CHOOSING IT TO 'UA' PREF. LEVEL AND ..........
0200           IF(ACT(B,6)-MAXSUM) 14,14,0
0201           MAXSUM = ACT(B,6)
0202  C  RESETS MAXSUM IF IT IS PREFERRED TO PREVIOUS ACTS
0203        14 CONTINUE
0204
0205           DO 15 B=1,AZ
0206           IF (ACT(B,4)-2) 15,0,15
0207  C  IF AN ACT IS POSSIBLE
0208
0209           IF(ACT(B,6)-MAXSUM) 0,145,15
0210           ACT(B,4)=0
0211  C  BUT GETS FEWER PREFS. , IT IS ELIMINATED
0212       145 X=X+1
0213  C  'X' COUNTS NO. OF ACTS RECEIVING MAXIMUM PREFERENCE
           15 CONTINUE
           IF(X-1)16,20,16
     C  THIS PART IS TERMINATED IF ONE ACT IS UNIQUELY PREFFERRED
           16 CONTINUE
```

```
0250        SUBROUTINE ISQUASH (II,IIZ)
0251        DIMENSION II(IIZ)
0252        J=0
0253      1 J=J+1
0254      2 IF (J-IIZ) 0,5,7
0255    C IF J INDICATES A PLACE IN VECROR II......
0256        IF (II(J)) 1,0,1
0257    C BUT THE PLACE IS VACANT......
0258        DO 3 K=J,IIZ-1
0259        II(K)=II(K+1)
0260      3 CONTINUE
0261    C THE VECTOR IS CONDENSED TO ELIMINATE THE SPACE........

0262      4 IIZ = IIZ-1
0263    C AND THE NO. OF INDS REDUCED ACCORDINGLY
0264        GOTO 2
0265      5 IF(II(J))1,4,1
0266    C DEALS WITH LAST PLACE IN II
0267      7 RETURN
0268        END
```

END OF SEGMENT, LENGTH   53, NAME   ISQUASH

```
0214        GOTO 20
0215  C IF SEVERAL ACTS ARE EQUAL AT EVERY PREFFRENCE LFVEL, THE NEXT SECTION (20)
0216  C WILL ARBITARILY SELECT THE FIRST OF THEN
0217  20 DO 21 B=1,AZ
0218        IF (ACT(B,4).EQ.2) GOTO 22
0219  21 CONTINUE
0220  C THE MOST PREFFERED POSSIBLE ACT IS ......
0221  22 ACT(B,4)=1
0222  C MARKED"4" AS SELECTED ......
0223        DO 23 J=1,IIZ
0224        IF(IND(II(J),B+3)-U) 0,0,23
0225  C AND THE UNDECIDED INDS WHO PREFER IT ......
0226        IND(II(J),3) = B
0227  C FIX THEIR CHOICES ......
0228        II(J)=U
0229  C AND COME OFF THE UNDECIDED LIST
0230  23 CONTINUE
0231        CALL ISQUASH (II,IIZ)
0232  30 IF(Y=1) 0,50,33
0233  40 DO 44 J=1,IIZ
0234        DO 41 K=4,AZ+3
0235        IF (IND(II(J),K)-U) 0,42,0
0236  C IF AN INDS U-PREFERENCE......
0237  41 CONTINUE
0238  42 IF(ACT(K-3,4)-1) 44,0,44
0239  C IS FOR A SELECTED ACT ......
0240        IND(II(J),3)=K-3
0241  C THEN HE FIXES HIS CHOICF ......
0242        II(J) = 0
0243  C AND COMES OFF THE UNDECIDED LIST
0244  44 CONTINUE
0245        CALL ISQUASH (II,IIZ)
0246  C FINALLY THE II VECTOR IS CONDENSED BY ISQUASH
0247  50 CONTINUE
0248  51 RETURN
0249        END
```

END OF SEGMENT, LENGTH 280, NAME VOTE

322

```
0294        SUBROUTINE LEAVE
0295        COMMON IND(99,11),I(30),IZ,IDUM(40),MINLOC,JDUM,LEFT
0296        LEFT = 0
0297        DO 5 J=1,IZ
0298        IF(MINLOC - IND(I(J),2))5,5,0
0299  C IF AN IND'S LOC DROPS BELOW MINLOC......
0300        I(J) = 0
0301        LEFT=LEFT+1
0302  C THAT INDIVIDUAL LEAVES THE GROUP......
0303      5 CONTINUE
0304        IF(LEFT) 7,7,0
0305        CALL ISQUASH(I,IZ)
0306  C AND VECTOR I IS REDUCED ACCORDINGLY
0307      7 RETURN
0308        END
```

END OF SEGMENT, LENGTH   41, NAME   LEAVE

```
0309          SUBROUTINE ACTION
0310          INTEGER ACT(8,6),AZ,B,X
0311          DIMENSION II(30)
0312          COMMON IND(29,11),I(30),IZ,ACT,AZ,MINLOC,MAXLOC
0313          B=0
0314     1    B=B+1
0315    C 'B' IS THE NAME OF THE ACR UNDER CONSIDERARION
0316          IF (B=A7)0,0,50
0317    C END IF 'B' IS NOT AN ACTIBITY
0318          IF(ACT(B,4)-1) 1,0,1
0319    C IF THE ACT HAS NOT BEEN CHOSEN, LOOK AT THE NEXT ACT
0320          IIZ=0
0321          X=0
0322          DO 2 J=1,IZ
0323          IF(IND(I(J),3)-B)2,0,2
0324    C ONLY INDS CHOOSING ACT B ARE CONSIDERED HERE
0325          IF(IND(I(J),2)-880)0,2,2
0326    C ONLY ACTIVE INDIVIDUALS ARE CONSIDERED
0327          IIZ = IIZ + 1
0328    C COUNTS INDS CHOOSING ACR B
0329          II(IIZ) = I(J) + IND(I(J),2)*100
0330    C PUTS THE NAME AND LOC OF INDS CHOOSING B INTO VECTOR II
0331          X=X+IND(I(J),2)
0332    C SUMS LOCS OF INDS CHOOSING ACT B
0333     2    CONTINUE
0334          IF(IIZ) 0,1,0
0335    C DEALS WITH THE CASE WHERE ALL INDS WHO CHOSE ACT B HAVE LEFT
0336    31   IF(X-(ACT(B,2)-2)) 24,20,0
0337          IF(X=(ACT(B,2)+2))20,20,27
0338    C TESTS FOR TOO LITTLE,THEN TOO MUCH COMMITTMENT
0339    C IF THE SUM OF LOCS IS WITHIN 2 POINTS OF THE ACTIVITY REQUIRED,NO ADJUSTMENT
0340    24   IF(X/IIZ-5)4,0,0
0341    C IF MEAN-LOC IS HIGH, INACTIVE INDS ARE CALLED IN
0342          DO 25 J=1,IZ
0343          IF (IND(I(J),2)-880)25,25,0
0344    C ONLY LOOKS AT INACTIVE INDS
```

324

```
0345           IND(I(J),2) = IND(I(J),2)-880
0346     C ACTIVATES THEM
0347           IND(I(J),3)= B
0348     C RESETS THEIR ALLOCATED ACTIVITY
0349           IIZ = IIZ + 1
0350     C ADDS REACTIVATED INDIVIDUAL TO TOTAL
0351           II(IIZ) = I(J) + IND(I(J),2)*100
0352     C PUTS REACTIVATED IND INTO VECTOR II
0353           X=X+IND(I(J),2)
0354     C RESETS LOC TOTAL
0355           GOTO 31
0356        25 CONTINUE
0357           GOTO 4
0358     C IN A CASE THERE ARE NO INACTIVE INDS
0359        27 IF(X/IIZ-5) 0,4,4
0360     C IF MEAN-LOC IS LOW, INDS ARE DE-ACTIVATED
0361           IRA = MINO(IND(II(1),AZ+3),IIZ)
0362     C IRA (RANDOM INTEGER) SELECTS AN IND TO DEACTIVATE
0363           LA = MOD(II(IRA),100)
0364     C NAME INACTIVATED INDIVIDUAL
0365           DO 28 J=1,IZ
0366           IF(I(J) - LA)28,0,28
0367           IND(I(J),2) = IND(I(J),2) + 880
0368     C AND MARKS HIM INACTIVE
0369           GOTO 30
0370        28 CONTINUE

0371        30 X = X = II(IRA)/100
0372     C REDUCES LOCSUM ACCORDINGLY
0373           IF (IRA - IIZ) 0,26,0
0374           DO 29 J=IRA,IIZ-1
0375           II(J) = II(J+1)
0376     C REDUCES VECTOR II AFTER LOSS OF INACTIVE INDIVIDUAL
0377        29 CONTINUE
0378        26 IIZ = IIZ - 1
0379     C REDUCES NO. OF INDS. IN II
```

```fortran
      GOTO 31
    4 DO 7 J=1,IIZ
C THIS LOOP PUTS INDS IN VECTOR II IN INCREASING ORDER OF LOC
      K=IIZ-J
      MARK=0
      DO 6 L=1,K
      NEXT=L+1
      IF(II(NEXT)-II(L)) 0,6,6
C NO CHANGE IF L IS SMALLER THAN ITS SUCCESSOR
      M=II(L)
      II(L) = II(NEXT)
      II(NEXT) = M
C IF L IS LARGER THAN IRS SUCCESSOR, TREY CHANGE PLACES
      MARK=1
C AND THE CHANGE IS RECORDED
    6 CONTINUE
      IF(MARK) 0,8,0
C IF THERE WERE NO CBANGES , THE ORDERING IS FINISHED
    7 CONTINUE
    8 IF(X-(ACT(B,2)*2))0,0,12
C THE NEXT PART DEALS WITH T8E CASE OF INSUFFICIENT COMMITTMENT
      DO 10 J=1,IIZ
      K=IIZ+1-J
      IF((II(K)/100)-10)0,10,0
C IGNORE INDS WHO HAVE MAXIMUM LOC ALREADY
C THEN INCREASES COMMITTMENT OF MOST COMMITTED INDS.
      N=MOD(II(K),100)
C MOD EXTRACTS NAME (NUMBER) OF INDIVIDUAL
      M=MINO((II(K)/100)*2,10)
C DOUBLES THAT INDS LOC TO A MAX OF 10 IN II
      II(K)= N+M*100
      X = X + (M - IND(N,2))
C SETS NEW LOC TOTAL
      IF(X-(ACT(B,2)-2))10,16,16
C TESTS TO SEE IF NEW LOC TOTAL IS SUFFIVIENT
   10 CONTINUE
      GOTO 1
C IN CASE LOC TOTAL IS NEVER SUFFICIENT
```

```
0418        12 DO 14 J=1,IIZ
0419     C DEALS WITH THE CASE OF TOO MUCH COMMITTMENT
0420           N=MOD(II(J),100)
0421     C EXTRACTS NAME OF LEASE COMMITTED INDIVIDUALS FIRST
0422           M=MAXU((II(J)/100)/2,2)
0423           II(J) = N+M*100
0424     C HALVES WITH A MIN OF 2, THE LOC OF LEAST COMMITTED INDS.
0425           X=X-IND(N,2)+M
0426     C SETS NEW LOC TOTAL
0427           IF(X-(ACT(B,2)+2)) 16,16,14
0428     C TESTS TO SEE IF NEW LOC TOTAL IS SUFFICIENTLY REDUCED
0429        14 CONTINUE
0430        16 DO 17 J = 1,IIZ
0431           IND((MOD(II(J),100)),2) = II(J)/100
0432     C PUTS NEW LOC LEVELS INTO IND MATRIX


0433        17 CONTINUE
0434        20 ACT(B,5)=1
0435     C MARKS ACT AS COMPLETED
0436           GOTO 1
0437        50 RETURN
0438           END
```

END OF SEGMENT, LENGTH   430, NAME   ACTION

```
        SUBROUTINE DISSONANCE
        INTEGER ACT(8,6),AZ
        COMMON IND(99,11),I(30),IZ,ACT,AZ
        DO 10 J=1,IZ
        IF (IND(I(J),2)-880)    0,10,10
C  IGNORES INACTIVE INDIVIDUALS
        IPREF = IND(I(J),IND(I(J),3)+3)
C  IPREF GIVES PREF. LEVEL OF I'S SELECTED ACT
        IF(ACT(IND(I(J),3),5)-1)0,5,0
C  IF THE ACT CHOSEN BY AN IND HAS BEEN COMPLETED,GOTO 5, IF NOT, CONTINUE....
        IF(IPREF - AZ) 0,10,0
C  IF AN INDS LAST PREF. ACTIVITY HAS NOT BEEN COMPLETED , MAKE NO CHANGES
        DO 2 K=4,AZ+3
        IF(IND(I(J),K) - (IPREF+1)) 2,0,2
C  SELECT THE LESS PREFERRED ACTIVITY.......
        IND(I(J),K) = IND(I(J),K) - 1
C  AND INCREASE THAT INDS. PREF, FOR IT  ....
        IND(I(J),IND(I(J),3)+3) = IPREF + 1
C  WHILE DECREASING HIS PREFERENCE FOR THE UNCOMLETED ACT
        GOTO 10
C  THEN LOOK AT THE NEXT INDIBIDUAL
      2 CONTINUE
      5 IF (IPREF - 1) 0,10,0
C  IF AN INDS FIRST PREF. ACTIVITY HAS BEEN COMPLETED, MAKE NO CHANGES
        DO 7 K=4,AZ+3
C  OTHERWISE .....
        IF(IND(I(J),K) - (IPREF-1)) 7,0,7
C  FIND THE MORE PREFERRED ACTIVITY ....
        IND(I(J),K) = IND(I(J),K) + 1
C  AND DECREASE THAT INDS PREF. FOR IT
        IND(I(J),IND(I(J),3)+3) = IPREF -1
C  WHILE INCREASING HIS PREFERENCE FOR THE COMPLETED ACT
        GOTO 10
C  THEN LOOK AT T8E NEXT INDIVIDUAL
      7 CONTINUE
     10 CONTINUE
        RETURN
        END
```

END OF SEGMENT, LENGTH 136, NAME DISSONANCE

328

```
0477          SUBROUTINE JOIN
0478          INTEGER ACT(8,6),AZ
0479          COMMON IND(29,11),I(30),IZ,ACT,AZ,IDUM(3),JOINED,ICOMP,INEXT,
0480         1DUM,ENTER
0481          ICOMP= 0
0482          ITOT = 0
0483          JOINED = 0
0484          DO 1 J=1,IZ
0485          IF (IND(I(J),2)-880)  0,1,1
0486   C IGNORES INACTIVE INDIVIDUALS
0487          IF(ACT(IND(I(J),3),5) - 1) 1,0,1
0488   C IF AN INDS. CHOSEN ACT IS COMPLETED......
0489          ICOMP = ICOMP +1
0490   C ONE POINT IS ADDED TO ICOMP.
0491          ITOT = ITOT + IND(I(J),2)
0492      1   CONTINUE
0493          IF (ICOMP - 1) 5,5,0
0494          ENTER = (ITOT/ICOMP-1)/10.0
0495          JOE = ICOMP*ENTER
0496   C JOE IS NO. OF I'S WHO MIGHT JOIN
0497      2   IF(JOE-1)5,0,0
0498          DO 4 K=1,JOE
0499          IZ = IZ+1
0500          IF(IZ-30)0,0,5
0501          I(IZ) = INEXT
0502   C INEXT JOINS
0503          JOINED = JOINED+1
0504          INEXT = INEXT + 1
0505          IF (INEXT-100)0,5,5
0506   C ENDS IF POOL OF INDS EXHAUSTED
0507      4   CONTINUE
0508      5   RETURN
0509          END
```

END OF SEGMENT, LENGTH   111, NAME JOIN

```
0510          SUBROUTINE SUMMARY
0511          COMMON IDUM(1175),DUM(2),ICYCLE,NSTORE(50,5)
0512          WRITE(2,1)
0513        1 FORMAT(6H1CYCLE,3X,2HIZ,6X,4HTURN,4X,4HNACT,4X,5HICOMP,3X,6HTOTLOC
0514       1,2X,5HAVLOC)
0515          DO 10 J=1,ICYCLE
0516          M = (NSTORE(J,5)/NSTORE(J,1))
0517          WRITE(2,2)J,(NSTORE(J,K),K=1,5),M
0518        2 FORMAT (3X,7(I2,6X))
0519       10 CONTINUE
0520          RETURN
0521          END

END OF SEGMENT, LENGTH    47, NAME  SUMMARY


0522          FINISH
```

Author Index

Subject Index

334